CRACKING THE DIGITAL CEILING

Is computing just for men? Are men and women suited to different careers? This collection of global perspectives challenges these commonly held Western views, perpetuated as explanations for women's low participation in computing. By providing an insider look at how different cultures worldwide impact the experiences of women in computing, the book introduces readers to theories and evidence that support the need to turn to environmental factors, rather than innate potential, to understand what determines women's participation in this growing field. This wake-up call to examine the obstacles and catalysts within various cultures and environments will help those interested in improving the situation understand where they might look to make changes that could impact women's participation in their classrooms, companies, and administrations. Computer scientists, STEM educators, students of all disciplines, professionals in the tech industry, leaders in gender equity, anthropologists, and policy makers will all benefit from reading this book.

Dr. Carol Frieze works on diversity and inclusion in Carnegie Mellon's School of Computer Science. She focuses on culture and broadening participation in computing. She is co-author of *Kicking Butt in Computer Science: Women in Computing at Carnegie Mellon University* (2015). Frieze is winner of the 2016 AccessComputing Capacity Building Award and the 2017 winner of the Computing Research Association's A. Nico Habermann Award.

Dr. Jeria L. Quesenberry is an associate teaching professor of information systems at Carnegie Mellon University. Her research interests include cultural influences on IT students and professionals, social inclusion, and broadening participation. She is co-author of *Kicking Butt in Computer Science: Women in Computing at Carnegie Mellon University* (2015).

Cracking the Digital Ceiling

Women in Computing around the World

Edited by

CAROL FRIEZE

Carnegie Mellon University

JERIA L. QUESENBERRY

Carnegie Mellon University

CAMBRIDGE
UNIVERSITY PRESS

University Printing House, Cambridge CB2 8BS, United Kingdom

One Liberty Plaza, 20th Floor, New York, NY 10006, USA

477 Williamstown Road, Port Melbourne, VIC 3207, Australia

314-321, 3rd Floor, Plot 3, Splendor Forum, Jasola District Centre, New Delhi - 110025, India

79 Anson Road, #06-04/06, Singapore 079906

Cambridge University Press is part of the University of Cambridge.

It furthers the University's mission by disseminating knowledge in the pursuit of
education, learning and research at the highest international levels of excellence.

www.cambridge.org
Information on this title: www.cambridge.org/9781108740074
DOI: 10.1017/9781108609081

© Cambridge University Press 2020

First published 2020

A catalogue record for this publication is available from the British Library

Library of Congress Cataloging in Publication data
Names: Frieze, Carol, 1947– editor. | Quesenberry, Jeria L., 1977– editor.
Title: Cracking the digital ceiling : women in computing around the world / edited by
Carol Frieze and Jeria L. Quesenberry.
Description: Cambridge, United Kingdom ; New York, NY : Cambridge University Press,
[2019] | Includes bibliographical references and index.
Identifiers: LCCN 2019011014 | ISBN 9781108497428 (hardback : alk. paper) |
ISBN 9781108740074 (pbk. : alk. paper)
Subjects: LCSH: Women in computer science. | Women in information science. |
Computers and women.
Classification: LCC QA76.9.W65 C7 2019 | DDC 004.082–dc23
LC record available at https://lccn.loc.gov/2019011014

ISBN 978-1-108-49742-8 Hardback
ISBN 978-1-108-74007-4 Paperback

Contents

Contributors

Monica P. Adya
Department of Management, Marquette University

Sally A. Applin
School of Anthropology and Conservation, University of Kent

Cynthia Bennett
Human Centered Design & Engineering, University of Washington

Sue Black
Department of Computer Science, Durham University

Brianna Blaser
DO-IT, University of Washington

Sheryl E. Burgstahler
DO-IT, University of Washington

Palma Buttles
Software Engineering Institute, Carnegie Mellon University

Maria Charles
Broom Center for Demography, University of California – Santa Barbara

Tiffany Chow
Department of Sociology, University of California – Santa Barbara

Carol Frieze
School of Computer Science, Carnegie Mellon University

Nancy J. Hafkin
Women in Global Science and Technology

Orit Hazzan
Education in Science and Technology, Technion

Sophia Huyer
CGIAR Climate Change, Agriculture and Food Security Programme

Evgeniy (Eugene) K. Khenner
Department of Information Technologies, Perm State University, Russia

Richard E. Ladner
Department of CS & Engineering, University of Washington

Catherine Lang
Department of Education, La Trobe University

Rodziah Latih
Department of IS & Technology, University Kebangsaan Malaysia

Sinna Lindquist
FOI – Swedish Defence Research Agency

Arminda Guerra Lopes
Department of Informatics, Polytechnic Institute of Castelo Branco

Jennifer Mankoff
Department of CS & Engineering, University of Washington

Ingrid Melinder
Department of CS and Communication, KTH Royal Institute of Technology

Efrat Nativ-Ronen
Registration and Admissions Department, Technion

Mazliza Othman
Department of CS & Information Technology, University of Malaya

Joyojeet Pal
Microsoft Research India

Jeria Quesenberry
Information Systems Program, Carnegie Mellon University

Eileen M. Trauth
College of Information Sciences & Technology, Pennsylvania State University

Tatiana Umansky
The Statistics Laboratory, Technion

Fred Valdez, Jr.
Department of Anthropology, University of Texas at Austin

Roli Varma
School of Public Administration, University of New Mexico

Yichun Yin
Noah's Ark Lab, Huawei Technologies

Ming Zhang
Department of Electronics Engineering and CS, Peking University

Acknowledgments

The editors wish to express our gratitude and appreciation to those who helped make this book possible. We especially wish to thank our authors for their encouragement, insights and excellent contributions to the book. This group of authors are leaders in advancing the visibility of the barriers to and catalysts for success that women in computing encounter around the world. We acknowledge the great work of the many educational, governmental and organizational institutions throughout the world who empower women in computing. Many leaders in the effort are identified throughout the chapters in this book. We thank Carnegie Mellon University for their institutional support and the value they place on inclusion and diversity. In particular, we want to acknowledge the work of Carnegie Mellon CS professor and Founder of Women@SCS, Lenore Blum, who initiated and led the way for cultural change in Carnegie Mellon's School of Computer Science.

We also thank Kaitlin Leach and her team at Cambridge University Press for their interest and support of this project. Their contributions throughout the whole process from inception of the initial idea to final publication have been invaluable. We also appreciate the attention to detail that Stephanie Sakson put into the copyediting efforts. Thank you to our external reviewers who provided constructive and comprehensive feedback.

We dedicate this book to Carol's granddaughters Maisie, Molly, Gracie, and Sophie, and Jeria's daughter Ella. We hope this book will inspire their lives in the ways other women have inspired ours.

Introduction

In 1882 renowned English scientist Charles Darwin announced that "[t]he chief distinction in the intellectual powers of the two sexes is shewn by man's attaining to a higher eminence, in whatever he takes up, than can woman" (Darwin, 1871, p. 564). This belief in women's inferior intellect was not new,[1] but as an eminent scientist, Darwin's proclamations held great sway in his time and place – and since – although nowadays few would admit to this. Or would they? Jump forward to 1992 and we see the arrival of John Gray's *Men Are from Mars, Women Are from Venus*, which became a phenomenal best-seller (selling more than fifteen million copies globally[2]), and continues to be so. While the book is not as forthright in saying women's intellect is inferior, it does explain the many ways in which men and women differ – including the ways they think (Gray, 1992).

The mindset that assumes men and women have different intellectual abilities and capabilities has a strong hold on public thinking in the United States and many parts of the Western world. Such thinking feeds our stereotypes and our biases and is used to explain why men and women "choose" different areas of study, different careers, and hold different aspirations – including how they relate to computing; computer science (CS); informatics, information, and communication technologies (ICTs); information systems (IS); information technology (IT); and related fields.

This book includes a collection of perspectives that challenge the *pink brain, blue brain*[3] myth and provides voices from multiple cultures and countries. Our inspiration and motivation for this book came from working with computer science majors at Carnegie Mellon University (CMU) in the United States and recognizing that for women to be successful in computer science we did not have to change the curriculum to suit "women's ways of thinking" – women can do the intellectual work as

1

well as their male peers – *but we did need to change the culture* (Frieze and Quesenberry, 2015).

Thus, our goal with this book was to collect a range of global perspectives to show that women's participation in computing[4] is largely determined by cultural factors. To accomplish this goal we have brought together a landscape of researchers and educators in this edited volume. We have included brief summaries and quotes of some of their work throughout this introduction to set a foundational understanding of the topics at hand. In the final section of this introduction we have also included a guide to the chapters and their highlights, to help our readers navigate the organization of the contents.

We showcase the role of cultures, which can vary even within one country, and illustrate how a multitude of cultural factors influence women's participation in computing. Along with cultural heterogeneity, women and men are not single separate categories – we are all shaped by intersectionality and complex identities including such factors as race and ethnicities, disabilities, socioeconomic backgrounds, sexual orientation, and religious beliefs. Our experiences are subject to the values, attitudes, and behaviors of cultures at large as well as the micro-cultures we inhabit such as our families, schools, workplaces, and peer groups.

WOMEN IN COMPUTING: DATA ON PARTICIPATION

Gender balance in itself can have particular impact on the individual experiences of women in computing. As one Swedish computer scientist explained, being one of very few women "had the quite strange side effect of [me] quickly becoming a familiar face to almost everyone in the program – on good days it felt like being a celebrity, on bad days it felt like being a zoo animal" (Linquist and Melinder, Chapter 11). Being the only woman on the software engineering team, or being the only girl in the computer science class, can mean being seen as representative of all women and not as another engineer or student. It can also lead to feelings of isolation and non-belonging – and at its extreme to leaving the field.

What we find as we explore the data from different countries and cultures is that women are seriously underrepresented in computing in many parts of the world. This would appear to support a commonplace American belief that computing is a boys' field. Consider that in 2016 in the United States, only 19% of computer science undergraduate degree recipients were female (Zweben and Bizot, 2017) and women held only 26% of computing occupations (Bureau of Labor Statistics, 2017).

For minority women the situation is worse. For example, African American women represented just 3% and Latinas 6% as recipients of computer science degrees (Zweben and Bizot, 2017). African American women and Latinas hold slightly less than 10% of computing occupations in the United States (National Science Foundation, 2017).

But now consider this:

- 50% of CS majors at Carnegie Mellon University in the United States are women (Frieze and Quesenberry, 2015).
- 55% of CS majors at Harvey Mudd College in the United States are women (Alvardo et al., 2012).
- 59% of students enrolled in CS studies in Saudi Arabia are women (Alghamdi, 2016).
- 50% of engineering graduates in Cyprus are women (UNESCO, 2017)
- 55% of entrepreneurs in the Internet industry in China are women (PRCSCIO, 2015).
- 50% of undergraduates in computing at University of Malaya and Universiti Kebangsaan Malaysia in Malaysia are women (Othman and Latih, Chapter 15).
- 40%, 65%, and 50% of students in CS/computer engineering at the undergraduate, master's and doctorate levels, respectively, in India are women (Huyer, Chapter 2).

While women are seriously underrepresented in computing fields in the United States, and in most of the world, *the situation is not universal* as the above data, and some of the chapters in this book, illustrate. Additionally, women have shown themselves to be strong participants in many fields that were once closed to them on the grounds of biology and perceived innate characteristics. In the United States and Portugal, we can look to medicine as examples of this change. In both countries there is near gender equality in the medical profession (e.g., AAMC, 2017; Lopes, Chapter 12). Furthermore, in 2016, 57% of *all* bachelor's degrees went to women in the United States, while 50.3% of science and engineering bachelor's degrees went to women in 2013 (Girls Collaborative Project, 2016; National Center for Education Statistics, 2016). We see a similar picture emerging globally. For example, in Russia women outnumber men in overall graduation rates, with women gaining 56% of postsecondary degrees (Khenner, Chapter 13). In Portugal in 2009, 59.3% of the total higher education graduates were women. Similarly, the Organisation for Economic Co-operation and Development (OECD) reports that women earn more postsecondary degrees than men, and a UNESCO analysis of women in science, technology, engineering, and math (STEM) fields found that women represent 53% of the graduates in tertiary education in bachelors and master's programs (OECD, 2017; Huyer, Chapter 2). Such data illustrate women's intellectual potential to succeed in any field and it seems reasonable to suggest that this should include computing. It also suggests that data tell us only part of the story. To get a better understanding we need to pay immediate and close attention to the cultural factors that might be enabling or deterring women's participation in computing. "Cultural understanding is crucial to an understanding of gender influences and barriers because gender is experienced through culture" (Trauth, Chapter 3).

One of the most interesting discussions relating to data challenges some of our expectations and has serious implications for women in computing in the West. Studies have found that affluent, developed countries that *feature highly in gender equality rankings* are more likely to have the *lowest* participation of women in computing (Chow and Charles, Chapter 1). According to a recent study the gender gap in STEM increases with increasing levels of gender equality (Stoet and Geary, 2018). The World Economic Forum (2016) ranked Scandinavian countries as the most equitable of societies.[5] While Scandinavian countries like Norway, Finland, and Sweden are leaders in gender equality they have the largest gender gaps in college degrees in STEM fields (Stoet and Geary, 2018). Meanwhile, Saudi Arabia has good representation of women in high school computing and yet very low ranking – 141 out of 144 – for gender parity according to the World Economic Forum (2016).

GENDER THEORIES: ESSENTIALISM, SOCIAL CONSTRUCTIONISM, AND INTERSECTIONALITY

Historically, there are at least three major theoretical perspectives typically used to explain women's participation in computing: essentialism, social constructionism, and intersectionality theory.

Essentialism is the belief that people have properties that are essential to their composition. This suggests that all members of a particular group (e.g., gender, race, sexual orientation) innately share a common set of fixed, unified characteristics that form the primary components in understanding human actions (Wajcman, 1991). Hence, at the core of essentialism is the belief that since men and women are inherently different in their physical bodies, they are also different in the ways in which they act, behave, *and think* – and in how they relate to computing.

The essentialist way of thinking carries serious, negative repercussions for countries where women are poorly represented in computing. In *Occupational Ghettos: The Worldwide Segregation of Women and Men,* researchers argue that *essentialism* is still entrenched in the dominant culture of many advanced industrial countries where a deep-seated belief in gender differences is maintained and supported by a culture that values individual preferences and self-expression (Charles and Grusky, 2005). Even though such cultures no longer hold that men are *better* than women, they still subscribe to a belief that men and women are *very different.* This continuing belief in difference means boys and girls are more likely to follow gendered studies and career paths even in countries perceived as very progressive on gender issues.

Some fascinating research that challenges essentialism and beliefs in intellectual gender differences has emerged from the field of neuroscience. Lise Eliot, professor of neuroscience at the Chicago Medical School of Rosalind Franklin University of Medicine and Science, debunks the belief that brain differences account for gender stratification in intelligence and capacity for scientific thinking. Eliot's exhaustive review of the scientific literature on human brains from birth to adolescence is explained in her book *Pink Brain, Blue Brain.* She concluded that there is "surprisingly little solid evidence of sex differences in children's brains" (Eliot, 2009, p. 5). Indeed, the work of Eliot and other researchers has shown that men and women are not as different in their intellectual potential as popular wisdom would have us believe (Barnett and Rivers, 2005; Fine, 2010; Halpern, 2000; Hyde, 2005; Hyde and Linn, 2006).

Social construction is the belief that human behavior is rooted in historical and cultural interaction and practices. The central concept of Berger and Luckmann, explained in *The Social Construction of Reality* (1966), is that social systems are based on interactions that eventually develop into habitualized norms and roles. Over time these interactions become institutionalized, and, hence, meaning is embedded in individuals and society such that when a woman enters a male-dominated field she is seen as "stepping out of line" in terms of cultural expectations. Sandra Bem's cognitive theory of *schemas* explains how social norms start early in life and become entrenched unconscious guides to our behavior and attitudes (Bem, 1981). Bem suggests that gender schemas help solidify cultural stereotypes. They provide an "easy" way of perceiving the world around us while we struggle to identify with gender constructs in the cultures in which we find ourselves.

Many suggest that a social construction perspective is key to under-standing cross-cultural variation in gender roles and expectations. American-based authors Henry Etzkowitz, Carol Kemelgor, and Brian Uzzi provide a life-course analysis (based on interviews and surveys) of women in the sciences from an early childhood interest, through univer-sity, to graduate school, and finally into the academic workplace in their book *Athena Unbound*. They conclude that despite recent advances women still face a special series of gender-related barriers to entry and success in scientific careers.

Intersectionality theory provides a framework to address the many ways in which women (and men) are not one single separate category. Our identities capture a range of interconnections, similarities, and differences that influence how we experience the world. The term "intersectionality" has been credited to Kimberle Crenshaw in her essay "Demarginalizing the Intersection of Race and Sex: A Black Feminist Critique of Antidiscrimina-tion Doctrine, Feminist Theory and Antiracist Politics," in which she discusses the multidimensional experiences of black women (Crenshaw, 1989). While women are undervalued generally in our culture, individual factors, such as race, socioeconomics, sexual orientation, and ethnicity, can add levels of further marginalization. The theory also reminds us that identities are not fixed but are subject to the changing situations and micro-cultures in which we live our personal and professional lives. For instance, Trauth (2002) uses the "Individual Differences Theory of Gender and IT" to characterize how individual women respond in a range of specific ways to the interplay between individual characteristics and envir-onmental influences.

Intersectionality is particularly important to reflect on in this book of global perspectives, but we have one caveat: we are as guilty as anyone for using the binary terms "women" and "men" in our writings. We are limited by our language and have yet to find a more efficient way to explain our ideas as we address the global situation for women in computing. The chapters in this book represent a variety of theoretical underpinnings – but common to all the perspectives is the acknowledgment that cultural factors – not innate biological considerations based on sex – play a role in the shaping of gender.

This may be a good time to let our readers know what we are not saying. We are not saying that men and women are the same – that there are no differences – clearly our bodies indicate this – but we are saying that in some environments there may be more similarities than we realize. Several psychologists have pointed out that "a focus on factors other than gender is needed to help girls persist in mathematical and scientific career tracks" (Hyde and Linn, 2006, p. 599). Most importantly we agree that "gender differences are not general but specific to cultural and situational contexts" (Linn and Hyde, 1989, p. 17).

CULTURE

We use the term "culture" to refer to the complex and broad set of relationships, values, attitudes, and behaviors (along with the micro-cultures and counter-cultures that may also exist) that bind a specific community consciously and unconsciously (Frieze and Quesenberry, 2015; Williams, 1958). This community can be localized in the micro-culture of a school or department, or as extensive as the culture of a nation. Culture is bound by context and history and we are born into specific cultures with prevailing values and structures of opportunity.

Gender is first and foremost a cultural issue, not simply a women's issue, and we need to address the underlying cultures in which opportunities and values are situated. It is also the potential "ordinariness" of culture, rife with implicit gender-difference assumptions that can jeopardize our thinking. Gender-difference beliefs easily become mistaken for deep-rooted characteristics appearing to be completely natural while actually being socially constructed in specific cultures.

A cultural perspective can both broaden and focus our thinking. It can broaden our thinking to encompass learning from different cultures, and it can focus our thinking as we identify specific factors affecting specific situations. Galpin (2002) describes the participation of women in under-graduate computing in more than thirty countries, concluding, "The reasons that women choose to study computing will vary from culture to culture, and from country to country" (p. 94). She also reminds us that when we are "seeking solutions for women's low participation in comput-ing, it is important to consider all cultural and societal factors that may affect this participation" (p. 94). German professor Britta Schinzel (2002) also looked at female enrollment in CS around the world, reporting it as "culturally diversified" and noting a multiplicity of reasons accounting for higher and lower rates of female participation. As gender is often constructed differently in different cultures, taking a cultural approach allows us to see quite clearly and convincingly that many characteristics ascribed as natural to men and to women are actually produced in a culture.

We acknowledge that our Western worldview and our own cultural experiences have influenced this work. Our perspective for defining culture is United States–centric and it is difficult for us to step outside our own cultures, which makes this collection both challenging and riveting. One of our authors asks us to consider this interesting cross-cultural question: As computing becomes more ubiquitous, when we see similar cultural obstacles for women across nations, are we seeing a branding based on Silicon Valley computing culture? "When the Silicon Valley behavioral cultural frame is applied as a template to other geographic areas, it spreads some of the same problems with regard to opportunities, power, and financial inequality for women and others in the computer industry" (Applin, Chapter 8).

Many of us are impatient for change regarding the participation of women in computing. But history shows us that culture is mutable and dynamic, shaping and being shaped by those who occupy it, in a synergistic diffusive process. We believe it is at the level of culture that the most effective changes can occur and lead to women's successful participation in computing.

HISTORY

Western history represents a particularly interesting cultural case that clearly shows the importance of context. Historically women have played a very important role in the development of the field of computing, a role largely determined by the culture, social needs, and trends of the times. Here, we touch on this very briefly (mostly from a Western perspective), and suggest readers refer to the works of specialists (including among others J. Abbatte, D. Gurer, W. Isaacson, and K. Kleiman).

In the early history of computing, Ada Byron Lovelace, a mathematician, played a significant part in the development of the concept of computation, translating a lecture, on Charles Babbage's design of the analytical engine, from French to English. Lovelace added her own notes, which ended up being more expansive than the original article. The collaboration of Lovelace and Babbage on the difference and analytical engine could be seen as leading to the forerunner of the modern computer. Lovelace developed structures that resemble today's programming structures. She visualized how to program the engine to calculate and how to store sequences of operations (Gurer, 2002; Matsui and Chilana, 2004).

A big jump forward to the mid-twentieth century shows how wartime often provides us with good examples to illustrate the changing levels of women's contribution in predominantly male fields. During the 1940s in World War II, women played a major role as code breakers in the top-secret efforts going on at Bletchley Park in England. Dr. Sue Black (interviewed in Chapter 10), worked to save this famous landmark when it was in danger of being dismantled. She also had the pleasure of interviewing several of the surviving women code breakers.

In England and in the United States many women worked alongside men on calculating weapons trajectories at a time when people were the "computers." In 1943 almost all "computers" were women, and, ironically, women were perceived as best for the job: "Programming requires lots of patience, persistence and a capacity for detail and those are traits that many girls have" (Gurer, 2002, p. 176). Gurer suggests that, historically, praise for computer pioneers has tended to focus on hardware (developed by men), while ignoring the early programmers and inventors of programming (women), but she points out that "[t]oday's achievements in software are built on the shoulders of the first pioneering women programmers" (Gurer, 2002, p. 120). The Hollywood movie *Hidden Figures* documents another often ignored group – African American female mathematicians and "computers" who contributed to the space race. The movie is based on the non-fiction book *Hidden Figures: The American Dream and the Untold Story of the Black Women Mathematicians Who Helped Win the Space Race*, by Margot Lee Shutterly, which immortalized women such as Katherine Johnson (Shutterly, 2016).

Admiral Grace Hopper was an American pioneer in computing. She designed the first compiler for programming languages and was one of the first programmers for the Harvard Mark I computer, used in the war effort for World War II. Grace Hopper and her team were credited with coining the computer terms "bug" and "debugging," after discovering a moth stuck in the workings of a computer. Her name and contribution have inspired the greatest global gathering of women in computing: the Grace Hopper Celebration of Women in Computing,[6] which attracted 20,000 participants in 2018.

A CASE EXAMPLE: THE CARNEGIE MELLON UNIVERSITY STORY

Our initial motivation for this collection of perspectives from a wide range of countries and cultures came from observations and studies of undergraduate students in the computer science major at Carnegie Mellon University. This inspired us to challenge the *pink brain, blue brain* mentality that we believe has become a major obstacle to gender balance in the field of computing in the United States and many parts of the Western world.

We found that women are "kicking butt"[7] in CS in some environments in the United States. The percentage of women enrolling and graduating in computer science at Carnegie Mellon has exceeded national averages for many years. Indeed, the school hit the news in fall 2017 when an unprecedented 49.7% new women entered the CS major followed by the 2018 entering class with 50% women. But Carnegie Mellon is not alone – other institutions in the United States have also had success in addressing the gender gap. Harvey Mudd College, for example, went from 10% women in CS in 2006, the year Maria Klawe (a highly respected computer scientist) took over as college president, to 40% women in CS by 2012 (Alvarado et al., 2012). Schools that are investing in cultural change may be quite different, and have different approaches, but they share some straightforward practices that have proven to be successful in the United States: they pay attention to the situation; they assess which interventions will work in their particular environments; they have institutional and financial support for diversity and inclusion efforts; they value and believe in women; they are open to change from the status quo; and they have multiple levels of commitment. They are living proof that – as Carnegie Mellon CS professor and Founder of Women@SCS, Lenore Blum says – increasing the participation of women in computing "is not rocket science!"

At Carnegie Mellon the critical strategies for changing the culture were threefold: *institutional support* (involving deans, faculty, staff, administrators, funding, values, and the school's philosophy); *student leadership* through our energetic and creative women's organization, Women@SCS, endorsed by the school and central to the culture (providing leadership, mentoring, encouragement, and peer-to-peer programs involving both undergraduates and graduates); and *leveling the playing field* (to ensure women, and others, do not miss out on valuable social, academic, and professional opportunities and experiences). Overall we have strived to take a holistic approach, recognizing that both academic life *and social life* work together for students to be successful (Veilleux et al., 2013; Walton and Cohen, 2007). Women@SCS has helped provide a strong shield against isolation, a primary factor negatively impacting the experience and performance of women and minorities in computing (Etzkowitz et al., 2000; Smith, 2010; Taylor, 2002).

Since 2002 we have carried out a series of studies to monitor the attitudes, experiences, and perceptions of our CS majors, watching for issues that need attention. What continues to surprise us is how similar the men and women are (Blum and Frieze, 2005; Frieze and Quesenberry, 2015). Undergraduate students in the CS environment at Carnegie Mellon show a spectrum of attitudes toward the field. We have found many variables among students' experiences, attitudes, and expectations, and a complex spectrum of gender similarities and differences that exist among, and between, men and women – *but no significant gender divide.*

Since 2000 we have learned many valuable lessons about women in CS at Carnegie Mellon. In a nutshell, what stood out to us are the following: for women to be successful in CS we did not need to change the *curriculum* to be focused on so-called women's interests in computing but we did need to change the *culture and environment* (Frieze et al., 2011; Frieze and Quesenberry, 2015). Indeed, gender-difference approaches have not provided satisfactory explanations for the low participation of women in CS, and beliefs in a gender divide may actually be deterring women from seeing themselves in male-dominated fields.

ORGANIZATION OF THE BOOK

One of the most interesting and fun elements of working on this book has been the collaboration with authors who bring their perspectives from around the world. We are delighted to include chapters from twenty-nine experts, practitioners, researchers, educators, and activists who are leaders in understanding how culture shapes women's participation in computing. The authors also represent a variety of different disciplines – including anthropology, computer science, human–computer interaction, information sciences/systems, informatics, policy, sociology, and statistics – which lends to the richness of the work and to their conclusions. The authors raise interesting questions and use a variety of theories, methods, and interventions in their chapters. You may notice that we purposefully kept the authors' language and colloquialisms to add to the richness of the analysis and highlight the diversity of cultural context.

Each chapter includes five to ten discussion questions that we hope will continue the conversation and generate ideas for future considerations.

In organizing the book, we cast a wide net to include as many cultural perspectives as possible and we are pleased to include analyses of more than fifty separate countries across the globe. Yet we do not see this as an end in itself. There are many countries and cultures that unfortunately are not represented in this book. Furthermore, our authors bring a diversity of perspectives to their chapters, but they are not speaking for the full community they represent. Their work is derived from and situated in their particular cultural community, but by no means is intended to represent a generalization for their entire community. All of our authors faced a tremendous task knowing from our own experience that little global research has been done on women in computing.

Table I.1 gives an overview of the topics covered in each chapter, along with high-level descriptions and keywords. The guide to the chapters includes additional details not summarized in the following paragraphs where we describe the parts of the book and identify themes that are raised among the chapters.

This book is organized in four parts that present perspectives on women's interest, pursuit, and persistence in secondary schools, post-secondary schools, and careers in the computing field. Part I, "Global Perspectives," includes research that explores cross-national comparisons of women in computing from more than a single country perspective. In this part, the authors present fascinating data and analyses of the global picture of women in computing ranging from some of the poorest, least developed countries to the highly modernized. We are fortunate to have chapters from authors who have done exceptional research for many years to increase our understanding of women in computing from a cross-cultural perspective.

Tiffany Chow and Maria Charles show data that challenge our assumptions as we learn that increased gender equity, higher education, and modernization do not lead to higher rates of women in computing. Sophia Huyer summarizes data from a recent UNESCO report showing that while there are opportunities for women to enter STEM fields, a range of cultural barriers (namely, family and childcare considerations) constrain their participation. Eileen M. Trauth complements the previous chapters' quantitative findings as she uses qualitative interviews from field studies in Europe, North America, Africa, and Asia-Pacific to explore how individual variations play a role in responding to cultural considerations. We also see that women's careers often hit obstacles and challenges as they attempt to advance. The reasons for this vary by country but demonstrate how culture plays a central role in the shaping of women's participation.

Part II, "Regional Perspectives," includes research that explores cross-national comparisons of women in computing from a regional perspective. This part includes three chapters that stand alone geographically, but share some of the similarities and differences explored throughout the book. For example, Palma Buttles and Fred Valdez, Jr. argue that women from Latin America and the Caribbean have a shared regional culture, but are still multidimensional and varied. Orit Hazzan, Efrat Nativ-Ronen, and

Table I.1 *Chapter overview*

	Overview	Topics covered
Part I: Global Perspectives		
1 An Inegalitarian Paradox: On the Uneven Gendering of Computing Work around the World *Tiffany Chow and Maria Charles*	Provides a new descriptive mapping of the gender segregation of information and communication technology (ICT) occupations in fifty countries and examines how observed differences map onto variation in socioeconomic modernization, women's educational and economic status, and other relevant country-level characteristics.	Global perspectives, modernization, occupational segregation, work, ICT
2 A Global Perspective on Women in Information Technology: Perspectives from the "UNESCO Science Report 2015: Towards 2030" *Sophia Huyer*	Summarizes a UNESCO report on the global situation of women in STEM fields that found women are well represented at the tertiary level in bachelors and master's programs, but not at the PhD, post-doc, researcher, and manager levels. The data indicate similar cultural issues, and patterns persist across the globe, with some exceptions such as Turkey and Malaysia.	Global perspectives, UNESCO, culture, leadership, employment, family, work–life balance, ICT
3 Field Studies of Women in Europe, North America, Africa, and Asia-Pacific: A Theoretical Explanation for the Gender Imbalance in Information Technology *Eileen M. Trauth*	Presents an empirical analysis of field data from Europe, North America, Africa, and Asia-Pacific that is used to support the "Individual Differences Theory of Gender and IT." The theory argues that within-gender variation in exposure to, experience of, and response to gender messages and barriers about women can explain women's low representation in the IT field.	Europe, North America, Africa, Asia-Pacific, gender theory, individual differences theory of gender and IT, social inclusion, IT workforce

Table I.1 (*cont.*)

	Overview	Topics covered
Part II: Regional Perspectives		
4 Sociocultural Complexities of Latin American and Caribbean Women in Computing *Palma Buttles and Fred Valdez, Jr.*	Illustrates the complexity surrounding the gender gap in computing in Latin America and the Caribbean and identifies potential lines for future inquiry, arguing that women are not homogeneous, but rather are varied and multidimensional.	Latin America, Caribbean, Mexico, Brazil, sociocultural factors, socioeconomic factors, machismo, marianismo, stereotypes, CS
5 A Gender Perspective on Computer Science Education in Israel: From High School, through the Military and Academia to the Tech Industry *Orit Hazzan, Efrat Nativ-Ronen, and Tatiana Umansky*	Describes the story of Israeli female participation in CS from both a gender and a sectorial perspective. Critical to the analysis is understanding the similarities and differences among two cultural groups: Jewish and Arab women.	Israel, Israel Defense Forces (IDF), diversity, Jewish women, Arab women, female representation, culture, CS education, tech industry
6 Factors Influencing Women's Ability to Enter the Information Technology Workforce: Case Studies of Five Sub-Saharan African Countries *Sophia Huyer and Nancy J. Hafkin*	Presents case studies from five countries in East and West Africa – Ethiopia, Kenya, Rwanda, Senegal, and Uganda – which assesses the economic, cultural, infrastructural, and policy factors influencing women's ability to enter the IT workforce in the region.	Africa, Ethiopia, Kenya, Rwanda, Senegal, Uganda, culture, leadership, employment, family, work–life balance, STEM, IT education and workforce
Part III: Cultural Perspectives from the United States and Europe		
7 Against All Odds: Culture and Context in the Female Information Technology Professional's Career Choice and Experiences *Monica P. Adya*	Introduces female IT professionals who have overcome a variety of odds with regard to their choice of, and success in, IT careers. The analysis shows that grit and resilience to cultural influences such as gender-stereotyping of IT careers are central components of female persistence.	United States, career barriers, computing self-efficacy, entrenchment, resilience, career mentors, role of family

Table I.1 (cont.)

	Overview	Topics covered
12 Portugal: Perspectives on Women in Computing *Arminda Guerra Lopes*	Presents two case studies of Portugal – one at the high school level and one at the polytechnic and university level – with women interested in CS. The results show that Portuguese sociocultural influences bring many challenges, but promises for the future can be found.	Portugal, history, sociocultural factors, fascism regime, colonial war, high school students, polytechnic students, university students, CS
13 Women in Computing: The Situation in Russia *Evgeniy K. Khenner*	Provides a detailed description of the history and participation of women in computing in Russia. The study shows the underrepresentation of women is, in large part, due to stereotypes of the profession. The analysis also includes reflections of several female pioneers in the Russian computing field.	Africa, Ethiopia, Kenya, Rwanda, Senegal, Uganda, culture, leadership, employment, family, work–life balance, STEM, IT education and workforce
Part IV: Cultural Perspectives from Asia-Pacific		
14 More Chinese Women Are Needed to Hold Up Half the Computing Sky *Ming Zhang and Yichun Yin*	Examines how women's participation in the Chinese computing field is influenced by deeply rooted attitudes from China's traditional Confucian-based ethics, the intense pressures of balancing work and home, and the prevailing male-dominated environment.	China, Chinese traditional ethics culture, gender diversity, Chinese female practitioners, entrepreneurship, computing industry
15 How the Perception of Young Malaysians toward Science and Mathematics Influences Their Decision to Study Computer Science *Mazliza Othman and Rodziah Latih*	Analyzes the results from a follow-up study of post-secondary students in Malaysia and concludes that young Malaysian men and women do not hold different perceptions of their ability to succeed in CS.	Malaysia, gender similarities, gender differences, gender disparity, computer science education

16 Women as Software Engineers in Indian Tamil Cinema *Joyojeet Pal*	Discusses the emergence of women as software engineers in Indian Tamil cinema. The analysis describes how the role of female software engineers captures the complexity of Indian society's aspirations, prejudices, and fears alike, while offering a positive change in the cinematic representation of women in the workplace.	India, Indian Tamil cinema, social shaping, tradition, middle class, software engineer, technology
17 Women in Computing Education: A Western or a Global Problem? Lessons from India *Roli Varma*	Presents a case study of women in computing in India that shows how computing and gender are constructed more diversely than assumed in Western research. The analysis shows that women are attracted to the computing field, but face challenges that are specific to the Indian social context.	India, confidence in mathematics, geek mythology, Indian female students, patriarchy, underrepresentation of women, CS
18 Challenging Attitudes and Disrupting Stereotypes of Gender and Computing in Australia: Are We Doing It Right? *Catherine Lang*	Provides an overview of the gendered nature of computing in Australia and initiatives to challenge attitudes and societal stereotypes. The analysis also critiques what Australia is "doing right" and identifies areas for future improvement.	Australia, Indigenous youth, student course choices, teacher education, interventions, gender and computing

Tatiana Umansky explore how regional differences in Israel influence the experiences of Jewish and Arab girls and women in the country. Although their chapter focuses on the country of Israel, we felt the cultural themes they explore between Jewish and Arab girls and women are indicative of varied cultural backgrounds of the region. Sophia Huyer and Nancy J. Hafkin describe how in several African countries childcare and maternity policies are inscribed in a nation's constitution to contribute to women's equal opportunities in the workplace. As in several chapters, the significance of representation and stereotypes appears, with examples that serve to reinforce stereotypes, while others challenge our expectations.

Part III, "Cultural Perspectives from the United States and Europe," includes research that explores country case studies from primarily a Western viewpoint and that of Russia.[8] Chapters in this part range broadly, not only by location but also by perspectives. Many of these perspectives emerge from individual interviews and reflections from female pioneers in the computing field. We hear the voices of women who have often been forgotten – women who have played a major role in the history of computing, women with disabilities for whom gender is just one factor in their marginalization, women who moved westward for improved opportunities, women who moved into a culture "branded" by their male colleagues.

This part includes three chapters focused on the United States, yet these chapters highlight various subcultures within the American context. Monica P. Adya investigates female IT professionals who have overcome a variety of odds with regard to their choice of, and success in, IT careers. Her analysis compares and contrasts the experiences of South Asian and American women in the United States workforce. Sally A. Applin gives an in-depth analysis of Silicon Valley's computing culture and its influence on the rest of the world. She identifies cultural biases that have influenced women and speculates as to how these factors will evolve and continue to shape computing worldwide. Brianna Blaser, Cynthia Bennett, Richard E. Ladner, Sheryl E. Burgstahler, and Jennifer Mankoff provide an overview of disability history to highlight the struggles that individuals with disabilities have had with obtaining access to education and careers. They include a discussion with women with disabilities in computing education and careers and found that many of these women feel isolated and marginalized – thus they conclude with steps that can be taken to make the field more welcoming and accessible overall.

Part III also includes several chapters from a European perspective, highlighting four unique country perspectives from the United Kingdom,

Sweden, Portugal, and Russia. Sue Black discusses her work as a leader for gender parity in computing in the United Kingdom where among her many efforts she started #techmums and the British Computer Society's Specialist Group BCSWomen, and perhaps is most well known for initiating – and succeeding – in saving Bletchley Park, as the title of her book reflects. Sinna Lindquist and Ingrid Melinder present a history of the Swedish educational system along with facts and figures on gender divergence for different academic tracks and levels. In doing so, they describe the reasons why women might pursue a career in computing. They also share the perspectives of successful women in computing who discuss how their upbringing and background impacted their choice of education and career path. Arminda Guerra Lopes presents two case studies from Portugal (at the secondary and post-secondary levels) that help to explain the motivation for women to study or pursue a career in computer science. Her analysis concludes that the Portuguese sociocultural influences on women are difficult to overcome and unfortunately do not fully coincide with the concept of a computing professional. Evgeniy K. Khenner provides a detailed overview of the gender imbalance of women in computing in Russia – starting with a summary of the history – and then providing statistics and explanations at the secondary, post-secondary, and employment levels. He suggests that the imbalance is based on both discrimination and female perceptions of "fit" in IT.

Part IV, "Cultural Perspectives from Asia-Pacific," includes research that explores country case studies from an Eastern viewpoint and that of Australia. In this part we include some computing cultures in which women are well represented. Ming Zhang and Yichun Yin describe historical and cultural issues related to women in China's computing communities. They discuss an interesting situation in that women represent a very small percentage of the Chinese computing industry, yet they represent a relatively high proportion of senior positions and entrepreneurs. Mazliza Othman and Rodziah Latih provide an update on their earlier study of women in computing in Malaysia. In their current study, they continue to find that Malaysian women have a markedly different attitude toward science and mathematics compared with their Western counterparts. They conclude that computing is not viewed as a masculine field by young Malaysians and thus there is no gender imbalance. Joyojeet Pal presents a cultural analysis of the emergence of women as software engineers in Indian Tamil cinema. He suggests that the cinematic representation of women in the workplace has played a positive role, while accommodating traditional values, in shaping the perceptions of women in the Indian computing field. Roli Varma adds to the Indian perspective and in doing so presents a case study that shows how the perceptions of computing are welcoming to women in India since the field offers lucrative jobs, high salaries, professional careers, safe office working environments, and economic independence. Yet women still remain marginalized due to patriarchal values. Catherine Lang summarizes the underrepresentation of women in Australia and reflects on why interventions over the last several decades have had little impact on improving the participation rate of women in the computing field. She suggests that educational institutions should empower teachers to be more creative and to build opportunities for computing competence that spans the silos of traditional educational disciplines.

Throughout Part IV we hear about contexts where traditional patriarchal social expectations create barriers to women's sustained participation. But this is not always the case. In some, despite such challenges, the field of computing opens up new career possibilities for women along with increased confidence and independence. Further, Western stereotypes about the field and perceptions of "fit" are socially constructed and not pervasive in all regions of the world. One important consideration in the part on Asia-Pacific is a reminder that the terminology we use and how we name the various fields of computing may have an impact on perception and participation. Furthermore, the stereotypes and perceptions of the computing field are specific to the social context and not a universal problem that many times is generalized in mainstream media and academic literature.

References

Alghamdi, F. (2016). "Women in Computing in Saudi Arabia." In *Proceedings of the 3rd ACM-W Europe Celebration of Women in Computing.* Retrieved from https://uu.diva-portal.org/smash/get/diva2:971716/FULLTEXT01.pdf.

Alvarado, C., Dodds, Z., and Libeskind-Hadas, R. (2012). "Increasing Women's Participation in Computing at Harvey Mudd College." *ACM Inroads,* 3(4), 55–64.

Association of American Medical Colleges (AAMC). (2017). "More Women than Men Enrolled in U.S. Medical Schools in 2017." AAMC News, press release, December 18. Retrieved from https://news.aamc.org/press-releases/article/applicant-enrollment-2017/.

Barnett, R., and Rivers, C. (2005). *Same Difference: How Gender Myths Are Hurting Our Relationships, Our Children, and Our Jobs.* New York: Basic Books.

Berger, P. L., and Luckmann, T. (1966). *The Social Construction of Reality: A Treatise in the Sociology of Knowledge.* New York: Doubleday.

Bem, S. L. (1981). "Gender Schema Theory: A Cognitive Account of Sex Typing." *Psychological Review,* 88, 354–364.

Blum, L., and Frieze, C. (2005). "The Evolving Culture of Computing: Similarity Is the Difference." *Frontiers: A Journal of Women Studies, Special Issue on Gender and IT,* 26(1), 110–125.

Bureau of Labor Statistics (2017). "Labor Force Statistics from the Current Population Survey." Retrieved on April 13, 2019, from www.bls.gov/cps/cpsaat11.htm.

Charles, M., and Grusky, D. (2005). *Occupational Ghettos: The Worldwide Segregation of Women and Men (Studies in Social Inequality).* Redwood City, CA: Stanford University Press.

Crenshaw, K. (1989). "Demarginalizing the Intersection of Race and Sex: A Black Feminist Critique of Antidiscrimination Doctrine, Feminist Theory and Antiracist Politics." *University of Chicago Forum,* 1989(1), 8.

Darwin, C. (1871). *The Descent of Man, and Selection in Relation to Sex,* 2nd edition. London: John Murray.

Eliot, L. (2009). *Pink Brain, Blue Brain: How Small Differences Grow into Troublesome Gaps – And What We Can Do About It.* New York: Houghton Mifflin Harcourt.

Etzkowitz, H., Kemelgor, C., and Uzzi, B. (2000). *Athena Unbound: The Advancement of Women in Science and Technology.* Cambridge: Cambridge University Press.

Fine, C. (2010). *Delusions of Gender.* New York: W. W. Norton.

Frieze, C., and Quesenberry, J. L. (2015). *Kicking Butt in Computer Science: Women in Computing at Carnegie Mellon University.* Indianapolis, IN: Dog Ear Publishing.

Frieze, C., Quesenberry, J. L., Kemp, E., and Velaszquez, A. (2011). "Diversity or Difference? New Research Supports the Case for a Cultural Perspective on Women in Computing." *Journal of Science Education and Technology,* 21(4), 423–439.

Galpin, V. (2002). "Women in Computing around the World." *ACM SIGCSE Bulletin – Women in Computing,* 34(2), 94–100.

Girls Collaborative Project. (2016). "The State of Girls and Women in STEM." Retrieved from https://ngcproject.org/sites/default/files/ngcp_the_state_of_girls_ and_women_in_stem_2016_final.pdf.

Gray, J. (1992). *Men Are from Mars, Women Are from Venus.* New York: HarperCollins.

Gurer, D. (2002). "Pioneering Women in Computer Science." *ACM SIGCSE Bulletin – Women in Computing,* 34(2), 120.

Halpern, D. (2000) *Sex Differences in Cognitive Abilities.* Mahwah, NJ: Lawrence Erlbaum Associates.

Hyde, J. S. (2005). "The Gender Similarities Hypothesis." *American Psychologist,* 60(6), 581–592.

Hyde, J. S., and Linn, M. C. (2006). "Gender Similarities in Mathematics and Science." *Science,* 314(5799), 599–600.

Linn, M., and Hyde, J. (1989). "Gender, Mathematics and Science." *Educational Researcher,* 18, 17–27.

Matsui, H., and Chilana, P. (2004). "The Rise and Fall: Women and Computer Science." Canadian Coalition of Women in Engineering, Science and Technology (CCWEST) Conference, St. Catharines, Ontario.

National Center for Education Statistics. (2016). "Digest of Education Statistics." Retrieved from https://nces.ed.gov/programs/digest/d16/.

National Science Foundation (NSF). (2017). "Scientists and Engineers Working in Science and Engineering Occupations: 2015." *Women, Minorities, and Persons with Disabilities in Science and Engineering Digest.* Retrieved from www.nsf.gov/statistics/2017/nsf17310/digest/occupation/overall.cfmm.

Organization for Economic Cooperation and Development (OECD). (2017). "Health at a Glance 2017." *OCED Indicators.* Retrieved from www.oecd.org/health/health-at-a-glance-19991312.htm.

People's Republic of China State Council Information Office (PRCSCIO). (2015). "China White Paper on Gender Equality and Women Development."

Schinzel, B. (2002). "Cultural Differences of Female Enrolment in Tertiary Education in Computer Science." In *Proceedings of the IFIP 17th World Computer Congress – TC3 Stream on TelE-Learning: The Challenge for the Third Millennium.* The Netherlands: Kluwer, 201–208.

Shutterly, M. L. (2016). *Hidden Figures: The American Dream and the Untold Story of the Black Women Mathematicians Who Helped Win the Space Race.* New York: William Morrow.

Smith, E. (2010). "The Role of Social Supports and Self-Efficacy in College Success." *Pathways to College Network,* Fall 2010. Retrieved from www.collegeaccess.org/images/documents/R2P/SocialSupports.pdf.

Stoet, G., and Geary, D. C. (2018). "The Gender-Equality Paradox in Science, Technology, Engineering, and Mathematics Education." *Psychological Science,* 29(4), 581–593.

Taylor, V. (2002). "Women of Color in Computing." *ACM SIGCSE Bulletin – Women in Computing,* 34(2), 22–23.

Trauth, E. M. (2002). "Odd Girl Out: An Individual Differences Perspective on Women in the IT Profession." *Information Technology and People,* 15(2), 98–118.

United Nations Educational, Scientific and Cultural Organization (UNESCO). (2017). "Women Still a Minority in Engineering and Computer Science." Retrieved from www.unesco.org/new/en/unesco/themes/gender-equality/resources/single-view-gender/news/women_still_a_minority_in_engineering_and_computer_science/.

Veilleux, N., Bates, R., Jones, D., Crawford, J., and Floyd Smith, T. (2013). "The Relationship between Belonging and Ability in Computer Science." In *Proceeding of the 44th ACM Technical Symposium on Computer Science Education, (SIGCSE '13).* New York: ACM, 65–70.

Wajcman, J. (1991). *Feminism Confronts Technology.* University Park: Pennsylvania University Press.

Walton, G. M., and Cohen, G. L. (2007). "A Question of Belonging: Race, Social Fit, and Achievement." *Journal of Personality and Social Psychology,* 92(1), 82–96.

Williams, R. (1958). "Culture Is Ordinary." In A. Gray and J. McGuigan (eds.), *Studies in Culture: An Introductory Reader.* London: Arnold, 5–14.

The World Economic Forum (2016). "The Global Gender Gap Report 2017." Retrieved from www.weforum.org/reports/the-global-gender-gap-report-2017.

Zweben, S., and Bizot, B. (2017). "2016 Taulbee Survey." *Computing Research Association,* 29(5), 3–51. Retrieved from http://cra.org/crn/wp-content/uploads/sites/7/2017/05/2016-Taulbee-Survey.pdf.

Part I

Global Perspectives

1

An Inegalitarian Paradox

On the Uneven Gendering of Computing Work around the World

Tiffany Chow and Maria Charles

INTRODUCTION

Previous research has revealed surprising cross-national differences in the gender composition of information and communication technology (ICT) fields. In 2001, for example, women's representation in ICT degree programs was weakest in the world's most affluent and reputably gender-progressive societies (Charles and Bradley, 2006). Historical trends in the ICT sectors of affluent democracies seem, moreover, to have gone in the direction of more, not less, gender segregation. Despite dramatic increases in female labor force participation and university attendance, US women's share of bachelor's degrees in computer science decreased from 28% to 18% between 2000 and 2015 (NSF, 2018, appendix 2-21), with similar declines documented in Europe for the 1990s (Schinzel, 2002).

But ICT work is not male-dominated everywhere, and contemporary Western understandings of computing as geeky, asocial, and inhospitable to women are not universal. Computer programing in the United States transitioned from stereotypically low-skilled and feminine work in the postwar decades to a respected and strongly male-dominated profession in more recent years (Abbate, 2012; Ensmenger, 2015). In Malaysia and India, by contrast, computing is today regarded as a highly desirable career pathway for women due to its good pay and safe indoor work environments, and undergraduate computer science degree programs boast near gender-parity (Othman and Laith, 2006; Lagesen, 2008; Frehill and Cohoon, 2015; Varma and Kapur, 2015; Mehta, 2016).[1]

These patterns of cross-national and historical variation are difficult to reconcile with popular beliefs and sociological theories that posit continuous declines in all forms of gender inequality with advancing socioeconomic modernization.[2] Instead of across-the-board improvements in women's status, the available evidence suggests that women's expanded *access* to public-sphere institutions often coincides with persistent, and sometimes even growing, gender segregation *within* these institutions (Bradley, 2000; Charles, 2011a,b; Huyer, 2015).

The dramatic underrepresentation of women and some racial and ethnic groups in computing and technical fields has sparked considerable concern and countless research and policy initiatives by governments, non-governmental organizations, and industry leaders worldwide. Motivating these initiatives are interests in diversifying employment opportunities in lucrative, high-status occupations and in ameliorating acute labor shortages that may threaten national economic development and competitiveness.

The present chapter provides a new descriptive mapping of how women's representation in computing occupations varies around the world. Applying occupational data from 2017, we document differences across fifty countries in the gender composition of ICT occupations, and we describe how these differences map onto variation in socioeconomic modernization, women's educational and economic status, and other relevant country-level characteristics. Results suggest little change from patterns documented for earlier decades: socioeconomic modernization is again found to coincide with more, not less, gender segregation of computing-related fields. We discuss possible explanations in the concluding section.

DATA AND METHODS

The primary data for our analysis are taken from cross-classifications of occupation by gender that were provided to the International Labour Organization by national governments (ILO, 2018). We use figures from the most recent year available, which is 2017 in almost all cases.[3] Occupations were coded to the 2008 version of the International Standard Classification of Occupations (ISCO-08), a four-level hierarchically structured classification that assigns occupations into one of 436 "unit groups." These are in turn aggregated into 130 minor groups, 43 sub-major groups, and 10 major groups (ILO, 2012). ISCO-08, a revision of the earlier ISCO-88, provides a means of harmonizing national census data to a common classificatory system. Especially relevant for present purposes is that this most recent version for the first time allows identification of ICT workers at the sub-major group level.[4] This means that we have an opportunity to compare women's representation among ICT "Professionals" (sub-major group 25) and ICT "Technicians and Associate Professionals" (sub-major group 35) across a large number of countries. Professionals (major group 2) are distinguished from Technicians and Associate Professionals (major group 3) by their skill levels, with the former requiring higher education of longer duration (e.g., at least a bachelor's degree vs. an associate's or vocational degree). The occupations included in sub-major groups 25 and 35 are shown in Table 1.1.

After eliminating countries and territories with missing data on ICT occupations and with extremely small ICT sectors (i.e., with fewer than 5,000 workers in groups 25 and 35 combined), we arrived at a sample of

Table 1.1 *ISCO-08 classification of information and communication technology (ICT) occupations*

---

2 Professionals (Major group)
  25 Information and Communications Technology (ICT) Professionals
    (sub-major group)
    251 Software and Application Developers and Analysts
        2511 Systems Analysts
        2512 Software Developers
        2513 Web and Multimedia Developers
        2514 Applications Programmers
        2519 Software and Applications Developers and Analysts Not
            Elsewhere Classified
    252 Database and Network Professionals
        2521 Database Designers and Administrators
        2532 Systems Administrators
        2523 Computer Network Professionals
        2529 Database and Network Professionals Not Elsewhere
            Classified

3 Technicians and Associate Professionals (Major group)
  35 Information and Communications Technology (ICT) Technicians
    (sub-major group)
    351 ICT Operations and User Support Technicians
        3511 ICT Operations Technicians
        3512 ICT User Support Technicians
        3513 Computer Network and Systems Technicians
        3514 Web Technicians
    352 Telecommunications and Broadcasting Technicians
        3521 Broadcasting and Audiovisual Technicians
        3522 Telecommunications Engineering Technicians

Note: 1-digit codes designate "major groups," 2-digit codes designate "sub-major groups," 3-digit codes designate "minor groups," and 4-digit codes designate "unit groups." Internationally harmonized data are available for ICT Professions and Associate Professions at the sub-major level are shown in italics.

Table 1.2 *Sample countries by United Nations regional group*

Africa: Ethiopia, Liberia, Mauritius

Asian-Pacific: Bangladesh, Cyprus, Israel, Myanmar, Philippines, Thailand, United
  Arab Emirates

Eastern Europe: Bulgaria, Croatia, Czech Republic, Estonia, Hungary, Latvia, Lithuania,
  Macedonia, Poland, Romania, Serbia, Slovakia, Slovenia

Latin America and Caribbean: Argentina, Brazil, Ecuador, El Salvador, Mexico,
  Panama, Uruguay

Western Europe and Others: Austria, Belgium, Denmark, Finland, France, Germany,
  Greece, Ireland, Italy, Luxembourg, Malta, Netherlands, Norway, Portugal, Spain,
  Sweden, Switzerland, Turkey, United Kingdom, United States

Note: All ILO data are from 2017, except for El Salvador (2016), Ethiopia (2013),
Liberia (2010), Mauritius (2016) Panama (2014), and Thailand (2016).

fifty-one countries.[5] We then omitted Peru because of concerns about data
reliability.[6] Although advanced industrial societies are strongly overrepresented in our country sample, the 50 countries included are economically
and culturally diverse and span all major United Nations regional groups,
with 20 located in the Western European group, 13 in Eastern Europe, 7 in
Latin America, 7 in the Asian-Pacific region, and 3 in Africa (see Table 1.2).
The uneven distribution across regions is attributable to the greater availability of harmonized employment data in more economically developed
societies. It is especially unfortunate that the relevant occupational data are
not available for India and China, two very large countries with significant
ICT sectors. Our country sample is nonetheless larger and more socio-
economically and regionally diverse than any used before to study the
gender segregation of ICT labor markets.

We measure gender segregation of ICT in two ways: as women's percentage share of workers in the respective occupational category (i.e., in
sub-major group 25 or 35), and using odds ratios. Although the latter are
less intuitively appealing, they have the advantage of allowing us to compare women's representation in ICT in a way that is independent of the
large differences across countries in women's share of the labor force.[7]
This is achieved for the professional group, for example, by normalizing
the woman-to-man odds ratio for ICT professionals (ISCO sub-major
group 25) against the woman-to-man odds ratio of professional workers
who are *not* ICT professionals.[8] The first panel of Appendix 1.1 shows
correlations among the four segregation measures.

We also assembled country-level data on diverse socioeconomic indicators. Given the patterns revealed by previous studies, we are particularly

interested in exploring how the gender composition of ICT occupations varies across countries characterized by different levels of socioeconomic modernization and different rates of female participation in labor markets, higher education, and politics. Our primary measure of modernization is the 2015 Human Development Index (HDI), a composite of national income, health, and education (UNDP, 2016). To ensure that findings are not sensitive to the measure used, we supplement HDI with a simple indicator of gross national income, measured in 2011 (UNDP, 2016). Because societal affluence often coincides with the development of democratic institutions, we also assess how the gender composition of ICT occupations varies with national political democracy, measured using an index constructed by Marshall, Gurr, and Jaggers (2014).[9] Indicators of public-sphere participation include women's percentage shares of the total labor force, the national parliament, national university graduates, and ICT degree recipients.[10] We supplement these measures with a summary index of 2017 gender equality, which is a composite of women's reproductive health, empowerment, and economic status (UNDP, 2016). Zero-order correlations among these covariates and their individual country scores are reported in Appendices 1.1 and 1.2.

HOW DOES THE GENDER COMPOSITION OF ICT OCCUPATIONS VARY?

Before describing country-level differences in the gender segregation of computing occupations, it is useful to examine variability across major geographic regions. Table 1.3 shows striking regional differences that correspond to the patterns revealed by previous cross-national studies (Schinzel, 2002; Charles and Bradley, 2006, 2009): *ICT professional work is most male-dominated in the economically developed regions of Europe and North America and least male-dominated in the African and Asian Pacific regions.*[11] African women's 31.3% share of ICT professionals is, for example, nearly twice that found in the group that includes Western Europe and the United States (16.9%). Differences are even more pronounced when regional differences in the gender composition of the professional labor force are taken into account. Professional women's odds of working in ICT (rather than in another professional occupation) are 17% lower than men's odds in Africa, 61% lower than men's odds in the Asia-Pacific region, and 84% lower than men's odds in Western Europe and the United States. The Latin American and Eastern European regions fall in between, but are closer to the lower than the higher scores. Regional

Table 1.3 *Gender segregation in ICT occupations by UN regional group, 2017*

	ICT professionals		ICT associate professionals	
	Women's % share	Women/men odds ratio	Women's % share	Women/men odds ratio
Africa	31.26	0.83	23.88	0.66
Asian-Pacific	30.41	0.39	21.72	0.69
Eastern Europe	19.83	0.14	21.68	0.25
Latin America and Caribbean	21.14	0.20	15.91	0.21
Western Europe and United States	16.94	0.16	16.22	0.22

differences are less pronounced in the associate professions, but follow a similar pattern, with more integration in the less affluent regions. One exception is the very low representation of women among Latin American ICT technicians.

The country-specific percentages and odds ratios that generate these regional differences are displayed in Tables 1.4 and 1.5 for the professions and associate professions, respectively. The tables are sorted in descending order according to women's percentage share of ICT professionals. *The top of the professional ICT list (Table 1.4) is mostly populated by low-income African and Asian countries, and the bottom is overwhelmingly European.* We find, for example, that women comprise 65.1% of ICT professionals in Myanmar and 45.4% in Ethiopia, but less than 11% in the much more affluent Western and Eastern European countries of Switzerland, Greece, Hungary, and Czech Republic. The United States and reputably gender-progressive Sweden fall somewhere in the middle of the distribution with 23.5% and 22.9% women, respectively. The seeming gender integration of Ethiopian ICT professions is especially striking given Ethiopian women's relatively small share of professional workers overall (33.9%). They are in this sense *over*represented in ICT professions, as reflected in the odds ratio of 1.63 in the second column of Table 1.4.

Women's representation among associate professional ICT workers (i.e., technicians) follows a similarly counterintuitive pattern. The negative affluence gradient is a little less obvious, however, because two Eastern European countries – Romania and Lithuania – precede Myanmar at the top of Table 1.5. The United States, where 26.8% of ICT technicians are women, falls between Serbia and Ethiopia on this ranking. Interestingly, another (more affluent) Eastern European country, Czech Republic,

Table 1.4 *Women's representation in ICT professions, 2017*

	Women's share	Women/men odds ratio	Women's share of all professionals
Myanmar	65.07	0.64	74.33
Ethiopia	45.37	1.63	33.85
Panama	37.75	0.41	58.68
Thailand	33.72	0.33	59.56
Philippines	33.62	0.25	65.23
Macedonia	32.02	0.35	55.95
Bulgaria	30.48	0.19	66.58
Liberia	27.08	0.61	37.61
Romania	25.22	0.23	57.43
Ecuador	25.15	0.25	56.37
Lithuania	25.12	0.13	69.63
Serbia	24.70	0.22	57.35
United States	23.55	0.22	54.27
Cyprus	23.15	0.23	54.87
Sweden	22.78	0.18	57.43
Ireland	21.77	0.20	53.89
Bangladesh	21.34	0.50	35.28
Mauritius	21.34	0.26	49.66
Finland	21.00	0.24	47.72
Brazil	20.90	0.16	60.33
Turkey	20.73	0.28	47.11
Israel	19.73	0.14	60.22
Spain	19.67	0.18	55.97
Denmark	19.41	0.16	55.73
Italy	19.34	0.19	54.33
Latvia	19.05	0.09	68.72
Estonia	18.85	0.10	64.53
Uruguay	18.79	0.13	60.88
France	18.06	0.18	51.43
Norway	17.84	0.12	59.40
Croatia	17.68	0.11	63.77
United Kingdom	17.57	0.19	48.89
Portugal	17.28	0.12	60.28
El Salvador	16.99	0.21	49.20
Slovakia	16.83	0.11	60.32
United Arab Emirates	16.28	0.62	23.74
Mexico	15.49	0.18	49.41
Netherlands	14.25	0.15	47.88
Austria	14.18	0.13	51.15
Poland	14.11	0.09	61.11
Germany	13.71	0.17	44.95
Argentina	12.91	0.08	63.45
Belgium	12.88	0.11	53.25
Slovenia	12.69	0.08	61.65
Malta	12.42	0.13	48.31

Table 1.4 (*cont.*)

	Women's share	Women/men odds ratio	Women's share of all professionals
Luxembourg	11.10	0.12	46.89
Switzerland	10.85	0.12	46.14
Hungary	10.82	0.10	51.87
Greece	10.40	0.10	51.89
Czech Republic	10.20	0.09	52.56

Table 1.5 *Women's representation in ICT associate professions, 2017*

	Women's share	Women/men odds ratio	Women's share of all associate professionals
Romania	38.72	0.50	21.12
Lithuania	35.11	0.36	24.17
Myanmar	32.29	0.93	15.95
Thailand	30.45	0.37	41.19
Latvia	29.96	0.27	47.30
Liberia	28.12	0.84	7.87
Serbia	27.42	0.30	46.78
United States	26.83	0.34	32.89
Ethiopia	26.08	0.81	15.29
Finland	25.41	0.23	43.88
United Kingdom	24.62	0.28	25.96
Bulgaria	24.56	0.36	26.84
Ireland	24.05	0.36	22.54
Macedonia	23.47	0.32	28.43
Mexico	23.01	0.29	36.99
Philippines	21.12	0.26	34.54
Denmark	21.11	0.30	30.66
Estonia	20.62	0.19	36.53
Slovenia	20.08	0.28	28.05
Belgium	19.59	0.26	26.24
Bangladesh	19.09	1.38	5.81
Cyprus	18.61	0.25	33.20
Sweden	18.02	0.27	28.62
Israel	17.62	0.19	27.60
Mauritius	17.44	0.32	45.43
Ecuador	17.37	0.24	27.67
Argentina	17.29	0.25	38.63
Croatia	16.95	0.24	36.79
Norway	16.94	0.27	25.23
Switzerland	16.61	0.19	39.42
Italy	16.31	0.28	46.41
Panama	15.86	0.18	32.71
Netherlands	15.59	0.16	31.85

Table 1.5 (*cont.*)

	Women's share	Women/men odds ratio	Women's share of all associate professionals
Spain	15.59	0.25	24.75
Uruguay	15.52	0.23	25.80
Portugal	15.01	0.20	28.50
Germany	14.73	0.13	70.80
Brazil	13.02	0.15	35.48
United Arab Emirates	12.85	1.48	6.12
Poland	12.80	0.13	34.67
France	12.53	0.14	54.47
Hungary	11.84	0.07	63.39
Slovakia	11.65	0.13	59.89
Malta	11.27	0.21	30.40
Greece	10.79	0.11	19.63
El Salvador	9.29	0.14	26.27
Czech Republic	8.63	0.10	52.25
Austria	8.46	0.10	51.43
Turkey	8.12	0.24	14.83
Luxembourg	2.73	0.02	25.35

occupies one of the *lowest* positions on the list. But women's 8.6% share of Czech ICT associate professional work still exceeds their shares in Austria, Turkey, and Luxembourg (8.5%, 8.1%, and 2.7%, respectively). Consistent with results in Table 1.3, we find very weak representation of women in the Latin American ICT associate professions; all Latin American countries but Mexico fall in the bottom half of the list in Table 1.5.

WHAT PREDICTS WOMEN'S REPRESENTATION IN ICT OCCUPATIONS?

Zero-order correlations between the ICT segregation measures and other country characteristics are shown in Table 1.6, first for the professions (columns 1 and 2) and then for the associate professions (columns 3 and 4). Consistent with the country values reported above, correlations with economic modernization, measured with both the Human Development Index (HDI) and gross domestic income, are consistently negative. These relationships attenuate modestly in analyses (not shown) that omit the four countries with lowest levels of economic development (Bangladesh, Myanmar, Ethiopia, and Liberia). Women's representation in ICT occupations is also weaker in societies that score higher on national democracy.

Table 1.6 *Correlations with ICT segregation measures*

	ICT professionals		ICT associate professionals	
	Women's % share	Women/ men odds ratio	Women's % share	Women/ men odds ratio
1. Human Development Index (HDI)	−0.64***	−0.73***	−0.31*	−0.57***
2. Gross national income	−0.50***	−0.35*	−0.31*	−0.18
3. National Democracy Score	−0.32*	−0.61***	−0.09	−0.61***
4. Gender Equality Index	−0.51***	−0.56***	−0.24	−0.48***
5. Women's % of labor force	−0.06	−0.25	0.25	−0.54***
6. Women's % of parliament seats	−0.21	−0.03	−0.13	−0.18
7. Women's % bachelor's degrees	−0.25	−0.68***	−0.09	−0.63***
8. Women's % bachelor's degrees in ICT	0.60***	0.69***	0.14	0.40**

Note: Values are zero-order correlations with pairwise deletion of missing values. Sample sizes vary from 44 to 50. * $p < 0.05$, ** $p < 0.01$, *** $p < 0.001$.

The scatterplots in Figure 1.1 confirm the negative association between HDI and women's share of professional ICT occupations, both with and without inclusion of the four very low-HDI countries. In short, *we find little support for arguments linking socioeconomic modernization and democratization to a generalized decline in labor market gender inequality.*

Evidence is similarly inconsistent with the notion that the mass incorporation of women into major public-sphere institutions (e.g., labor markets, higher education, politics) promotes a "degendering" of these institutions (Baker and Letendre, 2005). In fact, most of the standard measures of gender equality included in Table 1.6 show *negative* correlations with women's representation in ICT occupations.[12] Partial correlations (not shown) that control for HDI are also inconsistent with unidimensional accounts, although some coefficients become weakly positive.

Table 1.6 does reveal one consistently positive association, however – namely, that women are better represented in ICT occupations in countries where they earn a larger share of ICT degrees. This suggests that increased access to higher education alone is not enough to support the gender-integration of computing work; what is required is desegregation *within* educational institutions – specifically, expanded opportunities for women

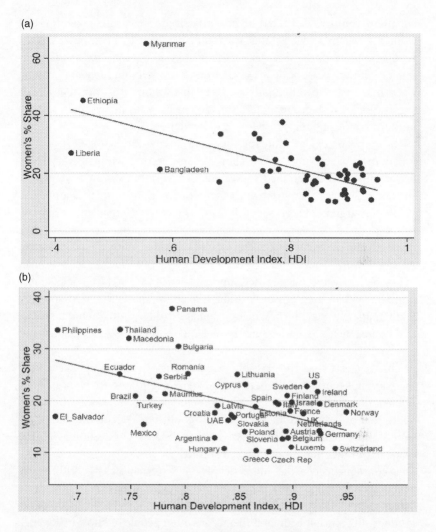

Figure 1.1 Women's share of ICT professionals by economic development: (A) all countries; (B) without outliers.

in ICT degree programs. Correlations with women's representation in ICT associate professions are generally weaker than those for the professions, but lead to similar conclusions.

CONCLUSION

This analysis of contemporary data on ICT occupations in fifty countries suggests little change in cross-national patterns since the end of the twentieth century. Contrary to popular evolutionary understandings of women's ever-improving status, we find no evidence that computer-related occupations become more gender-integrated with economic modernization or with the large-scale incorporation of women into higher education, labor markets, and other public-sphere institutions. Instead, the gender segregation of ICT occupations seems to coexist with many other positive indicators of economic prosperity and gender equality.

One obvious explanation for the highly male-dominated ICT sectors found in advanced industrial labor markets is that women everywhere prefer more people-centered and interactive work but simply have greater latitude to indulge these preferences under conditions of societal affluence. While this argument seems plausible on its face, *it is important to remember that career aspirations are themselves social products.* Comparative research shows that the gender gap in attitudes toward scientific and technical work also varies a great deal across time and space. Women living in less economically developed societies are in fact considerably more likely than their advanced-industrial counterparts to report enjoying mathematically related work, being good at it, and aspiring to mathematically related fields (Charles and Bradley, 2009; Charles, 2017; Stoet and Geary, 2018).

This suggests a second possible explanation for observed patterns (and these are not mutually exclusive): that *career aspirations are more strongly influenced by gender stereotypes in affluent societies.* There is much evidence that broad-based material security contributes to the rise and diffusion of individualistic, self-expressive value systems and declining cultural emphasis on the pursuit of material security (Inglehart and Norris, 2003). One consequence is that more people in "postmaterialist" cultures are encouraged to follow their passions and "do what they love" in choosing career paths – especially if they come from more privileged social backgrounds. But since it is often difficult for young people to know in advance what they will love or be good at, many develop beliefs about their aptitudes and affinities that reflect prevailing cultural stereotypes about the intrinsically masculine or feminine natures of specific types of work and the essential natures of men and women (Charles, 2017; Thébaud and Charles, 2018). The highly masculine "hacker" images surrounding engineering and computing work in the United States and other affluent Western societies are unlikely to attract girls and women seeking self-expressive career pursuits (Cech et al., 2011; Ensmenger, 2015; Varma and Kapur, 2015; Wynn and Correll, 2017). Neither are *all* men able to identify with the ICT "geek" culture; computing work is also highly stratified by race, class, and other social group axes in the United States (Alfrey and Twine, 2017; Kim et al., 2018; Ma, 2017).

The good news for those interested in diversifying the computing labor force is that stereotypes about STEM work can be counteracted by thoughtful policy interventions. Effects of cognitive gender biases may be reduced, for example, by policies that differentiate high school course requirements and weaken emphasis on individual curricular choice. Exposure to gender-atypical curricula gives girls and boys opportunities to learn directly about a wider variety of fields and to assess their own capacity to enjoy and excel in them (Varma and Kapur, 2015; Thébaud and Charles, 2018). To encourage a sense of belonging by members of under-represented groups, educators and policy makers must also attend carefully to the culture and organization of STEM classrooms and workplaces. Evidence suggests, for example, that work environments featuring diverse role models, supportive peer networks, and counter-stereotype programming can have dramatic effects on the representation of women in computer science degree programs (Margolis and Fisher, 2002; Cheryan et al., 2009). In short, girls and women are more likely to develop a passion for computing in cultures where they can more easily imagine themselves fitting in and enjoying this work.

Appendix 1.1

Zero-Order Correlations for 50 Countries

Panel A. Segregation Measures				
	1	2	3	4
1. Women's share of ICT professionals	1.00			
2. Women/men odds ratios for professionals	0.82***	1.00		
3. Women's share of ICT associate professionals	0.56***	0.41**	1.00	
4. Women/men odds ratio for ICT associate professionals	0.72***	0.78***	0.73***	1.00

Note: Extreme outliers on segregation measures are omitted: Ethiopia, Bangladesh, UAE. * $p < 0.05$, ** $p < 0.01$, *** $p < 0.001$.

Panel B. Other Country Characteristics

	1	2	3	4	5	6	7	8
1. Human Development Index (HDI)	1.00							
2. Gross national income	0.83***	1.00						
3. National Democracy Score	0.44**	0.11	1.00					
4. Gender Equality Index	0.85***	0.65***	0.45***	1.00				
5. Women's % of labor force	0.44*	0.08	0.64***	0.50***	1.00			
6. Women's % of parliament	0.27	0.29	0.28	0.39**	0.13	1.00		
7. Women's % bachelor's degrees	−0.05	−0.22	0.19	−0.08	0.34*	0.02	1.00	
8. Women's % bachelor's degrees in ICT	−0.58***	−0.31*	−0.57***	−0.64***	−0.60***	−0.23	−0.04	1.00

Note: Extreme outliers on HDI are omitted: Bangladesh, Liberia, Ethiopia, Myanmar. * $p < 0.05$, ** $p < 0.01$, *** $p < 0.001$.

Appendix 1.2

Country Scores on Explanatory Variables

	Human Development Index (HDI)	Gross national income, per capita	National Democracy Score	Gender Equality Index	Women's % of the labor force	Women's % of parliament	Women's % of bachelor's degrees	Women's % of bachelor's degrees in ICT
Argentina	0.83	20,945.12	9	0.64	42.96	37.08	61.85	31.14
Austria	0.89	43,608.82	10	0.92	47.20	30.33	58.67	14.30
Bangladesh	0.58	3,341.49	3	0.48	30.67	20.00	28.70	27.76
Belgium	0.90	41,243.31	8	0.93	46.38	42.38	61.14	5.63
Brazil	0.75	14,145.14	8	0.59	43.70	10.77	61.42	14.63
Bulgaria	0.79	16,261.26	9	0.78	46.80	20.42	–	40.05
Croatia	0.83	20,291.34	9	0.86	46.00	15.23	58.19	21.26
Cyprus	0.86	29,458.52	10	0.88	48.55	12.50	57.54	30.65
Czech Republic	0.88	28,143.98	9	0.87	44.27	19.57	63.58	15.27
Denmark	0.92	44,518.92	10	0.96	47.46	37.43	58.90	21.29
Ecuador	0.74	10,536.16	6	0.61	42.37	41.61	60.46	36.82
El Salvador	0.68	7,732.03	–	0.62	42.24	32.14	59.12	27.97
Estonia	0.87	26,361.89	9	0.87	48.97	23.76	64.74	26.99
Ethiopia	0.45	1,522.95	1	0.50	46.10	37.29	29.48	–
Finland	0.89	38,868.14	10	0.94	48.31	41.50	59.80	20.64
France	0.90	38,085.40	9	0.90	48.33	25.73	61.11	16.46
Germany	0.93	44,999.65	10	0.93	46.67	36.86	–	–
Greece	0.87	24,807.54	10	0.88	42.41	19.67	59.91	38.76
Hungary	0.84	23,394.32	10	0.75	45.47	10.10	62.25	18.82
Ireland	0.92	43,797.97	10	0.87	46.03	19.91	50.78	20.85
Israel	0.90	31,214.71	7	0.90	46.42	26.67	60.14	–
Italy	0.89	33,572.98	10	0.92	42.42	30.07	58.59	16.12
Latvia	0.83	22,589.17	8	0.81	51.16	18.00	63.91	23.68
Liberia	0.43	682.59	7	0.35	50.52	10.68	–	–
Lithuania	0.85	26,006.48	10	0.88	51.46	23.40	61.02	11.65
Luxembourg	0.90	62,470.59	10	0.93	46.59	28.33	54.67	19.59

(cont.)

	Human Development Index (HDI)	Gross national income, per capita	National Democracy Score	Gender Equality Index	Women's % of the labor force	Women's % of parliament	Women's % of bachelor's degrees	Women's % of bachelor's degrees in ICT
Macedonia	0.75	12,405.22	9	0.84	39.54	33.33	56.83	34.29
Malta	–	–	–	–	39.87	–	58.57	16.44
Mauritius	0.78	17,947.96	10	0.62	37.48	11.59	–	–
Mexico	0.76	16,383.11	8	0.65	38.37	40.58	54.13	32.18
Myamar	0.56	4,943.13	8	0.63	42.19	13.03	–	–
Netherlands	0.92	46,325.58	10	0.96	46.65	36.44	56.09	16.57
Norway	0.95	67,614.35	10	0.95	47.57	39.64	63.49	15.97
Panama	0.79	19,470.20	9	0.54	39.90	18.31	66.42	55.97
Philippines	0.68	8,395.09	8	0.56	37.93	27.07	59.75	48.13
Poland	0.86	24,116.99	10	0.86	45.07	24.82	65.05	17.90
Portugal	0.84	26,103.63	10	0.91	48.80	34.78	59.00	23.45
Romania	0.80	19,427.61	9	0.66	43.82	11.95	57.22	33.19
Serbia	0.78	12,202.13	9	0.82	44.22	34.00	57.40	25.76
Slovakia	0.84	26,763.62	10	0.82	45.41	18.67	62.95	12.39
Slovenia	0.89	28,664.21	10	0.95	46.37	27.69	58.49	15.52
Spain	0.88	32,778.52	10	0.92	45.63	37.99	59.23	14.02
Sweden	0.91	46,250.79	10	0.95	47.78	43.55	68.66	28.17
Switzerland	0.94	56,363.96	10	0.96	46.37	28.86	48.31	8.86
Thailand	0.74	14,518.64	0	0.63	45.54	6.09	63.03	47.85
Turkey	0.77	18,704.53	0	0.67	30.97	14.91	49.96	34.46
United Arab Emirates	0.84	66,203.30	0	0.77	20.48	22.50	54.50	57.78
United Kingdom	0.91	37,930.83	10	0.80	47.08	26.75	57.20	19.38
United States	0.92	53,245.08	8	0.80	46.91	19.48	57.21	23.61
Uruguay	–	–	–	–	45.16	–	–	22.33

DISCUSSION QUESTIONS

1. Why do the authors characterize cross-national differences in the gender composition of ICT as "surprising"?
2. What possible explanations have been offered for these differences?
3. Should we be concerned about women's underrepresentation in ICT occupations? Why or why not?
4. What is the relationship between a country's economic development and representation of women in ICT occupations?
5. What do the authors mean when they write, "career aspirations are social products"? Why is this important in explaining career differences between men and women?
6. What strategies may help women reach parity in computer science?

References

Abbate, J. (2012). *Recoding Gender: Women's Changing Participation in Computing.* Cambridge, MA: MIT Press.

Alfrey, L., and Twine, F. W. (2017). "Gender-Fluid Geek Girls: Negotiating Inequality Regimes in the Tech Industry." *Gender & Society* 31: 28–50.

Baker, D. P., and LeTendre, G. K. (2005). *National Differences, Global Similarities: World Culture and the Future of Schooling.* Stanford, CA: Stanford University Press.

Bradley, K. (2000). "The Incorporation of Women into Higher Education: Paradoxical Outcomes?" *Sociology of Education* 73: 1–18.

Cech, E., Rubineau, B., Silbey, S., and Seron, C. (2011). "Professional Role Confidence and Gendered Persistence in Engineering." *American Sociological Review* 76: 641–666.

Charles, M. (2011a). "What Gender Is Science?" *Contexts* 10: 22–28.

(2011b). "A World of Difference: International Trends in Women's Economic Status." *Annual Review of Sociology* 37: 355–372.

Charles, Maria. (2017). "Venus, Mars, and Math: Gender, Societal Affluence and Eighth Graders' Aspirations for STEM." *SOCIUS* 3: 1–16.

Charles, Maria, and Bradley, Karen. (2006). "A Matter of Degrees: Female Underrepresentation in Computer Science Programs Cross-Nationally." In Joanne McGrath Cohoon and Bill Aspray, eds., *Women and Information Technology: Research on the Reasons for Underrepresentation.* Cambridge, MA: MIT Press, pp. 183–203.

(2009). "Indulging Our Gendered Selves? Sex Segregation by Field of Study in 44 Countries." *American Journal of Sociology* 114: 924–976.

Charles, M., and Grusky, D. B. (2004). *Occupational Ghettos: The Worldwide Segregation of Women and Men.* Stanford, CA: Stanford University Press.

Cheryan, S., Plaut, V. C., Davies, P. G., and Steel, C. M. (2009). "Ambient Belonging: How Stereotypical Cues Impact Gender Participation in Computer Science." *Journal of Personality and Social Psychology* 97: 1045–1060.

Ensmenger, N. (2015). "Beards, Sandals, and Other Signs of Rugged Individualism: Masculine Culture within the Computing Professions." *OSIRIS* 30: 38–65.

Frehill, L. M., and McGrath Cohoon, J. (2015). "Gender and Computing." In Willie Pearson, Jr., Lisa M. Frehill, and Connie L. McNeely, eds., *Advancing Women in Science: An International Perspective*. New York: Springer, pp. 237–264.

Huyer, S. (2015). "Is the Gender Gap Narrowing in Science and Engineering?" In *UNESCO Global Science Report 2015*. Paris: UNESCO.

ILO (International Labour Office). (2012). *International Standard Classification of Occupations*. Geneva: ILO.

(2018). ILOSTAT. www.ilo.org/global/statistics-and-databases/lang–en/index.htm. Accessed July 31, 2018, via web download and personal communication.

Inglehart, R., and Norris, P. (2003). *Rising Tide: Gender Equality and Cultural Change around the World*. Cambridge: Cambridge University Press.

Jackson, R. M. (1998). *Destined for Equality: The Inevitable Rise of Women's Status*. Cambridge, MA: Harvard University Press.

Kim, H., Cho, Y., Kim, S., and Kim, H. (2018). "Women and Men in Computer Science: Geeky Proclivities, College Rank, and Gender in Korea." *East Asian Science, Technology and Society* 12(1): 33–56.

Lagesen, V. A. (2008). "A Cyberfeminist Utopia? Perceptions of Gender and Computer Science among Malaysian Women Computer Science Students and Faculty." *Science, Technology & Values* 33: 5–27.

Ma, Y., and Liu, Y. (2017). "Entry and Degree Attainment in STEM: The Intersection of Gender and Race/Ethnicity." *Social Sciences* 6: 89.

Margolis, J., and Fisher, A. (2002). *Unlocking the Clubhouse: Women in Computing*. Cambridge, MA: MIT Press.

Marshall, M. G., Gurr, T. R., and Jaggers, K. (2014). *Polity IV Project: Political Regime Characteristics and Transitions, 1800–2013. Dataset Users' Manual*. Vienna, VA: Center for Systemic Peace.

Mehta, B. S. (2016). "A Decent Work Framework: Women in the ICT Sector in India." *Information Development* 32: 1718–1729.

Ministry of Human Resource Development. (2018). *All India Survey on Higher Education, 2017–18*. New Delhi: Department of Higher Education.

National Science Foundation (NSF). (2018). *Science and Engineering Indicators 2018*. NSB-2018-1. Alexandria, VA: NSF, www.nsf.gov/statistics/indicators/.

Othman, M., and Laith, R. (2006). "Women in Computer Science: No Shortage Here!" *Communications of the ACM* 49(3): 111–114.

Polity Project. (2018). "Polity IV Annual Time-Series 1800–2017." www.systemicpeace.org/inscrdata.html. Accessed July 31, 2018.

Schinzel, B. (2002). "Cultural Differences of Female Enrollment in Tertiary Education in Computer Science." *Proceedings of the IFIP 17th World Computer Congress* 230: 201–208.

Stoet, G., and Geary, D. C. (2018). "The Gender-Equality Paradox in Science, Technology, Engineering and Mathematics Education." *Psychological Science* 29: 581–593.

Thébaud, S., and Charles, M. (2018). "Segregation, Stereotypes, and STEM." *Social Sciences* 7: 1–19.

Treiman, D. J. (1970). "Industrialization and Social Stratification." In Edward O. Laumann, ed., *Social Stratification: Research and Theory for the 1970s*. Indianapolis: Bobbs-Merrill, pp. 207–234.

UNDP (United Nations Development Program). (2016). "Human Development Data, 1990–2017." http://hdr.undp.org/en/data. Accessed July 31, 2018.

UNESCO (United Nations Educational, Scientific and Cultural Organization) Institute for Statistics. (2018). UIS. http://data.uis.unesco.org/. Accessed October 31, 2018.

Varma, R., and Kapur, D. (2015). "Decoding Femininity in Computer Science in India." *Communications of the ACM* 58(5): 56–62.

Wynn, A., and Correll, S. J. (2017). "Gendered Perceptions of Cultural and Skill Alignment in Technology Companies." *Social Sciences* 6(2): 45. doi:10.3390/socsci6020045.

2

A Global Perspective on Women in Information Technology

Perspectives from the "UNESCO Science Report 2015: Towards 2030"

Sophia Huyer

INTRODUCTION: DATA ON THE GLOBAL PERSPECTIVE

In 2015 the United Nations Educational, Scientific and Cultural Organization (UNESCO) published the latest edition of its Science Report. Published every five years, the Science Report maps the status of science, technology, and innovation and governance around the world. The 2015 edition was conceived as a response to the Sustainable Development Goals (SDGs) and the 2030 Agenda, which recognizes the role of science, technology, and innovation as an important contributor to global sustainability. This edition also included the first globally comprehensive presentation and analysis of global data on women's representation in science and technology outside Europe and North America. This chapter contains an overview of the main findings of the 2015 UNESCO Science Report chapter "Is the Gender Gap Narrowing in Science and Engineering?," as well as recent analysis of the factors encouraging and constraining women's participation in STEM fields globally.

A recent analysis of the global situation of women in STEM fields by UNESCO found that women are well represented at the tertiary level in bachelors and master's programs – and even outnumber men (they make up 53% of graduates). But after that, their numbers begin to consistently drop significantly at every subsequent step up the ladder. So while they are entering and succeeding at tertiary levels, women lose ground after that. Globally, they make up 29% of global researchers in all fields, although there is wide variation at the national and regional levels: in Central Asia they make up 48% of researchers, 45% in Latin America and the Caribbean, 40% in Central and Eastern Europe, 33% in North America and Western Europe, and 31% in sub-Saharan Africa. They make up less than

25% of researchers in East Asia and the Pacific (23%) and South and West Asia (18.5%).[1] At higher levels of seniority, management and decision-making, the numbers drop even further. For example, a global review of the representation of women in the membership and governance structures of national science academies found that the percentage of women academy members remains far below those of men – with an average of 12% women members overall. In the social sciences, humanities, and arts, representation is up to 20%, while in the natural sciences and engineering, women's membership remains well below 10%. On average, the largest share of women members (17%) was associated with academies in Latin America and the Caribbean. The average share of women serving on governing bodies was 20% (Ngila et al., 2017). Adams and Miller found that in Morocco, women make up half of students entering science, technology, and engineering at the tertiary level, but their representation in industry in the country drops to 20% or below (2016). This kind of analysis is important for other countries in the region, which also show high levels of women students and graduates in STEM fields, but where the retention levels may not be the same.

While UNESCO does not separate computer sciences and IT out of other science data categories, the Organisation for Economic Co-operation and Development (OECD) collects sex-disaggregated data on distribution of tertiary degrees awarded in information and communication technologies. In 2015, women made up more than 30% of graduates in these disciplines in only six countries for which OECD collects data – India (over 40%), Mexico, Indonesia, Turkey, Estonia, and Canada. The average for OECD countries is slightly below 25%.[2]

In looking at graduation rates in scientific disciplines – science, engineering, agriculture, and health – the numbers drop further in many regions. The good news is that the share of women graduates in scientific disciplines has been increasing worldwide. The bad news is that this is *not* the case in computer- and IT-related disciplines. While UNESCO does not publish sex-disaggregated data on this area separately from other sciences, other data sources indicate that enrollments in computer science have been decreasing since 2000, particularly in high-income countries. In Latin America and the Caribbean all countries reporting data showed a drop of women graduates in computer science by 2–13 percentage points (Huyer, 2015).

There are exceptions in different regions. In Turkey, the proportion of women graduating in computer science rose from a relatively high 29% to 33%. In Mauritius there was a rapid increase in enrollment of women in computer science (37%) and engineering (51%) between 1990 and 2003. This is attributed to a national culture where families placed a high value on women taking up IT careers (Adams, Baichoo, and Bauer, 2006).

There are some other exceptions where women are participating in computing at high levels. In Malaysia, for example, the IT sector is roughly at gender parity, with large numbers of women employed as university professors and in the private sector (Lageson, 2008). In 2008–2012, women made up over 60% of tertiary level students in science, math, and computing, but by 2017 this advantage was decreasing slightly (Goy et al., 2018). This is partly due to the predominance of women in the Malay electronics industry, the precursor to the IT industry. It is also a product of a national strategy to achieve a "pan-Malayan" culture beyond the three ethnic groups of Indian, Chinese, and Malay. Government support for the education of all three groups is available on a quota basis, and, since few Malay men are interested in IT, this leaves more room for women. The reason given for men's lack of interest is the attitude that engineering and media are not "real" IT because jobs are located in indoor spaces and hence are more suitable for women (Mellstrom, 2009). Additionally, families tend to be supportive of their daughters working in this profession, due to its prestige and high rates of remuneration, in the interest of upward mobility (Lagesan, 2008).

The reasons for these variations in trends are found in a range of factors that affect the potential for women to enter the IT workforce. They include sociocultural attitudes and expectations; workforce and professional environments and expectations about women's roles as mothers, daughters, and wives, and work–life balance; and government policy or programs relating to gender equality, education, and women in the workforce.

Cultural Factors

Some of the domestic and family expectations for women in different regions are similar to those that are well documented in North America and Europe – assumptions that women have primary responsibility for children and extended family, and that as a result marriage will affect their career trajectories and productivity.

The first barrier for women and girls can be the culturally constrained choice of parents and family to invest in their sons' over their daughters' education, since they are considered more important to the family livelihood and it is expected that the daughter will marry and have children rather than contribute financially to the family (Adams and Miller, 2016;

D'Mello, 2006). Hamilton et al. (2016) note that in many cultures, computing in particular is considered a male-dominated field that requires isolation, single-mindedness, and brilliance – all attributes that are considered inherent abilities, which are valued in men more than women, and which men are believed to possess more than women. In Africa, for example, it is often considered that mechanical skills are more suited to men than women (Beyene, 2015) and more "natural" for men. In Morocco, underestimation of women's abilities and intellect, by both themselves and family members, was said to constrain their educational and career choices (Adams and Miller, 2016).

Cultural traditions and gender norms can condition women's opportunities in general, and in particular for a career in STEM or IT. In Morocco, for example, a young woman in STEM was told by her father to get a job in academia rather than industry, for reasons of personal safety (Adams and Miller, 2016). In Malaysia, young women were encouraged to enter IT by their families because it was considered a more suitable and safe profession – office work is considered a woman-friendly space because it is seen as more safe and protected than, for example, construction sites and factories (Lageson, 2008). D'Mello (2006) notes that women in India are constrained by risks of traveling or living alone in hostels in urban areas, as well exposure to predominantly male peers, which opens them to suspicion about inappropriate sexual behavior.

Gender Roles and Expectations

The expectation that women will continue to oversee domestic and family life and that they will inevitably marry and have children restricts their career and education progress. Expectations of having families often require quitting or scaling back their career. In Morocco, the expectation that women will have children and stay home to care for them is a major constraint to their careers in STEM (Adams and Miller, 2016). Pretorius et al. note that in South Africa women are reluctant to enter the IT industry because of its association with long work hours and continuous learning requirements, conflicting with the traditional view of women as homemakers (Pretorius et al., 2015). Research in other cultures echoes this tension: in Singapore (Dutta, 2018); in Latin America, where women can self-select into "softer" IT positions that require less time commitment (ECLAC, 2014); and in India, where Thakkar et al. (2018) find a "precipitous exit" of women from computing due to family pressure, among other factors.

The expectations that women are primarily or solely responsible for household management, including child and extended family care, leads to a double workday of family and professional responsibilities in which they work, on average, longer hours than men worldwide (World Bank, 2012). Women spend more time in unpaid work in India and South Korea, while data for Brazil indicate that men spend 30% more time in unpaid work than women, in tasks such as gardening, washing the car, or household maintenance. However, closer examination reveals that this is actually a function of different definitions, since Brazil includes an additional category of "domestic work" – and women spend significantly greater amounts of time doing this type of work. A 2008 national pilot survey of time use found that 86.3% of women interviewed said they did domestic work, compared with 45.3% of men. The good news was that a comparison with earlier data found that the time spent by both women and men on household work was declining (with a greater decline for women), as a result of new technologies and infrastructure, such as increased access to water, electricity, and household equipment, as well as lifestyle changes such as decreasing family sizes and taking lunch outside the home during the course of a working day (Abreu, 2012).

In India, women work longer hours than men and carry the major share of unpaid household and community work. Women work nearly ten times as long as men on household and care-related activities: about ten times more time than men on household and care-related activities, about 2.1 hours per day on preparing food, and about 1.1 hours on cleaning the household and utensils, with nominal participation by men. Taking care of children is one of the major responsibilities of women, with women spending ten times more time than men in this area as well, about 3.16 hours per week, compared with 0.32 hours. Males spend 8 hours per week more than women on learning, leisure, and personal care activities (Nair, 2011).

In South Korea, women work five times more than men in unpaid work. In their culture, the pattern is for women to exit the labor market as a result of family childcare responsibilities. They generally do not return once they have children; but recently they have begun to reenter the labor market when their children go to school (Kim and Moon, 2011). In Mexico in 2011, 62% of women fourteen years and older were engaged in unpaid work in comparison to 26% of men (Zubieta and Herzig, 2015).

These gender roles and expectations extend beyond the household into the professional workplace. For example, the "work–home negotiations" of women in Singapore require them to balance expectations on both sides, and prioritize family obligations over attaining leadership positions.

Chinese Singaporean women particularly felt pressure to be the "Tiger Mom," that is, the "ideal mom" who manages the household and coordinates schedules, while balancing work requirements, all of which mitigates against the extra effort needed to attain a leadership role. Dutta notes that the strong emphasis on caring for the family as a respected activity for women in the three main Singaporean cultures (Chinese, Indian, and Malay) may lead women to value that role more than a larger or higher-level professional role (Dutta, 2018).

Added to restrictions caused by their expected roles in the household, women are constrained by norms governing their interaction with men outside the household or family. Gupta and Sharma (2002) point to patrifocality in Indian society that restricts interactions between female and male scientists. Professional contacts developed by women are restricted as a result to other female researchers, leading to less diverse, less extensive, and more locally oriented professional networks.

Constraints on Mobility and Travel

Inhibitions on travel and mobility are added constraints for women's scientific careers. Campion and Shrum (2004) found that the career prospects of women scientists were affected by perceptions that they are the primary caregivers at home. As a result, opportunities for fieldwork and travel are limited for women. Men, in contrast, were seen to be obligated to travel in their role as family providers.

The resulting restrictions on travel are major inhibitors of women's professional opportunities, both now and in the future, ensuring that women's professional networks and contacts tend to be local and national. D'Mello (2006) notes that mobility restrictions for women in India restrict their participation in informal workplace or professional networks that are important in career advancement. This connects to other observations that women's inability to travel due to their family roles limits their professional networks to local and national levels, inhibiting their ability to collaborate and publish in international, higher-prestige journals. Women scientists often do not have the same opportunity to travel abroad for advanced education or training and are less able to participate in international conferences (Campion and Shrum, 2004; D'Mello, 2006; Miller et al., 2012). As a result, women scientists can be less aware of the professional and funding resources available to them, and publish less in foreign journals. The repercussions of this situation have not been studied, although women with fewer publications in international journals likely are likely to be promoted less often. Additionally, Campion and Shrum

(2004) argue that as scientific networks become more global, differences in networks and results may restrict the scientific careers of women, even if their numbers are increasing.

Other travel barriers affect women's science careers on a daily basis – unsafe public transit, lack of transportation options after dark, and high costs of transportation can limit women's options for commuting to and from school or work. It can also prevent them from working in the evenings in laboratories or classrooms, hindering their research.

Career and the Workplace

As noted above, preconceptions about gender roles can affect women's employment prospects and, once they are hired, inhibit women from continuing in their careers. It can also relegate them to marginal positions and keep them from advancing in the sector (Wacjman and Lobb, 2007). Patel and Parmentier (2005) note that there has been an expectation that the participation of women in the workforce will contribute to a breakdown of traditional gender expectations, but find that in India, women's participation in the IT industry is based on and affected by a continuation of traditional gender roles. Employers may be reluctant to hire women on the expectation that they will later leave to marry and have children, or more simply that they will put their family obligations over their job. They also found that women tended to be hired in software or finance positions, which were less prestigious than hardware development, for example, or in data-processing positions rather than management. Lagesan (2008) notes that in Malaysia, hardware is considered a "male" field because it requires more mobile and physical activities, and involves outdoor exposure not suitable to women. Wacjman and Lobb (2007) comment that in the Vietnam software sector women tend to be concentrated in the less skilled jobs such as testing (rather than programming) and systems design. Despite concerns that women are relegated to software engineering in India rather than hardware development, other assessments find women are less involved in software development in general. An OECD (2018) analysis[3] of women's participation in digital occupations finds that 77% of the 12,000 R-based software packages[4] created during the period 2012–2017 were produced by teams of men, with women-only teams accounting for just 6% of packages, and the remaining 17% from mixed teams.

The existing literature on workplace environment globally also points to issues commonly experienced in North America and Europe: gender discrimination and lack of employment equity provisions in the workplace lead to unequal pay, rates of promotion, unfriendly work expectations, sexual harassment, and lack of access to legal recourse or human resources support to make complaints (Bonder 2015; D'Mello, 2006; Pretorius et al., 2015). Government regulation, policy, or programming to address these constraints varies from country to country, and for those countries where policy is in place, implementation may be limited by budget or structural constraints.

While there is not the same breadth of research on these issues in the global South, some trends are highlighted: In general, *publication rates* for women in lower-income countries tend to be lower than those of men, and access to ICT (email, internet) has not increased scientific collaboration engaged in by women (Miller et al., 2012; Nourmohammadi and Hodaei, 2014). In their global gender analysis of citations, Bonham and Stefan (2017) note that the gender balance in publications is close to parity in biology, but significantly imbalanced in favor of men in computer science as well as in computational biology. This imbalance exists for some of the same reasons as in industrialized countries, although there is little research on gender differences in productivity in lower-income countries (Miller et al., 2012).

Nevertheless, there are some reasons for optimism. Analysis of *patents* by women in 2014 (8.4%), shows an increase from 5.6% in 1994; interestingly, one of the areas where the greatest growth for women was seen is in patents related to ICT (OECD, 2018). Chun et al. (2018), in their analysis of the impact of ICT on jobs in Vietnam, posit that increased use by businesses of ICT is advantageous for women's employment in that increased ICT use increases the share of non-routine interactive tasks, tasks in which women have an advantage. However, the benefits for women decrease as the complexity of a business increases, likely due to the greater proportion of men who train in highly technical skills (Chun et al., 2018).

NATIONAL POLICY AND INITIATIVES TO SUPPORT WOMEN IN THE WORKPLACE AND STEM FIELDS

Policies on maternity leave, childcare, flexible work, and specific programs for women in the STEM workplace will affect the opportunities for women to enter and remain in the sector, along with policy related to research grants or breaks in education or employment. A review of policies to support women in the workplace and STEM fields in Brazil, India, and

South Korea found that women scientists rely on a mix of government-led, private sector–led, and/or traditional socioeconomic arrangements to balance their work and home lives.[5]

Maternity Leave

Brazil, India, and South Korea all have maternity leave policies of differing types. In Brazil, the Federal Constitution for 1988 expanded social rights (including pregnancy and maternity leave provisions), made provisions for women workers to take breaks to feed their babies, instituted support for six months of day care, and introduced paternity leave (although paid paternity leave is granted to only a very small percentage). The Indian Constitution requires the state to ensure just and humane conditions of work and maternal leave, with women entitled to twelve weeks of maternity leave. In South Korea, the Act on Gender Equality in Employment and Work-Family Reconciliation includes clauses on maternity support and work–family balance, including parental leave, reduced working hours for mothers with young children, and sharing of maternity leave between women and men. Employers are also required to grant child or family care leave at a generous level: parents are entitled to ninety days at 100% of their salary, followed by one year at 40%.

Childcare

The Republic of Korea has one of the strongest national policies on health care. Financial support has been ensured since 2001, where the lowest 50% of households with children aged 0–5 years received full childcare support in 2009, while richer households were reimbursed at 60% and 30% levels. At the end of 2008, 41.4% of children were in childcare of some sort, 64% of these benefiting from childcare grants. While India has a childcare policy, facilities are not widely available. Some regions and states institute programs, but this is not a general rule. The Indian Task Force on Women in Science in 2007 made a recommendation that daycare/nursery facilities should be made available at research institutions, with the resulting announcement in 2008 that the Department of Science and Technology would provide financial support to institutions to provide childcare facilities (Department of Science and Technology, 2009). In Brazil, some states or municipalities may provide local services. In principle, every firm of a certain size is required to offer childcare, but the policy is not widely implemented. For professional women in higher income groups, paid domestic workers take care of children and household duties, and private nursery schools are found in urban areas. For women in lower income groups, the extended family is relied on – a grandmother who provides care during the day, or a young female relative who lives in the household.

Flexible Work

Flexible work[6] policies are not common globally, although some countries have implemented incentives. The government of South Korea in 2010 has implemented a system for government employees that allows at-home work, telecommuting, and flex-time. This is a result of a goal to increase the number of women in the workforce to a rate closer to other OECD countries. This trend has not gained momentum in the private sector, although in 2018, 22% of local small and medium-based enterprises had adopted flex-work – in comparison to 69% in European countries and 53% in Japan (Yonghap News Agency, 2018). In India, the opposite pattern is seen: flexible work has been most widely adopted in the private sector, with no national government policy yet in place. Flex-time is not allowed by Brazilian labor law, and all formal work contracts are full-time.

Other Programs and Policies to Support Women in the Workplace

South Korea has established two main policies to promote women's participation in the workplace: the Basic Women's Development Act and the Act on Gender Equality in Employment and Support for Work-Family Reconciliation. The Basic Women's Development Act was enacted to promote the full development of women and facilitate equality of men and women in all aspects including political, economic, social, and cultural fields. The Ministry of Gender Equality and Family established the Basic Plan on Women's Policy to implement the objectives of the law through the following: expansion of women's participation in the politics and policy-making process; expansion of women's participation in public office; realization of equal employment opportunities; the obligation to take measures to prevent sexual harassment in the workplace; reinforcement of maternity support; realization of equality in the family, school, and social education; reconciliation between work and family; establishment of equal family relations; and the elimination of sexual discrimination in mass media (Kim and Moon, 2011). In 1998, an Employment Equity act was established in South Africa to redress discrimination in the workplace according to race and historical disadvantage (Thomas and Jain, 2004). The Department of Labour completed a strategic plan in 2012 that included in its goals promotion of equity in the workplace and increasing the number of women, youth, and people with disabilities employed in the country. The Science, Engineering and Technology for Women (SET4W) advisory group was established in 2003 as an advisory committee of the National Advisory Council on Innovation (NACI). It advised the Minister of Science and Technology on gender mainstreaming in the science, technology, and innovation environment. It was later folded into NACI, which has a gender mainstreaming mandate. The Constitution of India guarantees equality to all Indian women and no discrimination by the state, as well as equality of opportunity and equal pay for equal work. It also renounces practices derogatory to the dignity of women and just conditions of work and maternity relief. In Mexico, the Ministry of Labour and Social Support established a Policy of Equal Work to support equality of opportunities and the recognition of labor rights for both women and men. The Mexican Standard for Labor Equality and Non-Discrimination between Women and Men, established in 2012, is unique in Latin America in that it certifies both public and private social organizations that promote equality and non-discrimination, social provision and work–life balance, a suitable work environment, accessibility and ergonomic furniture, as well as the freedom to be a union member (Zubieta and Herzig, 2015).

Family-Friendly Policies and Programs for Women in Science

The countries examined here all recognize the importance of implementing targeted family-friendly initiatives in general, with varying degrees of implementation. Implementation of policies to support women in the scientific fields is much less evident. In one rare example, the South Korean government has produced Basic Plans for Fostering and Supporting Women in Science and Technology every five years since 2004. These plans support programs to encourage women and girls to enter the sector, establishment of recruitment and promotion policies, establishment of an officer in charge of women and gender issues at scientific institutions, research funds targeted to women scientists, and establishment of an Institute on Women in Science and Technology. The Daedeok Research Complex in Daejeon, which employs 20% of the country's female scientists and engineers, has a nursery school with 300 spaces (Kim and Moon, 2011).

Relevant policies in Mexico are the General Law for Equality between Women and Men and the Federal Law to Prevent and Eradicate

Discrimination. In May 2013, the government of the Federal District published a decree that granted paternity leave for fifteen working days with pay for men who become fathers (Zubieta and Herzig, 2015).

CONCLUSION

As research in non-OECD countries demonstrates, while there are opportunities for women to enter STEM fields, a range of barriers constrains their participation. Some of these barriers are cultural, in terms of expectations that women will continue to be responsible for children and household affairs even if working outside the home. They are considered to have different capacities to understand and participate successfully in STEM fields, and are regulated by what is considered acceptable behavior for a woman outside the home, affecting their interaction with male colleagues.

The demands of the workplace on women scientists in these countries pose another barrier. Few countries have policies to promote equal access to tertiary education, flex-time, maternity policies, childcare support, or pay equality. While some countries, particularly those with a well-established STEM policy framework, have established such policies, there may be gaps in implementation. Further progress in this area will be needed to help women overcome the barriers posed by cultural assumptions and family responsibilities.

DISCUSSION QUESTIONS

1. What in your view are the barriers and constraints in common to women across regions in entering and remaining in the IT sector?
2. What is the one highest barrier to women's participation in the IT sector, and what steps should be taken that would result in real change?
3. How do you overcome or change cultural gender norms to increase opportunities for women in the IT sector?

References

Abreu, A. (2012). National Assessment of Gender, Science, Technology and Innovation – Brazil Qualitative Report, Brighton, Canada: Women in Global Science and Technology (WISAT). Retrieved from http://wisat.org/wp-content/uploads/Brazil_Qual_GE-KS.pdf.

Adams, J. C., Baichoo, S., and Bauer, V. (2006). Women Embrace Computing in Mauritius. In *Encyclopedia of Gender and Information Technology*, ed. Eileen Moore Trauth. Hershey, PA: IGI Publishing.

Adams, S., and Miller, S. R. (2016). The Scissor Effect: Challenges and Response Strategies for Encouraging Moroccan Women to Pursue Engineering and Science Careers. *Journal of Women and Minorities in Science and Engineering, 22*(3): 245–257.

Baskaran, A. (July 2017). UNESCO Science Report: Towards 2030. Institutions and Economies, [S.l.], pp. 125–127. ISSN 2232-1349. Retrieved from https://ijie .um.edu.my/article/view/5039.

Beyene, H. (2015). *Final Report National Assessment: Ethiopia.* Brighton, Canada: Women in Global Science and Technology (WISAT) and the Organization for Women in Science in the Developing World (OWSD). Retrieved from http://wisat .org/wp-content/uploads/National-Assessment-on-Gender-and-STI-Ethiopia.pdf.

Bonder, G. (2015). *National Assessments in Gender and STI: Argentina Report.* Brighton, Canada: Women in Global Science and Technology and Organization for Women in Science for the Developing World (OWSD).

Bonham, K. S., and Stefan, M. I. (2017). Women Are Underrepresented in Computational Biology: An Analysis of the Scholarly Literature in Biology, Computer Science and Computational Biology. *PLoS Computational Biology, 13*(10): 1–12. https://doi.org/10.1371/journal.pcbi.1005134.

Campion, P., and Shrum, W. (2004). Gender and Science in Development: Women Scientists in Ghana, Kenya, India. *Science, Technology, and Human Values 28*(4): 459–485.

Chun, N., and Tang, H. (2018). *Do Information and Communication Technologies Empower Female Workers? Firm-Level Evidence from Viet Nam.* Manila: Asian Development Bank.

Department of Science and Technology. (2009). *Evaluating and Enhancing Women's Participation in S&T Research: The Indian Initiatives.* New Delhi: Ministry of Science and Technology, Government of India.

D'Mello, M. (2006). Gendered Selves and Identities of Information Technology Professionals in Global Software Organizations in India. *Information Technology for Development, 12*(2): 131–158.

Dutta, D. (2018). Women's Discourses of Leadership in STEM Organizations in Singapore: Negotiating Sociocultural and Organizational Norms. *Management Communication Quarterly, 32*(2), 233–249. https://doi.org/10.1177/0893318917731537.

Economic Commission for Latin America and the Caribbean (ECLAC). (2014). *The Software and Information Technology Services Industry in the United States: An Opportunity for the Economic Autonomy of Women in Latin America.* Santiago: ECLAC. http://selectusa.commerce.gov/industry-snapshots/software-and-information-technology-services-industry-united-states.

Georgetown University Law Center. (2006). *Flexible Work Arrangements: A Definition and Examples.* Washington, DC: Georgetown University Law Center.

Goy, S. C., Wong, Y. L., Low, W. Y., Noor, S. N. M., Fazli-Khalaf, Z., Onyeneho, N., . . . GinikaUzoigwe, A. (2018). Swimming against the Tide in STEM Education and Gender Equality: A Problem of Recruitment or Retention in Malaysia. *Studies in Higher Education, 43*(11), 1793–1809.

Gupta, N., and Sharma, A. K. (2002). Women Academic Scientists in India. *Social Studies of Science, 32*(5–6), 901–915. https://doi.org/10.1177/030631270203200505.

Hamilton, M., Luxton-Reilly, A., Augar, N., Chiprianov, V., Castro Gutierrez, E., Vidal Duarte, E., Hu, H. H., et al. (2016). Gender Equity in Computing: International

Faculty Perceptions and Current Practices. In *Proceedings of the 2016 ITiCSE Working Group Reports, ITiCSE 2016*, 81–102. https://doi.org/10.1145/3024906.3024911.

Huyer, S. (2015). Is the Gender Gap Narrowing in Science and Engineering? In *UNESCO Science Report*. Paris: UNESCO.

Kim, Y. O., and Moon, Y. K. (2011). *National Assessments on Gender and Science, Technology and Innovation (South Korea)*. Brighton, Canada: Women in Global Science and Technology (WISAT). Retrieved from http://wisat.org/wp-content/uploads/RepKorea_GE-KS.pdf.

Lagesen, V. A. (2008). A Cyber Feminist Utopia? Perceptions of Gender and Computer Science among Malaysian Women Computer Science Students and Faculty. *Science, Technology and Human Values, 33*(1): 5–27.

Mellström, U. (2009). The Intersection of Gender, Race and Cultural Boundaries, or Why Is Computer Science in Malaysia Dominated by Women? *Social Studies of Science 39*(6): 885–907.

Miller, B. P., Duque, R., and Shrum, W. (2012). Gender, ICTs, and Productivity in Low-Income Countries: Panel Study. *Science Technology and Human Values, 37*(1): 30–63. https://doi.org/10.1177/0162243910392800.

Nair, S. (2011). *National Assessment of the Participation of Women and Girls in the National STI System Based on the Gender Equality–Knowledge Society Framework, India*. Brighton: Women in Global Science and Technology (WISAT). Retrieved from: http://wisat.org/wp-content/uploads/India_GE-KS.pdf.

Ngila, D., Boshoff, N., Henry, F., Diab, R., Malcom, S., and Thomson, J. (2017). Women's Representation in National Science Academies: An Unsettling Narrative. *South African Journal of Science, 113*(7–8): 1–7. https://doi.org/10.17159/sajs.2017/20170050.

Nourmohammadi, H., and Hodaei, F. (2014). Perspective of Iranian Women's Scientific Production in High Priority Fields of Science and Technology. *Scientometrics, 98*: 1455–1471. https://doi.org/10.1007/s11192-013-1098-1.

OECD. (2018). *Empowering Women in the Digital Age*. Paris: OECD.

Patel, R., and Parmentier, M. J. C. (2005). The Persistence of Traditional Gender Roles in the Information Technology Sector: A Study of Female Engineers in India. *Information Technologies and International Development, 2*(3): 29–46. https://doi.org/10.1162/1544752054782457.

Pretorius, H. W., Mawela, T., Strydom, I., de Villiers, C., and Johnson, R. D. (2015). Continuing the Discourse of Women in Information Technology: A South African Perspective. *Gender, Technology and Development, 19*(3): 346–369. https://doi.org/10.1177/0971852415597100.

Thakkar, D., Sambasivan, N., Sudarshan, P. K., Yardi, P., and Toyama, K. (2018). The Unexpected Entry and Exodus of Women in Computing and HCI in India. In *Proceedings of the SIGCHI Conference on Human Factors in Computing Systems – CHI'18*, 1–12. https://doi.org/10.1145/3173574.3173926.

Thomas, A., and Jain, H. C. (2004). Employment Equity in Canada and South Africa: Progress and Propositions. *The International Journal of Human Resource Management 15*(1): 36–55. doi:10.1080/0958519032000157348.

Wajcman, J., and Lobb, P. L. A. (2007). The Gender Relations of Software Work in Vietnam. *Gender, Technology and Development 11*(1): 1–26. https://doi.org/10.1177/097185240601100101.

World Bank. (2012). *World Development Report 2012: Gender Equality and Development.* Washington, DC: World Bank.

Yonhap News Agency. (2018, April 14). S. Korean firms behind foreign rivals in workplace flexibility. Yonhap News Agency, Seoul. https://en.yna.co.kr/view/AEN20180408003800320.

Zubieta, J., and Herzig, M. (2015). *Participation of Women and Girls in National Education and the STI System in Mexico.* Mexico: CONACYT. Retrieved from www.researchgate.net/publication/267880725_Participation_of_Women_and_Girls_in_National_Education_and_the_Science_Technology_and_Innovation_System_in_Mexico.

3

Field Studies of Women in Europe, North America, Africa, and Asia-Pacific

A Theoretical Explanation for the Gender Imbalance in Information Technology

Eileen M. Trauth

INTRODUCTION

Diverse perspectives coming from a diversity of people in the information technology (IT) profession yields benefits both in terms of products and services provided to consumers and in terms of employment opportunities presented to those who would work in this field (Trauth et al., 2006a). In this regard the gender imbalance presents an important challenge to researchers, teachers, and employers. Overcoming the barriers to greater diversity in the field also requires an understanding of the context in which they occur and can be addressed.

This chapter draws on qualitative research conducted in countries around the globe into the gender imbalance in the IT field. This research has sought both to understand the diversity of barriers that women encounter and to characterize the ways that women have successfully overcome them in pursuit of an IT career. The findings from these field studies are used in this chapter to advance an argument for taking context into account when attempting to understand gender barriers and how to address them. The chapter begins with an overview of a theory that incorporates within-gender variation in barriers and responses to them. This theory has informed fieldwork, the findings from which are presented in the following section. It provides examples of the kinds of cultural variation in gendered messages and barriers that should be considered in developing meaningful interventions to address the gender imbalance.

THEORIZING WITHIN-GENDER VARIATION IN IT CAREER CHOICE AMONG WOMEN

Research on gender in the IT field has been conducted for more than twenty-five years (Trauth, 2017). Hence, it has moved beyond the stage of exploratory, pre-theoretical or a-theoretical research in which data are collected and analyzed so as to learn about a phenomenon in advance of theorizing about it (Trauth, 2006, 2011). Thus, theory in gender and IT research is needed (1) to guide the collection, analysis, and interpretation of data (whether it is positivist, interpretive, or critical research) and (2) to inform the understanding of research findings in which gender is the main or a subsidiary factor (Gregor, 2006; Trauth, 2013).

Until quite recently, in the information technology research literature the most typical way of conducting gender research has been to look for *gender differences* between men, as a group, and women, as a group. This is, in part, an artifact of methodology: positivist research (the most typical kind of IT research) tests hypotheses about differences among groups. This dichotomous approach to gender research also reflects a monolithic perspective on gender: there are only two genders and all members of each gender group are the same. The assumption is that women are all the same in their relationship to IT careers for either bio-psychological reasons or because all women experience the same societal influences (Trauth, 2002). The bio-psychological explanation for the gender imbalance is captured in the concept of gender essentialism. It posits that the underrepresentation of women in the IT field is a function of women's biology and/or psychological makeup. The other monolithic perspective on the gender imbalance is social construction, which assumes that all women, everywhere, experience the *same* societal influences and barriers to participation in the IT profession. However, reflection on one's own experience of human variation can quickly challenge both of these stereotypes. First, in the twenty-first century the assumption of a gender binary has given way to a recognition of gender fluidity. Further, since women, everywhere, are not all the same, it stands to reason that they are not all the same with respect to interest in, recruitment into, and retention within the IT profession. If women were all the same with respect to societal influences, then there would be *no women* in the IT field. Therefore, explanations for the gender imbalance need to be sought elsewhere.

This leads naturally to seeking explanations for differences *among women* in terms of factors that might encourage or inhibit IT career choice. The examination of differences in the factors that positively influenced women to participate in the IT career versus those that inhibited participation can then suggest interventions to address the gender imbalance. It is from this perspective that a theory emerged that recognized the wide range of influences on women and girls that can account for the gender imbalance in the IT field. It is called the "Individual Differences Theory of Gender and IT" (Trauth, 2002, 2006; Trauth et al., 2004, 2008a,b, 2009b). This theory has been used to explain women's participation in the IT field by focusing on variation in the ways that women are exposed to, experience, and respond to gender relations in the IT profession (Trauth and Quesenberry, 2007). *Exposure* refers to whether or not a woman or girl received a particular gendered message about IT careers. *Experience* refers to the degree to which she might internalize this barrier. *Response* refers to what she did as a result of encountering a disempowering message or outright barrier.

This theory conceptualizes gender relations in the IT field at two different levels of analysis. One level is concerned with gender group biases that women encounter. The other level of analysis deals with the variation among women with respect to how they respond to gender group biases. This variation is posited as resulting from differences in demographic traits, personalities, and individual and sociocultural influences. According to the Individual Differences Theory of Gender and IT, the underrepresentation of women and gender minorities in the IT field can be explained by the interaction of three sets of factors or theoretical constructs that exert an influence on a girl's/woman's IT career choice and retention. The first factor is the *individual identity construct*, which accounts for variation in the influence of both personal demographics (e.g., age, ethnicity, sexual orientation, nationality, socioeconomic class, parenthood), and type of IT work (such as computer hardware development, software design, or user support). The second factor is the *individual influences construct*, which accounts for variation in the influence of both personal characteristics (such as educational background, personality traits, abilities, and personal agency) and personal influences (such as role models, mentors, and significant life experiences). The third factor is the *environmental influence construct*, which accounts for variation in environmental or societal-level influences. These environmental influences include national and regional cultural attitudes (e.g., cultural norms about gender roles, attitudes about women, about women working, about women working in IT), economic factors (e.g., the availability of IT work in a region or country), infrastructure factors (e.g., the availability of child care), and policies (e.g., the existence of gender discrimination laws). The Individual Differences

Theory of Gender and IT argues that, collectively, these constructs account for the differences among women in the ways they relate to the IT field, and respond to gendered discourses about IT. The next section shows the ways in which this theory has been used to investigate variation in within-gender influences on women's IT career choice and retention in countries around the world.

VARIED ENVIRONMENTAL INFLUENCES LEADING TO WITHIN-GENDER VARIATION

This section probes in greater detail the third construct of the theory: within-gender variation in influences coming from the environmental context. To do so, results of research conducted in four parts of the world are used to demonstrate the variation in environmental influences with respect to gendered messages and barriers that women encounter about participation in the IT profession, and the variety of ways in which they respond to them. These locations are the United States (Kvasny et al., 2009; Trauth and Quesenberry, 2007; Trauth et al., 2008b, 2009b), Ireland (Trauth, 1995, 2000, 2004, personal communication), the Asia-Pacific region (Trauth 2002; Trauth et al., 2003; von Hellens et al., 2001), and South Africa (Trauth, personal communication). The results are organized around the four subconstructs of the theory: culture, economy, infrastructure, and policy.

Culture

Cultural understanding is crucial to an understanding of gender influences and barriers because gender is experienced through culture. It is a cultural construct. A culture – whether national, regional, or institutional, whether dominant or marginalized – reflects norms and values regarding gender and gender relations. It communicates an understanding about masculinity, femininity, and overall gender roles. More specific to the present discussion, culture reveals attitudes about women in general, women working in the paid labor force, and women working in technical fields such as IT. The examples below illustrate the varied cultural influences affecting the participation of women in the IT profession.

In the United States, variation in cultural influences was revealed through examination of three specific regions of the country: eastern Massachusetts, central North Carolina, and central Pennsylvania. Each of these regional cultures was shown to exert different influences on women with respect to participation in the IT field (Trauth et al., 2008b). For example, women in eastern Massachusetts were influenced by the overall value placed on diversity in the region as well as the abundance of women's role models resulting from the size of the high-tech sector there. In contrast, women in North Carolina were experiencing migration from a predominantly rural culture with defined gender roles toward a diversified economy accompanied by new cultural norms about women's role in society and the labor force. The regional culture of central Pennsylvania was shown to be rooted in the gendered occupations of the railroad and coal mining industries and agriculture. But, like North Carolina, it too is undergoing a cultural transition that is accompanying a more diversified economy and employment opportunities for women. And within each of these regions, further variation occurred in the messages and barriers women experienced as a function of race and ethnicity. That is, the journeys of the African American women who participated in the study spoke of barriers based on the intersection both gender and race (Kvasny et al., 2009). Witness Sandra's encounter with racial stereotypes about African American single mothers at a job interview:

He said, "You are going to get pregnant and quit." Then we will have to hire somebody else, or train somebody else to fill in while you are on maternity leave." I said, "I already have two children and I am not [currently] married and I am not planning on having any more children." And he said, "You will ... and then we will be stuck here." I was not hired for that position.

In Ireland variation in cultural influences on women in the IT profession was examined over time in conjunction with broader cultural changes in the society as it became an open economy with an increasing focus on information-age occupations, specifically, employment in the information technology industry. The women who worked in the Irish IT sector in the 1970s and 1980s were the product of a culture in which women's role was in the home. Work in the paid economy was intended for young, single women. Those who continued to work outside the home after marriage and motherhood were sometimes perceived as taking a job away from a man who needed to support his family (Trauth, 1995, p. 141). In the 1990s economic necessity was making it more acceptable for married women to work outside the home just as employment opportunities in the IT sector were growing (Trauth, 2000, p. 107). By the 2000s cultural norms about the acceptability of women working in the IT sector had changed so much that young Irish women were not even aware of some of the cultural barriers to married women working outside the home (Trauth, 2004). Indeed, parents were encouraging both their sons and their daughters to take up IT careers (Trauth, personal communication).

Varied cultural influences on gender and the IT profession in the Asia-Pacific region can be witnessed through the lens of the considerable cultural differences in the countries that comprise this region. Data were collected from women who had lived and worked in India, Japan, China, Vietnam, Australia, New Zealand, and South Pacific islands. Three women who worked in Australia but who were educated in communist countries observed that socialist ideologies were historically more open to women choosing engineering and other technical professions than was the case in the capitalist societies in which they had lived (Trauth et al., 2008a). Charlene, an Australian woman who grew up during Poland's communist era, observed:

I feel coming from a communist country, I was raised in a little bit different way than girls are raised [in capitalist Western cultures]. There was more expectation on us to get to any field we wanted and gender was not really an issue. And because of economical reasons, our mothers had to work. As such, they were also our bread winners as much as our fathers. I guess, there was a bigger awareness or let's say, acceptance, of women [working].

Likewise, Cynthia, a Chinese woman working in Australia, observed:

I think more women in China study engineering than [in Australia]. In China, our country says a woman and a man are equal. There is no [stereotype that IT] is men's work.

In some countries, such as China, the choice of an IT career was heavily influenced by test scores on secondary school exit exams (Trauth et al., 2006b). An Indian woman noted that exam scores in her country determined what a woman *could be* but cultural norms determined what she *should be* (Trauth et al., 2009a). A woman interviewed in New Zealand explained the educational barriers that existed in the early days of the computer industry in that country. When IT work first came to the country, because no one was formally educated about IT work, lateral entry from other fields was possible. This gave women an opportunity to choose an IT career as an adult. But over time, entry to IT careers became increasingly dependent on formal credentials. Hence, women's participation declined as a result of gendered norms in schools about careers that were suited for a woman to pursue (Trauth, 2002).

Insight into gendered cultural influences about the IT profession in South Africa came from student comments in a graduate course on gender and the IT profession in which both men and women were enrolled

(Trauth, personal communication). The context of class discussions was the significant cultural change occurring in post-apartheid South Africa, which was then under way. One discussion was about the effects of a quota system for employment in all professions, which related not just to race and ethnicity but also to gender. One issue that women raised was concern that they would be perceived as filling a quota rather than being duly qualified for their IT positions. Other discussions revealed cultural influences on women's IT careers that were particular to certain subcultures in South Africa. For example, one woman student who worked for a multinational IT company articulated the challenge she would encounter were she to be managing a man from her tribe.

Economy

One dimension of economic influence is the overall economic health of a region/country. For example, as mentioned earlier, in the early years of the emergence of Ireland's information technology sector (i.e., the 1970s and 1980s), when jobs in the country were scarce, there was a view that a married woman who worked outside the home in the paid economy was taking a job away from a man who needed to support a family (Trauth, 1995, 2000). In contrast, in the twenty-first century when the overall economy was robust, there was a very different attitude toward women working. It was becoming the norm for women to work outside the home, including working in the IT sector (Trauth, 2004). Irish students commented that their parents encouraged both their daughters and their sons to go into IT careers (Trauth, personal communication).

The size of the information economy, that is, the amount of IT employment available in the country or region, is another aspect of economic influence. This influence was in evidence in the three regions of the United States that were studied. During Boston's high-tech boom of the 1990s the IT workforce made up approximately 4% of the overall labor force. During that same time period, IT workers constituted 3.6% of the overall labor force in North Carolina, and 2.5% in central Pennsylvania (Trauth et al., 2008b). It stands to reason that the larger the IT industry is in a region, the greater is the opportunity for women to work in it. Cynthia, an American, made this point:

When I was in high school a lot of my parents' friends were in computing. So, my mother kind of tried to push me in that direction since she saw that it was a quickly developing field. And I think largely because of the monetary aspects. She actually encouraged me to take a programming class in high school. So, I did in my senior year.... I really liked the programming class so I contacted some of my parents' friends that worked at [computing company] and [computing company] and went on some industry visits with them, shadowing them, saw what they did. And then I said, "OK, maybe I will look into this some more." After looking at the different programs, I decided that I was going to major in computer science.

Infrastructure

In Ireland, prior to the 1990s much of the infrastructure was organized around the assumption of a stay-at-home housewife in each household. This assumption influenced the hours that stores were open as well as parent–teacher meetings in schools. Hence, it became an issue in families in which women worked outside the home. Women observed that when they went for parent–teacher meetings, there would be only one chair; it was assumed that the father would not be present because he wouldd be at work.

One aspect of infrastructure that emerged in the research conducted in every country was childcare facilities. But the variation came in terms of how it was provided. In Australia, for example, parents receive state subsidy to offset childcare costs. In contrast, in the United States, childcare is privately funded. These policy variations, in turn, result in different approaches to childcare in different countries, and can sometimes lead to unexpected consequences, as Mairead, an Irish woman, explains:

I know from friends of mine who are in a position to hire ... if they had a girl and a guy interviewing and they were roughly on a par, they would hire the guy because they would have to pay for maternity leave for the girl. They would never say it and are ashamed that they are discriminating against themselves essentially. But in the current economic climate, they can't afford to be paying, you know, where everybody is pinned as it is, you take somebody on, they work for two years and then they go out and spend the next two, three, four years taking maternity leave, so you are paying for cover for them. I know from that point of view people are more reluctant to hire a woman. I think you have to be better, that you are competing against that the men have a natural advantage. You have to really outdo them to get a job. If you are competing against a guy, your experience has to be better. You have to be a stronger candidate.

Policy

This aspect of varied environmental influences reveals different regional (e.g., state), national, and supranational (e.g., European Union) policies and regulations affecting women having careers in IT. Some policies that had an influence on women were not gender specific. An example is the policy of funding Irish students to study IT that was a part of the country's overall economic development policy. Aoife explains:

[I] did a two-year cert in programming. I think that I just decided to have a career and I thought that I would like programming. Thought would like it. I think that I just liked the logic aspect of it – the problem solving. It was also attractive because it was only a two-year course that was funded and it had a maintenance grant which made a huge difference as otherwise I wouldn't have been able to do it. And then as well I knew that I'd get a great job out of it. The course had a great record at getting jobs for graduates, that was the biggest influence.

However, some of these regulations are specific to gender. An example would be European Union gender-discrimination policies that apply to EU countries. An example of varied national policies related to gender appear in the form of parental leave policies. Irish women receive twenty-six weeks' paid and sixteen weeks' unpaid maternity leave, and Irish men qualify for two weeks' paid paternity leave. Women in Australia are entitled to eighteen weeks of paid maternity leave, whereas women in New Zealand receive twenty-two weeks. In both of these countries, fathers/partners qualify for two weeks' paid leave. In contrast to these countries, in the United States there is both a difference with other countries and considerable variation in parental leave policies across states. At the US federal level, there is guaranteed, but unpaid, family leave of twelve weeks. Of the three states involved in this research, only Massachusetts provides paid maternity leave. Other policies are more indirect with respect to gender. An example of this would be tax regimes that favor a single wage earner in the family, thereby making it less cost effective for a woman to work outside the home.

CONCLUSION

While all women in a given society might be *exposed* to the same environmental messages and barriers, the interviews displayed evidence of variation in the degree to which they *experienced* or internalized these influences, which, in turn, affected their *response* to them. Some variation came from personal influences, either personal characteristics or influential people. For example, a woman in South Africa explained how she came to be working as an IT professional. She said that after the end of apartheid various IT companies were offering university scholarships to black South Africans as an incentive for them to enter the IT field. This woman had such a scholarship, but on her first day of university classes the professor in her engineering course pointed to the few women in the classroom filled with 200 students. He announced to the entire class of 200 students that these women wouldn't remain in the course because they wouldn't be able to keep up with the work. When asked how it was that she overcame this barrier, she invoked her personal characteristic of agency: she said that she intended for her grandmother to see her first grandchild graduate from university and there was nothing this or any other professor could say that would deter her from her goal (Trauth, 2008b)! Another source of variation in *experience* of gender barriers was shown in Australian research. Women who successfully pushed back against gender biases tended to have the support of a significant man – father, uncle, family friend – in her life (Trauth, 2002). In Ireland as the information economy became increasingly important to the overall economy, Irish women experienced fewer barriers than did the women who preceded them into the IT profession (Trauth, 2000). Regional cultural differences in the United States about women working outside the home and working in technical fields resulted in women experiencing and internalizing different messages and barriers (Trauth and Quesenberry, 2007).

The evidence provided in this chapter of within-gender variation in environmental influences on women's IT career choices and career paths directly challenges essentialist claims of characteristics of a "universal woman" as the explanation for the gender imbalance. Rather, the research presented here speaks to the need to consider the situation of women in particular contexts when developing interventions to address the gender imbalance. Indeed, the approach of institutions such as Carnegie Mellon University in addressing the gender imbalance through effecting cultural change shows that this approach is both feasible and successful (Frieze and Quesenberry, 2015).

DISCUSSION QUESTIONS

1. What examples could you use from your own experiences or observations that would challenge the stereotype that "all women are the same"?
2. Consider the culture in which you grew up. Think about cultural influences on girls and women. Now think about another culture in which you have lived or that you know about. Compare and contrast cultural influences on women in these two cultures.

3. Think about a particular society in which you live or that you know about. Now identify some differences in how women are treated based on their individual characteristics such as age, religion, sexual orientation, race, ethnicity, or disability.
4. Provide an example of how the presence or absence of role models could affect a girl's career aspirations.
5. What is an example of an intervention that could be developed to increase the number of women in the IT field?
6. How might the intervention in Question 5 be tailored to a different cultural context?

References

Frieze, C., and Quesenberry, J. (2015). *Kicking Butt in Computer Science: Women in Computing at Carnegie Mellon University.* Indianapolis, IN: Dog Ear Publishing.

Gregor, S. (2006). The Nature of Theory in Information Systems. *MIS Quarterly, 30,* 3, 611–642.

Kvasny, L., Trauth, E. M., and Morgan, A. (2009). Power Relations in IT Education and Work: The Intersectionality of Gender, Race and Class. *Journal of Information, Communication and Ethics in Society Special Issue on ICTs and Social Inclusion, 7,* 2/3, 96–118.

Trauth, E. M. (2000). *The Culture of an Information Economy: Influences and Impacts in the Republic of Ireland.* Dordrecht: Kluwer Academic Publishers.

Trauth, E. M. (2002). Odd Girl Out: An Individual Differences Perspective on Women in the IT Profession. *Information Technology & People,* Special Issue on Gender and Information Systems, *15,* 2, 98–118.

Trauth, E. (2017). A Research Agenda for Social Inclusion in Information Systems. *The Data Base for Advances in Information Systems, 48,* 2, 9–20.

Trauth, E. M. (1995). Women in Ireland's Information Industry: Voices from Inside. *Eire-Ireland, 30,* 3, 133–150.

Trauth, E. M. (2004). Women and Ireland's Knowledge Economy: Snapshots of Change. Keynote Presentation, International Women's Day Celebration, University of Limerick, Limerick, Ireland, March.

Trauth, E. M. (2006). Theorizing Gender and Information Technology Research. In E. M. Trauth (ed.), *Encyclopedia of Gender and Information Technology* (pp. 1154–1159). Hershey, PA: Idea Group Publishing.

Trauth, E. M. (2011). Rethinking Gender and MIS for the Twenty-First Century. In R. D. Galliers and W. L. Currie (Eds.), *The Oxford Handbook of Management Information Systems: Critical Perspectives and New Directions* (pp. 560–585). Oxford: Oxford University Press.

Trauth, E. M. (2013). The Role of Theory in Gender and Information Systems Research. *Information & Organization, 23,* 4, 277–293.

Trauth, E. M., and Quesenberry, J. L. (2007). Gender and Information Technology Workforce: Issues of Theory and Practice. In P. Yoong and S. Huff (eds.),

Managing IT Professionals in the Internet Age. (pp. 18–36). Hershey, PA: Idea Group.

Trauth, E. M., Nielsen, S. H., and von Hellens, L. A. (2003). Explaining the IT Gender Gap: Australian Stories for the New Millennium. *Australian Computer Society Journal of Research and Practice in IT, 35,* 1, 7–20.

Trauth, E. M., Quesenberry, J. L., and Morgan, A. J. (2004). Understanding the Under Representation of Women in IT: Toward a Theory of Individual Differences. In *Proceedings of the ACM SIGMIS Computer Personnel Research Conference.* New York: Association for Computing Machinery.

Trauth, E. M., Huang, H., Morgan, A., Quesenberry, J., and Yeo, B. J. K. (2006a). Investigating the Existence and Value of Diversity in the Global IT Workforce: An Analytical Framework. In F. Niederman and T. Ferratt (eds.), *IT Workers: Human Capital Issues in a Knowledge-Based Environment* (pp. 331–360). Greenwich, CT: Information Age Publishing.

Trauth, E. M., Quesenberry, J., and Huang, H. (2006b). Cross-Cultural Influences on Women in the IT Workforce. In *Proceedings of the ACM SIGMIS Computer Personnel Research Conference.* New York: Association for Computing Machinery.

Trauth, E. M., Quesenberry, J., and Huang, H. (2008a). A Multicultural Analysis of Factors Influencing Career Choice for Women in the Information Technology Workforce. *Journal of Global Information Management, 16,* 4, 1–23.

Trauth, E. M., Quesenberry, J., and Yeo, B. (2008b). Environmental Influences on Gender in the IT Workforce. *The Data Base for Advances in Information Systems, 39,* 1, 8–32.

Trauth, E. M., Quesenberry, J. L., and Huang, H. (2009a). Factors Influencing Career Choice for Women in the Global Information Technology Workforce. In M. G. Hunter and F. B. Tan (eds.), *Technological Advancement in Developed and Developing Countries: Discoveries in Global Information Management* (pp. 23–48). Hershey, PA: IGI Global.

Trauth, E. M., Quesenberry, J. L., and Huang, H. (2009b). Retaining Women in the U.S. IT Workforce: Theorizing the Influence of Organizational Factors. *European Journal of Information Systems,* Special Issue on Meeting the Renewed Demand for IT Workers, *18,* 476–497.

von Hellens, L. A., Nielsen, S. H., and Trauth, E. M. (2001). Breaking and Entering the Male Domain: Women in the IT Industry. In *Proceedings of the ACM SIG Computer Personnel Research Conference.* New York: Association for Computing Machinery.

Part II

Regional Perspectives

Sociocultural Complexities of Latin American and Caribbean Women in Computing

Palma Buttles and Fred Valdez, Jr.

DEFINING THE STUDY AREA

Latin America and the Caribbean is a vast area reaching two continents, North America and South America, and the islands in and around the Caribbean Sea. This region accounts for 8.6% of the world's population (UNESCO, 2016). Geographically, Latin America and the Caribbean commences in North America at the United States and Mexico border and terminates in South America at Tierra del Fuego in Chile. The Caribbean includes countries, dependencies, and territories in and around the Caribbean Sea. Latin America and the Caribbean includes thirty-three countries and thirteen dependencies and/or territories. Within Latin America are the geographically recognized larger sub-regions of North America, Central America, and South America. The Caribbean includes nine sub-regions. Within the Caribbean is the Caribbean Community (CARICOM), which is comprised of a grouping of twenty countries, all island states, but does not include all countries within the Caribbean (www.caricom.org).

THE IMPORTANCE OF THIS STUDY: THE DATA

Data point to a decrease in the number of women across Latin America and the Caribbean pursuing education in computer science. According to Huyer (2016), this decrease ranges from 2% to 13%. Computer science accounts for less than 1% of scientific specialization in Latin America and the Caribbean (UNESCO, 2016). Reports of underrepresentation of female tertiary graduates in science technology, engineering, and math (STEM), a field in which the computer science discipline belongs, are reported for Latin American and Caribbean countries (World Economic Forum, 2016). While the labor force participation rates of women in Latin America and the Caribbean remain steady, unemployment rates are on the rise for women (ECLAC, 2018; Gasparini and Marchionni, 2015; Huyer, 2016).

While the evidence and trend are disturbing, this concern becomes elevated when coupled with the fact that many countries across Latin America and the Caribbean are experiencing the "widest skills gap in the world" (Flores and Melguizo, 2018), especially impacting the largest economies of Brazil, Mexico, and Argentina (Flores and Melguizo, 2018; Melguizo and Pages-Serra, 2017; Schwalje, 2011; Tandon, 2012). Skills traditionally acquired through technical or vocational programs as well as tertiary education in computer science and related fields are critical to Latin American and Caribbean economies, and these skills remain in high demand (Schwalje, 2011). The World Economic Forum predicts that "future job growth will likely be in job families that currently employ few women, such as computer and mathematical roles as well as architecture and engineering" (World Economic Forum, 2016, p. 33).

According to Huyer (2016), Latin America and the Caribbean have some of the highest rates in the world of women pursuing science, so why is participation in computer science declining? It is important to understand, however, that "science" includes life sciences, physical sciences, mathematics, statistics, and computer science (Huyer, 2016). For the countries reporting data, female graduates account for 45% of all science graduates in Latin America and the Caribbean, but according to Huyer (2016, p. 94), "participation of women in science has consistently dropped over the past decade." This decrease is reported for Argentina, Brazil, Chile, and Colombia. However, Huyer (2016) further notes that this decrease may be due to women transferring to agricultural sciences. Some countries have seen a positive growth in female tertiary graduates in science, including in Guatemala, 75%, and in Panama, Venezuela, the Dominican Republic, Trinidad, and Tobago where women account for over half of similar graduates (Huyer, 2016).

The number of female graduates in science contributes in part to Latin America and the Caribbean having the second highest rate, 44%, in the world of women working in the research and development (R&D) sectors, surpassing the United States, which is currently at 32.3% (Huyer, 2016). Higher rates and gender parity in R&D sectors is reported for women in Bolivia at 63%, Venezuela at 56%, Argentina at 53%, and Paraguay at 52% (Huyer, 2016). The Caribbean is also experiencing increases in Cuba, 47%, while Trinidad and Tobago are at 44%. Although the data are positive in terms of female participation in tertiary education, it should be viewed as a good direction with many steps remaining.

In the larger context of Latin America and the Caribbean, the trend regarding women's participation in tertiary education is on the rise. For example, the enrollment of women in tertiary education between 2000 and 2013 has risen substantially in Guatemala, Chile, and Columbia (Avitabile, 2017). It should be noted, however, that in some countries enrollment of women has declined, including Argentina, Ecuador, and Paraguay (Avitabile, 2017). Data from the period of 2000–2012 indicate that women account for the majority of the two million bachelor's degrees awarded from Latin America and Caribbean countries reporting this data (Lemarchand, 2016). Unfortunately, of the two million graduates, six out of ten specialized in social sciences and only one out of seven in engineering and science (Lemarchand, 2016). These numbers serve to illustrate a reduced interest in "science" fields across Latin America and the Caribbean.

While women in Latin America and the Caribbean hold high political offices, have memberships in the National Academy of Sciences, serve as heads of universities, achieve full professor ranking, and serve as CEOs, a glass ceiling persists, in particular in the software and information services industry as well as in academia in Latin America and the Caribbean (ECLAC, 2014; Huyer, 2016). According to Huyer (2016), data from 2010 indicate that women in Brazil account for only 14% of university chancellors and vice-chancellors at Brazilian public universities (see also Abreu, 2011). In Argentina, women account for 16% of directors and vice-directors of national research centers (Bonder, 2015; Huyer, 2016). In the National Autonomous University of Mexico, women account for only 10% of directors of scientific research institutes (Abreu, 2011; Bonder, 2015; Huyer, 2016). Data from the Caribbean's University of the West Indies illustrate greater representation in academia with women accounting for 51% of lecturers and 32% of senior lecturers (Huyer, 2016). However, women account for only 26% of full professors (Huyer, 2016).

At a time when a skilled labor force, especially those with skills acquired through study in computing and IT fields, is required to support and enable Latin America's and the Caribbean's economic growth and participation in a digital economy, why are the numbers of women in computer science on the decline (ECLAC, 2014; Huyer, 2016)? Women's participation in science education and employment, including R&D, and membership in national academies of sciences suggests that *women are not shying away* from fields that have traditionally been dominated by men, and they are still underrepresented specifically in computer science.

This chapter does not seek to solve this complex issue or definitively identify all of the factors that contribute to the decline of women in computer science. Rather, it serves as conversation starter and a call for in-depth analysis of the downward trend of female participation in this important field. This study contributes to our understanding of cultural issues by illustrating the complexity surrounding the issue of low female participation and offering potential contextual and culturally relevant factors for future inquiry. In particular, we want to stress that women in Latin America and the Caribbean are not homogeneous; they are varied and multidimensional. There are many factors, including race, ethnicity, gender identity, sexual orientation, socioeconomic status, and religious affiliation, that should be considered when identifying causes contributing to this decline. Of importance also are the many cultural systems these women belong to and interact with, including their familiar culture. Of particular importance to women's pursuit of education and employ-ment are the cultures and subcultures of the educational institutions and the organizations in which they are employed (see Frieze and Quesenberry, 2015).

DATA LIMITATIONS AND CONTEXT

We provide quantitative and qualitative data derived from a variety of sources to identify potential sociocultural and socioeconomic factors contributing to the decline of women pursing education and employ-ment in computing and related fields. In some instances, non-triangulated qualitative observations or personal opinion/commentary are used, but should be treated as anecdotal. Data at the Latin America and Caribbean country level are significantly derived from the Eco-nomic Commission for Latin America and the Caribbean (ECLAC, or the Spanish acronym, CEPAL), the Organisation for Economic Co-operation and Development (OECD), the United Nations Educational, Scientific, and Cultural Organizations (UNESCO), and the World Eco-nomic Forum (WEF).

It is important to remember that identifying meaningful factors from varied and sometimes non-comparable data and from a large geographic area is inherently problematic. Making comparisons particularly problem-atic are characteristics such as date of the data, collection methods, and reliability of the data. For example, aggregated data at the Latin American and Caribbean level can vary in the countries included in the data set. In some instances, the more populous countries of Brazil and Mexico often receive separate and more detailed treatment. Furthermore, in some cases, it is not possible to separate data specific to women in computer science or related fields as some report data at the broader level of "women in sciences." This difficulty is partly due to the nomenclature used to describe academic programs that develop traditional computer science skills with great variety. Also relevant to future studies is the educational context.

While potential sociocultural and socioeconomic factors are best understood at the smallest context allowed by the data, it is the identification of factors at the larger Latin American and Caribbean contexts or sub-regions and country contexts that provides data that can be used to identify potential broad factors validated through focused analysis. Factors identified at the smaller context, including, for example, country, region, city, ethnicity, and socioeconomic status, allow for deeper insights that can be used to support broad trends. The cultural context can be used to inform culturally responsive programs and/or initiatives that may increase female participation in computing science and related fields (Ashcraft et al., 2017).

SOCIOCULTURAL CONSIDERATIONS

While Latin American and the Caribbean share some homogenous cultural attributes, extensive cultural variation regarding norms, values, symbols, beliefs, ideas, and so on are found, for example, by country, region, socioeconomic status, ethnicity, gender, and industry. Further variation is found within countries by region, cities, and ethnic groups; across socioeconomic lines, religious affiliations, sexual orientation, education, familial groups, and gender identity; and where these intersect. The cultural heterogeneity found across the Latin American and Caribbean landscape suggests that inquiry at a smaller cultural context is more likely to identify deep-rooted sociocultural and socioeconomic factors influencing women's participation in education and employment for computing and related fields.

Other influencing sociocultural factors can be linked to the cultures and subcultures of the education systems, organizations employing women in computing fields, and the field itself (Fouad et al., 2017; Frieze and Quesenberry, 2015; Hewlett and Luce, 2005; Misa, 2010; Snyder, 2014). Within the sociocultural context, social interactions and life experiences play an important role in shaping women's identities, including a "science possible self," defined as a belief held by adolescents that they could one day become "scientists" (Hill et al., 2017). We would like to extend this application to "a computer science possible self." These contexts and experiences may impact women's decision to pursue science and computer science in particular.

Gender Ideologies and Stereotypes

Gender ideologies include culturally bound norms that inform, for example, behavior and role expectations that directly affect the choices and decisions women make, whether free or constrained to pursue education and/or employment in computing fields. These may differ on multiple levels such as Latin America and Caribbean sub-regions, country, and by person. Here we seek to highlight, at a high level, select gender ideologies that can inform future research, specifically addressing participation in computing science and related fields. For the purposes of this chapter, we present broad generalizations with specific culturally bound examples.

Gendered expectations as expressed in stereotypes may constrain women's choices to pursue computing education and employment. The current decrease in women's participation in the labor force, seen across Latin America, may serve to reinforce traditional gender roles (Gasparini and Marchionni, 2017). The Latina generalized stereotypes are often contradictory. On one level, women are expected to embody behavioral attributes associated with piety and familial duty. At another juncture women are expected to be provocative and seductive (Correa, 2010). The generalization of Latinas in mass media has contributed to the perpetuation of these stereotypes and contributed to and reinforced stereotypical behavioral norms and gendered expectations, across Latin America and the Caribbean (Correa, 2010; UN Women/Unstereotype Alliance.com). The UN Unstereotype Alliance (unstereotype alliance.org) is leading an international campaign to raise awareness of stereotypes in an effort to combat their perpetuation. The extent to which women experience or are influenced by the Latina gender stereotype and the associated stereotypical behavioral norms varies, by country, ethnicity, socioeconomic status, level of education, religion, and familial and birth cultures.

Machismo and Marianismo Stereotypes

The gender ideologies of machismo and marianismo are deeply imbedded in Latin American culture and contribute to stereotypes portrayed in mass media and cultural norms of behavior (Correa, 2010; Diekman et al., 2005; Englander, Yánez, and Barney, 2012). According to Englander, Yánez, and Barney (2012) positive behavioral attributes of machismo include being a good provider, having dignity, and being responsible. Negative behavioral attributes include abuse, sexual domination, insults, and bravado. For marianismo, positive behavioral attributes include humility, caregiver, submissiveness, dedication, and saintliness (Diekman et al., 2005;

Englander, Yánez and Barney, 2012). The negative behavioral attributes include being petty, emotional, untrustworthy, and sexually promiscuous (Englander, Yánez, and Barney, 2012).

It has been demonstrated, however, that the perception of machismo- and marianismo-informed cultural norms of behavior are malleable and can change over short periods of time, in response to stimuli (Diekland et al., 2005). As observed in Brazil and Chile, when women assume traditional positive machismo roles, such as becoming head of households or by increasing their participation in the labor force, in the context of urbanization and industrialized economies, they are perceived as embodying positive attributes of machismo and decreasing in the positive attributes of marianismo (Diekland et al., 2005).

According to Cheryan, Masters, and Meltzoff (2015, p. 4), "in today's society, computer science and engineering stereotypes are perceived as incompatible with qualities that are valued in women, such as being feminine, people-oriented, and modest about one's abilities." These are all positive behavioral norms associated with marianismo. It has been observed that science career aspirations are formed early in adolescence (Hill et al., 2017). In a study examining mindsets about ability and gender biases during early adolescence, Hill et al. (2017, p. 3) state that "if being desirable, feminine, and sexy is perceived as incompatible with interest and achievement in sciences, girls may distance themselves from science and also fail to form friendships around science." Girls may distance themselves from science if they perceive it as being unfeminine, unsexy, and not people-oriented. These perceptions are in direct conflict with the negative marianismo computer stereotype and behavioral norms, especially those portrayed in mass media, including geekiness, poor hygiene, and sloppy dress. It is possible that the computer science stereotypes along with the positive and negative behavioral norms associated with marianismo may be a constraint on some women's choices to pursue computing as a career choice.

Cultural norms related to marianismo often dictate that women assume the role of primary caregiver and household manager. Analysis of time-use diaries of Mexican women indicate they spend 29.7% of their weekly hours as a caregiver versus 13.8% for men, and 27.2% on housework versus 6.2% for men (Carniado, 2000). Responsibilities outside of working hours can directly contribute to a reduction in work–life balance and as a source of stress that places women in sciences and research at a disadvantage (Bonder, 2015; Diekland et al., 2005; ECLAC, 2014).

The culture and/or subcultures of the organizations where women are employed contribute, in part, to the reduction in work–life balance and are a source of stress. For example, while organizations set formal guidelines and written norms regarding working hours, the unwritten norms usually trump those in writing and are what are reinforced and rewarded. When the unwritten norm is long work hours and weekend work, this places women whose lives are impacted by strong marianismo expectations at a disadvantage. These stressors have been shown to contribute to women in Latin American and the Caribbean leaving computing and IT fields (ECLAC, 2014). In the United States, another contributing factor related to family is the stress women feel who return to work after maternity leave (Snyder, 2014); indeed, many of the women who left their careers in tech after maternity leave cited stress as one of many factors (Snyder, 2014).

Factors beyond stereotypes that contribute to a gender gap in sciences may originate in adolescence, be significantly relevant, and should serve to inform future lines of inquiry. According to Hill et al. (2017, p. 1), factors originating during adolescence represent "a number of individual, inter-actional, and institutional mechanisms including gendered socialization, implicit biases, and discrimination."

Stereotypes and Behavioral Norms: View from Brazil

The results from a 2018 survey elevating the invisible gendered stereotypes led by the UN Unstereotype Alliance (UN Women/Unstereotype Alliance. com) provides confirmation that stereotypes are firmly embedded in Brazilian culture. Brazilian women indicated that 79% feel they are not fairly represented in society, and especially in the workplace. Of the women surveyed, 51% agreed that "they are told to be dutiful and obedient," a characteristic of the positive marianismo ideology and behavioral norms (Diekland et al., 2005). This was especially true for single black women, of which 63% agreed with this statement. Also of interest is that many women feel pressured to pursue careers and embody traditional stereotypes. In support of the latter, 39% of Brazilian women "felt they were always expected to look their best," aligning with the negative marianismo behavioral norm of being pretty (Diekland et al., 2005). This expectation increases with age of responders and for women with children. Further reinforcing the negative behavioral norms of marianismo that are portrayed in mass media is the expectation of 67% of women to be curvy and to accentuate curves through body shaping and minimal clothing, the provocative Latina. This number increases for unmarried women to 71% and to 75% for unmarried white women.

Marianismo can impact women's participation in the labor force in many ways. For example, cultural norms often dictate that women are the primary caregivers of children, which may impact their ability to pursue work outside the household and the ability to pursue or complete education. According to Gasparini and Marchionni (2015, p. 117), "on average 67% of prime-age women with no children under 18 participate in the labor market, that share falls to 56% for those with at least a child under 5 years-old."

Stereotypes and Behavioral Norms: A View from Mexico
No specific research has been found regarding the impact of Latin American and Caribbean gendered stereotypes on women in computing. A study by Englander et al. (2012), however, examined gendered stereotypes for doctorate women geoscientists in a Mexican research institute and provides data relevant to this chapter. We must stress that the cultural context, including the culture and subcultures of the organization and the fields of study represented, are important factors than can influence results.

Findings suggest women scientists perceive that their interactions vary by gender and status within the organization. Of interest is the women's perception of themselves as "non-traditional" while working in an environment with traditional gender expectations (Englander et al., 2012). Women use language associated with positive and negative machismo and marianismo behavioral attributes to describe themselves (Englander et al., 2012), illustrating that these stereotypes inform perceptions of self and others, leading Englander et al. (2012) to posit that women working in male-dominated fields assume the behavior characteristics of machismo, both positive and negative.

SOCIOECONOMIC CONSIDERATIONS

Understanding the role of socioeconomic status and women's participation rates in the Latin American and Caribbean labor force is an important contextual backdrop to help frame women's education and employment in computing and related fields. Female participation in the formal skilled labor force has the potential to contribute to reducing the skills gap and labor shortage. Socioeconomic status and access to formal job opportunities can have a direct impact on the readiness, pursuit, access, and completion of primary, secondary, and tertiary education (Ferreyra et al., 2017; Gasparini and Marchionni, 2015).

According to Gasparini and Marchionni (2015, 2017) women's participation in the Latin America labor force was steadily trending in a positive direction during the last half-century. By the early 2000s, women's partici-pation rates began to decline, offsetting any previous progress toward gender equality. Gasparini and Marchionni (2017, p. 201) note that the decline is most noticeable "among married and vulnerable women, i.e. women with low levels of education, living in rural areas, with children and married to low-earnings partners." The decline touched women in all segments of society and education levels including women with tertiary education (Gasparini and Marchionni, 2017). In the 1990s, the labor force participation growth rate per year for women with a tertiary education was 0.24% and dropped to 0.13% in the 2000s (Gasparini and Marchionni, 2017). According to data from eleven Latin American and Caribbean countries, in 2017, the unemployment rate for women rose slightly higher than for men, but their participation rate remained the same (ECLAC, 2018, p. 17). Evidence indicates sharp socioeconomic disparities still exist as do gender inequities (ECLAC, 2018; Gasparini and Marchionni, 2015, 2017).

Latin America and Caribbean countries, in general, have been experi-encing a growth of the middle class and a decrease of the poor. The socioeconomic status distribution of the Latin American and Caribbean population includes 23.6% poor, 39.4% vulnerable, 34.5% middle class, and 2.5% affluent (ECLAC, 2018). Socioeconomic status and access to educa-tion are interconnected and thereby impacting women's access to educa-tion. According to Paz (2017, p. 84), "less than 10 percent of young people in the poorest percentile have access to higher education, the access rate grows to 22 percent for the median percentile, and jumps to approximately 64 percent for the richest one."

With a large portion of the Latin American and Caribbean population classified as poor or vulnerable, a sizable segment of society may have limited access to tertiary education. This illustrates an example of a constraint women face when making the decision to pursue education in computer science. Programs to address the needs of this segment of society are important and are being addressed in many Latin American and Caribbean countries through policy and initiatives (see Ferreyra et al., 2017; Gasparini and Marchionni, 2017; UNESCO, 2016). According to Avitabile (2017, p. 51), "growth in access rates has been faster for students at the bottom of the income distribution and for women."

Within Latin America and the Caribbean, the types of higher education institutions include technical training centers (two-year degrees), profes-sional institutes (four-year degrees), and universities (five-year degrees) (Urzúa, 2017). Socioeconomic status can influence the choice women make regarding where to study and their academic readiness (Englander et al., 2012; Paz, 2017). Many people, including women, choose to pursue computer related training at technical institutes and/or centers that offer a two-year degree. To increase the number of people enrolling and graduating from higher education, some countries, such as in Argentina, offer free public education or reduced tuition. However, Ferreyra (2017) suggests that "free tuition" does not incentivize people to graduate and may lead to an increase in dropout rates. It should be noted that technical training in a computing or IT field does not deliver the same knowledge, skills, and abilities as a degree in computer science from a higher education institution. In addition, socioeconomic and sociocultural factors may be constraints that impact women's choices, freely or otherwise, in pursuing a formal degree in computer science.

A COMPLEX ISSUE AND HOLISTIC SOLUTIONS

It is our hope that we have illustrated that women in Latin America are heterogeneous and should be viewed as such. We have highlighted examples of sociocultural and socioeconomic factors that can contribute to the decline of women in tertiary education in computer science. The choices women in Latin America and the Caribbean make, freely or constrained, are influenced and shaped early in life, during adolescence, by many factors, including family, friends, educational system, gender expectations, stereotypes, socioeconomic status, and the cultural systems in which they live and interact. These can lead to or deter the development of a "computer science self." The cultures and subcultures of the tertiary or higher education institutions can also be an influencing factor in selecting a degree program and sticking with that program.

The cultures and subcultures of the tertiary education system and the organizations employing female computer scientists can impact, in a positive or negative way, the development or sustainment of a "computer science self." Stereotypes in Latin America and the Caribbean impact gender expectations at home, school, and in the workplace. The level of impact is influenced by many factors including country, region, city, ethnicity, religion, and socioeconomic status. For example, the gender expectations placed on a poor woman by society or culture may be quite different for a middle-class woman.

It is apparent that the drop in the number of women graduating with computer science degrees in Latin America and the Caribbean cannot be attributed to a single factor or cause. Rather, it is a series of interrelated complex sociocultural and socioeconomic factors that require further detailed examination. This complexity suggests that, to address this decline, a holistic perspective and holistic solutions are required. By high-lighting potential factors, it is our hope that it may inspire future research to gain a deeper understanding of these factors and the role they play in influencing women's participation in computer science. This includes enrollment and graduation from computer science degree programs and employment in computer science and related fields. A deeper understand-ing may inform the development of culturally relevant policies and pro-grams. A better understanding may also serve to identify the work environment conditions, including the organizational culture and subcul-tures, which contribute to an increase in sustained employment in com-puter science and related fields. Increasing the number of women in computer science and reducing negative stereotypes in their various forms may lead to an increase in future generations of young women envisioning a computer science self.

DISCUSSION QUESTIONS

1. What role does the culture of an organization, or "work culture," play in a women's decision to work as a computer scientist?
2. Why do Latin America and the Caribbean need more women to pursue careers in computer science or related fields?
3. How would new or differing stereotypes of computer scientists contrib-ute to increasing women's participation in computing?
4. How do the images of women in television, print, and movies influence young girls' decisions to pursue or not pursue computer science?
5. How do ethnicity, gender identity, gender expectations, and socioeco-nomic status impact enrollment in computer science?
6. If you could write a television show starring a female computer scientist as the lead, what would she look like, what would be her position on the job, and what type of work would she do?
7. Why do women take on more traditional masculine behavioral attri-butes when working in male-dominated fields such as computer science?
8. What sociocultural and socioeconomic factors constrain women's deci-sions to enroll in education and in particular computer science?
9. How should the culture of educational systems and organizations change to support the increase of women in computer science?

References

Abreu, A. (2011). National Assessments of Gender, Science, Technology and Innovation: Brazil. Prepared for Women in Global Science and Technology and the Organization for Women in Science for the Developing World: Brighton (Canada).

Americas Society/Council of the Americas and Junior Achievers America. (2018). Overcoming the Skills Gap in Latin America: Challenges, Solutions, and Recommendations White Paper. www.as-coa.org/articles/overcoming-skills-gap-latin-america-challenges-solutions-and-recommendations.

Ashcraft, C., Edger, E. K., and Scott, K. A. (2017). Becoming Technosocial Change Agents: Intersectionality and Culturally Responsive Pedagogies as Vital Resources for Increasing Girls' Participation in Computing. *Anthropology & Education Quarterly*, *48*(3), 233–251.

Avitabile, C. (2017). The Rapid Expansion of Higher Education in the New Century. In *At a Crossroads: Higher Education in Latin America and the Caribbean*. World Bank Group.

Bonder, G. (2015). Nation Assessments in Gender and STI: Argentina Report. Women in Global Science and Technology (WISAT), the Organization for Women in Science for the Developing Worl (OWSD), the Elsevier Foundation, and Gender-InSITE (Gender in Science, Innovation, Technology and Engineering. https://genderinsite
.net/sites/default/files/Argentina_GE-KS.pdf

Carniado, P. M. (2000, October). Gender Issues in the Measurement of Paid and Unpaid Work. Paper presented at the United Nations Expert Group Meeting on Methods for Conducting Time-Use Surveys, New York City, New York. Retrieved April 2002 from www.un.org/Depts/unsd/timeuse/xptgrpmtg.htm.

Chen, L. Y. (2018). Chinese Investor Bet on Latin America for Next Tech Gold Rush. *Bloomberg.com*. www.bloomberg.com/news/articles/2018-03-04/chinese-startups-export-playbook-to-latin-america-for-new-riches.

Cheryan, S., Master, A., and Meltzoff, A. N. (2015). Cultural Stereotypes as Gatekeepers: Increasing Girls' Interest in Computer Science and Engineering by Diversifying Stereotypes. *Frontiers in Psychology*, *6*, 49.

Correa, T. (2010). Framing Latinas: Hispanic Women through the Lenses of Spanish-Language and English-Language News Media. *Journalism*, *11*(4), 425–443.

Costa, G (2018). Latin America Is Primed to Be the Next Global Tech Spot. World Economic Forum, https://techcrunch.com/tag/latin-america/2018/07/23/the-tech-investment-wave-has-reached-latin-america/.

Diekman, A. B., Eagly, A. H., Mlandinic, A., and Ferreira, M. C. (2005). Dynamic Stereotypes about Women and Men in Latin America and the United States. *Journal of Cross-Cultural Psychology*, *36*(2). http://dx.doi.org/ 10.1177/ 0022022104272902.

Economic Commission for Latin America and the Caribbean (ECLAC) (2014). *The Software and Information Technology Services Industry: An Opportunity for the Economic Autonomy of Women in Latin America*. Santiago: United Nations Economic Commission for Latin America and the Caribbean.

Economic Commission for Latin America and the Caribbean (ECLAC) (2018). Economic Survey of Latin America and the Caribbean 2018. Evolution of Investment in Latin America and the Caribbean: Stylized Facts, Determinants and Policy Challenges. Briefing paper.

Englander, K., Yáñez, C., and Xochitl, B. (2012). Doing Science with a Culture of Machismo and Marianismo. *Journal of International Women's Studies, 13*(3), 65–68.

Ferreyra, M. (2017). The Demands of Side of the Higher Education Expansion. In *At a Crossroads: Higher Education in Latin America and the Caribbean.* World Bank Group. http://dx.doi.org/10.1596/978–1-4648–1014-5.

Ferreyra, M., Avitabile C., Álvarez, J., Paz F., Urzúa, S. (2017). *At a Crossroads: Higher Education in Latin America and the Caribbean.* World Bank Group. http://dx.doi.org/10.1596/978-1-4648-1014-5.

Flores, M., and Melguizo, A. (2018). Latin America Has the Biggest Skills Gap in the World. Here's How to Bridge It. World Economic Forum, www.weforum.org/agenda/2018/03/latin-america-has-the-biggest-skills-gap-in-the-world-here-s-how-to-bridge-it/.

Fouad, N. A., Chang, Wen-Hsin, Wan, M., and Sing, R. (2017) Women's Reasons for Leaving the Engineering Field. *Frontiers in Psychology,* 8, Article 875. http://dx.doi.org/10.3389/fpsyg.2017.00875.

Frieze, C., and Quesenberry, J. L. (2015). *Kicking Butt in Computer Science: Women and Computing at Carnegie Mellon University.* Indianapolis, IN: Dog Ear Publishing.

Gasparini, L., and Marchionni, M. (2015). Female Labor Force Participation: The Evidence. In *Bridging Gender Gaps.* Gasparini and Marchionni, editors. Center for Distributive and Social Studies.

Gasparini, L., and Marchionni, M. (2017). Declaration in Female Labor Force Participation in Latin America. *Economía, 18*(1), 197–224.

Global Tech Firms and Investors Are Reshaping Latin America's Start-Up Environment. *Tech Crunch.com,* https://techcrunch.com/tag/latin-america/2018/02/27/global-tech-firms-and-investors-are-reshaping-latin-americas-startup-environment/.

Hewlett, S. A., and Luce, C. B. (2005). Off-Ramps and On-Ramps: Keeping Talented Women on the Road to Success. *Harvard Business Review, 83,* 43–46.

Hewlett, S. A., Luce, C. B., Servon, L. J., Sherbin, L., Shiller, P., Sosnovich, E., et al. (2008). *The Athena Factor: Reversing the Brain Drain in Science, Engineering, and Technology (Harvard Business Review Research Report).* Boston: Harvard Business Publishing.

Hill, P. W., McQuillan, J., Talbert, E. J., Spiegel, A. N., Gauthier, G. R., and Diamond, J. (2017). Science Possible Selves and Desire to be a Scientist: Mindsets, Gender Bias, and Confidence during Early Adolescence. *Social Sciences, 6*(2), 55.

Huyer, S. (2016). Is the Gender Gap Narrowing in Science and Engineering? *UNESCO Science Report: Towards 2030,* 2nd revised edition. United Nations Educational, Scientific and Cultural Organization.

Lemarchand, G. A. (2016). Chapter 7: Latin America. In *UNESCO Science Report: Toward 2030,* pp. 174–209. UNESCO Publishing.

Melguizo, A., and Pages-Serra, C. (2017). In Latin America, Companies Still Can't Find the Skilled Workers They Need. World Economic Forum on Latin America. www.weforum.org/agenda/2017/03/in-latin-america-companies-still-can-t-find-the-skilled-workers-they-need/.

Misa, T. J. (2010). *Gender Codes: Why Women Are Leaving Computing*. IEEE Computer Society. Hoboken, NJ: John Wiley & Sons.

Paz, F. (2017). Equity, Quality, and Variety of Higher Education. In *At a Crossroads: Higher Education in Latin America and the Caribbean*. World Bank Group. http://dx.doi.org/10.1596/978-1-4648-1014-5.

Schwalje, W. (2011). The Prevalence and Impact of Skills Gaps on Latin America and the Caribbean. *Journal of Globalization, Competitiveness, and Governability*, 5(1), 16–30.

Snyder, K. (2014). Why Women Leave Tech: It's the Culture, Not Because "Math Is Hard." *Fortune.com*, http://fortune.com/2014/10/02/women-leave-tech-culture/.

Tandon, N. (2012), A Bright Future in ICT Opportunities for a New Generation of Women. Digital Inclusion, International Telecommunication Union (ITU). www.itu.int/ITU-D/sis/Gender/Documents/ITUBrightFutureforWomeninICT-English.pdf.

UNESCO. (2016). *UNESCO Science Report: Toward 2030*. UNESCO Publishing.

Urzúa, S. (2017). The Economic Impact of Higher Education. In *At a Crossroads: Higher Education in Latin America and the Caribbean*. World Bank Group. http://dx.doi.org/10.1596/978-1-4648-1014-5.

World Economic Forum (WEF) (2016). *The Global Gender Gap Report 2016*. Insight Report. Switzerland.

5

A Gender Perspective on Computer Science Education in Israel

From High School, through the Military and Academia to the Tech Industry

Orit Hazzan, Efrat Nativ-Ronen, and Tatiana Umansky

INTRODUCTION

This chapter focuses on computer science (CS) education in Israel, which is known as the "Start-Up Nation" due to its high level of technological innovation and high number of start-ups in the country (Sensor and Singer, 2009). It tells a story, from a gender perspective, that starts in high school, passes through the military service and university stages, and concludes with what happens to female computer scientists in the job market, whether it be in academia or industry. We show that, as expected, external characteristics and cultural aspects matter in determining women's participation in CS education and CS professions.

This chapter further supports Blum et al. (2007), who found that "the notion of a gender divide in how men and women relate to computing, traditionally attributed to gender differences, is largely a result of cultural and environmental conditions. Indeed, the reasons for women entering – or not entering – the field of CS have little to do with gender and a lot to do with environment and culture as well as the perception of the field" (p. 109).

As mentioned, we demonstrate this phenomenon in high school, in the Israel Defense Forces (IDF), in academia, and in industry. In high school, our conclusion is largely based on research by Eidelman and Hazzan (2005, 2007, 2008), supported by current data published by the Israeli authorities, which reveal differences between Jewish and Arab female high school students who choose to study CS at the highest matriculation level. On the university level, we focus on our own institution – the Technion – Israel Institute of Technology. In addition to general data about our students, we present data from a survey distributed to the 1,800 Technion freshmen who started their studies in the 2018 winter semester. We further show how university acceptance rates to study CS continues to influence the proportion of female students at the higher levels, that is, graduate students and faculty members, as well as in the high-tech industry.

Israel is a small country in the Middle East; it is smaller in size than New Jersey. With a population of nine million people, Israel encompasses two main population sectors: Jews and Arabs (about 20%). The Jewish population is not homogeneous, and it includes a group of ultra-Orthodox Jews who do not participate in the secular education system. Thus, about 20% of Israel's school students in the Jewish sector do not study high school-level STEM.

This makes Israel's story very interesting, as this chapter will reveal.

WHY IS IT INTERESTING TO EXPLORE ISRAEL FROM THE CS PERSPECTIVE?

The story of Israel is interesting for several reasons that stem from several education systems: the Jewish and the Arab, the army service, which is compulsory only for the Jewish sector, and the advanced tech industry.[1] Specifically, the following points characterize the education system in Israel.

1. Putting aside the ultra-Orthodox, Israel has two education systems, which deliver the same CS curriculum, in two languages: the Jewish majority (studying in Hebrew) and the Arab minority (studying in Arabic). According to recent data[2] provided by the Israeli Central Bureau of Statistics, the Israeli Ministry of Finance, the IDF, and other Israeli entities, as published in May 2018 in *The Marker*;[3] while women comprise 56% of high school graduates eligible for matriculation diplomas, only 32% of high school students studying high-level CS are female. This includes both Jewish and Arab sectors. Within the Arab education system, however, the proportion of female Arab students choosing CS is higher. Indeed, in the Arab sector, which comprises roughly 20% of the population of Israel, the same percentage of female students tend to study CS in high school as their male counterparts.

2. Military service (in the IDF) is compulsory in Israel for the Jewish sector only, both male and female, and takes place after high school and, in most cases, before attending university. Army service is about two years for women and three years for men, and if special training is involved, service duration is longer. Some IDF candidates proceed

to university before their army service, and later on serve in positions relevant to their field of study, mostly in technological fields. However, the majority of youth will not study toward a degree prior to their army service. Some combat positions are open to men only, but both men and women can serve in most technological positions. Candidates for army service can apply for certain positions and are tested for their suitability to those positions. In other cases, no choice is given and positions are assigned after the army takes into consideration the candidate's abilities, IDF needs, and the candidate's preferences. IDF has its own training facilities for technological professions, thus allowing excellent candidates to study subjects they have never before encountered. Such technological courses vary from short training sessions to longer courses that span several months. This service contributes to female exposure to technological topics in general, and CS in particular. Nevertheless, the low rate of female participation in high school CS classes in the Jewish sector leads to low participation rates of females in these units as well. While women constitute 34% of IDF soldiers, they comprise only 17% of soldiers in all IDF technological units.

3. While women represent 59% of the undergraduate body in all Israeli universities in all disciplines, they comprise only 31% of CS students.[4] Similar representation rates are evident in other (mainly Western) countries (see for example, the US case described in Main and Schimpf, 2017).

4. In the job market – high-tech industry and academia – the gender gap widens once again, due to social reasons, such as the work culture and the role of venture capital firms. Specifically, in Israel, family values are important, and most Israeli women, including scholars and professionals, have families; indeed, the average number of children per woman is 3.1, the highest among the Organisation for Economic Co-operation and Development (OECD) countries. Clearly, in such a society, the work–family conflict, for both men and women, intensifies in general, and especially in Israel's technological and competitive leading international tech hub. Within this environment, the percentage of women in the high-tech industry is similar to that of women in high school CS – 32%; however, the proportion of women working in core tech jobs is only 26%.[5]

Figure 5.1 presents a graphic illustration of this procession, which is described in detail in the following four sections.

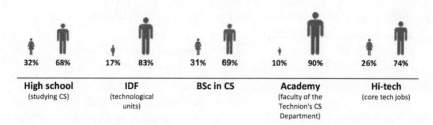

High school	IDF	BSc in CS	Academy	Hi-tech
(studying CS)	(technological units)		(faculty of the Technion's CS Department)	(core tech jobs)

Figure 5.1 Gender in computer science.

CS EDUCATION IN HIGH SCHOOL

Our journey starts in high school. The Israeli matriculation system is composed of several mandatory subjects and several high-level subjects chosen by the student from a variety offered by the school. The final exams and curricula are planned on a nation level by the Ministry of Education. High school students in eleventh and twelfth grades choose to study two or three subjects at a higher level. These can range from art and geography to science and technology. One such elective subject is CS. Students who choose to study technological and science subjects (such as CS) at the highest level usually study high-level mathematics as well.

The Israeli high school CS curriculum is considered worldwide to be a leading curriculum.[6] It provides students with a broad perspective of the field, including programming skills (in at least two paradigms), theory (computability and other advanced topics), and project development experience. The success of the Israeli high school CS education is explained by its structure, which consists of a nation-wide curriculum and syllabus (including learning materials), many designated teacher preparation programs, mandatory teaching certificates, and extensive research in CS education (Hazzan, Gal-Ezer, and Blum, 2008). It is important to mention that Israel is a pioneer in this context, as it began teaching CS in high schools about forty years ago (in the 1980s) concurrently with the establishment of the first CS departments in Israeli universities. It seems that the blossoming of the high-tech industry in Israel can be partially explained by this exposure of high school students to the field of CS, which began many years ago.

According to data published by the Central Bureau of Statistics,[7] about 7.8% of *all* high school students graduating with a matriculation diploma in 2016 studied CS in high school. Specifically, by gender, 11.2% of all male high school students who graduated with a matriculation diploma studied CS, compared with only 4.6% of all female students. Further, 36% of high school students who graduated with a matriculation diploma with CS in 2016 were female students.

Although the Jewish and Arab education systems teach the same CS curriculum, female participation in high schools varies between sectors. While both genders are equally represented in CS in the Arab sector (53%), in the Jewish sector, female students are underrepresented (27%). This picture of high school CS has *not* changed dramatically over the years.

Eidelman and Hazzan (2005) found several explanations for this difference, and their conclusion is unequivocal: female Arab high school students receive much more encouragement to choose CS than do their Jewish counterparts. Specifically, Eidelman and Hazzan found that female Arab high school students are encouraged more by their mothers (56% vs. 40%), fathers (44% vs. 40%), siblings (44% vs. 16%), friends (44% vs. 20%), acquaintances who have studied CS (50% vs. 20%), and – with the greatest difference – their teachers (56% vs. 8%) than are female Jewish students. This broad-based network of encouragement given to female Arab students is supported by additional research data.

We note that parental support is crucial in encouraging students to choose STEM. In a longitudinal research carried out in the United Kingdom, this factor was dominant for both gender and ethnicity groups (DeWitt et al., 2010).

The interesting question we pose now is: *How does the selection of CS in high school affect the selection of CS at the undergraduate level?* In Israel, unlike in most other countries, as mentioned earlier, there is another stage before Jewish high school graduates attend college or university.

CS IN THE ISRAEL DEFENSE FORCES

The IDF provides many talented young soldiers with a wide range of opportunities to acquire technological knowledge and become experts in CS and other innovative technologies. One example are graduates of the famous IDF intelligence unit "8200," many of whom have become entrepreneurs, establishing countless start-ups and maintaining close networking relationships. Furthermore, technology exchange processes between the IDF and the free market are a well-known phenomenon.

Since the service in the IDF is compulsory only for the Jewish sector, we ask whether the gap in gender participation evident in high school between the Jewish and Arab sectors is reduced during the Jewish youngster's IDF service. In other words, does IDF provide similar opportunities for both genders to be exposed to advanced technological topics in general and to CS in particular? This is especially relevant due to the fact that only students with high qualifications are accepted for service in these elite technological units.

As it turns out, the answer is no. In the 2018 *TheMarker* report mentioned above,[8] the IDF provided the following data: female soldiers comprise only 17% of soldiers serving in technological units in programming and development roles, compared with 34% female soldiers serving in all IDF units. Furthermore, male soldiers of high socioeconomic status are overrepresented in these units, relative to their representation in the IDF as a whole, while female soldiers are equally represented in the technological units and in the IDF as a whole.

The education system plays a significant role in shaping this picture. Specifically, since prior knowledge in computing is an advantage in these units, and parents of high socioeconomic status provide their *boys* with enrichment education in CS, those young males gain a competitive advantage in the selection process to these units. Since, as we saw, female Jewish students are not encouraged to study CS in high school, they are less likely to serve in elite IDF technological units in CS-related roles, a fact that continues to influence their future careers in the field.

CS IN HIGHER EDUCATION

The CS departments in Israeli universities are among the best in the world.[9] This fact also contributes to the success of the Israeli high-tech industry. As it turns out, gender participation is not equal among sectors. According to recently published data provided by the Council of Higher Education, 40% of undergraduate CS Arab students are women, while in the total population of CS students, only 31% are women.[10]

We focus here on our institution, the Technion – Israel institute of Technology, which offers studies in engineering, science, medicine, and architecture. The Technion ranks first in the world in providing its students with digital skills.[11] According to Frenkel and Maital (2012), 24% of Technion graduates are either CEOs or VPs.[12] Another 41% fill management positions and some 18.4% of all Technion graduates currently work, or worked at one time or another, in a start-up company. Finally, nearly 25% of all graduates initiated a business at one time (yet only some 15% of Technion's female graduates have ever launched a business).

Technion: Undergraduate Studies

We now take a detailed look at the undergraduate program offered at the Technion, and specifically at its department of CS. The CS department is the second largest academic unit in the Technion, with about 1,700 undergraduate students (about one-sixth of the total number of Technion undergraduate students). The demand for the department is huge, and students who are accepted into it are among the best at the Technion and in Israel. The department supplies the Israeli high-tech industry with its most talented graduates, and it is therefore argued that it has played a central role in Israel becoming the "Start-Up Nation" (Sensor and Singer, 2009). The department's unique standing with the Israeli high-tech industry enables structured interaction between the department and Israeli and international high-tech industries, and its graduates are sought after by many high-tech companies.

An interesting picture emerges when it comes to gender participation in CS undergraduate studies. Since the average proportion of female students for the years 2008–2017 was 27%, we asked: Does the cohort of CS freshmen reflect the high school CS matriculation rates?

The answer is yes; high school participation in CS is evident in the proportions of females in the CS department over the years. While at the Technion, the proportion of *all* female students in CS was 27% on average for the years 2008–2017, 57% of them studied CS in high school (compared with 66% of the male students). Table 5.1 summarizes and compares the gender proportions for Israeli high school graduates and Technion freshmen in 2017. For both genders, the rate of CS high school graduates is higher in the CS undergraduate programs than in all other undergraduate Technion programs. This paints a clear picture: *Student exposure to CS in high school is relevant for their future selection of CS as a major in their higher education.*

Table 5.1 *Gender proportions for Israel high school graduates and Technion freshmen in 2017*

		Among Israeli high school graduates	Among Technion freshmen	Among Technion CS department freshmen
Students who studied CS in high school	Male	11.4%	38%	60%
	Female	4.6%	20%	52%
Females in BSc studies		59%, 31% in CS	41%	27%

Table 5.2 *Distribution of responders (N) by gender and sector (511 responses)*

Department	Arab		Jewish	
	Male	Female	Male	Female
CS	9	3	60	24
Other departments	15	33	205	162

We now add a gender analysis of freshmen CS students. At the beginning of the 2017–2018 academic year (fifth week of the first semester), we distributed a comprehensive anonymous survey to some 1,800 freshmen students, of whom 511 completed the survey. The survey addressed the question: Who comes to study at the Technion? In addition to demographic data, the survey analyzed the students' choice to study at the Technion, what they did prior to attending the Technion, what their impression of the studies at the Technion was so far, and how they envision their future professional development. See Table 5.2.

One of the questions was about the student's mother tongue, enabling us to identify the sector. In the following analysis, we overlook the Arab sector (both male and female) due to its small size in the survey. Thus, the following analysis examines students from the Jewish sector only.

Female CS students participated in informal science and technology frameworks more than male CS students. Such activities include She Codes,[13] the Chemistry Club, and regional and national science competitions. During their high school years, 29% of female CS students participated in extracurricular STEM activities, compared with only 15% of female students in other faculties who participated in such activities.

About 78% of female CS students who served in the IDF served in STEM-related positions, compared with only 48% of male CS students.[14] This suggests that serving in STEM-related positions in the IDF increases CS awareness among female students and, we might cautiously add, may enhance their self-efficacy in dealing with CS and technological professions (Bandura, 2001). It is apparent that the IDF influenced female students: 48% of female students studied CS in high school, but 78% served in STEM-related positions. As for the male students, their choice of profession seems to be determined as early as high school – 78% of them studied CS in high school.

Being aware of the importance of diversity, both on the individual level and on the national level, the Technion facilitates several activities to attract more women to the Technion. The following are several examples on an institutional level.

- TechWomen[15] is an annual event held on International Women's Day in March. In this event, hundreds of female high school students from all over Israel, who study mathematics and major in one of the sciences at the highest matriculation level, visit the Technion. The students hear the stories of both undergraduate and graduate female Technion students and visit the Technion research groups and labs in the different departments.
- The website women.technion[16] presents information for all Technion females – undergraduate, graduates, faculty members, and alumni. Among other things, the website contains the personal stories of female students and faculty members, with special emphasis on women's achievements in science and engineering, as well as activities and social networks.
- The Technion hosts national initiatives to encourage female students to study STEM subjects, such as She codes and QueenB.

The following are several examples on the departmental level.

- The Department of CS nominates its excellent female students for the Google Scholarship[17] (formerly the Anita Borg scholarships) competition; and, they win (almost) every year.[18]
- The Department of Electrical Engineering organizes an annual event to expose high school females to the field of electrical engineering and its vast range of subdomains, in order to change their perception of the profession (Hazzan, Levy, and Tal, 2005).

Technion: Graduate Studies

The consequences of the low participation of women, of both sectors, in the CS undergraduate program were reflected in the May 2017 *Women and Men at the Technion: Students and Faculty* report for 2016: only 32% of the newly registered master's students and 14% of the newly registered doctoral students in the CS department were women.

On the national level, according to a recent report published by the Knesset[19] Information and Research Center,[20] only 27% of all students who earned a doctoral degree in mathematics and CS in 2015–2016 were women.[21]

The Technion is active also on the graduate level to attract more female students, mainly to the faculties in which their representation is extremely low. This is especially crucial in Israel, since in order be a faculty member in one of the leading universities, one must hold a one- to two-year postdoc position abroad (in most cases in the United States). This demand is a challenge when the candidate's spouse also has a demanding job. To acknowledge this complexity and find ways to cope with it, the Technion facilitates several activities. One of them is an annual leadership workshop for female doctoral students.[22] The workshop aims to provide the female doctoral students with leadership skills and to establish a network of influential women in science and engineering research.

THE ISRAELI JOB MARKET

We divide our investigation in this section into academia and the tech industry. Due to the limited data available on Arab women in the high-tech industry, which does not enable a thorough analysis, this section concentrates on gender differences only.

Academia

The annual report of the Technion reveals that women comprise only 10% of all CS faculty members. This proportion is similar to that of some faculties like electrical engineering (9%) and is lower than other faculties like industrial engineering (21%) and biotechnology engineering (44%). On the national level, 12% of all faculty members in mathematics and CS in 2014–2015 were women.[23]

Industry

As mentioned, Israel is a very small country with a population of about 9 million people. Still, at its high-tech economic peak during the 1990s, Israel was one of the world's leading centers of technological start-ups and innovations. Despite its small population, Israel had, at that time, about 3,000 start-ups,[24] and came in third (after the United States and Canada) on the list of countries with the highest number of companies listed on NASDAQ. It is estimated that there are about 6,000 start-ups in Israel today.

Three main factors contributed to this prosperity (see Sensor and Singer, 2009). The first was the national security and military needs that led to the development of cutting-edge technologies. Since its establishment in 1948, Israel has been forced to invest huge budgets and efforts to maintain its military advantage in order to survive. In particular, designated army units exist that specialize in technological innovations. As mentioned, many of Israeli's high-tech entrepreneurs started their careers in the Israeli army.

The second factor that contributed to the success of the Israeli high-tech industry was a massive immigration wave of Russian engineers from the former Soviet Union during the 1990–2000 decade. This addition of engineers to the Israeli population made Israel the country with the highest number of engineers per capita in the world.[25]

The third factor was mentioned above: the high level of the CS departments in the Israeli universities, established about forty years ago.

With respect to gender differences, women hold only 26% of the core jobs in the high-tech industry.[26] Furthermore, a recent study, published by Mazuz-Harpaz and Kirl (2017), found a gap between women and men who studied CS and electrical engineering, in terms of their rate of employment (68% vs. 76%, respectively). In terms of salary, they found a 7% difference in favor of male engineers at the beginning of the career, which increased to up to 18% around the age of forty.

In addition to the lower participation of female soldiers in the elite technological units and their lower representation in CS academic programs, additional factors cause women to continue being underrepresented in the high-tech industry as well. Those factors are mainly cultural – the long work hours that characterize the high-tech industry and motherhood. Indeed, while in many developed countries, the marriage age for women is rising and the number of births is declining, in Israel women are still heavily pressured to marry and give birth to more than one child (as mentioned earlier, the average number of children per woman in Israel is 3.1, the highest among the OECD countries).

Indeed, motherhood plays a central role in women's satisfaction and participation in the Israeli high-tech industry. Different studies have come to different conclusions about working moms. Frenkel (2008) investigated Israeli *mothers and non-mothers* in the high-tech industry and found, among other things, that average income of a mother in the Israeli high-tech industry is higher than that of a non-mother. Mothers in this industry are more satisfied with their work than their non-mother counterparts, but higher levels of stress and the lack of leisure time the price that mothers in this industry pay. Frenkel concluded, however, that the family–career combination is more rewarding than each one alone, that is, career or motherhood. It should be emphasized that this study was quantitative; the women who participated were approached via the internet, and it included only those women who were still working in the high-tech industry and not women who had given up their high-tech careers.

A qualitative study, conducted by Hazzan and Levy (2006), further supports the above assertions about the dominance of social factors in determining women's participation in CS occupations, namely, that motherhood and long work hours intensify the work–family conflict. This pressure increases when children arrive and one of the spouses must decide to forfeit his or her career in order to maintain the home; in all cases encountered in their study, this person was the mother. In addition, some of the women interviewed tried to compensate for their need to leave work early (due to their responsibilities at home) by arriving at work earlier than most of their colleagues. Such attempts, however, do not help them shatter the image of not being totally dedicated to work.

Furthermore, even when a woman wants to become an entrepreneur and establish her own company, barriers exist due to the need to find a venture capital (VC) fund that will find the start-up idea worthy of investment. In these VC firms, 34% of employees are women (in a variety of occupations), but only 15% are real investors – the ones who decide on the actual investment. It is assumed that since investors tend to invest in entrepreneurs with similar characteristics to themselves, the cycle continues and the pipeline is further narrowed.

CONCLUSION

As we saw, student exposure to CS in the high school is highly relevant for their choice to study CS at the undergraduate level. We also saw the crucial role CS plays in the Israeli IDF and industry. In this context, Israel has recently launched several programs aimed at exposing more youth to CS. We mention three specifically. First, middle schools in Israel are now starting to teach CS, and elementary schools are exploring ways to start teaching CS even earlier. Second, to further its goal of increasing female participation in CS, Israel is also encouraging other underrepresented groups in Israel to study CS and related topics. These groups include ultra-Orthodox students and students from peripheral regions. Third, the Israeli Council for Higher Education is attempting to attract more students to CS and is encouraging academic institutions to find ways of increasing the number of students studying CS. In addition, a program to expose all students in Israel to concepts of the high-tech industry has been launched recently.

DISCUSSION QUESTIONS

1. Describe the data discussed in this chapter as it pertains to your own country.
2. Choose three countries from one continent and describe their CS-related activities.

3. Look at job advertisements that target CS graduates. What can you learn about the profession?
4. Find five firms in your country that employ CS graduates. Describe the roles that CS graduates hold. Is there a difference between female and male roles?
5. Imagine you are a manager of a high-tech company. Lay out five rules that reduce the work–family conflict for both genders.

References

Bandura, A., Barbaranelli, C., Vittorio, C., and Pastorelli, C. (2001). Self-efficacy Beliefs as Shapers of Children's Aspirations and Career Trajectories, *Child Development*, *72*(1), 187–206.

Blum, L., Frieze, C., Hazzan, O., and Dias, B. (2007). Culture and Environment as Determinants of Women's Participation in Computing. In *Reconfiguring the Firewall: Recruiting Women to Information Technology across Cultures and Continents*, C. J. Burger, E. G. Creamer, and P. S. Meszaros (eds.), pp. 109–133. A K Peters, Ltd.

Dewitt, J., Archer, L., Osborne, J., Dillon, J., Willis, B., and Wong, B. (2010). High Aspirations but Low Progression: The Science Aspirations–Careers Paradox amongst Minority Ethnic Students. *International Journal of Science and Mathematics Education*, *9*(2), 243–271.

Eidelman, L., and Hazzan, O. (2005). Factors Influencing the Shrinking Pipeline in High Schools: A Sector-Based Analysis of the Israeli High School System. In *Proceedings of SIGCSE 2005 – The 36th Technical Symposium on CS Education*, St. Louis, MO, pp. 406–410.

(2007). Eccles' Model of Achievement-Related Choices: The Case of CS Studies in Israeli High Schools. In *Proceedings of the 38th Technical Symposium on CS Education*, Covington, KY, pp. 29–33.

(2008). Sectoral and Gender-Wise Analysis of the Choice of CS Studies in Israeli High Schools. *Journal of Computers in Mathematics and Science Teaching*, *27*(4), 391–422.

Frenkel, A., and Maital, S. (2012). *Technion Nation: Technion's Contribution to Israel and the World*. Samuel Neaman Institute. www.neaman.org.il/en/Files/technion-nation.pdf.

Frenkel, M. (2008). Reprogramming Femininity? The Construction of Gender Identities in the Israeli Hi-Tech Industry between Global and Local Gender Orders. *Gender, Work and Organization*, *12*(4), 352–374.

Hazzan, O., Gal-Ezer, J., and Blum, L. (2008). A model for High School CS Education: The Four Key Elements That Make It! In *Proceedings of the 39th Technical Symposium on CS Education*, Portland, OR, pp. 281–285.

Hazzan, O., and Levy, D. (2006). Women, Hi-Tech and the Family-Career Conflict. In *The Encyclopedia of Gender and Information Technology*, E. Trauth (ed.), pp. 1297–1302. Hershey, PA: GI Publishing.

Hazzan, O., Levy, D., and Tal, A. (2005). Electricity in the Palms of Her Hands: The Perception of Electrical Engineering by Outstanding Female High School Pupils. *IEEE Transactions on Education, 48*(3), 402–412.

Main, J. B., and Schimpf, C. (2017). The Underrepresentation of Women in Computing Fields: A Synthesis of Literature Using a Life Course Perspective. *IEEE Transactions on Education, 60*(4), 296–304.

Mazuz-Harpaz, Y., and Kirl, Z. (2017). *Springboard to the Hi-Tech*, Ministry of Finance, Israel. http://mof.gov.il/ChiefEcon/EconomyAndResearch/Pages/ArticlesSet.aspx; http://mof.gov.il/ChiefEcon/EconomyAndResearch/ArticlesSet/Article_10092017.pdf (in Hebrew).

Sensor, D., and Singer, S. (2009). *Start-Up Nation: The Story of Israel's Economic Miracle*. Twelve.

6

Factors Influencing Women's Ability to Enter the Information Technology Workforce

Case Studies of Five Sub-Saharan African Countries

Sophia Huyer and Nancy J. Hafkin

INTRODUCTION

This chapter focuses on five countries, assessing the economic, cultural, infrastructural, and policy factors influencing women's ability to enter the IT workforce. The National Assessments on Gender, Science, Technology and Innovation, coordinated by Women in Global Science and Technology (WISAT), is a cross-national research project analyzing country-level data to assess the readiness for and participation of girls and women in a global world defined by knowledge. The assessments look at health, social status, safety and security, economic status, resources, agency, and opportunity and capability dimensions of women's lives in the context of an enabling policy environment, in order to assess the implications for and outcomes related to women's participation in knowledge-related sectors, decision-making, and education. Recently, five national studies were undertaken in East and West Africa – Ethiopia, Kenya, Rwanda, Senegal, and Uganda. These studies found the economic, policy, and cultural factors affecting women's participation in the IT workforce to vary considerably. While there are commonalities, these differences in national context result in different patterns of female participation in the STEM labor force.

ETHIOPIA

Ethiopia's Constitution espouses the equality of men and women in the social, legal, economic, social, and political realms. It mandates the rights of people before the law and prohibits sex-based discrimination. Women's equal rights are affirmed during marriage, divorce, and in decision-making within marriage. To further ensure women's equal rights to men, the Constitution mandates affirmative action in response to historical discrimination against women, outlining the state's obligation to eliminate traditional customs that harm women's minds or bodies. Affirmative action for women takes the form of "special attention to women so as to enable them to compete and participate on the basis of equality with men in political, social and economic life as well as in public and private institutions." The state is also obligated to "ensure the participation of women in equality with men in all economic and social development endeavors." Fully paid maternal leave is guaranteed, including prenatal leave, as part of women's right to family planning education and access. Women's rights are also affirmed in hiring, promotion, pay, the transfer of pensions, and equal rights for equal work. In terms of labour legislation, pension rights of female employees have been protected in both public and private sectors. Women's and young people's rights are guaranteed in the formation of an employment contract, while sex-based discrimination in compensation and employment is prohibited. However, there are no laws relating to sexual harassment. Finally, the national Science, Technology and Innovation Policy (STIP) calls for increasing "the number of females enrolling in engineering, science and TVET [technical and vocational education and training] institutions" (Beyene, 2015).

However, cultural barriers to the participation of women and girls in society pose severe constraints: there is son, not daughter, preference in property inheritance, while traditional practices such as female genital mutilation (FGM) and early marriage are still common. The national literacy rate for women is low by global standards, at 41%, and only 72% of women in the wealthiest quintile are literate. Gender parity has been reached in primary school enrolment, and in TVET. By 2011 girls' enrollment overtook that of boys for grades nine and ten (ending with the Ethiopian school leaving exam, the EGSECE). However, the proportion of females drops in higher education to about 30% (Beyene, 2015).

In several of the countries, no sex-disaggregated data are collected at the national level on participation of women in the IT workforce; however, some available data give an indication of the national trends. In Ethiopia, data collected by the Central Statistical Agency in 2013 indicate that women made up 37.5% of people employed in information and communication professions, approximately 22,500 workers. In fields such as publishing and computer programming as well as the consultancy and information service field, women comprise 52% of publishing activities and 58% of computer programming, consultancy, and related activities.

Women were also well represented in programming and broadcasting, and information and communication: 45.3% and 38.3%, respectively. Telecommunication had the lowest female representation in 2013, at 22.3%. In the manufacturing sector, women accounted for 41% of the computer, electronic, and optical products manufacturing workforce in 2013. Although in many specific industries such as civil engineering, manufacturing of electrical equipment, and manufacturing of machinery, gender parity has not been achieved – women made up between 30% and 40% of the labor force of most sub-sectors – the numbers reflect a national goal of 30% female representation in various sectors. While the data are encouraging, however, it is not clear why women have such a significant presence in these fields, which runs counter to international patterns. It is not clear if the government's affirmative action policy can explain this, and information on the data definitions for these categories is not provided. More information is needed to assess if women are making real strides in the information and communication industry or if they are playing subordinate and traditional roles such as administrators and low-level workers in these settings (Beyene, 2015).

In the private sector, Ethio Telecom, the largest information and communication technology (ICT) provider in the country, has made a concerted effort to expand the role of women and increase the number of female employees with an affirmative action goal of 40% female employment. Data from May 2015 indicate that out of 11,893 employees, slightly more than 25% were women. This is an increase from 2012, when women made up 14% of the workforce. However, most women employers are in the customer service department, reflecting trends elsewhere of women migrating to "soft" communications or social tasks. In addition, they are concentrated in the lowest four levels (of eight). Only 33 women compared with 265 men are in the fifth level, and as levels rise, women simply disappear. For instance, at the second highest level, there is one woman and fifteen men, and the top manager is a man (Beyene, 2015).

KENYA

In Kenya, the Constitution of 2010 enshrines equality as an essential value: "Women and men have the right to equal treatment, including the right to equal opportunities in political, economic, cultural and social spheres." It also prohibits discrimination on any grounds, including race, sex, pregnancy, and marital status. The principle of affirmative action is in place to "redress any disadvantage suffered by individuals or groups" and extends to elective and appointive bodies in Kenya, where "not more than two-thirds of bodies shall be of the same gender"; that is, at least one-third of members are required to be women. This requirement extends to the boards of companies where the government has at least a 50% share, leading to an increase in numbers of women on corporate boards (Republic of Kenya, 2010; Frosina and Mwaura, 2016). The Sexual Offences Act of 2006 defines sexual offences including rape, attempted rape, and sexual harassment, among others, and accompanying jail time for conviction of these crimes.

Cultural attitudes and trends that pose barriers to women's participation in the public sphere and workforce include acceptance of domestic violence in marriage and economic dependence of women on their husbands, with 42% of women and 36% of men aged 15–49 agreeing that a husband is justified in beating his wife. Although FGM is illegal, it is still practiced in some regions of the country. Some 21% of Kenyan women aged 15–49 are circumcised. The gender division of labour is strongly entrenched, especially in the rural areas, where men spend up to 70% of their work time managing herds, while women's time is divided into farm work, running small businesses, caring for children, and collecting firewood and water. Wives work twice as many hours as their husbands. Women and girls are also primarily responsible for care of the sick, elderly, and dying. While they are legally allowed to take out bank loans, lack of collateral (due to limited land rights and property ownership) poses barriers. It is estimated that only 7% of women have access to credit in Kenya, although the universality of the microfinancing service M-Pesa in the country is changing this for women (Ndiaye, 2013). The female literacy rate in Kenya is 75%, and there is gender parity in primary school enrollments. The participation of girls decreases slightly more than boys at the secondary level (to 65%) and further at the tertiary level (Frosina and Mwaura, 2016).

In terms of women's participation in the STEM sector overall, enrollment rates are increasing gradually, although they remain quite low. The highest percentage of women graduate from programs in the social sciences and education, although the next two most popular programs are in the sciences: 12% of all females enrolled in tertiary education in Kenya are in health and welfare programs; 8.7% in science programs; 6.9% in engineering, manufacturing, and construction; and 5.8% in agriculture, forestry, and fisheries programs (UNESCO, 2012).

Kenya is known as "Silicon Savana" due to the high penetration of both mobile phones and mobile money, leading to an explosion of tech incubators such iHub.[1] Probably as a result, the Kenyan economy hosts one of the largest ICT sectors in Africa, with the value-added share of ICT services in GDP being 3.4% in 2013 (including telecommunications). However, while the use of mobile phones and mobile applications are increasing the ability of women to engage in distance and lifelong learning, this is not translating into the IT sector where women are "greatly underrepresented" (Chege, 2015). Some targeted gender tech initiatives have had some success: the well-known AkiraChix was founded by twelve women who had been working at iHub. AkiraChix enrolls young women from Nairobi's slums in a one-year training course on technology and entrepreneurship, and after the program they are given job placements or helped to start their own enterprises. Safaricom and Cisco have teamed up to form Women in Technology (WIT), a multitiered program that includes outreach efforts to encourage children and young women to pursue science and technology studies through programs that start at the age of five. WIT also manages a platform and network for women in the tech field to network (Frosina and Mwaura, 2016).

RWANDA

Rwanda has instituted several laws and policies relating to women's position in the workforce: Law No. 13/2009 of 27/05/2009 Regulating Labour in Rwanda establishes equal opportunities and equal pay for women and men, and prohibits gender-based violence, harassment, and discrimination on the grounds of gender, marital status, or family responsibilities. Maternity leave is granted for twelve weeks with full pay, and the payment of maternity leave benefits are made to the father or the guardian of the newborn in the case of the mother's death. VISION-2020 envisages Rwanda as a knowledge-based and middle-income country by 2020 with employment as one of the fundamental pillars. As part of this, the country has taken a special focus on TVET, higher education, and employment opportunities for women. The National Employment Program facilitates the creation of 200,000 off-farm jobs every year targeting mainly unemployed youth and women, especially those with no employable skills, people with disabilities, and women and youth cooperatives and medium, small and micro-enterprises that need technology and skills upgrading (Rwabuhihi, 2017).

Rwandan society is characterized by a patriarchal social structure and unequal social power relations between men and women, although policy and implementation mechanisms are being put in place with the intention to systematically address these inequalities. In 2014, 8% of adult women and 8.8% of adult men had reached at least a secondary level of education. The adolescent birth rate remains quite high at 33.6 births per 1,000 women between fifteen and nineteen years of age. Polygamy continues to be practiced in some parts of the country. Other indices indicate more positive trends: FGM is not practiced in the country, and there is no tradition of son preference. Women have access to land, and while early marriages are still in evidence, the rate is comparatively low. By 2009, inheritance by females and access for women to bank loans and property other than land were increasing. Literacy rates for women and men were 65% and 72%, respectively, in 2012, and gender parity has been achieved at the primary level, with a small disparity in favor of girls at the secondary level. This pattern reverses at the tertiary level, with men making up 55% of tertiary-level students (Masanja et al., 2016).

To reduce gender disparity in ICT, a focus has been placed on encouraging and training women in ICT skills. An initiative to develop web content development that is of direct interest to women and girls has been initiated as part of the Education Master Plan of the Ministry of Education. Many tertiary-level institutions target female enrollments in ICT-related programs. The Ministry of Public Service, Skills Development and Labour has implemented an ICT staff recruitment and promotion policy that aims to encourage women in ICT-related careers within civil and public service, as part of the Integrated ICT-Led Socio-Economic Development Plan for Rwanda 2006–2010 (Masanja et al., 2016).

There is little information on women with high-level computer skills in Rwanda. Data are also scarce on shares of women among information technology workers. However as indicated in the policies and laws described above, the government does have a policy to promote women's advancement in the workplace. Access to tertiary education has mostly been and still is easier for male than female students, with a large gender gap, especially in science-based disciplines. Although the government and higher learning institutions have put in place mechanisms to improve the gender balance among students, data from the Education Statistics Year Book 2014 show that in 2013 the number of male students at the tertiary level per 100,000 male inhabitants was around 900, while the corresponding figure for female students was 670 (Masanja et al., 2016).

Analysis of women's representation in science-based disciplines is shown in Table 6.1. The STEM discipline with the highest representation of women is health and welfare, followed by agricultural sciences and sciences in 2012, the first year for which sex-disaggregated data are available, and 2016, the latest year available. Overall, women's representation is

Table 6.1 *Proportion of women students in Rwandan tertiary education by discipline*

	Sciences	Engineering and technology	Health and welfareelfare	Agricultural sciences	Social science	Humanities
2012	32%	24%	52%	33%	52%	30%
2016	34%	23%	50%	34%	52%	28%

Source: National Institute of Statistics Rwanda (NISR), 2013 and 2016.

at 30% or above, with the exception of engineering and technology, at 23% in 2016. The participation of women students increased in sciences and slightly in agriculture, while it decreased in health and welfare and human-ities. Total enrollment decreased in most fields except for social sciences and health and welfare.

SENEGAL

In West Africa, Senegal is known as a leader in gender equality. The Constitution of Senegal of 2001 strengthened the principles of gender equality and the elimination of all forms of discrimination against women; since 2010 Article 7 stipulates: "All human beings are equal in the eyes of the law. Men and women have equal rights."

 . Specific laws have been designed to promote gender equality, such as one on parity that requires equal representation of men and women in elective and semi-elected bodies. Various instruments of economic and social governance (PRSP II 2006–2010 to the DPES 2011–2015, and the SNDES 2012–2017) take into account the gender dimension. Relating to education, gender disparities are still significant, particularly in access to knowledge and use of technology. The new General Policy Letter for the Education and Training Sector covering the period 2012–2025, through its Program for Improving Quality–Equity–Transparency (PAQUET), attaches great importance to the gender dimension. The government has also established excellence scholarships for young girls specializing in science, vocational training, and technical training.

The main cultural barriers for women include inequality in domestic workload compared with men. They engage in domestic work, involving cleaning, laundry, cooking, babysitting, care for the elderly, home main-tenance, fetching firewood and water, and shopping for the family, with seven hours per day spent on domestic work, compared with thirty minutes for men. While son preference is not a strong trend in the country, family code continues to advantage men and husbands, while approximately 30% of women on average are circumcised. Literacy rates remain comparatively low in the country, at 38% for women and 53% for men, although these rates are improving rapidly among the younger population. There is a small gender disparity in primary school enrollment and retention in favor of girls, although rates of transition to secondary school are more favorable for boys than girls and also subsequently to tertiary levels (Sarr and Wade, 2017).

Despite these laws, women's representation in the formal labor force is low, but they are highly represented in informal employment. Most women work on their own account or collaborate in family businesses. Reasons for this include lack of qualifications (education), and focus on family or household-related activities (Sarr and Wade, 2017). Regardless of the age group considered, the level of labor force activity is higher for men than for women at 57.4% for men and 37.8% for women in the population aged ten and over, and 65.8% and 42.7%, respectively, in the age group fifteen and over (ANSD, 2015). The salaries of women in the formal sector labor force are above the world average as a percentage of male salaries, but not equal to those of men for equal work in Senegal, where women make 93.8% of the wages of men (ANSD, 2016). This compares favorably to the global gender wage gap of 58% (WEF, 2016). However, as has been seen, fewer women than men in Senegal are in salaried employment.

Among the professionals in the ICT sector, the female population is younger than the male group, with nearly 83% of women between the ages of fifteen and thirty-five, compared with 38% of men in the same age bracket. More than 41% of men in the sector, compared with 15% of women, have more than ten years of experience. Women enter ICT employment with more training and education in ICT than men but enjoy substantially less capacity building while employed. They also receive less financing and equipment to do their jobs. Men generally have more access to training and benefit more from capacity building as well as greater access to finance and equipment, resulting in higher salaries than those of women (Groupe d'experts associés, 2017). Men are somewhat more likely than women to benefit from permanent jobs and self-employment, an area that women have not entered to date, while women are more likely to be in temporary employment and working as trainees (Sarr and Wade, 2017).

UGANDA

The constitution of Uganda provides for recognition of the rights of women and promotes and protects social justice and equality of all

Ugandans. The national Gender Policy of 2007 gives a mandate to the Ministry of Gender, Labour and Social Development and other line ministries to mainstream gender in all sectors, with a set of priority areas of action at the national, sectoral, district, and community levels. The policy notes that sustainable development calls for maximum and equal participation of both men and women in economic, political, and sociocultural development. The Equal Opportunities Commission is mandated to eliminate discrimination and inequalities against any individual or group of persons on the ground of sex, age, race, color, ethnic origin, tribe, birth, creed or religion, health status, social or economic standing, political opinion, or disability, and take affirmative action in favor of groups marginalized on the basis of gender, age, disability, or any other reason created by history, tradition, or custom for the purpose of redressing imbalances that exist against them. Other relevant laws include the Divorce Act 2004, Domestic Violence Bill, 2010, and Female Genital Mutilation Act, 2010. The National ICT Policy recognizes the goal of "lifelong education for all" and aims to address literacy and human resource capacity-building with strategies that include integrating ICT into mainstream educational curricula and other literacy programs to provide for equitable access for all students regardless of level, developing and managing ICT centers of excellence to provide basic and advanced ICT training, setting up mechanisms that promote collaboration between industry and training institutions to build appropriate human resources capacity, and promoting the twinning of training institutions in Uganda with those elsewhere to enhance skills transfer (Murungi et al., 2015).

Cultural barriers for Uganda differ from those of its neighbors in some ways. There is almost no incidence of FGM reported in the country, although it is estimated that half of Ugandan women have experienced physical violence since the age of fifteen. Early marriage remains a problem, with 16% of girls married before the age of fifteen, and 53% married before the age of eighteen. Son preference exists in the country, with a population slightly skewed in favor of males (51–49% females). Boys tend to be valued for their role in carrying on the family lineage. Gender inequalities in the control and ownership of productive resources/assets exist: only 20% of women own land. Cultural attitudes favor men over women in traditional land inheritance, and no laws are in place to protect women's rights to land. As a result, women's access to credit is restricted, although initiatives to improve this access are showing results. Similarly to Kenya, Uganda has gender parity at the primary education level, with subsequent decreases in the proportion of girls at secondary and tertiary levels. Literacy rates are quite high, at 86% for females and 90% for males (Murungi et al., 2015).

While women in STEM earn 33% more than women in other jobs, they hold a disproportionately low share of STEM undergraduate degrees, particularly in engineering. Seven universities and colleges in Uganda had a total student enrolment of 21,467 in 2009, with women making up 51% overall and 18% of enrollments in science, engineering, and technology (SET). Female professional and technical workers were 35% of total in 2006, according to the International Standard Classification of Occupations (ISCO-88), which includes physical, mathematical, and engineering science professionals; life science and health professionals; teaching professionals; and other professionals and associate professionals. The number of women in computing has fallen from 35% in 1990 to 26% in 2015.[2]

CULTURAL INFLUENCES AMONG THE FIVE COUNTRIES

In general, the five countries studied tend to be characterized by rigid gender norms and inequalities, for example, the preference of sons over daughters in property inheritance. In addition, women tend to have higher rates of unpaid and domestic work, leaving them with a longer workday than men. There was substantial male–female time-use gaps, with women's workday extending to 15–19 hours in some countries and sometimes twice that of men.

In Ethiopia, women have heavy domestic workloads in both urban and rural areas. In urban households, women were solely in charge of water (80%) and firewood (70%) collection, while rural women carry out 78% of water and 81% of firewood collection. Urban men (20%) share domestic responsibilities slightly more than rural men (10%). Females are engaged in more caregiving services to household members than men, with most of the caregiving focused on children. Married women spent about 1.5 hours per day more than men in caregiving activity as well, with 45% of married women involved in caregiving, spending about 3.6 hours per day, compared with 21% of married men, who spent 2 hours. Usually, men are responsible for services outside the residential home, including community services, although unpaid community services fell more heavily on women.

These gender imbalances in daily workload have great significance for women's and girls' opportunities, leaving them little time to pursue education and seek out information to advance their skills and pursue better opportunities. In both urban and rural areas, women and girls expended less time on learning activities and non-productive/leisure activities, although urban women spend more time in such activities than their rural counterparts. Men in both rural and urban settings had more time to consult information sources and media and had more leisure-time activities such as recreation, cultural events, and sport activities. In urban settings, 54% of men compared with 48% of urban women spent time utilizing mass media, while in rural areas, where overall participation rates of mass media use were much lower, gender disparities persisted, with a 9% rate for men and 4% for women.

In Uganda, gender norms mean that boys are prized by families for carrying on the family lineage, while girls tend to be preferred as a source of wealth from bride price. Most women, especially the poor, work between 12 and 18 hours per day, with an average of 15 hours compared with an average of 9 hours per day for men. However, this does not take into account the hours women spend on domestic work, including childcare and social activities, among others. As a result, many women end up working more than the national recommended normal working hours of 40–48 hours per week.

In Senegal, women's overload from domestic work, involving cleaning, laundry, cooking, babysitting, care for the elderly, home maintenance, fetching firewood and water, and shopping for the family, has been well documented (CREFAT, 2014). Estimates show that the average time spent on domestic work is seven hours for women as compared with about thirty minutes per day for men. Some 67% of the economic value of domestic labor in Senegal is generated from the domestic work of women from ten years of age to over sixty-five years. Unpaid domestic work in Senegal would account for 30% of the gross domestic product if calculated in the system of national accounts. This share is higher than that of the primary (15.5%) or the secondary sector (23.3%).

GENDERED EMPLOYMENT TRENDS AMONG THE FIVE COUNTRIES

All of these five countries see high rates of women's labor force participation, including salaried, self-employed and unpaid work. In general women work at lower positions than that of men, and much of their work is unpaid. All countries continue to have gender gaps in wages, with women's equivalent work paid 30% less than men's in Ethiopia and Uganda. In all, the numbers of women in salaried employment is low and gender segregation in occupations is a continuing tendency. Women are far more likely than men to work in the informal sector, and are increasingly becoming entrepreneurs and self-employed, particularly in Uganda.

In Ethiopia, in fields such as information technology, for instance, average monthly male earnings outpaced women's by 671 birr. Women's average monthly income in professional scientific and technical activities is also lower than men's: the former earn on average a monthly income of 1,960 birr as compared with 2,466 birr for men (Beyene, 2015).

Kenya's wage gap is not as wide, with women making 92% of men's wages, or 92 cents for every dollar earned by men.

The proportion of females in Rwanda participating in the labor force in 2012 was 71.4% for females, while that of men was 75.6%. In 2014, the proportion of female in self-employment was 74.5% and that of males was 67.2%. The Rwanda Demographic and Health Survey of 2014–2015 indicates that 87% of married women are employed, with 44% of those paid both in cash and in kind, 13% paid in cash only, and 14% paid in-kind only (NISR, 2015).

In Uganda, according to the Ministry of Finance, Planning and Economic Development (2015–2016), the average monthly wage of women is about 30% less than the average wage of men. The economically active population is made up of 59.8% males and 45.7% females. The percentage of female participation is less than that of males by 14.7%, although in urban areas the labor force participation rate for males is higher than that of females. Unemployment is higher among women, at 13.1%, compared with 5.8% among men, and unemployment among women in urban areas is twice that of men. Women's participation in the formal labor market is below that of men and as a result women earn less compared with men. According to the Uganda National Health Survey (2015–2016), 47.1% of women and 32.4% of men are subsistence farmers. In 2012–2013, 61% of women were self-employed, compared with 46% of men, while more women are contributing family workers than men. Some 40% of women compared with 54% of men were in paid employment, while 40% of men were employers and 50% were own-account workers. In 2015–2016, 46% of women and 28.3% of men were paid employees in agriculture. The gaps in mean earnings from self-employment are substantial everywhere (50% in favor of men on average) and wider than those observed in wage employment (15% on average). In 2012/2013, on average men earned 220,000 Ugandan shillings (in urban areas) and 110,000 Ugandan shillings (in rural areas), while their female counterparts earned 150,000 Ugandan shillings (in urban areas) and 66,000 Ugandan shillings (in rural areas) (UBOS 2014, 2017).

In Senegal, the concentration of women in low-income jobs in the country and their exclusion from lucrative economic sectors makes it very difficult to access employment that offers opportunities to improve professional skills. These factors constrain the participation of women in fields such as science and technology. To illustrate this point, although women make up the majority of the population, they are a minority in the labor force: regardless of the age group considered, in those fifteen and older, the level of labor force activity is higher for men (65.8%) than for women (42.7%) (ANSD, 2015). The salaries of women in the formal labor force are above the world average as a percentage of male salaries, but not equal to those of men for equal work in Senegal. Government statistics of 2016 reported an average monthly salary of 116,164 West Africa CFA francs (FCFA) for men as compared with 108,984 FCFA for salaried women (93.8% of the wages of men) (ANSD, 2016). This compares favorably to the global gender wage gap of 58% (WEF, 2016). However, as has been seen, fewer women than men in Senegal are in salaried employment. Few women are employers, and they are very poorly represented in the paid workforce as well. Most women work on their own account or collaborate in family businesses (Sarr and Wade, 2017).

CONCLUSION

As in other parts of the globe, cultural perceptions pose a barrier also in the African countries highlighted here, where cultural/religious laws and practices on divorce, inheritance, and property ownership constrain women's opportunities. Added to this are cultural conceptions of women's capacity for participating in these fields. Further, economic and educational barriers for women's participation in STEM remain high. As a result, with the exception of Ethiopia, which demonstrates some positive trends in parts of the sector, the African countries presented here show low participation of women in STEM and ICT. While women are highly represented in the workforce of each country, they predominate in the informal sector and in low-skilled employment. As a result, it is more difficult for them to enter professional jobs in general, including STEM. Ethiopia is the sole exception, with comparatively high percentages of women in some ICT and professional fields.

Additionally, where there is a gender policy environment, pervasive cultural constraints render the policy insufficient to promote greater gender parity in these fields. While all countries showed some mainstreaming of gender in national policy, only Ethiopia and Rwanda have developed science, technology, and innovation policies that refer specifically to the importance of the inclusion of women. In the East African countries, constitutional and policy commitments to gender equality and inclusion often fall short, in omissions in sector policies, in program and project implementation, or through deference to cultural/religious laws and practices on divorce, inheritance, and property ownership that uphold patriarchy. This is true also for Senegal. While policy in these countries may promote gender equality and participation of women in nontraditional areas of society and economy, budgets and programming to support implementation of policy are not always in evidence. We can see that cultural attitudes have a significant influence on women's participation in IT in these countries, as well as others represented in this review. However, the lack of supporting budgets or programs to overcome barriers of culture, education, and participation in the formal economy may also be important factors.

DISCUSSION QUESTIONS

1. What are the cultural attitudes toward women's aptitude for STEM and IT in the countries in this chapter, and how do they compare with similar attitudes in other regions?
2. Are the constraints on girls and women from studying and working in science, technology, and innovation similar from country to country?
3. What is your assessment of girls and women in science, technology, and innovation in your country? Is it different from the experience of those countries detailed here?

References

ANSD. (2015). Senegal: Demographic and Continuous Health Survey (DHS-Continuous) 2014. Dakar. www.dhsprogram.com/pubs/pdf/FR305/FR305.pdf.

ANSD (2016). Report on National Survey on Employment in Senegal, 2015. Dakar. www.ansd.sn/index.php?option=com_ansd&view=titrepublication&id=33.

Beyene, H. (2015). *Final Report National Assessment: Ethiopia*. Brighton, Canada: Women in Global Science and Technology (WISAT) and the Organization for Women in Science in the Developing World (OWSD). Retrieved from http://wisat .org/wp-content/uploads/National-Assessment-on-Gender-and-STI-Ethiopia.pdf.

Chege, N. (2015). How Women in Tech Are Changing IT Training. *The Nation*, July 25.

CREFAT. (2014). Domestic Work in Senegal: 30% of GDP to Be Valorised, Policy Brief no. 2. https://crefat.univ-thies.sn/img/uploads/1415310849crefat.pdf.

Frosina, N. L., and Mwaura, G. M. (2016). *An Assessment of Gender Mainstreaming in STI and the Knowledge Society in Kenya*. Brighton, Canada: Women in Global Science and Technology. Retrieved from http://wisat.org/wp-content/uploads/National-Assessment-on-Gender-and-STI-Kenya.pdf.

Groupe d'experts associés (DEA). (2017). Enquête Intégration du genre dans le secteur des TICs (Survey on the Integration of Gender in the ICT Sector). 2017. Unpublished. Dakar.

Masanja, V. G., Masanja, J. K., and Masanja, R. K. (2016). *The Gender Equality and the Knowledge Society (GE-KS) in Rwanda*. Brighton, Canada: Women in Global Science and Technology. Retrieved from http://wisat.org/wp-content/uploads/National-Assessment-on-Gender-and-STI-Rwanda.pdf.

Muringi, I., Bukare, A., Atim, S., Boyle, A., and Dauvergne, M. (2015). *Final Report for the GEKS Uganda National Assessment* (Vol. 256). Brighton, Canada: Women in Global Science and Technology. Retrieved from https://owsd.net/sites/default/files/National Assessment on Gender and STI - Uganda_1.pdf.

National Institute of Statistics Rwanda (NISR). (2013). Statistical YearBook 2013. Retrieved from www.statistics.gov.rw/publication/statistical-yearbook-2013.

National Institute of Statistics of Rwanda (NISR). (2015). [Rwanda], Ministry of Health (MOH) [Rwanda], and ICF International. 2015. *Rwanda Demographic and Health Survey 2014–15*. Rockville, MD: NISR, MOH, and ICF International.

National Institute of Statistics Rwanda (NISR). (2016). Statistical YearBook 2016. Retrieved from www.statistics.gov.rw/publication/statistical-yearbook-2016.

Ndiaye, Oumy Khairy. (2013). "Is the Success of M-Pesa Empowering Kenyan Rural Women?" *Feminist Africa*, no. 18: 156–161.

Republic of Kenya. (2010). *The Constitution of Kenya*. Nairobi.

Rwabuhihi, R. (2017). *Republic of Rwanda Labour Market Policies, Gender and Poverty Eradication: The Experience of Rwanda*. Kigali: Republic of Rwanda.

Sarr, F., and Wade, A. (2017). *Assessment of Gender Equality in the Knowledge Society in Senegal*. Brighton, Canada: Women in Global Science and Technology and the CGIAR Climate Change, Agriculture and Food Security Programme (CCAFS). Retrieved from http://wisat.org/wp-content/uploads/NH-EN-Senegal-_Final.pdf.

Uganda Bureau of Statistics (UBOS). (2014). *Uganda National Household Survey 2012/2013*. Kampala, Uganda: UBOS.

Uganda Bureau of Statistics (UBOS). (2017). *Uganda National Household Survey 2015/2016*. Kampala, Uganda: UBOS.

United Nations Educational, Scientific and Cultural Organization. (2012). Economic Empowerment and Functional Adult Literacy Programme. Country Profile: Kenya. www.unesco.org/uil/litbase/?menu=4&programme=145.

World Economic Forum. (2016). *Global Gender Gap Report*. Economic Opportunity and Survival, Educational Attainment, Health and Survival, and Political Empowerment. http://reports.weforum.org/global-gender-gap-report-2016/results-and-analysis/.

Part III

Cultural Perspectives from the United States and Europe

Against All Odds

Culture and Context in the Female Information Technology Professional's Career Choice and Experiences

Monica P. Adya

INTRODUCTION

Since 2006–2007, I have interviewed numerous women in technology careers to understand their motivation for choosing their careers and their experiences in the technical workforce. While the intent of an initial study that emerged from some of these interviews (Adya, 2008) was to compare and contrast the experiences of South Asian and American women in the US workforce, the stories of some of these women were more broadly impactful. Some of these women were inspiring in how they overcame barriers and eventually succeeded in information technology (IT) careers, and others in how they changed the course of their lives, sometimes away from IT careers and into others that they felt they could grow into.

I met, for instance, Olivia,[1] who was bothered by how her users sought to maintain gender-stereotyped roles (Ahuja, 2002), for example, by expecting males to solve technical issues more efficaciously than her. As she noted:

A couple of times they [users] sounded specifically disappointed when they heard my voice on the phone saying, "Well I need to talk to someone about networking," and said, well I can help you with that.. . . Every once in a while I have had that when I have not been able to figure out something, people have said, "Well, let's just get Nate to help." And I am, like, that's not the issue. It's not that I don't know any more than he does. I'm like he would have the same trouble as I would in trying to figure this out.

After some years in an IT career, Olivia chose to leave the IT workforce completely and, at the time of her interview, intended to start a new career in publishing.

During that same time frame, I interviewed Amy, an IT professional in the military, who was raised, with three brothers, by a father. While in the military, Amy had struggled with workplace stereotypes and bureaucracy from her immediate supervisor, who had relegated her to seemingly insignificant work in a "remote corner" of her campus so she would be out of his way. She reacted to her supervisor's negative attitude to her by confronting him but realized early that she could not fight the bureaucracy. She decided her best way was to "get back" by educating herself further and building a successful career in IT: "You either say something to him or quit the job. You have to work with them and get along [or] have to move on. Grow up." Amy believed that being in the military toughened her. At the time of my interview with her, she had completed her BS in computer science and was working as a Unix administrator in the healthcare industry. She projected long-term commitment to her IT career and aspired to move up the ladder rapidly.

The stories of these two women, and those of many others, not only serve to highlight the numerous barriers that women continue to face in their decisions to become and remain technology professionals in the United States; they also emphasize how some women continue to push and aspire against all odds. Whereas their career paths were full of challenges, the successes of these women were the result of the complex interplay of individual, environmental, social, and structural factors. This intricate mesh of context and culture that shapes the particular successes of some women in IT is the central theme of this chapter.

My own path to a career in IT has been influenced by many of these elements. Born into a family of three daughters in India, I was never raised to believe that a technical career was out of reach for me. Rather, in an environment where others often lamented that there was no "son to carry [my father's] name forward," our parents raised us to break these stereotypes and pursue any career with the aspiration of attaining the highest degree in our chosen fields. My mother's response often was "our daughters will be raised no less than sons." As I explored courses in programming and tech support in India, the thought that I was entering a male-dominated profession never crossed my mind. IT is not viewed as a masculine field in India. It was only when I came to the United States and joined academia that I, along with my colleagues such as Jenny Preece and Kate Kaiser, noted concerns about the small percentage of female students in our IT classes. Since then, conversations and interviews with many college students and female IT professionals in the United States and in India have elicited contrasts and similarities around perceptions of, and experiences in, IT careers in these two cultures. Some stories are shared here.

I first begin with a brief review of some of the existing literature that points to the underrepresentation of women in IT careers. The section that follows elaborates on common traits and experiences I found in these women as well as individual factors that contributed to their success in IT careers. Illustrative stories are woven through the section, a majority of which reflect experiences in the US workforce. Occasionally, there are stories of women in other countries. The chapter concludes with some brief recommendations for how more women could be encouraged to pursue and succeed in IT careers against the odds that they face.

UNDERREPRESENTATION OF WOMEN IN IS/IT CAREERS IN THE UNITED STATES

In the United States, concerns around the gender gap in IT careers remains persistent and has not been alleviated between the 1990s (Cole et al., 1994) and today (Armstrong et al., 2018) despite a variety of interventions and incentives targeted at both women and girls. A 2017 survey by PwC,[2] a global professional services provider, noted that only 3% of females indicate a career in technology as their first choice. Well over 78% noted that they could not name a famous female working in technology careers. The deficit of female role models in leadership positions seems to suggest to women that technology careers are male-dominated. Over a quarter of the women surveyed by PwC indicate that they have been discouraged from the career in technology due to its perception as a male-dominated field. Indeed, only 16% of women in this survey indicated that a technology career was suggested to them, as opposed to 33% of men. This recent survey is one of many that continue to suggest that seeds for low female participation are sown early, often in middle school (sixth grade onward), while poor experiences in a field perceived to be male-dominated further perpetuate lower female retention in IT careers. Before we delve deeper into the contributory factors, however, it would be beneficial to understand the variety of theories that have been proposed to explain low female participation in technical careers.

Macro- and Micro-Level Theories in IT Work Participation

Most frequently, three macro-level theories have been used to explain the underrepresentation of women in certain occupations (Anker, 1997).

Neoclassical/human capital theories suggest that lower training and experience in specific fields contribute to inadequate female representation in the workforce. Labor market theories, in contrast, note that markets are segmented and that overcrowding of women in certain professions tend to drive wages down, making these professions unattractive to men (Anker, 1997). Finally, feminist theories attribute the disadvantaged position of women in certain occupations to patriarchy and women's subordinate social position (e.g., viewing women as homemakers and care providers).

In contrast to macro theories that attribute low female participation to socioeconomic factors, micro-level theories tend to emphasize individual differences and contexts to understand the same phenomenon. The essentialist paradigm, for instance, suggests that inherent biological and psychological differences between males and females impact their willingness and ability to participate in certain careers (Kirby, 1991), such as might be the case in a technical career. An alternative viewpoint is presented in the theory of social construction (Burger and Luckman, 1966), which suggests that socially constructed beliefs and attitudes may explain female participation and experience in certain careers. For instance, societal perception of IT as a masculine career (von Hellens et al., 2003) may deter women from choosing IT careers. A third theory used to explain female participation, or lack of it, is the theory of individual differences (Trauth, 2002), which posits that the group-level emphasis of essentialism and social constructivism force generalizations that may not adequately represent the impact of institutional and cultural factors on the individual. This theory recognizes "similarities between men and women as individuals, and the variations between members of each gender with respect to IT skills and the inclination to participate in the IT sector" (Trauth, 2002, p. 103).

Why are these theories important to understand? The theoretical lens applied to understand the phenomenon not only can distinguish the rationale provided for underrepresentation in IT careers but also can shape the nature of macro- and micro-level interventions designed to overcome the challenge. In this chapter, I view female participation in IS/IT careers through the lens of individual differences, which suggests that while female participation in the IT workforce is a complex reciprocation of factors, changes in structural, environmental, and social factors can improve recruitment and retention of women in such careers. These individual differences also highlight stories of women who are able to, against the odds, demonstrate success in IS/IT careers. The next few sections are built on literature as viewed through this lens with particular emphasis on women in the US IT workforce.

Barriers to Female Participation in IS/IT Careers

The above theories point to a variety of barriers that contribute to the shortage of women in IS/IT careers and impact not merely the recruitment of women into technology careers but also their long-term retention and success. Studies point to societal stereotypes, insufficient role models, peer pressures, and weak influence of teachers and counselors on girls' choices as some of the many factors that shift girls' choices away from technical careers to those that are considered more normative. At the same time, a growing body of literature points to the challenges of retaining women who have chosen IT careers. For instance, women might feel greater isolation in the IT work environment due to higher presence of male professionals, dearth of female leaders and mentors, challenges of keeping abreast with changing technologies, work–life imbalance, and workplace stereotypes perpetuated by managers and user groups.

Table 7.1 summarizes some key barriers to female participation and success in IT careers. These factors are categorized according to the primary influences – recruitment of women into IT careers, their retention and success in such careers, or both. Contrary to the intent of the chapter, Table 7.1 focuses on factors identified as barriers to women's participation and success in IT careers.

AGAINST ALL ODDS: CONTEXT AND CULTURE IN WOMEN'S SUCCESS IN IT CAREERS

In this section, I focus on stories of success, of women who have overcome barriers and demonstrated persistence in IT careers. Throughout my professional journey, I have encountered women who have struggled with, and eventually left, their careers in IT. During the same course, however, I have met those who have pushed against the odds and established long and successful IT careers, who serve as role models to other women, and who are challenging and positively deconstructing the stereotyped viewpoints of their male peers and supervisors. Whereas the circumstances of each of these women are unique, some within their control and some beyond, some common themes emerge among the women who persisted and succeeded. At the same time, there is evidence of particular influencers that make the stories of each of these women unique.

Table 7.1 *Cultural barriers to women's recruitment, retention, and success in IS/IT careers*

Barriers	Primary influence on	Key sources of barriers
Family	– Recruitment	– Lack of parental and sibling role models in STEM careers – Limited family resources to support STEM careers – Perpetuation of gender stereotypes in parental roles
Educational environment and access	– Recruitment	– Limited access to education – Limited access to technology – Teacher/counselor stereotypes
Role models and mentoring	– Recruitment – Retention and success	– Insufficient female role models – Predominance of role-models in non-IT roles – Media bias and stereotypes
Career expectations	– Recruitment – Retention and success	– Gender stereotyping of STEM careers – National culture of encouraging non-STEM over STEM careers – Perceived roles of women at home vs work
Perceptions of IS/IT as masculine fields	– Recruitment – Retention and success	– Predominance of males in the field – Insufficient females in leadership position – Supervisor and peer perceptions – Media stereotypes – Misdirected teacher/counselor guidance
Individual barriers	– Recruitment – Retention and success	– Personality traits – Attitudes – Preference for work–life balance
Organizational support	– Retention and success	– Gender-stereotyping of females in softer IT roles – Supervisor and manager attitudes – User group and peer attitudes

Common Factors in IS/IT Career Success

Whereas there is opportunity for a greater range of factors common to successful women in IT, three traits and attitudes, in particular, stand out as critical. *First, adverse conditions require grit and resilience, a trait that many women IT professionals represent.* Whereas most IT professionals handle high levels of job stress, "particularly because of the key role that IT plays in most organizations, the unrelenting demand for IT systems to work well, and constant pressure for greater efficiency and faster turn-around of results" (Lounsbury et al., 2007, p. 173), girls and women often face additional stressors that stem from gender-stereotyping of their roles, perceived isolation in a male-dominated field, and insufficient female mentors and role models.

A second factor, perceived self-efficacy in IT professions, often emerged as a second common success factor. This is consistent with studies (e.g., Michie and Nelson, 2006) that have pointed to males as having greater self-efficacy for IT and related occupations than women and the persist-ence of traditional work role expectations. Successful women in IT careers tend to break through these persistent beliefs and build their technological efficacy or develop abilities to fulfill gaps with a complementary skill set.

Finally, women who persist in IT demonstrate a commitment and career entrenchment that can stem from a variety of factors including investments in careers, psychological costs of career change, and low opportunities outside one's career (Carson et al., 1996). Whereas all of these were manifest at various points across the women who stayed in IT careers, investments in higher education and specialized degrees seemed to pre-dominate, particularly among South Asian women in the US workforce who typically had specialized degrees at undergraduate and graduate levels.

Grit and Resilience. Successful women in IT must overcome a variety of stereotypes to succeed in their careers. Most crucial, and one they encoun-ter early, often in middle school, is the gender stereotyping of IT careers. The social construction of IT as a masculine field (Trauth, 2002) as evidenced in the predominance of males in the profession begins early in middle and high school (Adya and Kaiser, 2005). The media continue to characterize IT careers as nerdy and male-dominated (Choudhury et al., 2010). Even IT artifacts, for example, the numeric keyboard's association with math, another field that has been stereotyped as masculine (Beise et al 2003), reinforce IT as a male-dominated field in the United States. Career profile tests taken in middle and high school use stereotypical items to push women toward non-STEM careers but are more likely to recommend STEM careers to boys because they like building things or playing video games as opposed to interacting with people. As fewer girls choose IT careers in response to these stereotypes, their representation in the work-force remains slim and bolsters the masculine nature of the IT profession. As Olivia's example early in the chapter highlights, these stereotypes then continue to perpetuate into supervisors and user groups.

Women who experience such gender-stereotyping of their careers tend to respond in one of two ways – they either rebel and fight against the odds or they conform and, in some cases, leave the chosen field. The girls and women I met who were successful in IT careers demonstrated a grit and resilience that enabled them to counter the many stereotypes and challenges they encountered in their work environment. Alexa, who worked as an IT project manager, noted how she needed to be "aggressive" in a male-dominated space, otherwise she could "never get the project done." The males she supervised "just did not want to listen to [her] because [she] was a female giving them orders." She sensed that this aggressive attitude had become a part of her and that she carried that style as she moved from one role or firm to another. "But," she noted, "it's the only way I can get things done when everyone around you is a male."

Self-Efficacy and Self-Confidence. Women who chose IT careers demonstrated a self-confidence in their ability to be successful in any career, irrespective of any gender stereotypes. Such confidence and perceptions of self-efficacy can shape the careers that girls pursue as well as those they disfavor (Bandura et al., 2001). Among the women I met, there were three common sources of self-efficacy – their access to and accomplishments in education, family, and social structures, and positive, reinforcing experiences. Self-confidence in these women emerged from academic success in middle and high school, particularly in math, science, and technology. Fundamentally, this meant they had access to education and technological resources. For instance, in interviews with her subjects, Trauth (2002) notes stories of women who were "toppers" in their academic careers and demonstrated a parallel confidence in being able to succeed in any career, including IT careers.

However, not all women are "toppers," have exceptionally strong academic credentials, or even have access to quality education. Often other factors are at play in enhancing their sense of self-efficacy and confidence in career choice. For some of these women, their self-confidence related to career success was often reinforced through social and familial interactions. Lilian, for instance, was one of two girls in her family, both raised by a mother who did not work. Her mother's regret in not being workforce-ready was redirected to encouraging Lilian and her sister to pursue any career and strive to be successful in their chosen path. Lilian commented on how frequently her mother reminded them that a successful career was a "pathway" for reduced dependency on spouses and partners. Inspired by the success and flexibility of her aunt's small but successful IT consulting firm, Lilian chose to develop her career in IT and became an IT project manager at a healthcare firm.

Other women discover their confidence and efficacy in IT roles through work opportunities. Positive reinforcements of their ability not only to successfully use technology but also to deliver value frequently serve to enhance their chances of shifting to IT careers. Jeanine, for instance, came into an IT career only indirectly. Her primary role within her organization was in finance. About two years ago, she was asked to lead a major Enterprise Resource Planning (ERP) systems initiative at one of the plants within her organization, primarily because of her financial knowledge and project management competency. She came into this temporary role with little technical background and was paired with the technical lead on this project. Through this implementation, she began moving into other IT projects with greater confidence. Her first ERP project was completed successfully, and she was subsequently asked to implement at a second plant. When I interviewed her, she had approached her manager and asked to continue to work on additional IT projects. Her desire to move into the IT area, she claimed, came from the understanding that she could be "successful with technology projects because [she] not only understood financial and technical sides but also ... successfully managed change," especially with factory floor workers who were initially wary of this implementation.

Entrenchment. Women who demonstrated a long-term commitment to IT careers also demonstrated a career entrenchment that differentiated them from others who chose to leave the profession. Career entrenchment is defined as an individual's feeling of "immobility resulting from substantial economic and psychological investments in a career that make change difficult" (Carson et al., 1996, p. 274). Career entrenchment often emerges from a variety of factors, not all of which are positive. Women may recognize that their investments and effort in an IT career are too high to make a career switch; they may have limited career options; or they may be unwilling to bear the emotional costs of career changes (e.g., loss of professional networks).

In my interactions with female IS professionals, a common source of entrenchment came from educational accomplishments. Women who pursued IT-specific degrees at the undergraduate or graduate levels tended to remain in IT careers for the long term. This was particularly so for those who attained more technical degrees such as those in computer engineering or computer science. In fact, it was not uncommon to find that these women preferred to remain in technical roles as opposed to moving into managerial roles (i.e., they demonstrated a persistent technical orientation).

Isabel, for instance, had an undergraduate emphasis in systems development. On the birth of her first child, she left the workforce but returned after nearly fifteen years, at which point no other career was an option for her, even though technologies had dramatically changed over that time. She also felt that in returning to an IS/IT career she would serve as a strong role model for her teenage children. Starting with part-time project management and support roles, she gradually made her way back to a large firm as a business analyst. Isabel modeled not only did the career entrenchment but also the grit that is necessary to return to a career in an ever-changing field.

There are, however, women who demonstrate career entrenchment even without the investments in a technical degree or a prolonged career in a specific firm or industry segment. A good example of this was Ishika, who started out with a career in journalism and decided to move to a managerial role in an IT security firm in the United States where she worked her way toward a vice president's role. She spoke of three challenges that she most frequently encountered – the stereotype associated with her lack of a technical degree, the fact that she was the only woman in the boardroom and had no female peers or mentors, and the compromises she had to make in her personal life where she never got to "pick up her kids or volunteer in school." Ishika demonstrated an entrenchment that came more from the economic and emotional aspect of her role as opposed to career investments. She understood that she had reached her position because of the respect she had garnered through the "measurable impact on [her] company's bottom line." She felt a "sense of accomplishment in a male-dominated field." As she noted, "I feel like if you put in your years, you will get a break." Although she missed journalism, she recognized that each field "has its own challenges and so changing careers at this point would not make sense." Today, after about seven years from our initial meeting, Ishika is a senior VP in the same firm and continues to be one of few but respected women in the boardroom. Perceived job rewards are often critical in enhancing job satisfaction and mitigating turnover intentions (Lawler, 1986).

By contrast, women who came into IT indirectly or as a second career tend to express a desire to leave IT with greater frequency. It is unclear whether, having switched their career once, the decision to switch again was less of a deterrent or whether they wanted to make their way back to the careers in which they started. Jasmine, who upon encouragement from her IS professor added IS as a second major to marketing, decided to shift back to marketing after four years in an IT role. In her new role with social media and digital marketing, she felt she had found her "happy spot" and had leveraged the IS major as best as she could. She had "started out in marketing and that is where [her] heart" was. "This is who I am but I am not an IT person – I just don't see myself that way for the long haul."

Family and work–life balance issues can, however, shake the foundations of entrenchment, especially if women perceive their ability to devote sufficient time to family is hampered by work pressures. Chetana, for instance, who did not have an IS degree but earned her work through organizational training, felt that the pressures of her technical role interfered with care of her newborn child. When I met her, she had left her programming role and was considering reskilling herself for a non-IT role. Such expressions may come as a surprise considering the telecommuting options and work flexibility being afforded by many firms today.

A variety of social, economic, and structural factors seemed to be at play in shaping these women's grit, self-confidence, and entrenchment toward their careers. However, I say this with a caveat. It also takes grit and determination to leave a chosen profession and start a new one, and a good number of women who chose to go that way noted how they would not let their IT careers die quietly. Grace, who experienced her manager's bias toward "male, white Americans promoting each other," called herself a "troublemaker" and eventually quit her job but not without challenging her supervisor and the human resources department on their equitable work practices.

Individual Factors

Whereas the above factors seemed to be common among successful women I have met in the IS profession, there are some individual traits and environmental factors that contribute to women's persistence in IS careers. I consider these "individual factors" because they and their manifestation can be distinct across individuals.

The Influence of Family. Whereas the influence of familial role models on choice of STEM careers is well established (Craig et al., 2018), women often specified the contributions of their family members not only in choice but also in persistence in the IT workforce. The influence of family appeared to be foremost in terms of providing the grit and self-confidence to choose and persist in an IT career. Some women noted the influence of their mothers in enhancing their self-confidence that they could pursue and be successful in any careers of their choice. For many of these women, their mothers either had never worked or had left their careers to raise families, and, often for that reason, they encouraged their daughters to pursue and persist in careers of their choice. Nayla's mother, for instance, never had a career but went back to college to retrain herself when her children started school. Thereafter, she built a successful career in education over 30 years. "My mother was really my role model," Nayla noted, "because she's the one who showed me I could do anything and be successful as long as I didn't let roadblocks along the way bother me."

Women frequently attribute their choice of careers to their fathers, particularly those who have STEM careers, who often discuss career options with their daughters and encourage them to pursue math and science careers, whether by engaging them in inquiry and activities related to STEM discipline (Craig et al., 2018) or by exposing them to STEM opportunities. Nayla, for instance, graduated with a degree in business at a time when computer Sscience and information technology had just begun appearing as new careers on the horizon. Her father encouraged her to take a programming course during the summer before she graduated from college and to learn typing, because everyone he saw using computers seemed to type well. This combination of programming and keyboarding skills set Nayla up for her first part-time job in data entry, which eventually pointed her to a degree in management information systems. Thirty-one years later, she has successfully persisted in her IS career and now serves as a mentor to a number of female colleagues. Nayla's story represents an interesting interplay where the mothers often provide psychosocial support for career success whereas fathers are more directive with regard to career paths that their daughters might choose (Adya and Kaiser, 2005).

Older siblings, especially brothers, in STEM careers motivate female participation in similar careers (Alexander et al., 2011). Because boys face fewer stereotypes in choice of technical careers, they are able to share these opportunities with their female siblings – essentially paving a path for them to follow. Amanda, for instance, is the youngest of four siblings. Her oldest sibling, a male, decided to major in IS and successfully leveraged that path to pursue an IS-related career. He encouraged each of his siblings, including Amanda, to consider IS or add it as a second major in college. All four eventually majored or minored in IS, even as a dual major. Today Amanda is in a successful IT career at a large firm after having completed her IS major.

Peer and Mentor Groups. A number of women I met highlighted the significant influence of role models and mentors in their choice and persistence in IT careers. However, the value that these mentors provide varied greatly. For some women, their mentors were peers who provided psychosocial support to manage and deal with workplace stereotypes. For instance, Lalita, who worked for a satellite communications firm in the United States and held advanced degrees in engineering, felt confident about the professional aspects of her role. She did not feel discriminated in the workplace based on her gender. Rather, she commented on the fact that she often experienced positive stereotypes in the United States because she was from India and had an engineering background. However, she was in her forties, and as the only "female, non-Caucasian project manager who [had] to manage a bunch of twenty-somethings," she felt isolated in her workplace. Lalita often turned to her female peers in other functional areas for advice on how to manage team issues, including understanding cultural and generational differences. Without her peer mentors, she would have struggled with regard to the social aspects of her work.

Such peer-based psychosocial support contrasts with the workplace mentoring that other women desired in order to succeed professionally (i.e., support for advanced or more meaningful roles in IS). For this, they often sought mentors who were IT professionals in roles senior to themselves. For instance, Lalita relied on a senior, male mentor for advice on professional growth and development, likely because there were few females in roles higher than hers. This is exemplified by a comment from Bhavana, an Oracle administrator in a healthcare firm, who noted that "in our entire software division there were only two other women in a group of about twenty to twenty-two people." She considered three managers – two females and a male – as her mentors. However, she turned more frequently to the female mentors because her male mentor, she felt, at times was "distracted" by her appearance.

Mentoring literature suggests that relying on a panel of mentors has greater benefits than reliance on a single mentor (Scandura and Pellegrini, 2007). Panels of mentors lend multiple perspectives to the mentee's career and can add value in different ways. Nayla attributed her success to two mentors, a male and a female, who were several years her senior – the female was in the same IT profession, whereas the male was in an indirect, supervisory role. The female mentor played a crucial role in introducing her to a broader network of female professionals, while the male mentor provided beneficial guidance on how to navigate the political environment and relationships within the organization. Both, she indicated, had measurable impact on her entrenchment and success in the IT career as well as her organization.

Teacher/Counselor Influence. Lexie began her undergraduate program as a marketing major with the intent of eventually starting her own company. As she moved through her junior year, she took a required introductory course in information systems. Lexie had frequent conversations with her female professor around the value of IS to marketing functions. In these one-on-one conversations, Lexie's professor encouraged her to consider careers at the intersection of marketing and IS. Three years ago, Lexie graduated with a double major in marketing and IS, and currently works for her family business with primary focus on marketing analytics and social-media marketing. Lexie notes how her impact on her family business was dramatically improved as she initiated IT-driven efficiencies in other non-marketing functions.

Lexie's story is one of many where both female and male professors have played a formative role in encouraging greater female participation in IT careers. Teachers and counselors can expose students to IT careers and technologies in ways that can gender-neutralize these careers. They can enhance self-efficacy related to computer use through design of effective curricula and hands-on projects that emphasize user interactions, insert creative design elements in software projects, and highlight demonstrated impact of IT on individuals, organizations, and societies (Weber and Custer, 2005).

It is noteworthy that teachers can also negatively enhance gender stereo-typing of roles and choices through such interactions as well. They run the risk of spreading the impression that boys are inherently better at com-puters or math-related fields than girls (Sanders and Stone, 1986). In such cases, teachers often attribute certain expertise to boys and may let them have priority over girls in computer use (Volman and van Ech, 2001). This often holds true for both male and female teachers. Girls in IT are found, most often, to be discouraged by teachers, guidance counselors, and male professors (Turner et al., 2002) from choosing IT careers, although women who moved from non-IT to IT careers later in life often indicated male professors to be a strong, positive influence in that move (Canes and Rosen, 1995). Middle- and high school teachers and counselors tend to feel comfortable advising in more traditional fields, possibly because they do not have sufficient IT backgrounds to be aware of career paths (Freeman and Aspray, 1999). College professors may have a broader, more integrative perspective of IT career opportunities to better direct students. Considering the potentially strong influence of teachers on women's par-ticipation in IS careers, there may be value added in providing greater career awareness to K-12 teachers and counselors.

Access to Education and Accomplishments. As with other factors, the issue with education and impact on choice of STEM/IT careers is a complex interplay of socioeconomic factors. It begins with the fundamen-tal problem of unequal access to education for girls and women, particu-larly for those in developing countries (Sanchez and Singh, 2018). Recent

World Bank figures indicate that globally only three in ten girls complete their lower secondary education (about nine years),[3] and a much smaller percentage of these women ever reach college. There is considerable evidence that access to education can bring cognitive enhancements that are essential to women's ability to "question, reflect on, and to act on the conditions of their lives and to gain access to knowledge, information, and new ideas that will help them to do so" (Kabeer, 2005, p. 13). As such, girls who lack access to good quality education begin on an unequal footing regarding any career choice but particularly so with STEM careers.

Even with access to education, girls and women may still be constrained by a variety of factors, such as limited resources, lack of technology and learning opportunities outside school, and social expectations related to their support roles within their homes (Adya and Kaiser, 2005). Women may not pursue further education at later stages of life for a variety of reasons, such as preoccupation with raising a family, not having the means to go back to college, or cultural expectations regarding the acceptability of going to college late in life. While these effects are often attributed to women in developing countries, the high cost of college education in Western countries coupled with access to viable career options without such degrees may dissuade women from pursuing advanced degrees in the United States as well (Adya, 2008). As one of my interviewees noted, some of her colleagues did not have the money to study in the United States and, as such, decided to pursue two-year courses and degrees, which made it tough for IT careers "because you [need to get] your degree and [only] then you get a job."

Once again, there are illustrative stories of women who have countered these odds to pursue successful careers in IT. In particular, stories of two women stand out. Marge, born and raised in the United States, was fortunate to have access to education and chose to specialize in and build her career as a medical professional. However, seeing workforce trends shifting toward technical careers, Marge began engaging with her database support team on small projects and found she enjoyed this aspect of her company's work. She decided to go back to her community college and obtain training on database administration, a skill that not too many members in her team possessed at that time. At the time I met her, she indicated she enjoyed her role as database administrator and, being about five years away from retirement, saw herself as ending her career in this technical role. Marge's story highlights one where access to education not only provided her a foothold in her early career as a medical professional but also opened up opportunities when she decided to make a career change later in life.

Contrast Marge's story with that of Bela, born and raised in a village outside of New Delhi, India. Bela's parents obtained admission for her in a non-profit school that served seven surrounding villages, one of which was theirs. Their intent was that Bela should be able to "read and write so [she] could raise a family." Most parents in India with this motivation will pull their daughters out of school as soon as they complete their elementary education. Bela was academically strong and, with some coaxing from her principal, her parents agreed to let her complete high school. The principal helped Bela obtain admission in well-established high school[4] where she received further encouragement to pursue higher education. Her principal, who continues to mentor her today, asked her to explore a career in engineering, which she did. Today, Bela works for a reputed IT service provider outside New Delhi and was hoping to get an opportunity to work in the United States through her firm. Bela's story highlights the value of access to education and guidance-based counseling on career choice. More crucially, it draws attention to the complex interplay of grit and resilience, the social structures that can constrain career growth, and the positive role of teachers/counselors in furthering women in STEM careers.

STANDING TOGETHER TO CHANGE THE ODDS IN FAVOR OF WOMEN

Recognizing that women who have been successful in IT careers have worked against numerous odds in doing so, what are our responsibilities as individuals, corporations, governments, and societies to change these odds in favor of women? Previous sections have made note of the complex mosaic of social, economic, and structural factors that have defined women's experiences in IT careers. Quite naturally, this suggests that increasing female participation in the IT workforce will require consideration of these complexities as well. Whereas a variety of suggestions are provided across other chapters, herein I provide some recommendations that stem directly from the emphasis in this chapter.

Recently, I visited the National Museum for Women in the Arts, in Washington, DC. During the same visit, I had a chance to see the National Archives. Both institutions highlighted two points: (1) the fight for women to get an equal place with men in their careers has had a long history, and (2) we have made great strides in bringing the rights of men and women closer. It drew parallels for me in terms of my experiences with female participation and support in IT careers – we have come a long way and we have a long way to go. Most critically, however, a third aspect that these visits highlighted was the grit and resilience of these women and the power of the collective in bringing greater equality for all. The shared voices and persistence of women are what will stand us in good stead in IT careers in the long run. Some collective actions must include the following.

- Standing together as a society in reminding our daughters, siblings, and peers that no career is out of bounds for anyone. This can happen only if teachers, counselors, mothers, fathers, siblings, and other family members not only are educated on career options in IT but also are able to challenge and tactfully extinguish related stereotypes. In an environment that is getting increasingly dogmatic, the relevance of data and facts in overthrowing these stereotypes becomes even more crucial to opening up equal opportunities for women.
- Making ourselves available as mentors and role models in the work-place. Too often it is easy to slip into our work demands and forget to put ourselves out there for others. Getting involved in, or starting, a mentor group for female IT professionals is a positive start for both female mentors and mentees, who can benefit mutually.
- Identifying and educating males who might also serve as strong and supportive mentors. Too often we draw attention to the shortage of female role models and mentors. Until that issue is fixed, women will need to develop positive mentoring relationships with males who are aware and empathetic to the gender gap (Sawyer and Valerio, 2018). Further, there is growing evidence that formal mentoring programs designed specifically for women "may at the same time reinforce masculine discourses which position women as deficient in relation to the invisibly male norm that is implicit within contemporary working practices" (Dashper, 2018, p. 1).
- Being collective in our voice for raising consciousness around the issues related to overt and covert stereotypes related to women in IT work – not merely stereotypes that stem from supervisors and managers but also those that are perpetuated by peers and user groups.
- Engaging actively in defining organizational and government policies that speak to female participation and experiences for women in IT in the workplace. Good practices and policies of one organization are often replicated by another. Such cross-pollination of best practices will lead to a collective improvement for women.
- Developing strategies for elevating the voice of other women. For instance, Elaina noted in her organization that when a male would

reiterate a suggestion or idea that a female had already stated a few minutes earlier in meetings, the contribution would be attributed to the male. They decided that, going forward, if a woman put forth an idea, another woman would reiterate that comment immediately while attributing it back to the original female contributor. The strategy seemed to work, as women started getting greater visibility for their contributions and opportunities for leadership.

CONCLUSION

This chapter has underscored the significance of culture and environment on the representation and, more importantly, the underrepresentation of women in IT and STEM careers. The stories of many women from the US IT workforce shared here highlight this. Girls in the United States are often faced with stereotypes about IT careers as being nerdy, too computer-oriented, or not creative enough even though numerous girls' camps have attempted to highlight the variety of opportunities in IT (Choudhary et al., 2010). Similarly, IT careers are viewed as synonymous with math careers even though studies show that many girls underestimate their abilities in both fields (Zeldin et al., 2007). Women who end up choosing IT careers often are faced with stereotypes in the workplace, a sense of isolation in a male-dominated work environment, and a shortage of role models and mentors to guide their development in the workplace. Do we risk that the discouraging experiences of these women will pass on to the next generation of girls?

But then there are those women who persist and are successful in their IT careers. These women share some common traits – grit, resilience, self-efficacy, career entrenchment – that are of great benefit in countering negative cultural effects. They are also shaped by their many unique experiences that are manifest in their career success. In supporting these women as they march toward the pinnacle of their careers, we benefit from developing for the next generation of girls strong women who can serve as inspirations and role models for successful IT careers. This will be our collective choice – a charge not merely to women but also to men in their personal and professional lives.

This chapter was written to focus on stories of these women, recognizing that below the surface of these successes also lie many struggles that these women IT professionals have borne out. In recognizing these successful women, this chapter also acknowledges those who were left behind, deterred from participating or persisting in IT careers because of the very same barriers. It is a reminder that we have a long way to go even as we look back and see how far we have come.

DISCUSSION QUESTIONS

1. The literature review in this chapter discusses a range of macro and micro theories that have been used to explain underrepresentation of women in STEM fields. Take one macro- and one micro-theory and discuss what solutions for underrepresentation might emerge from the application of these theoretical lenses. For instance, what solution might an essentialist propose as opposed to a labor market theorist?
2. Consider your own situation. Irrespective of whether you have chosen an IS/IT career or not, what factors discussed in this chapter have played the most significant role in your choice of career? How were your own circumstances different from that of your parents?
3. Identify a female IT or computer science professor in your college or university. Set up a meeting with her and ask her questions related to her career choice, challenges she faced in getting to where she is, and what led her to persist in her career. Relate her comments back to those identified in this chapter. What was common? What was different about her circumstances?
4. Low access to education and opportunities in IT education have usually been associated with developing countries. However, the chapter suggests that rising costs of higher education in the United States may also deter women from getting access to education and exposure to IT careers. Do you agree with this? Why? In what ways do you think organizations and governments are encouraging better education opportunities for women?
5. In all this discussion about female participation in IT, do you think male IT professionals are being marginalized? Discuss and explain your position.
6. The chapter highlights various stories of successful women in IT along with a few that struggled. Which of these stories had the most impact on you? Why?
7. The end of the chapter describes a situation where women in an organization decided to elevate the voice of their female peers in meetings. What other strategies have you observed, or might you recommend, for elevating the voices of women in society or within their organizations?

References

Adya, M. P. (2008). Women at Work: Differences in IT Career Experiences and Perceptions between South Asian and American Women. *Human Resource Management, 47*(3), 601–635.

Adya, M., and Kaiser, K. M. (2005). Early Determinants of Women in the IT Workforce: A Model of Girls' Career Choices. *Information Technology & People, 18*(3), 230–259.

Ahuja, M. K. (2002). Women in the Information Technology Profession: A Literature Review, Synthesis, and Research Agenda. *European Journal of Information Systems, 11*(1), 20–34.

Alexander, P. M., Holmner, M., Lotriet, H. H., Matthee, M. C., Pieterse, H. V., Naidoo, S., and Jordaan, D. (2011). Factors Affecting Career Choice: Comparison between Students from Computer and Other Disciplines. *Journal of Science Education and Technology, 20*(3), 300–315.

Anker, R. (1997). Theories of Occupational Segregation by Sex: An Overview. *International Labor Review, 136*(3), 226–254.

Armstrong, D. J., Riemenschneider, C. K., and Giddens, L. G. (2018). The Advancement and Persistence of Women in the Information Technology Profession: An Extension of Ahuja's Gendered Theory of IT Career Stages. *Information Systems Journal, 28*, 1082–1124.

Bandura, A., Barbaranelli, C., Caprara, G. V., and Pastorelli, C. (2001). Self-Efficacy Beliefs as Shapers of Children's Aspirations and Career Trajectories. *Child Development, 72*(1), 187–206.

Beise, C., Meyers, M., VanBrackle, L., and Chevli-Saroq, N. (2003). Challenging Dualisms in Female Perceptions of IT Work. *Australian Journal of Information Systems, 10*(2), 105–114.

Berger, P. L., and Luckmann, T. (1966). *The Social Construction of Reality: A Treatise in the Sociology of Knowledge.* New York: Doubleday.

Beyer, S., Rynes, K., Perrault, J., Hay, K., and Haller, S. (2003). Gender Differences in Computer Science Students. *ACM SIGCSE Bulletin*, February 19–23, Reno, NV.

Canes, B. J., and Rosen, H. S. (1995). Following in Her Footsteps? Faculty Gender Composition and Women's Choices of College Majors. *Industrial & Labor Relations Review, 48*(3), 486–505.

Carson, K. D., Carson, P. D., Phillips, J. S., and Roe, C. W. (1996). A Career Entrenchment Model: Theoretical Development and Empirical Outcomes. *Journal of Career Development, 22*(4), 273–286.

Choudhury, V., Lopes, A. B., and Arthur, D. (2010). IT Career Camps: An Early Intervention Strategy to Increase IS Enrollments. *Information Systems Research, 21*(1), 1–14.

Cole, A., Conlon, T., Jackson, S., and Welch, D. (1994). Information Technology and Gender. Problems and Proposals. *Gender and Education, 6*(1), 77–86.

Craig, C. J., Verma, R., Stokes, D., Evans, P., and Abrol, B. (2018). The Influence of Parents on Undergraduate and Graduate Students' Entering the STEM Disciplines and STEM Careers. *International Journal of Science Education, 40*(6), 621–643.

Dashper, K. (2018). Challenging the Gendered Rhetoric of Success? The Limitations of Women-Only Mentoring for Tackling Gender Inequality in the Workplace. *Gender, Work & Organization.* https://onlinelibrary.wiley.com/doi/full/10.1111/gwao.12262.

Diekman, A. B., Brown, E. R., Johnston, A. M., and Clark, E. K. (2010). Seeking Congruity between Goals and Roles: A New Look at Why Women Opt Out of

Science, Technology, Engineering, and Mathematics Careers. *Psychological Science, 21*(8), 1051–1057.

Freeman, P., and Aspray, W. (1999). The Supply of Information Technology Workers in the United States. *Computing Research Association*, Washington, DC. Available at http://archive.cra.org/reports/wits/cra.wits.html (accessed August 30, 2018)

Gupta, U. G., and Houtz, L. E. (2000). High School Student's Perceptions of Information Technology Skills and Careers. *Journal of Industrial Technology, 16*(4), 1–8.

Joshi, K. D., and Schmidt, N. (2006). Is the Information Systems Profession Gendered? Characterization of IS Professionals and IS Career. *The DATA BASE for Advances in Information Systems, 37*(4), 26–41.

Kabeer, N. (2005). Gender, Equality, and Women's Empowerment: A Critical Analysis of the Third Millennium Development Goal. *Gender & Development, 13*(1), 13–24.

Kirby, V. (1991). Corporeal Habits: Addressing Essentialism Differently. *Hypatia, 6*(3), 2–24.

Lawler, E. E. (1986). *High-Involvement Management.* San Francisco, CA: Jossey-Bass.

Lounsbury, J. W., Moffitt, L., Gibson, L. W., Drost, A. W., and Stevens, M. (2007). An Investigation of Personality Traits in Relation to Job and Career Satisfaction of Information Technology Professionals. *Journal of Information Technology, 22*(2), 172–183.

Michie, S., and Nelson, D. L. (2006). Barriers Women Face in Information Technology Careers: Self-Efficacy, Passion, and Gender Biases. *Women in Management Review, 21*(1), 10–27.

Sanchez, A., and Singh, A. (2018). Accessing Higher Education in Developing Countries: Panel Data Analysis from India, Peru, and Vietnam. *World Development, 109*(3), 261–278.

Sanders, J. S., and Stone, A. (1986). *The Neuter Computer: Computers for Girls and Boys.* New York: Neal-Schuman Publishers.

Sawyer, K., and Valerio, A. M. (2018). Making the Case for Male Champions for Gender Inclusiveness at Work. *Organizational Dynamics, 47*(1), 1–7.

Scandura, T. A., and Pellegrini, E. K. (2007). Workplace Mentoring: Theoretical Approaches and Methodological Issues. In *The Blackwell Handbook of Mentoring: A Multiple Perspectives Approach*, 71–91.

Trauth, E. (2002). Odd Girl Out: An Individual Differences Perspective on Women in the IT Profession. *Information Technology & People, 15*(2), 98–118.

Turner, S. V., Brent, P. W., and Pecora, N. (2002), *Why Women Choose Information Technology Careers: Educational, Social, and Familial Influences.* New Orleans, LA: Annual Educational Research Association.

Volman, M., and van Ech, E. (2001). Gender Equity and Information Technology in Education: The Second Decade. *Review of Educational Research, 17*(4), 613–634.

Von Hellens, L. A., Nielsen, S. H., and Beekhuyzen, J. (2003). Women Working in the IT Industry: Challenges for the New Millennium. *International Journal of Applied Business and Economics Research, 11*(1), 21–32.

Weber, K., and Custer, R. (2005). Gender-Based Preferences toward Technology Education Content, Activities, and Instructional Methods. *Journal of Technology Education, 16*(2), 55–71.

Zeldin, A. L., Britner, S. L., and Pajares, F. (2007). A Comparative Study of the Self-Efficacy Beliefs of Successful Men and Women in Mathematics, Science and Technology Careers. *Journal of Research in Science Teaching, 45*(9), 1036–1058.

8

Cultures and Context in Tech

A Dynamic System

Sally A. Applin

INTRODUCTION AND BACKGROUND

Silicon Valley draws many cultures together from nearly all facets of computing to a single, sprawling 1,854-square-mile geographic location, and as of 2017, Silicon Valley boasted a population of more than three million people with over 37.5% of Silicon Valley residents having been born outside the United States (Joint Venture Silicon Valley, 2017). Silicon Valley has created a legend that has attracted people – so much so that they leave countries and continents behind to relocate there to work.

Historically, Silicon Valley was comprised of farmlands and orchards. Pellow and Park (2002) describe the history of the area after World War II. At the time, Stanford University and the US government partnered to increase technological development in a concentrated location around the new technologies of the transistor and microprocessor. Stanford leased land to new electronics firms in order to lure lucrative technology contracts to the area, with agreements of resultant endowments to the university to further research, and it recruited professors and students with the allure of working on world-class technology and communications in a temperate climate. Stanford had restrictions on wanting professional labor in its tenants, and crafted messaging that suggested new transplants to the area should "blend in" (p. 62) to the suburban environment. The expectation that these workers were men was likely implied by the times. Over time, Palo Alto and its surrounding area has instantiated the messages of these "professional-class" workers being paid well, and living well, while creating humanity's technological future, thus, planting the seeds of the Silicon Valley "brand."

Since then, Silicon Valley has developed into a place of legend. Those who are able to live and work in Silicon Valley are accorded a higher global social status for being "cutting-edge pioneers" making humanity's future. For consumers, this status has been partially communicated to them through the brand messaging of the devices and services they have come to rely on for computing and communications. For example, as early as 1984, Apple Computer, Inc. connected its brand and products to the ideas of "independent rebels" and later "thinkers" (mostly shown as men) to their messaging (Apple Computer, Inc., 1997; Hayden, 2011; Siltanen, 2018). By printing "Designed in California by Apple" on its devices and packaging, Apple has extended its image and brand of Silicon Valley technology by connecting its productions to modern design (Budds, 2017), while leveraging the early pop culture and Hollywood mythology of California as a sunny, fun, creative destination. McGuirk (quoted in Budds, 2017) states, "One theme stands out in particular: the idea of personal liberation.... The ad for Apple's PowerBook 100, for instance, has a one-word slogan: 'Freedom.' The notion that a computer could be as portable as a book was presented as liberating. Technology, then and now, is perceived as enabling you to do anything, anywhere" (Budds, 2017, para. 7). As an extension of these campaigns and marketing devices, people are drawn to the region by "Designed in California" marketing, the lore and legend of Stanford University, the lure of financial reward from a wealthy and growing industry, and the dream of a place that flaunts rules and regulations and offers "freedom" as part of its ethos. People move to Silicon Valley from all over the world and from the United States for the opportunities that the technology industry in Silicon Valley promises (largely to men, by the numbers) – even if it means that they find themselves in an area with some of the highest priced real estate, lowest available housing inventory in the world (Scheinin, 2017), and fierce competition for housing as well as top jobs.

Silicon Valley's reputation evolved to be that of touting freedom from conventional workplace rules and regulations (again, mostly for men). These cultural values have created a climate of imbalance with regard to opportunities for women in computing. Women do not reap as much of the benefit of the Silicon Valley boom directly, even though women such as Rear Admiral Grace Hopper, who invented the compiler, were core pioneers and contributors to the industry long before mass marketing of the Silicon Valley myth became known worldwide. The foundation of today's software engineering management is based on organized, methodical, quantified, and fairly rigid models, derived from factories, government, and military processes (Cusumano, 1988). How this translated into a sense of freedom from rules through adhering to the cultural practices embedded in the software design process is worth examining, for the "Silicon Valley" brand of "fun, freedom, and entrepreneurship" (again, mostly for men) is grounded historically in standardization and conformity.

To understand the tension between a software practice still grounded in manufacturing processes, combined with a nearly opposite "brand message" of freedom and "disruption," the history of software development and of women in technology, particularly the messaging of how programmers were defined and represented after World War II, must be explored. In the 1960s and 1970s as its defense contracts were reduced, Rand, an early government defense computing contractor based in Santa Monica, California, became interested in how to standardize software production to increase the number of customers in the private sector they could serve to remain profitable, as well as to "attract new business and hold talented employees with higher salaries ... [and] to abandon the nonprofit status" (Cusumano, 1988, p. 4). Rand created the System Development Corporation (SDC) as a separate, spin-off division. Cusumano (1988) describes SDC as one of the first computing companies, designed to be "specialized in large-scale, real-time application systems ... [and was] the first attempt in the US to launch a factory-type organization for software production" (p. 1) with a goal of "methodological, standardized engineering approach to software development" (p. 8). For background on how RAND/SDC was going to organize labor to support this effort, Chang (2018) writes that the

System Development Corporation ... enlisted two male psychologists to scout recruits. The psychologists, William Cannon and Dallis Perry, profiled 1,378 programmers, only 186 of whom were women. They used their findings to build a "vocational interest scale" ... they concluded that people who liked solving puzzles of various sorts, from mathematical to mechanical, made for good programmers.... Based on data they had gathered from the same sample of mostly male programmers ... they concluded that programmers "dislike activities involving close personal interaction; they are generally more interested in things than in people."

(para. 14)

Critically, Chang (2018) identifies that the research from this study, in particular the "vocational interest scale" that was derived from studying mostly men, "speculatively" (para. 14) concluded that not "lik[ing] people" (para. 15) was a requirement for "good" programmers, which then planted seeds that not only grew but perpetuated during a "critical juncture" (para. 16) as the computer industry was evolving.

Chang (2018) adds that the Cannon and Perry studies and their subsequent eighty-two-page report used the word "men" (para. 16) to describe participants, and that their research was used in "large companies for decades" (para. 17). Combining the SDC standardizing computing practices to codify and streamline software development with a study and report changing the gender of desired "good programmer" characteristics attributed to males, and SDC's male leadership sourced from manufacturing and the military (Cusumano, 1988), the seeds of both a regimented industry staffed by "ideal male programmers" became a cultural value and practice. As the study results became a part of vocational testing and other industries such as marketing, the vector of programming shifted toward men, and helped to create the eventual widespread messaging that computers, and especially programming, were for men and the boys who would become them.

These notions were not limited to larger computing company staffing. As personal computers were developed, manufacturers wanted to sell them globally and created campaigns early on that showed men using them in the home for "work," sharing calculations with young boys. Women were shown infrequently in PC advertising, using computers in a work context, but few ads featured young girls or young women using PCs. Many ads featured only hardware, and those with people (if shown at all) showed men in powerful or commanding positions standing over or supervising women in clerical roles, or showed women admiring men doing something advanced. Sometimes women were shown in ads, nude except for the hardware. Apple seemed to have more balanced ads some of the time, including one early ad that featured a nude "Adam"; however, this was only one out of many other ads in the industry that featured women in subordinate, non-technical roles. This type of advertising effects culture and ideas, particularly when applied to new, not-yet adopted technology in a culture. These ads were globally distributed, meaning that their messages of "computing is for men and boys" were spread widely.

Additionally, even though some ads showed women using computers as a work tool, none showed women or girls programming. Although women had been early programmers and developers of large mainframe computers, as a result of cultural messaging and resources, they were given even fewer opportunities with the new PC technology. Chang (2018) illustrates that as the computing industry grew, teaching resources in computer science were scarce due to demand, and admission to these programs was favored for men rather than women. Cultural messaging through vocational tests based on the poorly interpreted and presented data from Cannon and Perry surveys, combined with advertising messaging, continued to funnel boys toward computers and largely ignored girls.

These early biases in the US computer industry created a strong message that was perpetuated through media, marketing, and both corporate and societal culture, and, as such, created the biases and stereotypes that perpetuate today.

As a result, over time, women in the computing industry were not often included as core members of the teams inventing and building the technologies that rocketed Silicon Valley into its current stature. The adoption of the web created even more fragmentation in the workplace, as more rogue start-ups worked on technologies and web development often with limited (or without) HR departments or compliance for legal, fair, and balanced hiring practices.

In 2018, women are part of the computer industry workforce in Silicon Valley, but less as creators of core technologies, or as high-level managers. The majority of women in Silicon Valley are found in human resources, marketing and PR, and as program or project managers, bookkeepers and accountants, attorneys, administrative assistants, social media managers (Duffy and Schwartz, 2017), and user experience designers or graphic designers, among other social-interaction and/or supporting type roles, with recruiting language biased toward females for those roles (Duffy and Schwartz, 2017; Hempel, 2018). There are still very few women leaders in top technology companies or in charge of top technical teams or high-status projects, and women-founded start-ups are woefully underfunded. In 2017, female founders received only 2% of all venture capital dollars (Zarya, 2018). The cultural confluence in the region of Silicon Valley creates a richness of ethnic and gender diversity that is seemingly ignored in the power structure of the computer industry. From a core technical creative (e.g., lead programmer, architect) and power perspective, its mostly men, all the way down.

To some extent, the gender bias in Silicon Valley is an effect of cultural productions that emerged in the United States through education and advertising (and through strongly influential branding), but it can also be exacerbated from migration in the local locale combined with globalization. English-Leuck (2002) wrote that, broadly, gender roles migrate to Silicon Valley by coming from other cultures and that this impacts Silicon Valley's workplace culture. That is, when people migrate to Silicon Valley from other cultures, they bring biases reflecting cultures where women, men, and other genders are treated differently (division of labor by gender is almost universal, but the content of gender divisions is not) in the workplace (and elsewhere). Additionally, when people are in one location, and are imagining others they form ideas of what those cultures may be like from being exposed to what media sources show or describe the other culture as being. These views can be biased (because they originate through an interpreted media frame), and can become further diffused and/or changed when they are interpreted within other cultures who perceive them through media in their locations no matter where (e.g., Iceland, New Hampshire, Alabama, Bombay – or anywhere else). Thus, when people migrate, they bring with them not only their own cultures and biases, but also their interpretations of these media-influenced biases, to places where people from different cultures co-exist and also have their own interpretations and biases. This contributes to a highly heterogeneous, and often incorrect assumption about people and their cultures. In particular, this can influence expectations about what women can, and cannot do in society.

In some countries, women are afforded even less equality in legal institutions than they are in the United States (McCune, 2014; Lacey, 2017). They may be "permitted" or even encouraged to be engineers, but they may not be promoted or treated very well in their home countries. Conversely, some technical women may be treated advantageously in their home countries (Werft, 2017) and may find themselves working in Silicon Valley within a company culture whose management expresses a cultural bias against women in core technical positions. If men reared with certain cultural or programmed media biases against women in certain types of technical roles relocate to the United States and hold management positions where they are directing women at work, this can be a disadvantage for everyone – despite the formal legal framework in that country. The "loopholes" in legal gender equality are exacerbated when these also accommodate expressions of male biases from other cultures.

Cultural norms are, in part, expressed in laws that citizens, companies, and governments are required to follow. As such, people who have moved to a new place and have lived there for a long enough duration to adapt to its laws are more likely to assimilate to new cultural norms. However, this is not always true, even for the cultures that originally contributed to law that is more inclusive than the cultural antecedents. When a culture is highly heterogeneous, the norms are harder to parse, and the legal framework expressing these may be overspecified.

Moreover, as M. D. Fischer explains:

The presence of the US disjunctions from gender equality are what makes room for people from other cultures within Silicon Valley to express their own related biases. The heterogeneity of many different gender biases coming together within a framework that already expresses gender biases makes it even harder to create uniformity in practices. Also problematic is that a lot of this is maintained because women, coming from the same cultures as the men, may share exactly the same biases, and thus, accommodate some of the practice.

(personal communication, August 21, 2018)

However, the legacy of hiring patterns in power positions (management and venture capital funding) based on male succession, as well as preferred educational affiliations (Mohan, 2018) outside legal rights, seems to persist. It can be very hard indeed for women to compete for coveted technology positions in engineering, the C-suite, or even to raise venture funding for their own start-ups, in spite of data confirming that female founders produce higher yield for their investors (Kowitt, 2018).

This chapter examines the impact of Silicon Valley's cultural frame on the rest of the world. If Silicon Valley is held up as a model of innovation, as it has been for decades in computing, then the cultural baggage that disenfranchises women may be continuing to be replicated as a type of "brand template" (Applin, 2016, p. 14) that is distributed worldwide via communications technologies. This template includes such biases as "young men in hoodies are the only ones who can write code," "men must be the only venture capitalists," "people over 30 are useless," and other fictitious sayings created and perpetuated by younger men in the computer industry and by venture capitalists with extraordinary power, who see themselves in these younger male reflections. The gender-biased findings from Cannon and Perry's "vocational interest scale" were not only misinterpreted over generations, but have been dispersed widely through iterations of vocational testing spanning decades. As a result, those same biases have persisted in the vocational tests and results and, as such, have been continually reinforced, woven into advertising and marketing messaging that is targeted to both men and boys and women and girls. This unfortunate misinformation has perpetuated unfair bias against women in computing, and continues to place social and cultural limits on girls and women studying computing. The current Silicon Valley brand continues to transmit these biases against women today, limiting the real contributions that women can provide and, in turn, their income, livelihoods, and opportunities for advancement.

DYNAMIC MIGRATION IN THE COMPUTER INDUSTRY

The Industrial Revolution created an incentive for workers to gather in a central location for production of goods. Prior to this, workers stayed in their villages and homes, working and producing locally. When machines were developed and deployed in centralized locations to improve the speed of manufacturing, workers were needed to operate them, and many in search of employment, adventure, a new beginning, or simply work migrated to cities for financial opportunities and to learn new skills.

Prior to the PC revolution and the development of the internet, people who worked with computers required large cooperative mainframe machines to program and calculate their experiments, conduct research, and process data for other projects. The first uses of big computers were within governments to expedite calculations to support ballistics efforts for World War II. The governments running these labs needed laborers to help these machines run calculations and to maintain the mechanical workings required to process the paper tape for calculations. Both the Mach1 and later the Eniac in the United States, and the Colossus Mark 1 and Mark 2 in the United Kingdom, required collaborative computational labor, much of which was done by women, who came from other fields such as mathematics, accounting, or with no training. In the United States, many women were hired to work on computers as part of the Women Accepted for Volunteer Emergency Service (WAVES) during the World War II war effort, in which women were deployed to industry to replace the jobs men had held and had to leave. In those early days of computing, "computer science" did not exist as a discipline. Computers were room-sized and centrally located, and the people who were interested in computing, needed a job, or were assigned to labs via military channels first migrated to educational and/or government institutions to work. For commercial uses, companies utilized more big computers and mainframes internally than they do now, and many had contracts with computing corporations, such as Rand, to handle those computing requirements via consultants or consulting relationships. As a result, computer technicians and scientists were co-located with machines in centralized computer labs. Later, as still large but increasingly popular computers became more widespread, people could move further afield to areas where they could practice their profession. After the war, when men returned to work, the WAVES were no longer needed. However, women trained in computer skills were still valuable and became programmers, providing other computational support to this growing field. This changed as men gained skills and power in the marketplace, as SDC standardized computing practices, and again through the PC revolution, when PCs became branded as a home appliance for men, and their advertising was targeted to men.

As PCs were developed, deployed, and became more reliable, and as the internet expanded and was adopted, people who studied and were interested in computer science had more options for where they might work. In spite of that, Silicon Valley remained a top destination due to its increasing reputation as an innovation center.

Over time, Silicon Valley communities have become increasingly more diverse, and the population has continued to grow. Nearly every country and US state is represented in Silicon Valley and many global companies consider it a point of pride to have a Silicon Valley office. Governments, as well as many universities, have offices and outposts in Silicon Valley, hoping to profit from the technological transfer of research to start-ups, to create wealth and/or opportunities for their citizens overseas.

In 2018, most companies in any industry have some computers on-site. Businesses that are data-centric and rely on enormous server farms may store some or all their data off-site in locations with more affordable real estate and power. Labor within the computer industry is divided between those creating the code and algorithms (mostly men), those productizing and marketing those outcomes (mostly women), and those doing the lower level maintenance of server farms (mostly men), which are largely located outside Silicon Valley in more rural areas where land is less expensive. Other factors contribute to where a person in Silicon Valley may work. Depending on their job, people may telecommute to Silicon Valley from their homes there or from a more remote locale, and people regularly collaborate with overseas partners and programming teams in India, China, and elsewhere, an outcome of companies seeking cheaper labor outside the United States. This not only makes the dynamic nature of the computer industry more pronounced, but also illustrates the cultural issues that are not regulated when an individual in the United States may be working with someone in a different cultural framework overseas. This is particularly true for women in technical roles, which could produce good or bad outcomes, depending.

Furthermore, physical migration is not fixed or singular to people arriving and staying in Silicon Valley. Some people eventually move and return to their home countries, go to new ones, or balance their lives between Silicon Valley and elsewhere. Saxenian (2007) describes the "regional advantage in a global economy" from studying Silicon Valley inhabitants who commute between Silicon Valley and their native countries, leveraging each one's practices for the benefit of business and profit. These "new argonauts" benefit from Silicon Valley by exporting its "system of open networks and decentralized experimentation" (p. 325) while simultaneously collaborating locally. This action dynamically redistributes resources and labor worldwide, and creates what Saxenian refers to as a "dynamic network of specialized and complementary regional economies" (p. 325). Not only are the economies dynamic, but the values and behaviors found within Silicon Valley culture are as well, and that is what is spread as people travel and learn about Silicon Valley via the media and the internet.

THE BRANDING OF CULTURAL PATTERNS: WHEN CULTURE BECOMES A TEMPLATE FOR REPLICATION

In most anthropological definitions, culture relates to behaviors, beliefs, or values shared within a group. This could be a group in a given place, a small group of people who interact with each other directly, or a group of people with a specific interest or religion. We each belong to many groups and negotiate aspects of many cultures simultaneously.

Projections of culture can broadly be separated into cultural practices (how people enact beliefs within a culture) and cultural values (the values people share within a group, but may or may not express in a given context). For example, a given social group may associate a cultural value favoring independence to women that differs from cultural values associated with a religious group. This could differ from cultural values associated with a workplace group the woman participates in. The practices of that woman and others may change as they shift participation within and between these groups. M. D. Fischer noted that "most people know how to avoid missteps when they are out of [a] culture, as far as cultural practices go," but cultural values "are much harder to leave behind, and must usually be remapped" between contexts (personal communication, August 21, 2018).

Cultural values are often described as biases, particularly when negatively framed. However, "bias" simply describes the fact that many things are not random and instead are directed in particular ways. Bias does not explain why, or whether, something described is productive or inhibitory, though bias is often used in that context. M. D. Fischer states that "a bias can shape a practice, but most people conform to [situational] norms and drop the appearance of a bias in cross-cultural situations" (personal communication, August 21, 2018). This means that as people become aware of biases that conflict with practices (or values) of those around them – if there are legal, moral, ethical, social, or other reasons to compel them – they will suppress expressing these as practices in favor of cooperation within a system's norms. Even so, biased values can still emerge in other ways in other contexts, or when people are caught off-guard and fail to recognize an inhibitory context.

Thus, cultural practices and cultural values can be hard to separate for people, and while we try, we often revert, causing conflict and confusion. It can be tempting for us as people (though not recommended) to maintain cultural consistency by staying within groups that are like-minded.

This is also likely part of why some men in technology appear to prefer and hire other men in technology, since although they may come from many different cultures, their cultural practices and cultural values associated with "being men in tech" may be relatively similar, producing a context where it becomes easy to "acceptably" remap their cultural values into the present circumstance. In these circumstances, to achieve a path whereby women are included and respected equally, even though potentially holding various cultural values and cultural practices, a mechanism is required that can transcend culture and "glue" people together, giving them new cultural values and a new cultural practice that can account for gender differences and approaches in more equitable ways. In many cases it is apparent that workplace regulations and a broader legal context are not sufficient to achieve this.

In my doctoral thesis (Applin, 2016), I developed a theory of brands as a basis for group formation and shared identity through creating and organizing local homogeneity through common symbolic resources (branding). For example, I propose branding as "a key mechanism for group formation, organization and reproduction for dispersed people with limited means to otherwise directly interact" (p. 2). Furthermore:

> In commercial terms, a brand is an association of a product or organization to a set of key ideas and relationships between these ideas, and an associated set of messages used to communicate or represent these ideas and relationships to represent the product or organization. As such, brands have become a common referent for many people – whether or not they use what has been branded.
>
> (p. 229)

I extend brands to model what motivates groups and subgroups and as a new form of categorization, meaning that brands can function as a way to share group behavior and remap these behaviors to individual values based on "common experience in the absence of shared experience" (p. 229). This creates new possibilities for understanding group dynamics, biases, and cultures beyond the conventional usage of the term "brands" relating to commerce. Branding helps people agree on a common experience, even when the experience is different for each person, and the valuation is based on a different remapping. Branding thus reconciles values between a range of people, often across differences, by providing many partial symbol elements that all subscribers can weigh in on and participate in, though which ones are chosen will vary. As such, brands become a candidate for explaining how Silicon Valley is developing a template, whose messaging is being distributed worldwide, and replicated in technology centers overseas. As I explain: "Designed Brands are the brands that are created by organizations for the purposes of differentiating a product or service and 2) Emergent Brands, brands ... are defined collectively and spontaneously as people with shared interests, passions, ideas, and/or hobbies, find each other and form groups" (p. 11).

In this chapter, the reference to brands includes designed brands (such as Silicon Valley and SDC's attempt to create a "software factory") or emergent brands that emerge from recognizing/marking commonalities between individual experiences (Applin, 2016, p. 243). To date, the Silicon Valley brand was "designed" early on at Stanford, and then became imbued with brand values today that are the result of intersecting cultural values toward women in labor roles (including the notion that many cultures reaffirm each other's position); narratives that single out young men (preferably under twenty-five) wearing a hoodie[1] as symbolic of an independent style of dress flaunting workplace style norms; a perpetuation of the "disruptor" narrative (e.g., someone or something that thwarts the function of a currently running system (analog, digital, or social) in order to create a new space for venture capital); coding smarts but less formal education (also a Zuckerberg influence); and/or an "entrepreneur," described as a person (usually male), who embodies the list above, but who may additionally have a full or partial formal education, in business, preferably "from either Stanford or Harvard" (also Zuckerberg) (Mohan, 2018). If we add a belief in technical solutions for all problems (including social ones), and within those technical solutions, mostly men being hired as the "right choice" to solve them, it forms a brand for Silicon Valley today that is grossly unfair for women and, perhaps unsurprisingly, seemingly based on Mark Zuckerberg, one of Silicon Valley's most famous (and wealthy) male icons.

Although many people do not fit the characteristics of the "Silicon Valley brand," described above, many people in computing affiliate themselves with its brand description and values in an aspirational fashion to align themselves with what they perceive to be "success" in the technology industry. This perpetuation of success equating to the Silicon Valley brand has become a "branded" context for cultural practice, and has persisted in the media in the form of television, print, advertising, and word-of-mouth messages. Furthermore, as people travel, this messaging has set up a monster that is influencing all types of industries. As a result, across the globe, people have added Silicon Valley brand cultural values and cultural practices to their existing values and practices. The brand of Silicon Valley has permeated the healthcare, automotive, supply-chain, retail industries, and countless others, as well as governance, becoming a broader player in all facets of human life, worldwide.

The changes in brand descriptions of women in computing and technology change worldwide processes and structures though the technology that is built, the messages associated with it via the Silicon Valley brand, and the real issues of software based on those brand values being deployed. These messages continue to suppress women's roles in technology and computer science and other industries, as the images from the Silicon Valley brand contain women not as creators but rather as supporters.

In 1971, journalist Don Hofler came up with the term "Silicon Valley" to describe the region and its technology, and "before long everyone wanted a 'Silicon Valley'" (Cameron, 2018, para. 1), and went about creating them – or at least renaming areas as technical centers – which could be interpreted as a way of designing a brand based on the existing designed brand of "Silicon Valley." In California, there is Silicon Valley in Northern California, Silicon Beach on the West Side of Los Angeles, Silicon Coast in Orange County, Silicon Shore in Santa Barbara, Silicon Surf in Santa Cruz, and Silicon Valley of the Sierras. There is Silicon Alley in New York; Silicon Forest and Silicon Shire in Oregon; Silicon Anchor in Virginia; Silicon Basin in Ohio; Silicon Bayou in Louisiana; Silicon Canal in Washington State; Silicon Harbors in South Carolina and Connecticut; Silicon Hill in Washington, DC; Silicon Hollar in North Carolina; Silicon Mountain in Colorado; and Silicon Peach in Georgia. In Massachusetts, there is Silicon River in Boston and Cambridge, and Silicon Sandbar on Cape Cod. There is a Silicotton Valley in Alabama. Silicon Prairie refers to several states in the US Midwest, with technology centers including Texas, Nebraska, Iowa, Wisconsin, South Dakota, Kansas, Minnesota, North Dakota, Missouri, Wyoming, and Illinois. There is Silicon Wadi on the coast of Israel; Silicon Canal, Alley, Beach, Mall, Pier, Shipyard, Spa, Walk, Fen, Glen, Corridor, Gorge, and Roundabout in the United Kingdom; Silicon Mountain, Cape, Lagoon, and Savannah in Africa and South Africa; Silicon Valley North in Ottawa, Ontario, and Silicon Vineyard in Canada as well; Silicon Hills and Silicon Gulch in Austin, Texas; Slopes in Utah; Silicon Gulf in the Philippines; Dubai Silicon Oasis in Dubai; Chilecon Valley in

Chile; Silicon Paradise in Costa Rica; Silicon Border in Mexico; Silicon Island in Japan; and Silicon Peninsula in China. There are Silicon Valleys of China, India, Indonesia, Taiwan, and Hong Kong; a Silicon Sentier in France; Silicon Saxeny, Woods, and Allee in Germany; Silicon Islands in Greece; Silicon Docks in Ireland; Silicon Fjord in Norway; Russian Silicon Valley, Silicon Sloboda, and Silicion Taiga in Russia; and Silicon Mallee and Silicon Street in Australia; and Silicon Welly in New Zealand. These are just some of the names with "Silicon" in them that developed around the Silicon Valley brand. There are other centers worldwide that mimic the Silicon Valley ethos in Bangalore, Israel, Turkey, Vietnam, Belgium, Denmark, Estonia, and many other places that don't use "Silicon" in their names, but all the same embrace the branding and aspirational nature of what the current Silicon Valley brand messaging transmits.

The reliance on Silicon Valley as a brand template may begin to change as technology develops in regions where a "Silicon Valley" was established, but over time, new inventions and technologies originating and emerging will create a separate character, cultural values, and cultural practices in each region.

This may already be evolving as Cameron (2018), the founder of the Washington think tank the Center for Policy on Emerging Technologies, writes: "The idea of establishing new Silicon Valleys to repeat the innovative efforts of the digital disruptors of the past 30 years is starting to look dated and even nostalgic. This is especially significant with Artificial Intelligence and the Internet of Things set to disrupt mature industries in almost every sector of the economy" (para. 10). De Vynck and Verhage (2018) describe the things that are unique to a technology industry rooted in New York, and its alternate advantages to what Silicon Valley has to offer, listing "the presence of other industries like finance, media and advertising, much more gender and racial diversity, and the metropolis's centuries-old status as a center of global commerce" (para. 3) as indicators of other ways innovation can arise outside what Silicon Valley has seemed to dictate. This can be good for women, especially those in technology and computer science.

The changing regional tones of "Silicon Valleys" as described by Cameron (2018) and De Vynck and Verhage (2018) describe the beginnings of my "emergent brands" (2016, p. 21) that evolve in organic ways and are shared remotely via the internet or other communications channels or by word of mouth:

The distribution of an emergent group across time, space, and locale boundaries affords it a robustness, and some degree of persistence on the Internet, which can then supplement local locale involvement. Thus, a hybrid model of group formation and social organisation evolves, that supports localisation while incorporating distributed global contributions and phenomena. This is based on social networks, social media, and distributed websites, which represent trending themes of emergent groups. The principles underlying emergent branding support additional means for understanding how humans organise and change in the context of a dynamic communications framework.

(p. 25)

Emergent brands differ from designed brands in that they are organic (Applin, 2016, p. 251). Silicon Valley was *created*, and over time, became a "designed brand" that evolved to have particular characteristics that were refined, characterized, and copied worldwide. By looking to the local locales, and their emerging innovations and cultures, each region will develop new ideas and new understandings of the role of everyone participating in technology and how they can contribute. Furthermore, as these new emergent brands evolve, unique physical regions and their contributions will in fact change and shape cultural values and practices. These will then be distributed via the internet, and on the devices and services created thus far by Silicon Valley, to inform technology industry practices worldwide in new ways, thus creating many more opportunities for women.

DISCUSSION QUESTIONS

1. As described in the chapter, how is the idea of "culture" dynamic?
2. Do cultural practices change because of legal frameworks?
3. The Cannon and Perry study perpetuated beliefs that changed opinions about women in computing. What were the mechanisms that were used to force that change? How were they adopted and spread into culture? What did the beliefs start as, and then eventually become?
4. What kinds of cultural values do you share with your classmates? Which ones don't you share? How do you modify your own cultural practices to get along with others in the classroom? In the lab?
5. How does the idea of a designed or an emergent brand perpetuate cultural meaning?

References

Apple Computer, Inc. (1997). *Apple –Here's to the Crazy Ones (1997)* [Video]. Retrieved August 29, 2018, from www.youtube.com/watch?v=tjgtLSHhTPg.
Applin, S. (2016). Disrupting Silicon Valley Dreams: Adaptations through Making, Being, and Branding. Doctoral thesis, University of Kent, Canterbury.

Budds, D. (2017). The Fascinating History of "Designed in California": The Apple Tagline Is Older than You Think. *Fast Company*. Retrieved August 29, 2018, from www.fastcompany.com/90129351/the-history-of-designed-in-california.

Cameron, N. (2018). Why Replicating Silicon Valley Is a Fool's Game. Blog. Retrieved August 29, 2018, from https://unherd.com/2018/08/replicating-silicon-valley-fools-game/.

Chang, E. (2018). Women Once Ruled the Computer World. When Did Silicon Valley Become Brotopia? *Bloomberg Businessweek*. Retrieved August 29, 2018, from www.bloomberg.com/news/features/2018-02-01/women-once-ruled-computers-when-did-the-valley-become-brotopia.

Cusumano, M. (1988). Systems Development Corporation: Defining the Factory Challenge. Working Paper 1887-87, Alfred P. Sloan School of Management Cambridge, MA. Retrieved August 30, 2018, from https://dspace.mit.edu/bitstream/handle/1721.1/49002/systemdevelopmen00cusu.pdf?sequence=1.

De Vynck, G., and Verhage, J. (2018). New York Will Never Be Silicon Valley. And It's Good with That. *Bloomberg*. Retrieved August 30, 2018, from www.bloomberg.com/news/articles/2018-02-27/new-york-will-never-be-silicon-valley-and-it-s-good-with-that.

Duffy, B. E., and Schwartz, B. (2018). Digital "Women's Work?": Job Recruitment Ads and the Feminization of Social Media Employment. *New Media & Society*, *20*(8), 2972–2989.

English-Lueck, J. (2002). *Cultures@Silicon Valley*. Stanford, CA: Stanford University Press.

Hayden, S. (2011). Brand Marketing "1984": As Good as It Gets. *Adweek*. Retrieved August 29, 2018, from www.adweek.com/brand-marketing/1984-good-it-gets-125608/.

Hempel, J. (2018). How Social Media Became a Pink Collar Job. *Wired*. Retrieved August 29, 2018, from www.wired.com/story/how-social-media-became-a-pink-collar-job/.

Joint Venture Silicon Valley. (2017). *2017 Silicon Valley Index*. San Jose, CA: Joint Venture Silicon Valley. Retrieved Aug. 29, 2018, from https://jointventure.org/images/stories/pdf/index2017.pdf.

Kowitt, B. (2018). Female-Founded Startups Generate More Revenue and Do It with Less Funding. *Fortune*. Retrieved August 29, 2018, from http://fortune.com/2018/06/07/female-founded-startups-revenue-funding/.

Lacey, N. (2017). To Understand Women's Rights We Must Look at Gendered Laws. Retrieved September 7, 2018, from www.opendemocracy.net/openjustice/gender-and-la.

McCune, E. (2014). 10 Examples of Gender Inequality in the World. *Borgen Magazine*. Retrieved September 7, 2018, from www.borgenmagazine.com/10-examples-gender-inequality-world/.

Mohan, P. (2018). Most VC's Are (Still) White Men, and 40% Went to Harvard or Stanford. *Fast Company*. Retrieved August 29, 2018, from www.fastcompany.com/90210794/most-vcs-are-still-white-men-and-40-went-to-harvard-or-stanford.

Pellow, D., and Park, L. (2002). *The Silicon Valley of Dreams*. New York: New York University Press.

Saxenian, A. (2007). *The New Argonauts*. London: Harvard University Press.

Scheinin, R. (2017). About Silicon Valley's Crazy Housing Situation: One Real Estate Exec Deconstructs the Market. *The Mercury News*. Retrieved August 29, 2018, from www.mercurynews.com/2017/09/25/about-silicon-valleys-crazy-housing-situation-one-real-estate-exec-deconstructs-the-market/.

Siltanen, R. (2018). The Real Story Behind Apple's "Think Different" Campaign. *Forbes*. Retrieved August 29, 2018, from www.forbes.com/sites/onmarketing/2011/12/14/the-real-story-behind-apples-think-different-campaign/#1ed5851a62ab.

Werft, M. (2017). 7 Feminist Laws Iceland Has That the World Needs. Retrieved September 7, 2018, from www.globalcitizen.org/en/content/7-iceland-feminist-law-women/.

Zarya, V. (2018). Female Founders Got 2% of Venture Capital Dollars in 2017. *Fortune*. Retrieved August 29, 2018, from http://fortune.com/2018/01/31/female-founders-venture-capital-2017/.

9

Perspectives of Women with Disabilities in Computing

Brianna Blaser, Cynthia Bennett, Richard E. Ladner,
Sheryl E. Burgstahler, and Jennifer Mankoff

INTRODUCTION

Popular media has recently given attention to sexist workplace culture and low rates of female employees within large tech companies.[1] Tech companies have released a plethora of diversity reports as part of a commitment to diversifying the workforce. Disability is largely absent from these companies' PR and resulting media coverage. Diversity and inclusion efforts – whether it is diversity reports to increase transparency, flexible benefits, or feminist stances meant to welcome women – rarely include disability specifically. When TechCrunch asked seven major companies – Intel, Apple, Twitter, Facebook, Slack, Google, and Salesforce – about the omission of disability from these reports, their responses were not reassuring (O'Hear, 2016). Facebook, Salesforce, and Google failed to respond. Intel and Slack pointed to their inclusion efforts related to disability and indicated they could release data in the future. Apple and Twitter pointed the journalist to their accessible products as evidence that they consider disability in driving innovation. Subsequently, Slack's 2017 diversity report highlighted that 1.7% of their employees identify as having a disability (Slack Team, 2017). In 2016 LinkedIn included disability in their diversity reporting, highlighting that 3% of their US employees have a disability (Wadors, 2016).[2] Otherwise, there is little attention given to individuals with disabilities, and, more specifically, women with disabilities in computing.

Meanwhile, there exist a plethora of programs designed to increase the participation of girls and women in computing. But, similar to the practices of the tech companies at which these programs hope their participants will work, very few of them address disability directly and many use technologies that are inaccessible to people with disabilities. There are a few notable exceptions. Women@SCS at Carnegie Mellon University has taken explicit steps to host their outreach programs at schools that serve students with disabilities, sponsored a capacity-building workshop to facilitate conversations about disability on campus, and recruited women with disabilities to participate in Opportunities for Undergraduate Research in Computer Science (OurCS). Girls Who Code, another notable example, has worked to ensure that girls have opportunities for participants to use accessible technology and invited speakers to talk to girls about careers in accessibility. The Grace Hopper Celebration's Under-represented Women in Computing Committee has worked to include women with disabilities in their programming. The National Center for Women in Information Technology (NCWIT) has resources related to women with disabilities such as the webpage *Equal Access: Inclusive Strategies for Teaching Students with Disabilities* (Barker and Frydman, n.d.). Similarly, the National Girls Collaborative Project has hosted webi-nars focusing on disability.

Recently, additional education and diversity efforts in computing have embraced disability. The Center for Minorities and Disabilities in Infor-mation Technology (CMD-IT) explicitly includes disability in its mission. They assert that ethnic minorities and people with disabilities have much in common with regard to underrepresentation in computing (Taylor and Ladner, 2013). CMD-IT is the presenting organization behind the Tapia Celebration of Diversity in Computing conference. As a result, Tapia has had an increased focus on disabilities. Recent years have seen multiple keynote presentations by individuals with disabilities including Annie Anton of Georgia Tech, Chieko Asakawa of IBM, Avani Wildani of Emory University, and Shiri Azenkot of Cornell Tech. Disability has had an increased presence at the conference in terms of attendees and program content. In 2018, the Computing Research Association made an effort to include students with disabilities in its first Grad Cohort Workshop for Underrepresented Minorities and Persons with Disabilities, which offered mentoring and professional development to graduate students with the hope of diversifying the ranks of senior professionals in computing research. CS Teaching Tips, which aims to help teachers anticipate stu-dents' difficulties and build on students' strengths through offering advice to educators, has worked to ensure their resources address disability.

In this chapter, we will define disability and consider the history of including individuals with disabilities in education through policy and activism. We will highlight some background on the inclusion of women with disabilities in computing education and careers in the United States and share findings from conversations with women with disabilities in computing education and careers. Finally, we will look at efforts to increase the participation of people with disabilities in computing education and careers and issue a call to action. There are some limitations to our discussion. Because little has been written about people with disabilities in computing education and careers, some information is drawn from our personal experiences in the field. Much of our discussion is based in the United States, drawing on US history, policy, and attitudes toward disability because that is where our own experiences and expertise are grounded. There are significant differences worldwide on these issues.

BACKGROUND ON DISABILITY RIGHTS

The World Health Organization (WHO) defines "disability" as an umbrella term covering impairments within the body, activity limitations, and participation restrictions (n.d.). "Impairments" include, but are not limited to, cognitive, chronic illness, developmental, mental health, physical, and sensory (hearing and vision) impairments. Activity limitations and participation restrictions occur when there are mismatches between impairments and the environment. For example, a mismatch occurs when a wheelchair user encounters stairs. Disability is not found in the person's body or in the stairs themselves, but in the interaction of their impairment and a product or environment. As such, better design infrastructure might place stairs and ramps near each other so people can move through the area as they prefer; better yet, a slow-incline ramp might eliminate the needs for steps at all. We use these definitions in this chapter for two reasons. First, healthcare-related organizations like WHO have traditionally defined disabilities according to medical diagnoses, as revealed in their classification system adopted in 2007. Their most recent definition of disability indicates an evolution in thinking about disability that medical care will not eliminate barriers for people with disabilities. Rather, it requires a combined effort by all sorts of entities including government institutions, companies, and community organizations. Second, as will be elaborated in the section that follows, this 2007 definition more accurately represents contemporary views about disabilities by people who have disabilities. There are several other ways to define disability. The Americans with Disabilities Act defines disability as "a physical or mental impairment that substantially limits one or more major life activities."

Despite changing attitudes, some people still perceive disabilities negatively. Considering the field of disability studies and the history of disability rights activism helps to frame and contextualize evolving perceptions of disability. Disability studies scholar Mike Oliver is well known for developing models of how disability is perceived by society (1990). He labeled the prevailing perception of disability in Western culture the "individual model." According to this model, disability is an undesirable bodily abnormality that, if possible, should be cured by medical and rehabilitation experts. When cure is not possible, this model considers it the individual's responsibility to adapt their life to fit into society regardless of the barriers it imposes. Oliver contrasted this perception with the "social model," which locates disability within societal structures such as physical infrastructure, attitudes about disability, and policy. According to the social model, accessibility is everyone's responsibility.

Disability studies scholars have debated how well these and other models represent the lived experiences of people with disabilities, arguing for a more nuanced view of disability (Shakespeare and Watson, 2001). For example, a narrow interpretation of the social model of disability, in not discussing bodies, takes away people's agency and incorrectly suggests that people with disabilities are opposed to healthcare for enhancing their health and well-being. The World Health Organization's definition of disability aligns with recent work by scholars including Alison Kafer (2013). These definitions do not focus on determining where disability is located, in the body or society, for example. Instead, they focus on how disability is revealed through interactions. In other words, disability occurs when features of a person's body mismatch features of an environment. This distinction contextualizes the importance of both individualized assistance for people with disabilities and overall societal improvements. For example, assistive technologies help people with disabilities integrate into society, but environmental and attitudinal improvements can make this integration easier and more welcoming. Likewise, it is important to apply accessible technology design strategies to ensure that mainstream technology is accessible to individuals with disabilities and is compatible with technology that specific individuals with disabilities may use.

Disability scholars have also explored appropriate language for talking about disability. Language is important because it has the power to shape perception and, ultimately, behavior. Some common framing problems that language scholars have attempted to address include talking about disability as a lack, a reason for pity, an inspiration, and a tragedy (Haller et al., 2006). Such language choices can reinforce stereotypes and perpetuate stigma. In response to this, the disability rights movement, elaborated below, has done two things. First, they introduced person-first language – for example, a person who has disabilities, a person who is blind – to emphasize that disability is only one aspect of a person's identity and does not define their personhood. At the same time, the disability rights movement has worked to reclaim the term "disability" and worked to transform its meaning into a positive statement about identity. Some communities of people with disabilities have taken up identity-first language – for example, autistic, blind, and Deaf people – to communicate pride in having disabilities (Sinclair, 2013). Still, language choices remain controversial. Some people with disabilities prefer person-first language, and some professional organizations doing work on behalf of people with disabilities stipulate that published materials adopt a specific convention. Thus, it is imperative, when possible, to ask individuals how they want to describe themselves in relation to their disabilities. In this chapter, we take a hybrid approach to language, using both person-first and identity-first language to honor the desires of multiple preference groups.

Activism led by people with disabilities has been an important force in improving perceptions of and opportunities available to people with disabilities (Linton, 1998). Like African Americans, LGBTQ+ people, and women, people with disabilities staked out protections in US law by engaging in civil disobedience protests in the 1970s and 1980s. Until that point, people with disabilities had to advocate persistently to attend schools for nondisabled students and to be hired; without policy backing, their efforts were largely thwarted by inaccessible infrastructure and cultural beliefs that people with disabilities should remain dependent at home in the care of family or housed in restrictive institutions.

The Independent Living Movement began a trend of preferred community programming to provide job training, assistive technologies, and attendant caregivers for people with disabilities (Shapiro, 1994). The movement was led by people with disabilities and intended to benefit people with disabilities. This activism characterized a shift to the perception that most people with disabilities can secure their own accommodations to integrate into society. The movement began in 1970 with disabled students at the University of California, Berkeley, who created the first of what are now called Centers for Independent Living. They offered advocacy training and community support for people with disabilities, including a wheelchair repair shop and a network of trusted care providers. There are now hundreds of Centers for Independent Living throughout the United States that provide an array of services for people with disabilities; these may include teaching daily living skills, arranging for accessible transportation, helping someone to modify an inaccessible house, and finding other community services they are eligible for (n.d.). Centers for Independent Living importantly do not require that people with disabilities be employed or looking for work; often, they can provide employment readiness training or services such as home modifications that would not be covered by a different federally funded resource, Vocational Rehabilitation, which provides workplace accommodations only.

One civil disobedience protest related to education for people with disabilities, popularly known as the 504 Sit-in, took place in 1977 (Schweik, 2011). Before this point, many people with disabilities separated themselves according to disability diagnoses, advocating for improvements specific to their own bodily impairments. However, this protest was notable because disability rights activists with many types of disabilities came together and occupied a federal building in San Francisco containing the US Office of Health, Education, and Welfare (HEW). The activists wanted to ensure that Section 504 of the Rehabilitation Act, which contained regulations requiring entities receiving government funding to become accessible, was signed and implemented by HEW Secretary Joseph Califano. Since the initial passage of Section 504 in 1973, disabled activists had waited on administrative personnel changes and heard concerns that Section 504 would be too expensive. During the sit-in, disabled activists moved into the building and picketed outside. The sit-in lasted for twenty-five days, ending when Califano signed Section 504. This historic protest brought people with disabilities together for a united cause, even if their specific diagnoses or barriers differed.

Passage of Section 504 began a transformation of schools, hospitals, and other government-funded institutions to make them accessible to people with disabilities. For example, housing entities receiving federal funding are required to be built accessible for people with disabilities, and K-12 and post-secondary institutions receiving federal funding had to make their programs accessible to students with disabilities. Importantly, Section 504 provided a precedent for other disability-related legislation in the United States including the Americans with Disabilities Act of 1990 and its 2008 amendments, which stipulate that people cannot be discriminated against based on their disability in regard to employment, interactions with state and local governments, and in any public place. Another important law influenced by Section 504 was the Individuals with Disabilities Education Act (IDEA), which codifies access to a free and appropriate public education for K-12 grade students with disabilities in the least restrictive environment. These laws play an important role in ensuring that individuals with disabilities have access to education and careers, including those in computing. For example, before IDEA, many blind students were forced to attend schools for the blind where they were trained to do one of only a few careers like caning chairs, tuning pianos, or massage (French, 1919; Omvig, n.d.). IDEA insures that any student with disabilities can study computing if they wish, and learn in the same classroom alongside their peers as much as possible.

Feminist disability studies scholars including Rosemarie Garland-Thomson (2005), Susan Wendell (2013), and Alison Kafer (2013) point out that the intersection of gender and disability should be included in feminist theory, and, likewise, that gender should be attended to in disability studies scholarship. Their work critiqued disability rights activism for being male-dominated and feminist studies for not addressing disability issues for women or presenting disability negatively in feminist texts. As such, research is only beginning to uncover concrete ways that disability affects women differently from men. For example, women are more likely than men to have a disability and live longer with disability than men do (Leveille, Resnick, and Balfour, 2002). Some 78% of individuals diagnosed with autoimmune disorders are women (Fairweather and Rose, 2004). It is unknown why this difference exists. Autism manifests differently in girls than in boys, and current diagnostic methods are likely to underdiagnose girls and women (Szalavitz, 2016). Females on the autism spectrum, comparative to men, may be diagnosed later, go undiagnosed, or be diagnosed with other conditions instead.

Recent activism focuses on diversifying representations of people with disabilities (Mingus, n.d.). Revisiting the 504 Sit-in with intersectionality in mind reveals more about how the protest was sustained for so long. Disabled black activist Brad Lomax enrolled the Black Panthers' support. The party's existing program, which fed breakfast mostly to children of color with low socioeconomic status, came in handy, delivering food to protesters while they maintained occupancy of the federal building.

An excellent example of intersectionality written in policy can be found in the Convention of the Rights of Persons with Disabilities (CRPD) adopted by the United Nations in 2006. The CRPD has fifty articles, with the purpose stated in Article 1: "The purpose of the present Convention is to promote, protect and ensure the full and equal enjoyment of all human rights and fundamental freedoms by all persons with disabilities, and to promote respect for their inherent dignity." Since adoption, 161 countries in the world are signatories to the convention. Among many issues, the CPRD addresses the need to develop and deploy technologies for people with disabilities and the need to include people with disabilities in the workforce, including the computing workforce (Ladner, 2014). Among the eight general principles guiding the convention is the statement: "Equality between man and women." Article 6 is specifically about women with disabilities, stating in part: "States Parties recognize that women and girls with disabilities are subject to multiple discrimination, and in this regard shall take measures to ensure the full and equal enjoyment by them of all human rights and fundamental freedoms." It is clear from the text of the CPRD that people with disabilities, including women, and their allies were involved in the creation of the CPRD. The CPRD is very much aspirational because the treatment of people with disabilities varies greatly around the world. Nonetheless, the CPRD stands as a beacon for changing attitudes and laws for the better around the world.

One aspect of intersectionality especially relevant to people with disabilities is health. Almost all of the disability literature makes the assumption that an impairment, once acquired, is a lifelong change to one's person. But there is often not a clear separation between illness and disability, and their interaction can have broad implications for how an individual with both is accepted (e.g., see Pinder's chapter "Sick-but-Fit or Fit-but-Sick? Ambiguity and Identity at the Workplace" [1996] and Gold and Duval's "Working with Disability: An Anthropological Perspective" [1994]). Working with a disability that has associated healthcare needs requires carving out time for doctors' appointments, dealing with setbacks and catching up, and other similar concerns. It may also be that impairment itself varies with the momentary intensity of the health condition. Often these changes are also invisible, creating complexity around disclosure and trust in interpersonal relationships. For example, if the appearance of someone's disabilities shifts, they may be disbelieved when they disclose. Others might assume that if they witness a task performed without accommodations once, this means that the requested adjustments are not actually important or necessary. Since more women than men have chronic health problems (Denton, Prus, and Walters, 2004), and this can feed into gender stereotypes (e.g., women are inaccurately perceived to exaggerate their symptoms [General Motors Corporation and Catalyst, 2006]), these issues are especially pertinent for women.

Finally, recent activism around disability and intersectionality has also advocated a shift in thinking around assistance from enabling independence to fostering interdependence (Mingus, 2010; Bennett et al., 2018). These activists believe independence can put undue pressure on people with disabilities to deny the assistance they need. This shift endeavors not to replace independence but to build on it with recognition that everyone needs help; and it is the assistance most useful for people with disabilities that we need to continue working toward. In this spirit, we highlight experiences of women with disabilities with attention to their challenges pursuing computing careers and the support systems that keep them healthy and motivated.

PARTICIPATION OF WOMEN WITH DISABILITIES IN COMPUTING

It is difficult to determine how well represented individuals with disabilities are in computing fields. This is due to factors that include differing definitions of disability in survey instruments, the variety of ways that educational institutions count and maintain data on disability, fear by disabled people that their disclosure will not remain confidential, a reliance on self-reporting, and the fact that individuals may acquire disabilities over the course of their education or career (Taylor and Ladner, 2011). Despite these limitations, some data exist. According to the National Center for Education Statistics, in the United States during the 2011–2012 school year, 11.1% of undergraduates overall had a disability and 10.6% of undergraduates majoring in engineering, computer science, or math had a disability (National Center for Education Statistics, 2015). Some 5.3% of graduate students overall and 4.8% of graduate students majoring in engineering, computer science, or math had a disability. Individuals with disabilities are more likely to attend two-year colleges than students without disabilities (National Center for Education Statistics, 2012).

Some barriers faced by women with disabilities pursuing computing education and careers are similar to barriers that individuals from other underrepresented groups might face, such as lack of role models and little encouragement from parents, educators, employers, and peers (Ladner and Burgstahler, 2015). Other barriers faced by women with disabilities in computing are unique to disability, but may not be unique to women. For example, women who are blind may encounter inaccessible technology, or those with learning disabilities may struggle with particular instructional approaches (Ladner and Burgstahler, 2015).

People with disabilities use a wide range of technologies to access computers, including screen-reading software, screen magnification, speech recognition software, word prediction software, mind-mapping or outlining software, or mouse or keyboard alternatives. In the classroom, students with disabilities utilize a variety of accommodations, the most common of which include captioning or sign-language interpreters, note takers, and extra time on tests. There are a variety of strategies that instructors can use to be more welcoming and accessible to people with disabilities. Universal design for learning calls for giving students multiple ways to gain knowledge, multiple ways to interact, and multiple ways to demonstrate knowledge (Burgstahler, 2015a,b). Adapting these strategies can benefit a range of students, not just students with disabilities. For example, providing scaffolding for a lecture not only benefits students with learning disabilities but also benefits any student who prefers to study using structured notes. Likewise, captioning videos can provide access to deaf or hard of hearing individuals, but are also particularly beneficial to non-native speakers of English as well as those who wish to see the spelling of technical terms (Gernsbacher, 2015).

Women with disabilities must make decisions about disclosing their disability in education and employment settings and how to advocate for their needs. Some women will encounter difficulties with technical interviews, whether it is a woman who is blind encountering an inaccessible format or a woman on the autism spectrum struggling to articulate her thought process. Relocating to a new city for school, internships, or employment may be difficult if it requires a woman to identify new healthcare providers or personal care support. This is particularly true for women who might depend on their families for some aspects of their care.

Of course, not all women with disabilities encounter similar experiences in their education and careers. Barriers differ with regard to specific disabilities and whether a woman belongs to other underrepresented groups. For example, women with disabilities from low socioeconomic status may encounter barriers in their education and careers related to cost. It can be cost-prohibitive to obtain adequate documentation of an invisible disability, such as a learning disability, to access accommodations. Travel to conferences can also be more expensive for individuals who need to cover salary or travel expenses for a personal care attendant (PCA) to travel with them. We have worked with students with disabilities who have received travel scholarships to conferences but do not receive funding for their PCAs' travel expenses. These students may be unable to partake in the conference and miss the learning and networking opportunities available to others. Captioning and sign-language interpreting are particularly expensive accommodations. Some students have encountered issues when they request captioning or interpreting at conferences and those organizations are reluctant to provide it.

Another barrier may occur when a student with a disability does not know what accommodations to ask for and, relatedly, has needs that are not well understood or supported. This is especially true for people whose disabilities are invisible (e.g., learning disabilities or chronic pain) and require compulsory documentation from a medical professional confirming they actually have disabilities (which is usually necessary before they can receive accommodations). Even once documentation is attained, the accommodations needed may be difficult to advocate for. Accommodations such as a flexible work schedule, work-at-home options, periodic rest breaks, and reduced stress are recommended for people with chronic health conditions such as lupus and chronic fatigue (National Resource Center on Lupus, 2018; Job Accommodation Network, n.d.), but asking for this flexibility can present barriers as existing accommodations request processes tend to assume all accommodations are tangible or accessible, like adapted office furniture or documents that can be readily accessed. In addition, for those working in an academic setting, there is also ambiguity about who pays for the accommodation. Within the university hierarchy, that could be the university, department, or individual faculty member (from grant or gift funds). The fundraising burden is highest for the smallest unit (the faculty member), but a faculty member has a great deal of freedom in deciding what accommodations to pay for if paying herself. In any case, it is not clear that payment responsibility is specifically delineated by the ADA. Not all universities are equally supportive or forthcoming about this.

Related to this is that needs may vary over time. Should a faculty member or student limit her work to what her normal capacity is when feeling unwell, allowing for steady but lower effort? If she instead works at what her normal capacity is when feeling well, she accomplishes more but has shifting needs, which may be more likely to lead to frustration and stereotyping, especially if her symptoms are invisible. The accommodations needed in either case shift as well – an overall lower workload versus a support structure that can fill in the gaps in the difficult weeks.

Another barrier to consider is that of awareness. Many people with chronic illness, or who acquire impairments later in life, do not identify as having a disability, and as a result do not have access to the advocacy and support resources of the disability community. Outreach to these people could help with this. This issue too may be more likely to impact women than men if more women are diagnosed with chronic illness, or women are more likely to assume it is their job to deal with it and not to "complain."

Despite barriers, there are people with disabilities who have succeeded in computing education and careers. Anecdotally, many have argued that in general people with disabilities develop significant problem-solving skills from encountering barriers in their everyday lives and that this experience may allow them to succeed in engineering fields (AccessEngineering, 2016). Considering specific disabilities, an individual who is blind may have particular expertise on screen-reading technology that can be invaluable to an employer looking to create accessible technology. Arash Zaghi argues that individuals with attention deficits may be able to make unique contributions to engineering fields because of their high levels of creativity and risk-taking potential (Zaghi et al., 2016).

STORIES HIGHLIGHTING WOMEN'S EXPERIENCES

Examining the experiences of women with disabilities in computing fields highlights the unique barriers they face and the creativity they bring to the field. In a discussion in an online mentoring community for students with disabilities in mid-2018, we asked women with disabilities to reflect on their experiences in computing education and careers. Members of the online community are high school, two-year-degree, four-year-degree, or graduate students, as well as recent graduates, with disabilities from across the United States studying computing-related fields such as computer science or information technology. Discussion in the community typically includes questions about accessibility, opportunities for professional development, internships, and other topics related to computing education and careers. The online community is diverse with regard to disability types, geographic location, and age. Because the online community is largely students and recent graduates, we also posed the same questions to a diverse group of professional women working in computing fields in our network. Twenty-two women shared their experiences and observations. We have used pseudonyms here to respect the privacy of participants.

We posed the following questions to the women to start the conversation. Women responded to the questions and to one another's comments.

- Women are a significant minority in computing majors and fields. Those with a disability are even a smaller minority. What positive or negative experiences have you encountered as either a woman or a person with disability that affected your participation in your major or field?
- How has your gender influenced your experiences with self-advocacy? Or your disclosure in education or employment?
- What else do you wish other people knew about women with disabilities in computing majors or fields?

Gender versus Disability Status

As women discussed how their gender or disability status or other factors of their identity impacted their education, many women noted that they cannot tell how various aspects of their identity have affected their particular experiences. Tia noted, "I live at the intersection of race, gender, and disability; I am an African-American woman and a quadriplegic, a minority, within a minority, within a minority. There are times when I cannot tell what bias is being triggered in the people I encounter (assuming only one bias is triggered at a time)." Mary felt similarly: "It is really hard to pick apart what aspects of my experiences are because of disability and which are because of gender. After all, people don't generally give thorough justifications when they're being discriminatory!" Mary went on to note that her disability, which is mobility related, seems to come up more often:

I do think that disability is something I have to consciously deal with more in my interactions with others. Maybe this is because there are fewer students with disabilities in computing then there are women. Maybe it's because disability is less socially accepted. Maybe it's because the practical access issues associated with disability are something that people can cling to as a "reason" to discriminate.

Other women also indicated that disability has been a more prominent issue. Abigail, who is blind, noted that her disability led to access issues and isolation: "Frankly I had to struggle so hard to meet basic access needs that most of the things the women in my group complained about didn't sound like real problems to me. I couldn't relate when one expressed discomfort that her class didn't contain many women. I would have been thrilled to have just one other blind student in the entire department to talk to." Kathy, a professional, had an interesting perspective. Although she views herself as "more of a Deaf person than a female," when she uses a male interpreter to speak for her in conference calls, "I feel that when they hear a male voice leading the meeting, I have the power." Jennifer, however, notes that she notices discrimination based on her disability, a visual impairment, only in certain settings but that "gender is always present."

Barriers to Participation

Isolation like that noted by Abigail was something a few women brought up. Mary noted, "I have extremely rarely encountered someone with similar issues.... This is extremely isolating. I have no role models. I have no similarly disabled peers. I do have people in my life who support me, but there are limits to how much they can understand without having their own lived experiences." Some women noted that they dealt with low self-confidence or impostor syndrome, which could be made worse when others also doubt their abilities, and also meant that access barriers they encountered were often dismissed. Grace, who has attention deficit hyper-activity disorder (ADHD) and a learning disability, noted, "I believed that women in general were perfectly capable of pursuing STEM [science, technology, engineering, and math] – just not me personally. As a result, I came to college behind my peers in math, and without prior program-ming experience outside of HTML and CSS."

Some women noted that they think gender may have influenced ways that they advocate for their needs. Mary remarked, "I'm also pretty sure that my social conditioning as a woman has made it a bit harder for me to develop self-advocacy skills, as our culture generally values women who are quiet and submissive." Jessica, who is deaf, noted, "It's a known problem that women typically need to walk a fine line between being perceived as 'assertive' (confident) vs. 'aggressive' (bossy and mean)." Jessica went on to express how self-advocacy is a positive thing in the workplace: "I believe people generally appreciate knowing what I need and having the chance to help others succeed. I also think they respect me more because they can tell I really want to do my best work, rather than sit back and shy away from asking for what I need."

For women with invisible disabilities, disclosure is a concern. Rosa, who has a mental health disability, noted, "I avoid telling employers and colleagues at work. I am in an employment-at will state, and am unfortu-nately concerned about any backlash.... My hometown was not accepting on my disability on a social level, making me paranoid about being seen as 'crazy' in a work environment as well." Hannah felt similarly: "People are allowed mistakes, but as a woman with a disability, I feel like I have no room for error – as if the world is betting on my failure." Lauren, who has a mobility-related disability, put a positive spin on the topic of disclosure: "Since my disability is so very obvious there's no option but to disclose my disability. I see it as an advantage to being memorable in interviews and situations. This viewpoint has helped me a lot in my career, and because I am extroverted I am able to use it this way."

Women described barriers related to accommodations and advocacy that impacted their education and careers. Jennifer noted, "I am visually impaired and although my disability is visible, I have always felt that I need to keep educating people about accommodations (e.g., digital copies of handouts or addressing needs during training). This can be exhausting over time or at least I have felt ignored in that I have to keep reminding the same people over and over." Others noted difficulties related to getting accommodations or access technology. Lisa, who has a mobility impairment, noted that a male teammate during a group project assumed she couldn't code because he was unaware that someone might utilize access technology to use a computer. Maggie, who is blind and autistic, also noted that others' lack of awareness about accessibility has created problems for her. When a programming assignment proved inaccessible, she said, "I contacted my professor for that class, but he had no experience with accessibility and really wasn't sure what to do. I also contacted the disability services office, but they didn't know about programming, so they had a hard time helping as well." Eventually, when everyone came together to talk, they were able to devise an alternative, accessible assignment.

Some women identified specific areas where they lacked support or mentors. Abigail shared, "I believe my programming skills atrophied as an undergraduate because I lacked access to advising and mentorships." Jasmine, who is autistic, participated in a high school robotics team with other students with disabilities and recalls hearing a parent voice "doubts, given the nature of the team, about the team's ability to produce a functional robot or anything beyond 'a pile of scrap metal' in the six-week building season." This motivated Jasmine to succeed.

Others noted difficulty finding jobs or internships. Beryl, who is deaf, said, "I am currently looking for a job and it is very hard to get an interview or pass through an interview." Purvi, who has a speech disability, noted, "I have been told that it would be very easy for me to find internships due to companies' diversity outreach and quota which meant that my talent didn't really matter; I was going to get hired no matter what. But the truth is, I have gotten rejected from companies [that] are known for their diversity outreach, because I wasn't technically prepared enough."

Some women shared the pressure they felt to be exceptional at what they do to justify their presence in the field. Grace noted that in her internships, "I often felt an obligation to prove myself and my abilities at the expense of learning new things." Likewise, Jessica noted, "When I observe how others communicate with efficiency and how they pick up knowledge in hallway conversations, it's easy to fall into the trap of thinking my deafness prevents me from doing the best job I could."

Sources of Support and Positive Aspects of Disability

Women pointed to various sources of support that have been important. For some students this included disability services offices at their institutions; others talked about faculty and staff in their departments, coworkers or managers, or organizations focused on broadening participation. One woman who is now employed after graduating noted the value of working on a supportive team.

Many women, however, also believed there were positive aspects of having a disability. Grace noted that when she got to college, "I was already used to struggling academically, and in many ways that prepared me to face academic difficulty. Whereas many of my peers had excelled during high school and were caught off-guard by the college workload, my grades had actually never been better." Mary said, "Navigating the world with a disability is often one giant problem-solving exercise! Those experiences can give us skills and perspectives that aren't obvious to others, and we should be valued for what we can contribute, not isolated because we are different." As Lauren put it, "I always have felt for me personally that being a woman in computing and being disabled has been my super power. I am able to bring a unique perspective to the table that most do not." Jessica indicated that positive aspects of being a woman with a disability include "being able to impact accessibility efforts in my company [and] bringing a unique perspective to my team and improving our communication style."

Jennifer argued that as a faculty member with a disability, having a disability allows her to prepare her students in a unique way. "It gives me a unique perspective compared to most of my colleagues, and so I try to bring that info to my classroom so that the students see that it is important to work with folks who are different from various perspectives." Kathy, a deaf professional, noted that her strategies to ensure she can access meetings make the meetings better for everyone. "Meetings tend to be of better quality if I am in control of leading them – I make sure one person speaks at a time, and to say his/her name before speaking."

We asked the women what they wanted others to know about women with disabilities. Women who addressed this indicated that they wanted to be seen as competent contributors who have a right to be in computing fields. Mary noted that there are accessibility issues in the field, and yet, "it is not our job to solve all of the field's accessibility problems. The responsibility to make the field accessible to all lies with the entire community." Indeed, awareness of issues that women with disabilities face and accessibility issues can serve to make computing fields a more welcoming place.

As this chapter looks to bring light to the unique experiences and challenges of women with disabilities in computing, our respondents had difficulty cleanly categorizing theirs. Several seemed to believe their disability presented more direct barriers to computing than being a woman, but social expectations for women to remain quiet compounded their disability-related marginalization. Additionally, inaccessible programs to raise participation of women in computing careers and expectations that they would at least find commonality with other women in their departments resulted in feeling more, rather than less, isolated. Respondents appreciated accessible support systems like those catering to students with disabilities, and, along with remaining assertive, they believed those two factors improved their confidence and opportunities. As such, encouraging women with disabilities' presence at events targeting women in computing more generally could help to increase their overall acceptance in the field and confidence in themselves.

DISCUSSION

As expected, some barriers that women with disabilities reported were similar to those that other underrepresented groups may encounter, such as those related to isolation, mentoring, and support. The women also noted barriers specific to accommodations and disclosure that are unique to individuals with disabilities. Our participants are active in an online community related to disability or otherwise involved in conversations around accessibility. Indeed, individuals who have encountered barriers related to accessibility may be more likely to seek out this sort of group. There are many directions that future work related to women with disabilities in computing could take. Little is known about how women experience disability in computing careers and education. There is ample room for research considering how disability impacts women's education and careers in computing, but also how disability impacts men and women in computing differently.

EXISTING EFFORTS ADDRESSING DISABILITY

There are efforts to increase the participation of people with disabilities in computing fields. Most of these efforts are in working with people with disabilities generally rather than focusing specifically on women with disabilities. Some of the efforts working on issues related to disability and computing are actually focused on increasing the accessibility of computing. We see this issue as intertwined with increasing participation of people with disabilities for multiple reasons. Increasing the accessibility of computing technology and tools is essential to increase the accessibility of computing education and careers. Moreover, accessible computing technology has a direct impact on the lives of people with disabilities (Ladner, 2009) and the population more generally (Ladner, 2009; 2015; Wobbrock et al., 2018). Some underrepresented groups, including women and people with disabilities, are attracted to STEM fields as a means for improving the world around them (Grandy, 1994; Margolis and Fisher, 2002; Blaser et al., 2011).

Our project AccessComputing, a National Science Foundation–funded program, has been working on both of these issues nationally since 2006. AccessComputing offers direct interventions for individuals with disabilities and supports institutional change to make education and employment more welcoming and accessible to individuals with disabilities. Through AccessComputing, high school students interested in computing majors and students pursuing postsecondary degrees in computing fields from across the country participate in an online mentoring community and professional development activities, as well as internships, research experiences, and conferences like the Tapia Celebration of Diversity in Computing and the Grace Hopper Celebration of Women in Computing. We have a variety of resources on our website to support educators and employers on diversity-related issues. We work directly with universities, companies, professional organizations, to broaden participation efforts across the United States and to create changes to make their organizations more welcoming and accessible and provide professional development to educators and employers.

Since 2014, our related project AccessCSforAll has been working to increase the accessibility of K-12 computer science through accessible tools and curricula. As computer science becomes integrated into the K-12 curriculum across the country and many are calling for computer science education for "all," it is important to ensure that students with disabilities are included (Ladner and Israel, 2016). Current efforts in this project include offering Advanced Placement Computer Science Principles professional development to teachers from schools that serve students who are blind, deaf, or have learning disabilities. Early exposure to computer science may encourage more individuals with disabilities to pursue education and careers in computing. One accessible programming language, Quorum, is used widely in schools for the blind and is designed to be accessible (Quorum, n.d.).

There are also efforts to ensure that accessibility is included in postsecondary computing curriculum. AccessComputing has made significant efforts in this area, conducting a research study to look at what is being taught with regard to accessibility in computing (Shinohara et al., 2018), developing resources to help faculty integrate this information in their courses, and leading efforts to integrate accessibility into classes taught in the University of Washington's Information School. Interestingly, the research study indicated that women are more likely than men to teach about accessibility in their courses. Some individuals with disabilities find that they take on the role of teaching coworkers about accessibility so that their companies can create accessible products. Teach Access (teachaccess. org), an initiative of tech companies and educational institutions focused specifically on increasing accessibility content in postsecondary computing education, has done significant work in this area. The companies represented in Teach Access have found it hard to locate employees with existing knowledge about accessibility, and so they are often training their staff. If postsecondary institutions taught this information, computing graduates would be more prepared for employment. Teach Access has provided grants as well as professional development to faculty, has initiatives regarding including language about accessibility knowledge in job ads, and has offered a study away program for students and faculty to learn about accessibility.

In industry, Microsoft's efforts related to disability and accessibility are particularly notable. In 2016, Microsoft appointed Jenny Lay-Flurrie as Chief Accessibility Officer. Lay-Flurrie, who is deaf, leads efforts related to accessibility and disability throughout the company. Microsoft has a disability hiring initiative as well as a focused autism-hiring program; the Disability Answer Desk, which provides specialized support for customers with disability; an annual Ability Summit; and a publicly available Inclusive Design toolkit. Microsoft Research also has a research team explicitly focused on ability. Other companies are also making significant efforts in this area. Several companies, including SAP, SAS, and Hewlett Packard have developed or are developing autism hiring initiatives. There has been significant growth in this regard in recent years. Many of these companies have been meeting annually as part of an Autism at Work Summit where they are able to share best practices in inclusive hiring.

CALL TO ACTION

Existing initiatives serve to create positive change with respect to disability, but these relatively sparse efforts make it imperative that others do more. Being mindful and explicit about addressing disability is important in inclusion and diversity efforts. Disability is often missing from these conversations (Harbour and Greenberg, 2017). It is important for educators, employers, and outreach efforts to take a holistic view of diversity and include disability in a meaningful way in their broadening participation activities. Recommendations include the following: Consider recruiting participants with disabilities, collecting data on the participation of individuals with disabilities in your programs, and be explicit about how individuals can request accommodations. Include people with disabilities in planning processes and get feedback about accessibility. Be proactive in making sure that websites are accessible, videos are captioned, and technology you develop is accessible. Learn about accessibility, universal design, ability-based design, and similar approaches and encourage others to do the same. We encourage funding agencies to be explicit about accessibility and disabilities in projects that they fund. By being more mindful about disability and accessibility, we can make computing fields more welcoming and inclusive of women with disabilities.

DISCUSSION QUESTIONS

1. This book seeks to illuminate the experiences of women with various intersectional identities in computing fields. Some of our participants identified aspects of their identity other than disability such as race and culture that impacted their experiences pursuing a computing career. How could you synthesize and integrate the experiences of our participants with those of some of the other chapters?

2. This chapter overviewed disability history and activism and noted the importance that intersectional perspectives has had on recent thinking about disability. What further research would you do on disability history and activism, while ensuring your search results include diverse experiences of people with disabilities?

3. What additional questions might you ask one of the interviewees in this chapter to learn how the varied aspects of their identity impacted them? Pick one woman whom you wanted to learn more about to make your answer more specific.

4. In this chapter, you learned that despite diversity and inclusion efforts in computing, women in computing report continued feelings of isolation and experiences with sexism and ableism. Design a new program to raise participation of women with disabilities in computing careers. Justify your choice of activities with evidence from the text. Be sure to include how your programming addresses challenges and incorporates support systems that have already been found to be successful.

5. Since designing a new program is not always practical or possible, explain how you would research an existing program meant to raise participation of either women or people with disabilities in computing fields to learn how the program could be improved to better serve women with disabilities. Then suggest possible program improvements based on the challenges faced by the interviewees in this chapter.

6. Interviewees in this chapter appreciated not only meeting other people who had similar experiences as them, but the support of allies who believed in them and worked to improve their experiences. Explain how you would research affective allyship with this population. Grounded in evidence from the interviewees' challenges and triumphs while leveraging different support systems, speculate on some ways people who are not women with disabilities can be affective allies.

References

AccessEngineering. (2016). Broadening Participation in Engineering to Include People with Disabilities. Video. Seattle: University of Washington. Retrieved from www.washington.edu/doit/videos/index.php?vid=71.

Americans with Disabilities Act of 1990, as amended, 42 U.S.C.A. § 12101, et seq.

Barker, L., and Frydman, A. (n.d.) Equal Access: Inclusive Strategies for Teaching Students with Disabilities. Retrieved from www.ncwit.org/resources/how-do-you-recruit-or-retain-women-through-inclusive-pedagogy/equal-access-inclusive.

Bennett, C., Brady, E., and Branham, S. (2018). Interdependence as a Frame for Assistive Technology Research and Design. Paper presented at *ASSETS'18: The 20th International ACM SIGACCESS Conference on Computers and Accessibility*. Galway, Ireland: ACM SIGACCESS.

Blaser, B., Burgstahler, S., and Braitmayer, K. (2011). AccessDesign: A Two-Day Workshop for Students with Disabilities Exploring Design Careers. *Journal of Postsecondary Education and Disability*, 25(2), 197–202.

Bureau of Labor Statistics. (2018, June 21). Persons with a Disability: Labor Force Characteristics – 2017. Washington, DC: Department of Labor. Retrieved from www.bls.gov/news.release/pdf/disabl.pdf.

Burgstahler, S. (2015a). *Equal Access: Universal Design of Instruction*. Brochure. Seattle: University of Washington. Retrieved from www.washington.edu/accesscomputing/equal-access-universal-design-instruction.

Burgstahler, S. (ed.) (2015b). *Universal Design in Higher Education: From Principles to Practice*, 2nd ed. Cambridge, MA: Harvard University Press.

Carnegie Mellon University. (n.d.). Women@SCS. Retrieved from www.women.cs.cmu.edu/.

Centers for Independent Living. (n.d.). What Is a Center for Independent Living? Retrieved from http://mtstcil.org/skills/il-3-background.html.

Denton, M., Prus, S., and Walters, V. (2004). Gender Differences in Health: A Canadian Study of the Psychosocial, Structural and Behavioural Determinants of Health. *Social Science & Medicine*, 58(12), 2585–2600.

Erickson, W., Lee, C., and von Schrader, S. (2017). *Disability Statistics from the American Community Survey (ACS)*. Ithaca, NY: Cornell University Yang-Tan Institute (YTI). Retrieved from Cornell University Disability Statistics website: www.disabilitystatistics.org.

Fairweather, D., and Rose, N. R. (2004). Women and Autoimmune Diseases. *Emerging Infection Diseases, 10*(11), 2005–2011. https://dx.doi.org/10.3201/eid1011.040367.

French, R. S. (1919). *The Education of the Blind: A Critical and Historical Survey with Special Reference to the United States of America*. Oakland, CA: University of California.

Garland-Thomson, R. (2005). Feminist Disability Studies. *Signs: Journal of Women in Culture and Society, 30*(2), 1557–1587.

General Motors Corporation (Sponsor) and Catalyst. (2006). *Women "Take Care," Men "Take Charge": Stereotyping of US Business Leaders Exposed*. New York: Catalyst.

Gernsbacher, M. A. (2015). Video Captions Benefit Everyone. *Policy Insights from the Behavioral and Brain Science, 2*(1), 195–202. https://doi.org/10.1177/2372732215602130.

Gold, G., and Duval, L. (1994). Working with Disability: An Anthropological Perspective. *Anthropology of Work Review, 15*(2–3), 1–2.

Grandy, J. (1994) *Gender and Ethnic Differences among Science and Engineering Majors: Experiences, Achievements, and Expectations*. GRE Board Research Report No. 92-03R. Princeton, NJ: Educational Testing Service.

Haller, B., Dorries, B., and Rahn, J. (2006). Media Labeling versus the US Disability Community Identity: A Study of Shifting Cultural Language. *Disability & Society, 21*(1), 61–75.

Harbour, W. S., and Greenberg, D. (2017, July). Campus Climate and Students with Disabilities. NCCSD Research Brief, 1(2). National Center for College Students with Disabilities, Association on Higher Education and Disability, Huntersville, NC. Retrieved from www.nccsdonline.org/uploads/7/6/7/7/7677280/nccsd_campus_climate_brief_-_final_pdf_with_tags2.pdf.

Job Accommodation Network. (n.d.). Chronic Fatigue Syndrome. Retrieved from https://askjan.org/disabilities/Chronic-Fatigue-Syndrome.cfm.

Kafer, A. (2013). *Feminist, Queer, Crip*. Bloomington: Indiana University Press.

Ladner, R. (2009). Expanding the Pipeline: Persons with Disabilities: Broadening Participation and Accessibility Research. *Computing Research News, 21*(2), 2–6. Retrieved from https://cra.org/crn/2009/03/persons_with_disabilities_broadening_participation_and_accessibility/.

   (2014). The Impact of the United Nations Convention on the Rights of Persons with Disabilities. *Communications of the ACM, 57*(3), 30–32. https://doi.org/10.1145/2566968.

   (2015). Design for User Empowerment. *Interactions, 22*(7), 24–29.

Ladner, R., and Burgstahler, S. (2015). Increasing the Participation of Individuals with Disabilities in Computing. *Communications of the ACM, 58*(12), 33–36. http://dx.doi.org/10.1145/2835961.

Ladner, R., and Israel, M. (2016). "For all" in "Computer Science for All." *Communications of the ACM, 59*(9), 26–28. https://doi.org/10.1145/2971329.

Leveille, S. G., Resnick, H. E., and Balfour, J. (2002). Gender Differences in Disability: Evidence and Underlying Reasons. *Aging Clinical and Experimental Research, 12* (2), 106–112.

Linton, S. (1998). *Claiming Disability: Knowledge and Identity*. New York: NYU Press.

Margolis, J., and Fisher, A. (2002). *Unlocking the Clubhouse: Women in Computing*. Cambridge, MA: MIT Press.

Mingus, M. (2010). Interdependency (excerpts from several talks). Retrieved from https://leavingevidence.wordpress.com/2010/01/22/interdependency-exerpts-from-several-talks/.

(n.d.). *Leaving evidence: A blog by Mia Mingus*. Retrieved from https://leavingevidence.wordpress.com.

National Center for Education Statistics. (2012). Table 2-6. Disability Status of Undergraduate Students by Age, Institution Type, Financial Aid, and Enrollment Status. In *National Postsecondary Student Aid Study*. Washington, DC: US Department of Education. Retrieved from www.nsf.gov/statistics/2017/nsf17310/static/data/tab2-6.pdf.

(2015). Table 311.10. Number and Percentage Distribution of Students Enrolled in Postsecondary Institutions, by Level, Disability Status, and Selected Student Characteristics: 2007–08 and 2011–12. In *Digest of Education Statistics*. Washington, DC: US Department of Education. Retrieved from https://nces.ed.gov/programs/digest/d15/tables/dt15_311.10.asp.

National Resource Center on Lupus. (2018). Workplace Accommodations and Applying for Disability Assistance. Retrieved from https://resources.lupus.org/entry/workplace-accommodation-and-disability.

O'Hear, S. (2016, November 7). Tech Companies Don't Want to Talk about the Lack of Disability Diversity Reporting. *TechCrunch*. Retrieved from https://techcrunch.com/2016/11/07/parallel-pr-universe/.

Oliver, M. (1990, July 23). The Individual and Social Models of Disability. Presented at the Joint Workshop of the Living Options Group and the Research Unit of the Royal College of Physicians on People with Established Locomotor Disabilities in Hospitals. Retrieved from https://disability-studies.leeds.ac.uk/wp-content/uploads/sites/40/library/Oliver-in-soc-dis.pdf.

Omvig, J. (n.d.) History of Blindness. *American Action Fund for Blind Children and Adults*. Retrieved from www.actionfund.org/history-blindness.

Pinder, R. (1996). Sick-but-Fit or Fit-but-Sick? Ambiguity and Identity at the Workplace. In C. Barnes and G. Mercer (eds.), *Exploring the Divide: Illness and Disability*. University of Leeds: Disability Press, pp. 135–156.

Quorum. (n.d.). *Quorum*. Retrieved from https://quorumlanguage.com/.

Schweik, S. (2011). Lomax's Matrix: Disability, Solidarity, and the Black Power of 504. *Disability Studies Quarterly*, 31(1). http://dx.doi.org/10.18061/dsq.v31i1.

Shakespeare, T., and Watson, N. (2001). The Social Model of Disability: An Outdated Ideology? In Sharon N. Barnartt and Barbara M. Altman (eds.), *Exploring Theories and Expanding Methodologies: Where We Are and Where We Need to Go*. Research in Social Science and Disability, volume 2. Bingley: Emerald Group Publishing, pp. 9–28.

Shapiro, J. P. (1994). *No Pity: People with Disabilities Forging a New Civil Rights Movement*. New York: Three Rivers Press, pp. 41–73.

Shinohara, K., Kawas, S., Ko, A. J., and Ladner, R. E. (2018). Who Teaches Accessibility?: A Survey of U.S. Computing Faculty. In *Proceedings of SIGCSE'18: The 49th ACM Technical Symposium on Computer Science Education*. New York: Association of Computing Machinery, pp. 197–202.

Sinclair, J. (2013). Why I Dislike "Person First" Language. *Autonomy, the Critical Journal of Interdisciplinary Autism Studies, 1*(2).

Slack Team. (2017, April 26). Diversity at Slack: An Update on our Data, April 2017. *Slack*. Retrieved from https://slackhq.com/diversity-at-slack.

Szalavitz, M. (2016, March 1). Autism: It's Different in Girls. *Scientific American*. Retrieved from www.scientificamerican.com/article/autism-it-s-different-in-girls/.

Taylor, V., and Ladner, R. (2011). Data Trends on Minorities and People with Disabilities in Computing. *Communications of the ACM, 54*(12), 34.

(2013). Computing Meets Culture. *CSTA Voice, 8*(6), 4–5.

Wadors, P. (2016, October 18). LinkedIn's 2016 Workforce Diversity. *LinkedIn*. Retrieved from https://blog.linkedin.com/2016/10/18/linkedin-2016-workforce-diversity-data.

Wendell, S. (2013). *The Rejected Body: Feminist Philosophical Reflections on Disability*. Abingdon, UK: Routledge.

Wobbrock, J. O., Gajos, K. Z., Kane, S. K., and Vanderheiden, G. C. (2018). Ability-Based Design. *Communications of the ACM, 61*(6) 62–71.

World Health Organization. (n.d.). Health Topics: Disabilities. Retrieved from www.who.int/topics/disabilities/en/.

Zaghi, A. E., Reis, S. M., Renzulli, J. S., and Kaufman, J. C. (2016). Unique Potential and Challenges of Students with ADHD In Engineering Programs. Paper presented at the *ASEE 123d Annual Conference and Exposition*. New Orleans, LA: ASEE. Retrieved from www.asee.org/public/conferences/64/papers/17281/view.

10

An Interview with Dr. Sue Black, OBE, Computer Scientist and Computing Evangelist

Carol Frieze and Jeria L. Quesenberry

INTRODUCTION

Dr. Black is perhaps most well known for initiating – and succeeding – in "saving Bletchley Park" (which is also the title of her book[1]). Bletchley Park[2] was a top-secret center for the famous World War II code breakers, including many women, whose work was credited with shortening the war by two to four years. The center deteriorated rapidly after the war and would most probably have been dismantled if not for the fundraising efforts of Dr. Black and her supporters. Bletchley Park is now a thriving visitors' center and is co-housed with the UK National Museum of Computing. Dr. Black's initial involvement with Bletchley Park inspired her to conduct an oral history project to capture the memories of the women who worked there. She met several of the surviving women code breakers; some shared their stories with her, others never revealed the details of their highly secret work.

In this interview Dr. Black provides insights into why the participation of women in computing in the United Kingdom is so low, suggesting it is "several things altogether that have created the situation that we're in now." According to HESA, a higher education statistics agency in the United Kingdom, "Fewer than 1 in 5 computer science and engineering & technology students are female"[3] and first-year UK enrollment in computer science is around 15% women (HESA, 2018). Dr. Black tempers her optimism for the future of women in computing but notes that "if we don't have women involved, if we don't have diversity at the heart of what we're doing, I think we're creating a world which is not a world that I want to really see."

AN INTERVIEW WITH DR. SUE BLACK

Carol Frieze: Can you tell us a little bit about your work in computer science?

Sue Black: I've been out of full-time academia for eight years now, I think. I spent ten or fifteen years as a computer science academic. And during that time, well, I've got a degree in computing, a PhD in software engineering. For my PhD I was specifically looking at code complexity and the impact of change within software systems. I carried that on after finishing my PhD. I also have done some research in the social media and software engineering kind of world in terms of software engineers using social media and how they use it to improve their code.

I've also done a bit of women in tech research and so I've been out of full-time academia for about eight years now. But I'm just about to come back in and I'm really looking forward to getting stuck in and doing some more research in those three areas, in software engineering, the social media area and also women in technology, and diversity in technology area.

Jeria Quesenberry: What do you enjoy the most about being a computer scientist?

Sue Black: Well, I enjoy everything about being a computer scientist. So it's hard to pick one thing. I mean I think that technology is changing the world around us. I think it just offers so many opportunities for so many people. Like, well, for people, for organizations and for countries as a whole. And I see computer science as underpinning everything that's happening in technology. So for me it's like creating the future I guess. And so that's one of the reasons why I think it's so important to have diversity of all sorts within computer science. Because if we're creating the future we want to create a future which is good for all of us and not just some of us.

Carol Frieze: Absolutely, tell us a bit about why you started #techmums.

Sue Black: I've had a career as a computer scientist for, I don't know, twenty years or so. And during that time, I've been in the press, in the media. Quite often they're very negative about technology and that always annoyed me.

And also, because I think technology is opening doors. It's offering opportunities to so many people, it's crazy to be negative about it all the time. And I think lots of people who aren't in the technology space really don't understand how beneficial it could be for them to know – to have some technology skills. And I think lots of the stuff in the press is all about, I don't know, robots taking over our lives or taking away our jobs or all that kind of thing.

Whereas, I see it as – so some jobs might go but it will create so many more jobs and they'll be much more fun and interesting than the jobs that were left behind. So I see it as changing the world. And so, for it to be reported on as negative all the time I just thought I want to do something about that. A few years ago, I started trying to work out what it was that I wanted to do. And I thought I want to flick a switch in people's heads from there's – I don't know if you've got it in the US but in the UK, we've got a comedy program called *Little Britain* which is like a sketch show.

Carol Frieze: I know it well.

Sue Black: And so, there's one sketch in there where there's one of the guys is dressed up as a woman and he's always sitting behind a computer. And anything that anyone ever says to him he basically always says *computer says no*. I think quite a lot of people think about computing in that way. And I thought what I really want to do is to flip that on its head and change it to computer says yes to show everyone what the opportunities are. I was thinking for some time how am I going to do that because I didn't really know what I was going to do.

And what I started doing was I started to try teaching. Before there was any coding in schools in the UK, I decided to try teaching coding to seven-year-old kids and teaching app design to seven-year-old kids. Basically, I put some workshops together and we ran them with, yeah, with lots of seven-year-olds. And what we found was – so when I got the parents to come in at the end of the day. The kids would do the workshops during the school day. The parents came in at the end. And I was encouraging the parents to like have a go at what their kids had been doing, the kids to show their parents.

And so, when I asked them to do that, in general – not everyone but in general the dads would step in and like have a look and like yes, what are you doing. And the moms, you could just see it on their faces. And again, not everyone but most of the moms were like oh my god. Please don't ask me to do that. So that started me thinking. If I want to affect the kids and how they see technology, if they get technology skills at school and they go home and their moms are negative about technology, we won't actually have got very far.

And it made me start thinking, well, maybe I should target moms with technology skills and maybe that could make a difference to everybody. I was trying to get to everybody but of course you can't start with everybody. I put some workshops together in basic IT skills – stuff like admin skills that you would use in an office like email, documents and spreadsheets, the Cloud, app design, web design, social media, how to stay safe online and a bit of coding in Python. I put together a program which is ten hours, five modules with all of that and got it accredited by e-skills in the UK and then found a school that was interested in running it and started running it.

And we actually had some great results straight away really. One of the moms that came on the pilot course, she'd come in to the focus group. So when I'd asked the moms in the group why are you here, why have you come along to this technology, why do you want to come on the #techmums program. She said that she was afraid of the keyboard. She said I know what these letter keys are but I don't know what are all of those keys at the top. I don't know what they are. And I'm scared if I touch one of them then something terrible is going to happen. So that was her. And I think loads of people feel like that. It's very common.

So that was one of our moms, Mina, who I'd got to know. The five modules are like two hours a week. The first module was like office admin stuff. The second module, I'm walking around the classroom chatting to everybody, asking how they're getting on with #techmums. And so, I started chatting to Mina. I said "How are you getting on?" She said, "Oh #techmums has changed my life." So I said, "That's amazing but how can it have happened so quickly? Like you just had two hours last week and here we are in the second week."

And she said that she runs a school uniform shop in the market down the road from the school in the east end of London. And for her to get her samples over to customers she parcels them up and her son comes over to the shop and takes them over to the customer site. She said, "But last week you taught us how to add attachments to emails and I realized that I can take photos of the garments and I can then email them across to the customers."

And so that's I think six years ago now. Last summer I went to visit Mina, see how she was getting on. And she said she's now got ten times the amount of customers that she had then. She also said that one of the things that #techmums taught her was that don't be scared of the computer. It's there to help you. And so if she doesn't know how to do something now she just Googles it because she knows that it's fine to do that and that nobody knows everything.

And I actually spoke to her a couple of weeks ago and she's now taking on more staff because she can't cope with the amount of business that she's got on her own. And of course, that's not only down to #techmums. She's obviously a great entrepreneur as well. But it's given her sort of the tools and the confidence to just get out there and do what she wanted to do. That's just one person that's gone through the program.

Jeria Quesenberry: Your work with mothers specifically I think is a really nice illustration of an intervention that can have a big impact. That's wonderful. I also have a seven-year-old so when you said seven-year-old coding I have like the utmost respect. That's a challenge.

Well, can you tell us a little bit about your life outside of computer science? What other interests, passions do you have?

Sue Black: Well, I guess do you want me to talk about setting up the UK's first online network for women in tech? Because that came from work but was outside ...

Jeria Quesenberry: That sounds very interesting.

Sue Black: When I was a PhD student, I was really shy I guess. Like I was shy growing up. And when I started my PhD, my PhD supervisor said to me that when you go to conferences you've got to network. It's not just what you know, it's who you know. And if you want to get your papers published it's – you stand a better chance if the people that you're submitting, that are reviewing your papers know who you are and have met you and had a conversation with you to sort of give you that extra edge in getting published and stuff like that.

For me the worst thing you could ask me to do at that time is like go into a room with hundreds of people and go and talk to someone I don't know. I was a bit horrified when he said that but I thought ok, he said I've got to do it so I've got to do it. The first conference that I went to was in computer science. I think it was about ninety percent men, ten percent women I'm guessing. I thought to myself ok, I need to talk to one person. That's like my target is to talk to one person because it really wasn't something I was used to doing.

And there was a guy that gave an interesting down-to-earth presentation. I thought I've got to chat to him in the break. In the break I went over, chatted to him for about fifteen minutes. We had a great conversation about research and stuff. But then for the rest of the conference every time I turned around he was staring at me and I was completely freaked out. And I'm sure it's down to my lack of emotional intelligence at the time but I just couldn't work it out. I thought I'd done something wrong. I couldn't work out what it was. And of course, because I was shy I wasn't going to go back to him and say, "Why do you keep staring at me?" So I'm just kind of stuck with my mind whirring around like what went wrong in that situation? I just don't understand it. I thought we had a nice chat and why is he staring at me all the time. I was terribly freaked out by that.

And then some time after that I went to a women in science conference in Brussels. Traveling over to this conference I can remember thinking to myself, "I hate conferences." I'm going to this but I hate conferences. I'm scared of talking to people I don't know. I was quite apprehensive walking in. So I went over to the registration desk when I got there, got my badge, went over to get a cup of tea. Some woman started talking to me. Some other women started talking. We all started talking. For the whole conference. I'd never had that kind of experience of everyone speaking to each other, chatting, having fun, introducing people to each other.

It was almost like a big party basically. And I think there were about ninety-eight women and two men or something like that. And that conference completely changed my life because it really helped me to realize that if you're in the majority life is just so much easier. And I think previously I was in the minority and there's also the whole "women approaching men" has got like connotations in our society which isn't that great. And it just completely changed my life because I just – I felt very, very empowered in lots of different ways from going to that women in science conference.

I came back from there thinking I've got to try and do something to create something so that all of the women in computing that want to talk to other women in computing, we can talk to each other even if we don't meet up in person. So I basically came back and set up – it was like an email list really because that's what it was at the time. This is twenty years ago now. It turned out to be the UK's first online network for women in tech and called it BCSWomen because I did it under the auspices of the British Computer Society (BCS). I set that up in 1998 and straight away loads of women joined it. Once I got everyone together I didn't quite know what to do next because I thought my aim was to get everyone together.

So I asked them what they wanted. They said that they wanted free training in internet technology and how to set up a website, because that wasn't commonly known at the time. I got the funding for that. We ran those classes. That did really well. And over twenty years it's gone from strength to strength really. They've done loads of different things, BCSWomen. I was chair for about seven years or something and then I passed it over to someone else. Different people have taken it different ways. Now there's so many things underneath the BCSWomen banner.

Like the Lovelace Colloquium every year which one of the committee, Hannah Dee, set up which is a big colloquium for female computer science undergraduates. About two hundred of them, two hundred is quite a lot in the UK. It's not like the seventeen thousand at the Grace Hopper conference 'cause we haven't got so many people here. But for female undergraduates there's a poster competition, lots of speakers. It's very empowering bringing female computer science students together. It was BCSWomen that led me up to Bletchley Park.

Carol Frieze: What would you say are the major reasons for the low participation of women in computing in the UK?

Sue Black: Well, it's a hard question to answer. I find it very interesting really that here in the UK in the fifties and sixties, maybe moving into the seventies it was a female-dominated industry. Looking back to the nineteen-sixties, I think at least half, possibly more than half of the programmers in the UK were women as far as I can tell. There were amazing pioneer women like Dame Stephanie Shirley who set up an organization called "F International" which was mainly moms programming from home and they produced software like the Concorde black box flight recorder. So like kind of safety-critical, really important software.

And people like Dina St. Johnston who I think in 1959 set up the world's first software house. Women were leading in this area in the UK anyway. So of course, it is quite depressing that that's not where we are now. I mean as far as I can tell from the outside and not really having lived through the seventies and eighties in computing because I came into it in the nineties really.

It seems that when big business realized that they could make lots of money, their more male-dominated business environment came in and tried to basically take over the market seeing that lots of money could be made. So I guess organizations like IBM came in and turned it into a more – rather than just the technical stuff but more kind of consultancy and that kind of thing around the whole computing industry. And at the same time, I think there was lots of advertising which mainly showed men and boys in computing.

And I think I mean I don't even know is the honest answer. Because I think unless you lived through that time it's quite hard to say in retrospect along with the fact that here we're only talking about the UK anyway. It's the whole personal computing theme as well. And so, in the UK schools there was a one computer per classroom kind of rule. Government gave funding to have one PC in every classroom. And I think because boys were more confident I guess they would just hog the computer so it meant that the girls didn't really get a chance to use the computer.

So there's that along with the whole gaming culture which has grown up and I guess because the people funding and writing the games in general were men to start with then that kind of culture permeated the whole of the gaming industry. It's like even now if you think about gaming I think more than fifty percent of the people that play online games are women. But even if I think about gaming I think about shooting 'em up games. I think we've got this whole perception that it's guys who play computer games and that they're all very macho even though I know that's not true.

There's all these stories and perceptions out there. And half the time you don't really know where they come from. But I think it just seems like from various different areas we're being told the story that it's mainly men that do these things. And the more that you're told that story, the more that it is mainly men that do it because women think, well, that's not for me, or girls think that's not for me. None of that's really based on a lot of facts I don't think. It just seems to me from being involved in the area for a long time that it's not one thing. Its several things altogether that have created the situation that we're in now.

Jeria
Quesenberry:
I agree. There are a lot of commonalities between the UK and here in the States such as the common perspective, and the gaming component.

I think we know the answer to the next question. Should we encourage more women to be in computing?

Sue Black:
Definitely not! (sarcastic) Yeah. Absolutely. I mean the thing is as we go forward into the future, technology/ computing is going to be everywhere around us. It feels like it is already but I mean it's just going to become more and more so. It's going to become more and more pervasive. All jobs are going to involve technology or interactions with organizations like our kids' school and stuff is all going to be technology related or we're going to get information through the internet, mainly online. Jobs are going to involve working with technology on computers.

We've got to have more diversity and we've got to have women involved in that because otherwise all of the products and services that are created will not be fit for purpose. If you don't have a diverse team creating products your product only serves one specific type of person.

And the only thing I can think of at the moment which is not technology is like the crash test dummies and how the dummies were. So women were getting injured in accidents or killed from air bags and stuff because the crash test dummies were all like male size. They didn't think about the fact that sometimes women might travel in cars. That kind of thing.

I think as technology is more and more pervasive we've got to have more diversity, more representation of everybody in terms of creating all of these products and services because otherwise they won't be fit for purpose. And as more and more people are using them that's going to affect more and more people. And we're kind of I think in an interesting stage at the moment in that we're going from I guess from lots of people using technology. Probably in the next five years – I feel in the UK anyway all the benefit system is going online.

In just a few years it's going to be everybody. And if you can't interact with technology you won't be able to have a productive and happy life really because you'll just be outside of everything. If we don't have women involved, if we don't have diversity at the heart of what we're doing, I think we're creating a world which is not a world that I want to really see.

Carol Frieze: We also have a few questions about Bletchley Park. We know you were instrumental in saving Bletchley Park from destruction. What sparked your initial interest in this and led you to devote so much time and energy to that work?

Sue Black: The first time I went to Bletchley Park was actually a British Computer Society meeting. So I was going up there, representing BCSWomen, the group that I set up. And at the time, 2003, I didn't really know much about Bletchley Park. All I knew really was that the code breakers worked there. And for some reason I had it in my head this picture of fifty old blokes wearing tweed jackets and smoking pipes, doing *the Times* crossword and then a bit of code-breaking on the side. I don't know how that got into my head but that's what I thought really.

That's what I was thinking about on the way up there. I didn't really know a lot more than that really. I went to the meeting and after the meeting – Bletchley Park is a twenty-six-acre site so it's a big site – so I thought, well, I want to go and have a look around and actually see what's here. I walked around, walked into one of the blocks there and there was a group of guys at the other end of the block and they were tinkering away on this sort of amazing feat of engineering. I couldn't really work out what it was. So being interested and curious I went over to have a look and started chatting to them.

I asked them all about what they were doing and it turned out that they were creating a rebuild of Alan Turing's bombe machine, one of the machines that was used to industrialize the code-breaking process. And so, I asked them everything about that, found that really interesting.

And then after a while they asked me why I was there. I said I'm here representing this group of women in computing. And they said, "Did you realize that more than half the people that worked here were women?" I was like no because I thought it was about fifty old blokes. I had no idea.

I said, "Well, how many people worked here?" And they said more than ten thousand. And I was just completely blown away because I'm interested in computing and the history of computing and the history of technology. I'm interested in the women's participation in that as well. So the fact that I've never heard about that was a real shock for me really so I just couldn't believe it. After our conversation I went away thinking, well, I've got to try to raise awareness of the fact that more than five thousand women worked at Bletchley Park because I've never heard about it. And I couldn't find anything online about it.

I eventually managed to raise some funding to run an oral history project to capture the memories of the women that worked there. And so that's what we did. I interviewed I think about fifteen of the women that worked there including code breakers. And at the launch of that project in 2008 I gave a talk about why I thought it was important. And then we had the director of Bletchley Park at that time give a talk and basically what he was saying was that he was really worried that visitor numbers might drop.

At that time their main revenue for Bletchley Park was from people visiting and paying on the door. And he said that there were lots of reports in the press at the time that there might be a swine flu epidemic. And so, he said that he was really worried that if there was a swine flu epidemic that the visitor numbers would drop. They weren't really managing to sustain them as it was. And he said if the visitor numbers dropped then their income would drop and if their income dropped they'd have to close Bletchley Park. And he said, and if we close, we won't be able to open again because it just wouldn't work. It was mainly run by volunteers. And so, he said basically if we close it will be forever. It's not going to open again.

And so, listening to that I thought well, that's terrible. All of those people worked there. It's a disgrace really. So then not long after that I got invited up to a reception at Bletchley Park and I did a full tour which I've not done before with one of the veterans who had worked there and was telling us about all of the major code-breaking achievements at Bletchley Park. And I heard all of these amazing facts and figures. And I just remember at the end of that tour we stood in front of hut six which looks very dilapidated and had like a blue tarp over one end which was there to stop the rain getting in and basically looked like it was going to fall down in the next few years.

And this guy was telling us about the major code-breaking achievements in that hut. And he said the work that was done here was said to have shortened World War II by two years. And at that time about eleven million people a year were dying. So potentially the work that was done here saved twenty-two million lives. And I just thought to myself, "and this place might close? That's terrible. That can't happen." I went away that time thinking I've got to do something about it.

And so, by that time 2008 I was head of a computer science department at the University of Westminster. And because I was head of department I was on an email list for all the heads and professors of computing in the country. So I sent an email around to everybody with a photo of the hut. Someone else had set up a petition on UK Prime Minister's website asking the government to help save Bletchley Park. So I pointed everyone to that petition and said, "Please sign it" and said, "We've got to save Bletchley Park."

And then I checked the petition site a few hours later and loads of really famous professors of computer science from around the country had signed the petition. I saw all their names on the petition. I just thought wow. It's not just me. All of these people, people that I think like "I'm not worthy" because they wrote the textbooks I used when I was an undergraduate, they were all signing it too. That was very exciting.

I chatted to my colleague at work who loved Bletchley Park as well saying, what else can we do to raise awareness. He said, why don't we write a letter to the *Times* newspaper? So he drafted a letter. I sent it round to everybody and about ninety-seven heads and professors of computer science signed it in a couple days. And then I thought, "I need to get more publicity." I contacted all of the journalists that I knew then which was probably only about four. But luckily one of them was the technology correspondent from the BBC, Rory Cellan Jones, who said, in a nutshell, he thought it was a story.

Then the next week he invited me up to Bletchley Park, interviewed me there saying I was "ashamed to be British. We should be looking after our heritage." And that went out on BBC News and across BBC America and was on the Today BBC radio 4 program which is the news program on the radio in the morning here. Within a week it had gone across the world as a story, which was great. But then after that like, I'm a computer scientist. I didn't quite know what I was doing– nothing much had changed.

There were no large amounts of money that had come into Bletchley Park or anything. I didn't know what else to do and it was only toward the end of 2008 that I started using Twitter and realized that just by typing Bletchley Park into the search box in Twitter I could reach anyone – I could see the tweets from anyone around the world that was tweeting about Bletchley Park. And I could start a conversation with them and encourage them to tell everybody they knew that Bletchley Park needed saving. I'd set up a blog as well kind of like telling the story and why we needed to save Bletchley Park.

I started tweeting about it, had a link to my blog in my bio on Twitter. Various people got in touch with me saying they wanted to help out with the campaign. And so, then we got Bletchley Park set up on Twitter and that sort of thing and using social media. And then in February 2009 I saw Stephen Fry tweeted a selfie of him with friends stuck in a lift in London in a tower block. And I saw that photo and I thought oh Stephen Fry, he must be interested in

Bletchley Park because I know he loves technology and history. I Googled "Steven Fry Bletchley Park" and he'd said things which assured me that he was interested.

And luckily, he was following me on Twitter so I sent him several direct messages basically asking him to get involved with the campaign. And the next morning he tweeted a link to my blog– normally I'd got about fifty hits a day on my blog and after one tweet from Stephen Fry I got eight thousand. So that really showed me what a big difference it can make getting key influential people on board with your campaign. So on that day I became the most retweeted person on Twitter in the world because so many people from Stephen Fry because he had such a following tweeting about it then I got lots of retweets as well. That was a crazy day. My Twitter went just completely mental.

I think when I started the campaign I thought it would take six months really to save Bletchley Park. Because I thought loads of people will realize we've got to save it and then they'll – I don't know – they'll do something. But by the time I'd been campaigning for three years I think I thought I'd just probably be doing this for the rest of my life. When the director actually said, "You don't need to say saving Bletchley Park anymore. It's saved."

I almost didn't believe him because I couldn't believe that after three years that it was all going to be ok. Bletchley Park got £4.1 million from the heritage lottery fund. Once they got a big substantial amount like that then we knew they'd be all right.

Jeria Quesenberry:	What a really wonderful story. Can you tell us a little bit more about the women of Bletchley Park? I know you interviewed some of them. What's surprised you? What were your favorite discoveries, that kind of thing?
Sue Black:	Yeah. Well, so the thing that surprised me the most was the amount of women that worked there. I mean I think it was nearly eight thousand. And of course, most of the men were away fighting as soldiers so I guess that's why the numbers of women were so high. I think that's the most surprising thing. I liked some of the stories of the women

who became code breakers like Mavis Batey (née Lever) and it was such – one of the great things about the campaign for me is that I met quite a few code breakers and got to know them.

Mavis Beatty was one of the code breakers. I think she was eighteen when she was there and she made one of the major code-breaking breakthroughs as an eighteen-year-old girl: she broke into Italian Naval Enigma. This led to the Royal Navy's victory at Cape Matapan in 1941. Her code-breaking work also contributed to the success of D-Day. She was an amazing and ridiculously modest woman.

And it's quite funny. She met her husband, Keith, at Bletchley Park; quite a lot of couples I think got together there. And she made me laugh because she said that when she started as a code breaker she had to walk past him in her office. And she said so I thought he was – she didn't say cute. I can't remember what she said but basically, she did think he was cute.

And so, she said that she decided to do the pencil test on him. And I was like, "So what's the pencil test?" And she said, "To find out if a boy, like if a man likes you, you walk past them and then you drop your pencil. If they pick it up, they're interested." She said so she did the pencil test. And I said, "And did he pick it up?" She said no. But they got married anyway and they were great. I met both of them together at Bletchley Park. They were really cool.

As part of what we did on the campaign was to go up to Bletchley Park every year for the veteran's Enigma Reunion meeting, that's held every September. And we were using social media back in 2009, 2010. Our idea was to capture as many memories as possible from the people that worked there. We interviewed many veterans, and it was quite interesting actually how many people just wouldn't talk about it at all.

I mean they just said I came here as an eighteen-year-old. I signed the Official Secrets Act. I'm just never going to tell anyone. So not lots of stories – and you can under-stand why. They've kept it all secret for such a long time from when they were teenagers. So how would they then as an eight-eight-year-old woman suddenly think it's ok to talk about it? Lots of them won't talk about what happened with good reason.

The sense that I got was they didn't talk to each other at work unless it was something that they had to talk about at work. They weren't allowed to talk about what they were doing. They didn't talk about what they were doing to anybody at any point. And so, for some of the women that was fine because they were billeted out, living at a stately home down the road. So lots of them were there together so they could get up to all sorts of things and go – they'd go into London for dances because the train is only thirty-five minutes into London. One of them talked about how they saw – was it the king? Yeah, it must have been the king I guess or Princess Elizabeth as she would have been then walking through the streets in London during the war. It was a very different time.

I think they had quite an exciting time if they were living with others in a group. But I think the other end of it was that some women would be billeted out on their own with a family. A lot of the people that worked there were on their own living with a family in the village in Bletchley. They couldn't talk to anyone at work about what they were doing. And of course, when you went back you couldn't talk to anyone about what you were doing. And the people in the local area didn't actually know what people were doing.

They had no clue it was code-breaking at all. I don't think. I think they just thought – I'm sure they called it like the looney bin or something. Yeah. They didn't quite know what was going on. And had a very sort of negative feel to it. I think they thought maybe they were cowards– the men should have been fighting at war and that kind of thing. I think some of the women had a very difficult time. Of the people that I met no one actually said that anyone committed suicide but they kind of alluded to the fact that some people couldn't cope with it and kind of went mad and stuff like that.

Because you can imagine you're an eighteen-year-old girl away from home for the first time. You're working on stuff which you can only just talk to the person next to you in a very operational way. No real chatting. You might go to get your lunch or whatever and might have a conversation but you can't talk about anything that you're doing at work. Then you go home to the family who kind of probably treat you with some suspicion because they don't know what you're doing. And then if they ask you, you can't tell them anything about what you're doing. I think it's like, "the best of times and the worst of times" depending on who you were and what you were doing, but it's a very mixed bag I guess.

And I think we'll never really know because most of the people have died now. There's some people still left around but lots of them don't really want to talk about it. It's like one of those periods in history where – like with me wanting to capture memories of the women that work there. I knew that we weren't going to get everything of course like the whole story which I think we're aware of really. But I just wanted to have some idea of what some of the women were doing and what their time there was like. Yeah. I mean it's kind of sad but at the same time it had to be like that for it to work I suppose.

Carol Frieze: You definitely raised awareness of the women that were there because so many didn't realize that.

Sue Black: Yeah, yeah. That's good.

Carol Frieze: It's important that it was you I think that did this because it could have been told in a different way.

Sue Black: True. Yeah. I guess so.

Jeria Quesenberry: We're just about out of time. We have one last question to ask. How has the work of Bletchley Park, both the book and everything that you've done, how has this changed your life?

Sue Black: I guess it's helped me to be more *me* if that makes sense. So like I was a computer science academic. I was doing stuff around women in technology. But I really am interested in social history. I'm really interested in the history of computing. I'm interested in the whole women's empowerment. And I'm not just – I love technology and computer science – but I'm not just a computer scientist and that's it.

I think it's enabled me to be more of a rounded person in my career I guess. So rather than just being someone who teaches and does research in computing and software engineering, because I ran the campaign people know me because of that. So it really helped me – I feel like social media changed my life as well as just the campaign because it connected me with so many people. I've probably met more than two hundred people first on Twitter and then second in real life.

And so, the social media aspect has really helped me connect with lots of people that aren't necessarily in computing but could be in any area who were early adopters on Twitter. And opportunities have come out of that I guess with connections that I've made. It's definitely enriched my life a lot.

Writing the book, I think, has led me to feel more confident. Because I didn't really know if I could write a book or not. So the fact I've done that, that's good. And it's led me into the book that I'm writing now. Penguin approached me after reading the book asking me to write a book for them. I guess it led to lots of different types of opportunities and really helped me to be more of my I guess kind of authentic self at work and just in life in general for it to be – all the stuff I do at work now, I love all of it. And it's not all specifically computer science. There's lots of things around it. It's enabled me to create I think a career which is what I wanted to be rather than just something that someone else defined.

Carol Frieze: What's your new book going to be about?

Sue Black: It's about coding. Penguin asked me to write *The Pelican Guide to Coding*. So it's like what is coding, how does it fit in with the world. I mean for me it's like showing why software is so important basically in our lives in so many different ways. It's kind of like my aim with the book to help get people on board who know that software is out there but don't quite see it. Because of course it's in almost everything around us but you don't actually see it in front of your face so I think a lot of people just don't realize. It's like banging the drum as an evangelist for software and the people that create it.

Jeria Quesenberry:	I can't wait to read it. It sounds wonderful.
Sue Black:	I've got to finish it.
Carol Frieze:	That's great, Sue. We really appreciate your time.
Sue Black:	No. Thank you. Thank you.

DISCUSSION QUESTIONS

1. How might Dr. Sue Black's story inspire other women to enter the computing field?
2. Why are there so few women in computing in the United Kingdom?
3. Why did Dr. Sue Black establish #techmums?
4. What are the positive impacts of #techmums?
5. How could the #techmums model be replicated in other contexts or cultures?
6. What role did Bletchley Park play in World War II?
7. Why is it important to share the story of female code breakers at Bletchley Park?
8. How did Dr. Sue Black use social media to save Bletchley Park?

References

Higher Education Statistics Agency (HESA). (2018). "Higher Education Student Statistics: UK, 2016/17 – Student numbers and characterisrics." Retrieved April 16, 2019, from www.hesa.ac.uk/news/11-01-2018/sfr247-higher-education-student-statistics/numbers.

11

An Overview of the Swedish Educational System with a Focus on Women in Computer Science

Looking Back to Learn for the Future

Sinna Lindquist and Ingrid Melinder

INTRODUCTION

Sweden is one of the most equal countries in the world and has been for several years (World Economic Forum, 2017; Swedish Institute, 2018). The ranking shows equality on a societal level, but in certain areas gender imbalance persists, for example, in education (Statistics Sweden, 2016). Education in Sweden, including postsecondary education, is free of charge for citizens of the European Union. Government financial contributions and favorable student loans are offered, as long as the study progress is satisfactory. Acceptance to study programs is based on grades from previous education, and in educational programs where practical skills are of importance such as art, design, and music, acceptance is also based on assessment of ability.

All educational programs strive to attract the most interested and capable students, obviously independently of gender and ethnicity. Girls perform better than boys in school in general (Swedish Secretariat for Gender Research, 2018), hence the number of women studying on university level exceeds the number of men. The question then is, Why it is still so difficult to attract women to, for example, computer science? Clearly, to change this gender imbalance, more needs to be in place than general gender equality and economic possibilities.

Since the shift from a centralized educational system during the 1990s in Sweden, where "the state took a great responsibility for educational outcomes in terms of the relationship between upper secondary education and higher education and the labour market" (Lund, 2008, p. 646), to a more decentralised system with more private alternatives, there is research on the reasons behind students' educational choices. On a general level students' choices depend on aspects such as parents' background and educational status and cultural preferences (cultural capital), and the specifics of those aspects (e.g., Broady, 2000; Börjesson et al., 2016). "Today, educational outcome is very much an individual responsibility," as concluded by Lund (2008, p. 646).

This chapter looks at the Swedish education system and the study preconditions, computer science in general, and the Royal Institute of Technology (KTH) in Stockholm in particular. Founded in 1827, KTH is the oldest and largest technical teaching and research university in Sweden (KTH, 2018a) with more than 13,000 full-time students, 33% of which are women. The figures from 2016 show the average gender balance through-out the education system, except on the professors' level, where only 15% are women out of the 310 chairs. (KTH, 2018b). As the largest technical university, it is important that KTH take a leading role in gender equality development in this field.

To provide specifics, we present experiences from six women who have found their way to KTH and computer science or closely related fields. The representation of different generations and experiences may reflect how things have changed, or not changed, over time. More specifically, issues such as dreams and ideas of what to become, plans for the future, decisions on education and the way ahead, expectations from relatives and society, treatment and support at the university, importance of relations and role models, and suggestions on what could be changed for the better will be discussed to shed light on the matter.

THE SWEDISH EDUCATIONAL SYSTEM: FACTS AND FIGURES

A short background on the Swedish educational system will show the development over the years of the opportunities for both men and women to study first at elementary school and currently at the university level. Still, engineering programs, especially computer science and IT, see few women applying despite the fact that women generally have higher grades than men (Swedish Secretariat for Gender Research, 2018). The gender imbalance was natural when engineering careers were generally thought unfit for women. In 1921, the same year that women in Sweden won the right to vote in general elections, KTH enrollment was opened to women. Seven years later the first woman graduated after four years' study. That was about a hundred years ago. The attitude toward women as engineers has changed dramatically since then. But the gender balance improves ever so slowly, although nowadays most businesses in these areas welcome women.

Elementary School and Upper Secondary Education

The law on general public education of girls and boys was passed on June 18, 1842, and was established in all of Sweden in 1850. In some small towns junior schools were set up even in the absence of qualified teachers. Before that, by a decree from 1726, the parson was required to hold "house hearings," to record reading abilities and knowledge of scripture of all residents in the homesteads.

The compulsory school was initially six years, extended in 1936 to seven years and in the early 1950s to eight years. In 1959 the nine-year school was introduced, becoming the current elementary school in 1962. Only 5% of the 1950s cohort graduated from upper secondary school. In the 1960s, the proportion rose to 10%, and a decade later to 30%. Today it is 80–85% that graduate.

University and Postgraduate Education

There is a coordinated admissions system to all university studies, that is, one standardized application for courses and programs at all universities in Sweden. Selection of university applicants is also centralized, based particularly on upper secondary school grades. Ties between equally qualified candidates are decided by ballot. That is sometimes problematic since it precludes using underrepresented gender as a criterion. Applicants seem to find this lottery a fairer method than using specific imbalances, such as gender imbalance, as a criterion.

Since 1977, the majority of students are women, but the proportion varies significantly between study programs. Computer science has very few female students, as illustrated by the figures below. In 2016–2017, 86,000 new students entered universities, 57% of which were female. A total of 400,000 students were enrolled, some 60% female. The national goal that 50% of a cohort should enroll in post-upper secondary school education is not yet fulfilled, but by the age of twenty-five, 44% have been or are enrolled.

Sweden recognizes two levels of postgraduate degrees: PhD, which is four years of research studies, and Licentiate, which is two years of

(a)

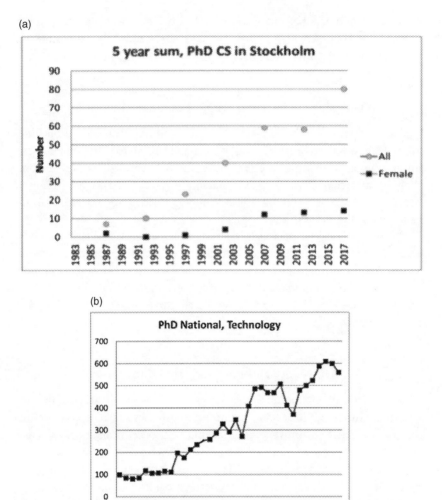

(b)

Figure 11.1 The total number of PhD degrees obtained in computer science and the percentage obtained by women.

research studies. The focus here is on doctoral degrees. Figure 11.1 is testimony to the national goal, that in a decade from the early 1990s there are double the annual number of PhD degrees. Here computer science includes numerical analysis and, since the year 1998, human–computer interaction (HCI). It is notable that the numbers of female doctors grow with the subject HCI.

(c)

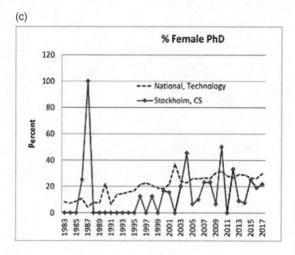

Figure 11.1 (*cont.*)

Figure 11.1a shows the total number of PhD degrees obtained in computer science in Stockholm, and on national level the total number of PhD degrees obtained in technology (Figure 11.1b) and the percentage by women (Figure 11.1c). Since the number of PhDs in computer science is so low, we present the result as the sum of five years. The official statistics are available only aggregated for the technologies area (SCB, 2018) for doctoral degrees in the years 1973–2017. The statistics for computer science in Stockholm have been compiled by the authors from tables in department reports and official lists.

COMPUTER SCIENCE AT KTH AND STOCKHOLM UNIVERSITY

Programming was initially taught in numerical analysis, an offshoot of mathematics in 1963. The first professor was Germund Dahlquist, a pioneer in the Swedish development of computers. He established the inclusive culture at the department and engaged a fair number of female teachers.

Computer science became a separate subject in 1983 with its first professor in the numerical analysis and computer science department (NADA) serving both KTH and Stockholm University. KTH established the engineering program in computer science in the same year. Most of the

(a)

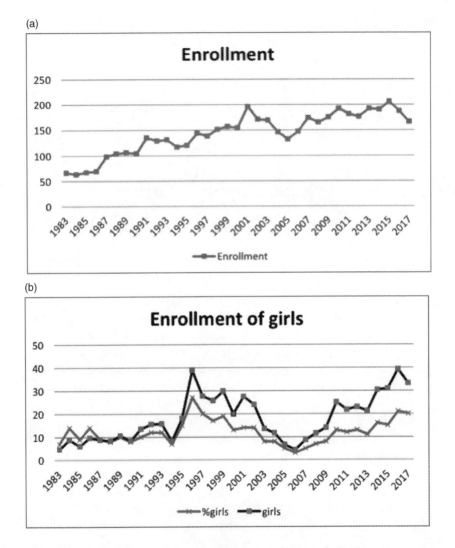

Figure 11.2 Total enrollment (a) and number and percentage of girls (b) in computer science at KTH.

faculty had backgrounds in engineering physics at KTH or numerical analysis at Stockholm University.

Only a few female students applied to the computer science program. Girls on average had – and have – better grades than boys (Swedish Secretariat for Gender Research, 2018). A determined recruitment effort saw the average growth from 8% to about 25% among the enrolled students, so that women's representation rose from four to forty in the year 1996. A few years after the IT dot-com crash, the female enrollment dropped again to a handful. When the number of enrolled students grew to 200, the grades of the last accepted student cohort fell noticeably. Then girls with high grades chose not to apply, which was interpreted as that they want a return on their hard-earned high grades. They want to join a program requiring high grades, and that would lead to a job perceived to help mankind and make the world a better place. The Dean at the School of Computer Science and Communication at KTH developed a tradition to talk to the female entrants about their background and experience, to get a deeper understanding of aspects that made them apply for an education in computer science. Unexpectedly, a common experience was that they were dissuaded from engineering careers, especially in IT or computer science, by school counselors. Anecdotally, female students commonly received comments like "Do you really think you are up to it?" from their counselors. Much has been done to promote a clearer picture of the value of studies in computer science and it seems that the negative trend has been broken and the number of women students have risen again, but it is far from balanced.

Figure 11.2 shows the entrants to the five-year engineering program in computer science at KTH, the total number (Figure 11.2a) and the number and the percentage of girls (Figure 11.2b). The share of the accepted girls is about the same as the share of the applicants. The summary has been done by the authors from tables in KTH yearly reports.

INTERVIEWS WITH WOMEN FROM DIFFERENT EPOCHS IN COMPUTER SCIENCE AND TECHNOLOGY

We interviewed six women from different epochs of the fast-moving computer science era. The focus has been on their personal upbringing and background, education and career, friendship, and role models, spiced with anecdotes from their lives. Based on their experiences, they have come up with thoughts and suggestions on what society in general needs to address to make a shift to gender neutrality in science and technology. And, more specifically, suggestions are provided on what needs to change to attract more women to computer science university educations. The presentations have been edited to highlight the diversity of aspects in the personal stories.

Listen to Learn and Make a Difference

Ingrid, PhD, numerical analysis, Stockholm University, 1979

Ingrid Melinder's grandfather's cousin was Hjalmar Strömer, who lived in the second half of the nineteenth century. Due to bad health he was a goat-herder instead of a lumberjack. At the age of seventeen he was invited by the pastor to study at the nearest village, and a year later was a teacher at the local school. He then walked some 200 miles to the nearest university to study natural science and at the same time to become a pastor. He admired his mother, who had taught him a lot and encouraged him to study astronomy. Convinced of men's and women's equal intellectual abilities, he even did experiments on the weight of brains of human beings and monkeys. The heaviest brain, from what must have been the most intelligent person, belonged to a woman. Hjalmar Strömer also taught in the first college for women in Sweden. In 1878 he said, "*Att hyllningen för qvinnan inte skulle bestå I vackra ord utan i detta att giva qvinnan vad henne tillkommer: mänskliga fri- och rättigheter*" (The tribute to the woman should not consist in nice words but to give her what belongs to her: human freedom and rights) (attributed to Rössborn). Strömer also stressed the importance of universal literacy for everyone to form her own opinion, and not to have to trust some local authority like the pastor ("*Undervisningen uteslutande från predikstolen ... i stället för upplysande*"). He, indeed, was a pioneer and among other things contributed to make it easier for women to study at high level.

Ingrid was born just about one hundred years after Hjalmar Strömer: "I had the opportunity to study at the university and even graduate as a PhD in Numerical Analysis, the very first PhD in the families of both my mother and father. That was possible because of the generous financing system in Sweden.... My father had a modest salary and my mother took care of the seven children." She continues: "From early years my plan was to become a physical training instructor, but the required grades to the program were too high.... My next plan was to become a veterinarian. I wanted to cure big animals like cows and horses. But the beer culture at the university was not for me, and very likely I would have ended up as a food researcher."

Unknown to all but the most initiated in the mid-sixties, programming was becoming a profession. It was taught in a branch of the mathematics program at the university, so Ingrid enrolled there. "I became very excited at an introduction seminar in numerical analysis about how easy it was to solve complex equations with an electronic computer using linear approximation and iteration." After only one year of studies in numerical analysis, she was asked to become a teacher assistant. That was the start of her academic career: "I completed the PhD on my spare time, met my husband at the department, and gave birth to three children. Then, at an age of 38, it was time for me to be more involved in the department."

That year she became head of the department, which was growing very rapidly. Soon the leadership took most of her time and concentration, so she dropped her own research. After twenty-five years as department head, Ingrid became dean of the School of Computer Science and Communications with 1,500 program students, 15,000 course students, 100 PhD students, and 330 employees.

Ingrid had the first Swedish professor in numerical analysis, Germund Dahlquist, as PhD advisor and later he hired her. He was a true humanist and his personality promoted a very friendly atmosphere at the department; he hired several women, so Ingrid always felt welcome and respected during the years. Ingrid reflects:

> In my position I came to listen to students and staff and heard many stories which gave invaluable insight. Not everyone felt respected and things had to be changed. We configured groups with students and faculty members to address issues in a way that I thought was successful. Nevertheless, as the department grew, there were students and employees who felt uncomfortable. For example, a much larger proportion of the female than male PhD students had unsatisfactory contact with and support from their advisors. We dealt with that at school and university level by educating the advisors, configuring advisor groups, and informing the students about their rights.

KTH policy is to encourage staff to retire at age sixty-five, so Ingrid did: "Since I retired in 2011, there is little interest in my experience and my influence has been marginal."

Searching for Challenges

Marie, MSc, computer science and technology, KTH, 1987

Marie Persson Björkman has since graduation been active in companies with focus on IT, multimedia, digital services, and related areas. She was Technical Attaché at the Swedish Office, Silicon Valley, San Francisco. In the last ten years Marie has founded and led as CEO the companies Movinto Fun AB, Six Feet Up AB, and Gobrilla Development AB. She has complemented her education in computer science with management, law, and leadership and is leveraging her long experience as business development consultant; she also serves as a board member in a variety of organizations and corporations.

Marie was one of the four women and fifty-six men in the new computer science and technology program 1983, the first new program at KTH in fifty years. She recalls:

Computer science and technology was in its infancy, [which was] one of the reasons why I chose the program at KTH which was brand new and explorative with all of the consequential pros and cons. Being in the first pilot group of computer science and technology students gave us the opportunity to participate in the actual design of the academic field itself.

Marie also highlights the importance of the commitment and support from the man behind the new program, Yngve Sundblad, one of the pioneers in computer science in Sweden. Also, the fact that KTH management strongly supported the program meant a lot: "We were in the spotlight to study new courses in new or different contents and formats. It matched my entrepreneurial soul and gave me strength to follow my own compass after my student years."

But at the time, the perspective of computer science and technology was narrow, partly because the field was new, and partly because it was hijacked by geeks among students and professors. There were no female role models at all, and few or no links between computer science and business areas other than technology companies.

That is still problematic. Universities ... do not stress the opportunities for technology and engineering enough towards other industries – in fashion, design, or healthcare for example.

Universities and companies are in the governance of men, which ...
means that we will not, as a society, gain all the advantages that
computer science could bring.... We need to broaden the
expectations of what computer science and technology embraces
and ... apply it to areas where women traditionally take interest and
work: educational solutions, support for gardening applications,
robot support for caring for the elderly, and so forth. With a more
shared and communicated approach of the field in combination with
common knowledge in the society, I hope for greater interest in
terms of women student recruitments. However, role models,
mentors, and networks as well as support from other women are
essential.

But career paths for women are not straight, nor is the playing field
level:

I'm glad that searching for challenges is a personal drive of mine,
otherwise I would have been more hurt from hitting and breaking
through glass ceilings during my working life. The first experience of
exclusion hit my self-confidence hard when a male colleague was
appointed CEO of my business area. I had in a few years built,
recruited, and developed a profitable business of e-learning and web
solutions, areas that the colleague did not master at all. His
appointment was incredibly surprising for most, not least for me.

I spent a couple of years in the industry before I realized the
structural pattern and understood how to fight it. The organizational
structures are shaped by men to support men. I expect that students
today get insight of these gender disadvantages during their
education. There are tools and methods to be learned and sisterhoods
to be built, for us to become stronger and more favorable in the
wonderful business of technology.

What has strengthened Marie in her career is that she actively sought
out and met with mentors, both men and women. In the same spirit, she
has always coached women:

The single most important thing is to build your own professional
network. We women are skilled at social networking around children
and family, but we do not use that ability in our professions. Today

it's my mission to support women to start using that superpower in their professional life, too.

Still after all the years in the computer science and technology business, my fascination is endless, and even stronger today – it's about the power and opportunity of the future. Which is both encouraging and challenging: both men and women are required to face and overcome the challenges.

Inspiration Can Vary

Danica, PhD, computer science, KTH, 2001

Danica Kragic Jensfelt is a professor at the School of Electrical Engineering and Computer Science at KTH, and the Director of the Centre for Autonomous Systems. Her research is in the area of robotics, computer vision, and machine learning. She holds an MSc in mechanical engineering from the Technical University of Rijeka, Croatia, in 1995, and a PhD in computer science from KTH, in 2001. As she relates:

Born and raised in Croatia with both parents working full time, I spent a lot of time with my grandmother who was a seamstress. She, and her customers, would talk to me as to a grown-up, wanting to know my opinion in different sometimes quite difficult matters. My parents did not make any specific demands on me. They would ask how school was but not "force" me to do homework and such. Instead, I learned that when I did something good, everyone was happy. I felt great freedom and confirmation, but sometimes I think . . . my childhood was too short.

To think and to work with one's hands is important and fosters creativity. "I would spend a lot of time at home, doing my homework, reading, watching TV documentaries or sewing. My mother always did something with her hands so I did too." She still designs and sews much of her *garderobe* (wardrobe).

Elementary school was a mixed experience:

I did not like school much because of the impersonal and harsh ambience. Teachers would call you by your last name, grades announced in front of the whole class, bullying children. But I had a very good math teacher. She would give me challenging tasks and really see me. I was good at math, and so the teacher sent me to a math competition. I really liked that: I always want to be the best!

Upper secondary school and university curricula were broad, with math, programming, mechanics, construction, and computer science including artificial intelligence and robotics, developing skills in solving theoretical as well as practical problems.

Danica was interested in microbiology, but eventually decided to do a master's in mechanical engineering, despite being advised not to because there were so few women there. The male dominance was indeed strong. Only two teachers were women, and as one of three women in class, Danica would stand out. She worked part-time as a model and wore "different" clothes. The teachers could be condescending and sexist. "'This theorem was discovered by a woman . . . you can imagine what she looked like,' chuckle chuckle, with me sitting in the front row. Teachers were . . . as they were . . . I also had to work harder than the boys to be accepted." But she was appreciated by classmates: "I was one of the three best students in class; the three of us became friends and we still are."

The university studies took most of her time. Danica quit the modeling job, deciding that finishing in time was more important than getting the highest grades. She managed both, and won a scholarship that would pay for books and board.

During summers she would do industry internships, which helped her decide what type of work she wanted. Also, through a student exchange organization, she experienced other cultures:

After graduation I traveled to Sweden with my boyfriend for his internship and then the plan was to go to Finland for mine. But he got a job and we decided to stay in Sweden. I started work as a paid housekeeper, and decided to learn Swedish and get to know the Swedish society by traveling the Stockholm subway.

She enrolled as a PhD student at the Center for Autonomous Systems in 1996. The supervisors were all men. The beginning was tough, with long hours, unclear expectations from supervisors, coping with being alone with no one to discuss research and life with, while trying to understand what PhD studies were all about: "I cried every night for six months! I was the only woman, I was the only foreigner, everyone else knew each other from previous studies at KTH, and they all came from well-off families. I just felt stupid."

After her first published article, it all fell into place. Today, Danica is a full professor, supervising PhD students from all over the world. She is a person anyone can talk to, about almost anything. It is very important to coach students in their careers, to think about if taking a post-doc in the academic field is the way to proceed or to work in industry. They need to understand the importance of sharing and networking.

Danica stresses that the "outreach" and promotion of science to the general public must be taken more seriously by academia. She herself appears on radio and TV shows and at Nobel Prize festivities as the knowledgeable researcher she is, although, she admits, "It is not acknowledged and you do not gain any academic merits from it."

Still finding time to sew, Danica appears on such occasions in designs of her own: "I believe it is important because that shows the variety in people. All these different things that I do are inspiring to me, and hopefully also to others."

Education Is Not Necessarily a Straight Path

Lindquist Sinna, PhD, human–computer interaction, KTH, 2007

Sinna Lindquist is a senior research position at FOI – Swedish Defence Research Agency, the department for Defence and Security, Systems and Technology, Decision Support Systems Unit, and at the Swedish Air Force Combat Simulation Centre.

I have always known that I would study at the university. My father . . ., a professor in cultural geography, would bring me along, even as a three-year-old, on excavations with his university students. When playing with my Lego, I would build churches and not houses. I liked sitting in my father's library reading or drawing.

My main driving force in life was to "have fun," meaning that I liked to learn new things, meet new people and get to know new contexts. . . . At some point I wanted to be a restorer and worked as an apprentice preserving polychrome wood.

The importance of a proper education was passed on to her, and Sinna took courses in subjects such as archaeology, ethnology, and the history of arts. "Alongside my university studies I took several classes in art which was my main interest in life and perhaps still is."

But it was hard to find a job to suit her qualifications and ambitions:

> In the 1992 economic crisis in Sweden, I gave birth to my first child and had no "proper" work, despite all university courses and a bachelor of arts in archaeology. The Swedish educational economic system offered expedient loans ... so I went to the university a second round to "upgrade." I have always liked huge heavy things like bridges and oversized mine trucks and thought that engineering might be fun.

At the time, most computer programs and applications were extremely poorly designed, with triple negations in error messages, no auto save in fill-in forms, etc. Sinna saw that her skills and broad education could make a difference: "If they had just asked someone with knowledge about people and not only programmers, a person like me," she thought.

A multidisciplinary project course in user-centered software development at KTH was just opening. Students from different universities and from psychology, computer science, media, design and anthropology were working together to do design for a specific group, using cooperative and participatory design methods. In the course, Sinna found use for knowledge and experience gained from previous studies: human–computer interaction would be her field.

For a student with a background in the humanities, KTH was an alien workplace. She even lectured on the topic "What does an ethnologist do at KTH?", and the answer was to work as a researching ethnographer in different projects. Other things were more troubling: "My salary was about half of an engineer's. Was it because my major was in the humanities and 'cultural studies' and not in some technical subject matter?"

PhD study was initially a rocky road, partly because of technical difficulties in getting credits for her undergraduate courses: anthropology or human factors would serve, but how were her ethnology courses related to that?

The projects were not necessarily in line with her research questions but rather with her academic profile: "I was 'tossed' into any project needing user studies and cooperative design methods."

Sinna needed to learn how to program, to speak with programmers in programmers' language. But she was told by a professor that she was too old (!): "to be a good programmer you have to start at a young age." This did not stop her for long, and the "Java for dummies" programming course broke the spell.

Sometimes life is unpredictable, and in 2011 she started work as a senior researcher at the Swedish Defence Research Agency in projects regarding decision support systems. "Today I work at the Swedish Air Force Combat Simulation Center with development of fighter pilot training in national and international projects." She finds this delightful since her teenage dream was to become a fighter pilot.

Inspired by Making a Difference

Meidi, MSc, computer science and technology, KTH, 2014

Meidi Runefelt Tönisson has been working as a software engineer in a few different fields, primarily focusing on mobile application development. She is currently employed as a software engineer at Doctrin, a Swedish e-health startup company: "I grew up in a tech savvy family.... Typing on the computer made it fun and easy for me to express myself as I learned to read and write. In other words: computers have been familiar and ubiquitous to me as far back as I can remember."

Even though Meidi pretty much grew up in front of a computer screen, she didn't even consider a career in computer technology, but "strongly identified with the social sciences and the arts, which I felt conflicted with my interest in technology."

Keen on learning new things but easily tiring of old interests led her to linguistics and film theory. After a few years of various university courses and odd jobs, she took a preparatory year of natural sciences classes, thinking that she might find something exciting in the world of "hard science." "At some point during this time, I came upon a pamphlet for a new master's degree program in computer science being offered at KTH – one with the possibility to add French to the syllabus." It showed that "merging of 'soft' and 'hard' science interests would indeed be possible. I sent in the application, and didn't really know what to expect."

Expectations of very few women enrolling in the program were correct – there turned out to be 13 out of 180. But thoughts "that the people . . . would be dry, anti-social and generally severely lacking in life skills" were wrong – she did meet many interesting people. And programming was unexpectedly creative: "Learning the tools to construct something out of nothing more than my own thoughts and ideas was exhilarating."

Being one of very few women "had the quite strange side effect of [me] quickly becoming a familiar face to almost everyone in the program – on good days it felt like being a celebrity, on bad days it felt like being a zoo animal."

The environment had other effects: "a sense of obvious belonging through my other female classmates" did not materialize. Instead, "I found myself having absorbed so many of the implicit stereotypes that surrounded me that I would subconsciously expect female classmates to be bad at programming." The conclusion was that she also, being a woman, must lack in programming skills.

This feeling of professional non-belonging is often called *imposterism*, and it added an extra layer of anxiety to every intellectual performance, since she was representing herself as not only a programmer and computer science major, but also a *woman*.

This feeling is still to be fought off "five years after graduating from university. I've spent those five years working full-time as a software engineer at a few different companies, and done quite well the entire time, but I can still find myself seriously doubting my own skills from time to time . . . 'maybe I'm just not meant to do this,'"

With professional achievements, she now is able to take a more realistic view of her performance: "Maybe I'm not the best software engineer in the entire world – so what? Not everyone can be! That doesn't mean I'm not good at what I do. I think that many people, minorities especially, fall into the trap of thinking they need to be absolutely perfect in order to be any good at all."

The motivation for Meidi is the delight that her craft – programming – brings her, but not only that.

The ability to make a difference is also something I've found to be an incredible source of inspiration.... Being able to use what I've learned in order to build something that could potentially help millions of people is something that kind of amazes me.... This is what ultimately brought me into medtech, after having spent a few years as an app developer.... Having not only the immediate sense of satisfaction that software craftsmanship gives me but also a deep sense of purpose is incredibly fulfilling.

Computer Science Is Relevant to Everyone

Hanna, MSc, machine learning, KTH, 2016

Hanna is a research engineer at FOI, Swedish Defence Research Agency, and she exemplifies the female engineer who chose and pursued a career seemingly unaffected by gender issues or glass ceilings: "I have to admit that the gender imbalance issue is not one I have been contemplating a lot over the years, probably due to the fact that it has never really troubled me on a personal level.... Women (or girls) being in minority has been the reality for me since secondary school, and not surprisingly still is where I work today. On a personal level I have never had a problem with this, but from a societal perspective it is obvious there is much room for improvement."

From a family of engineers, her educational journey led straight to an MSc in machine learning, with no detours or false starts: "I have never felt pressured by anyone around me to follow a certain path in terms of education, the decisions have been mine alone.... A couple years after graduating and now looking back at this string of decisions, there is not one of them I wish I would have done differently."

To Hanna, the field of engineering and technology was a given in her choice of career, and applicability swung the balance toward computer science. She chose not to enter academia, instead going into research and development somewhat closer to industrial applications, and joined the Swedish Defence Research Agency straight after graduation. "The applicability perspective is certainly something that appeals to and interests me."

The gender imbalance at the government agency is less pronounced on managerial levels than in typical tech companies, in part due to stronger influence of national goals for gender equality:

I do what I do at work because of the competence that I have. As far as I know, the fact that I am a woman does not come into that equation at all. And frankly speaking I would expect nothing less.... In my view gender equality means equal opportunity, which may or may not result in equal numbers.

When reflecting on the ways and means of improving gender equality over time, her perspective is that to some extent the problem will solve itself – in the long run" "a generation from now a lot more young girls are going to have a mother or an aunt or even a grandmother who does computer science."

One key to spurring girls' interest in computer technology, as interpreted also from interviews with high-schoolers and undergraduates in universities, is the application to real-life issues: "Obviously technology is big part of everyone's life today, much more so than a few decades ago. It makes computer science relevant to everyone, girls included."

Summary

To summarize, these stories illustrate many different experiences and driving forces with impact on education and career path choices. The educational system and government economic support constitutes a base for making these choices, but societal and cultural trends and ideas on gender equality have most certainly had impact too. Still, as was to be expected, individual stories as concrete examples cast light on the interplay of this background with upbringing, family traditions, and not least personal characteristics.

KTH STUDIES: INVESTIGATING WOMEN IN COMPUTER SCIENCE IN SWEDEN

KTH has conducted several quantitative and qualitative inquiries to get a deeper knowledge concerning girls' and young women's thinking of university studies and future careers. Below we will present parts of the results from investigations during the three years 2012 (Good, 2012), 2014 (KTH, 2014), and 2017 (Brännström, 2017).

The decisions of senior upper secondary school women students about future studies and career choices are heavily, but not necessarily consciously, influenced by expectations from family, friends, and established standards. They chose a technical or natural science upper secondary school program because it is broad and keeps many doors open. One reason for not applying to computer science programs is their insufficient knowledge about the programs. Still, they know that an engineering program will give many opportunities and high-quality jobs. Consequently, during the interviews the students become more curious in such programs when they realize that they can get the career they are looking for. They also become more interested when they understand that women are in great demand in most branches. It seems that the male dominance does not discourage their program applications. They are convinced that the gender imbalance will change in the near future.

The quantitative questionnaires to second-year upper secondary school students of all genders in the natural science programs show little gender difference. But the interviews reveal that girls seem more worried about choosing the "wrong" university education. Boys have a clearer picture of their future careers. The most important factors are that the work should be fun, highly paid, and meaningful, with a comfortable working environment and a good balance between work and privacy. Personal interest and the reputation of the university, including the quality of the teachers and the student environment, are also important factors in the search for the "right" university. About 95% of students plan to apply to a university. Females are more interested in natural sciences, especially biology and medicine; men more in technical sciences. Only about a third have a good idea about what an engineer is doing, but among women only one-fourth. Reasons listed for not applying to KTH specifically are that very high grades are thought necessary, that it is difficult to find a living place, and that KTH students are considered snobbish.

A big city problem, for Stockholm and Gothenburg in particular, is the scarcity of student apartments or rooms. In general there are very few dormitories at campus and the mobility in Sweden is low, which makes it more difficult to find an apartment. In Stockholm, many students choose to stay with their parents and therefore to study at a university nearby. Students are also looking for universities offering exciting environments in the city and on campus. They value a variety of activities and find it important to meet and talk to current students before they make their choice.

Student Suggestions

Many reasons why women are not choosing computer science have been the same for years. Although there have been several attempts to show the value of computer science to society at large, the KTH inquiries included questions regarding suggestions on how to change the gender imbalance. A summary of suggestions is presented here.

Suggestions that information about computer science programs should be more focused on the interest of girls and women have been raised. It means that there are certain areas where computer science is important and has impact, but is not covered in the course description. Further, there should be an honest and reliable description of the course content, as well as curriculum and study forms with examples from students' personal perspectives and of possible careers. In addition, computer science would benefit from new and illustrative ways of informing and presenting the subject matter, perhaps using computer science (e.g., animation and AI) to show its importance and expanse.

The common image of what people in computer science business actually do has to better reflect reality. The work is imagined as monotone, forcing employees to sit in front of the laptop all day long, in a factory-like environment with computers and cords everywhere. Hence, professionals showing new perspectives on computer science from practical experiences to pupils at elementary and upper secondary school may affect their choice of a future career. The students consider themselves intelligent, creative, ambitious, and determined and want an interesting and engaging job. Knowledge about the university computer science programs awakens curiosity and raises interest.

ACTIVITIES TO RAISE AWARENESS

There is an ongoing development on where and how to find information about study programs. On social media, administered from the university or individually, students tell their stories of and answer questions about the programs, environment, and social life. Further, in a complementary project, upper secondary school pupils are invited to KTH to follow a student around for a day. Student ambassadors also visit classes at upper secondary schools to share information about educational programs and university life.

The Tekla festival (Tekla, 2018) was organized after the music artist Robyn was awarded KTH's Great Prize in 2013. The festival was a two-day event in 2015 where 200 girls, aged 11–15, attended (Kreps, 2015). Robyn wanted to use the platform to inspire girls who might be intrigued about technology. The participants took part in workshops and lectures with samples from different areas of future technology in a fun and imaginative environment featuring robotics, music lab, scratch, and CAD. Robyn attended and also gave a performance. Due to the festival's popularity, attendance has doubled, and now the organization is trying to invite an even larger number.

The House of Science in Stockholm is for students of all ages from primary school to gymnasium/high school levels as well as their teachers. There are natural science and engineering students who will gladly guide them through various activities. A few years ago the focus broadened and now includes math and IT. School classes of all levels visits the lab for a day and do some experiments together with PhD students (KTH, 2018d).

The campaign "GIANTS" has been developed in collaboration between students, teachers, researchers, and professional communicators at KTH. The slogan is "The future needs GIANTS," and the campaign aims to attract more females to the programs within electrical engineering, computer science, and IT, using role models like Hedy Lamar, Ada Lovelace, and Edith Clarke. The event started with sixty women, and now, after a few years, it attracts 200 (KTH, 2018c).

SUGGESTIONS FOR THE FUTURE

Involve Media. Media, in the broad sense, should appreciate the importance of research and education and report about the results and value with the passion usually reserved for sports and culture. Today, science is given media space when groundbreaking results can be reported or when research has gone wrong or was found to be unethical. One idea is to arrange a conference with the title "Education and Research: The Engine in Society." The idea would be to invite leaders of leading media companies, representatives from universities, and politicians to discuss how media can better inform and report about the value of research and education for the society, not least the influence that IT has on everyone's life. Hopefully it will result in daily reports and eventually open people's eyes, especially the eyes of young people.

Introduce Programming in Elementary School. Young people's digital competence needs to be strengthened, in order for them to understand the world and to influence their environment and future. Hence, from July

2018, programming will be an identifiable compulsory element already in first grade elementary school (Government Offices of Sweden, 2017). Similar changes to curricula have been implemented in many other European countries. The credo is that "computational thinking" is becoming a key intellectual activity necessary for children to get along in a digital world. It is too early to assess the results. Several schools have introduced such elements earlier, and it was found there – in some classes – that girls liked the activities and expressed hope to work with IT.

Broaden the Understanding of What Computer Science and Technology Embraces. Computer science and technology have permeated most areas of industry and society, for example, in hospitals and healthcare, transportation, and education. To fill those areas with skilled people who have knowledge of the importance and impact of computer-based applications, computer science education needs diversity in people, skills, knowledge, and experience. The broad spectrum of what computer science entails and its diverse applications should be seen in the recruiting information material and, just as important, in syllabi and program curricula.

Role Models and Special Events. We believe role models play an important part in shaping people's dreams and goals in life. There is no lack of eminent women in computer science; they are just not recognized enough and visible in media and the public discourse. Depending on the target audience, such individuals could be TED talk speakers, inventors, businesswomen, gamers, bloggers, and YouTubers. Establishment of a role model with a computer science profile is not something that simply can be ordered; it might require a shift in perspective and a different focus. When, for example, an organization is searching for speakers for conferences (or when they are recruiting teachers or business leaders), *they might need to look beyond the easiest and most obvious choice.*

Depending on purpose and scale, special events such as conferences or recruiting events could be targeted specifically to women. On the one hand, such activities give women in the field more opportunities to find role models and be inspired by, or inspire, other women and to connect and share experiences. On the other hand, there is a risk that too much attention on women as a distinct subgroup tends to strengthen the idea of some fundamental difference between men and women in the field. This is part of a dilemma that we face.

Show Variation in Order to Inspire. People have interests besides their professions, and academics are no exception. It is important to show variety, and in computer science business, which deals with all kinds of applications, it is especially important to take advantage of double competence. "The third tasks," where professors and researchers spread their results to a broader audience, is not acknowledged as an academic merit, although it is a demand. Hence, the majority of university teachers and researchers are not showing the broad spectrum of what an academic career might entail, how different skills or interests can give new perspectives on fruitful ideas to teaching and research and, through that, to attract students with "other" genders or backgrounds.

Make Computer Science an Obvious Choice. Computer science (AI, programs, apps, data management, decision support systems, control systems, etc.) plays a role everywhere in society. It is strange, and possibly dangerous, that on a general level in society, in families, and among individuals, there is ignorance regarding computer science as a subject matter. It seems that computer science is for a chosen (nerdy) few. If you are not a computer science person yourself, you do not know what computer science studies entail, what it takes and who is suited to study computer science, and what to do with computer science knowledge.

All citizens should be educated in the subject matter, and the importance of computer science should be common knowledge. And when it comes to bringing more women into tech, make CS an obvious choice: encourage girls and young women at an early age that going into tech is fun, creative, and doable.

CONCLUSION

In principle, everyone in Sweden has the economic possibility to afford university education. The majority of university students today are women. Yet, despite the efforts done by the universities to show the variety of opportunities these subjects entail, there is a continuous struggle to attract women to computer science and information technology.

The stories of the six women illustrate how the educational path is not necessarily straight. Further, the openness of who can be a computer scientist, in society in general, and within schools, and among family and friends in particular, is important. Sadly, the unfair treatment of women at school, university, and work is still to be expected. Unacceptable behavior hinders our efforts to obtain a gender-balanced workforce in technology-centered workplaces. We must not tire in our quest to "make CS an obvious choice" for both men and women.

DISCUSSION QUESTIONS

1. Universities at different countries use various systems in their selection among qualified applicants. For instance, you can use grades from high school, interviews, special tests, or a mix. Reflect on which consequences different systems will have for getting a gender-balanced class. Do you have a suggestion for a special system to achieve such a class?

2. For decades, many activities have been done to attract women to university programs in computer science and in IT to get a better gender balance (read: attract the best students). There are more female students in these programs today, but there is still more that needs to be done to get a gender-balanced education. Reflect on why this is, why things are moving so slow in this direction, and what can be done to change it.

3. In Sweden, women in high school generally perform better than men, in terms of grades. Interview and questionnaire data show that they hesitate to apply to university programs in computer science, because they think the qualification are too high, while men, with generally lower grades, do not hesitate to apply. Reflect on the reasons behind this phenomenon.

References

Börjesson, M., Broady, D., Le Roux, B., Lidegran, I., and Palme, M. (2016). Cultural Capital in the Elite Subfield of Swedish Higher Education. *Poetics*, 56, June, 15–34.

Brännström. (2017). *Inställning till KTH och valet av högskoleutbildning – En kvalitativ undersökning*. Stockholm: KTH (In Swedish).

Broady, D. (ed.). (2000). Skolan under 1990-talet. Sociala förutsättningar och utbildningsstrategier. Rapport till kommittén Välfärdsbokslut (in Swedish). Sociology of Education and Culture, SEC, Reports/Rapporter från Forskningsgruppen för utbildnings- och kultursociologi, No. 27 "The School during the 1990s" (title translation: "Social Preconditions and Education Strategies. Report to the Committee Welfare Closing").

European Institute for Gender Equality. (2017). Gender Equality Index 2017 – Measuring Gender Equality in the European Union 2005–2015. http://eige.europa .eu/rdc/eige-publications/gender-equality-index-2017-measuring-gender-equal ity-european-union-2005-2015-report. Retrieved August 23, 2018.

Good. (2012). Målgruppsundersökning 2012 – Kvinnliga presumtiva studenter.

Government Offices of Sweden. (2017). www.regeringen.se/pressmeddelanden/2017/ 03/starkt-digital-kompetens-i-laroplaner-och-kursplaner/. Retrieved August 23, 2018; in Swedish.

Kreps, Daniel. (2015). Robyn to Host Tekla Festival Encouraging Women in Technology. *RollingStone*, www.rollingstone.com/music/music-news/robyn-to-host-tekla-festival-encouraging-women-in-technology-56783/. Retrieved August 23, 2018.

KTH. (2014). Unga kvinnor om teknisk vidareutbildning – En kvalitativ undersökning november 2014. https://intra.csc.kth.se/polopoly_fs/1.530313!/Ungakvinnortekniskastudier.pdf. Retrieved August 26, 2018; in Swedish.

KTH. (2018a). This Is KTH. www.kth.se/en/om/fakta. Retrieved August 13, 2018.

KTH. (2018b). KTH in Figures. www.kth.se/en/om/fakta/kth-i-siffror-1.3488. Retrieved August 13, 2018.

KTH. (2018c). The Campaign: GIANTS. www.kth.se/profile/gabher/page/the-campaign-giants. Retrieved August 24, 2018.

KTH. (2018d). The House of Science. www.kth.se/en/larande/vh/vetenskapens-hus-1.804301. Retrieved August 26, 2018.

Lund, S. (2008) Choice Paths in the Swedish Upper Secondary Education: A Critical Discourse Analysis of Recent Reforms. *Journal of Education Policy*, 23(6): 633–648.

RAPPORT. (2013, July 1). *Diarienummer V-2013-0466*. Stockholm: KTH (in Swedish).

Rössborn, Sten. (1965), *Nils Hjalmar Strömer 1849–1886, Föreläsare och Samhällskritiker*. Östersund: Bokmalen (in Swedish).

SCB. (2018). Doctoral Degrees in the Years 1973–2017 by Fields of Research and Development of Sex. www.scb.se/en/finding-statistics/search/?query=webb_doktexlsiff_1973-2017.xlsx&lang=en. Retrieved August 16, 2018.

Statistics Sweden. (2016) Women and Men in Sweden 2016. www.scb.se/Statistik/_Publikationer/LE0201_2015B16_BR_X10BR1601ENG.pdf. Retrieved August 10, 2018.

Strömer, Hjalmar. (1885, 1981). *Bedragna och bedragna in Varför hade Hjalmar Strömer så bråttom? Texter i urval*. Föllinge: Nordjemtlandica Förlag (in Swedish).

Swedish Institute. (2018). Sweden and Gender Equality. https://sweden.se/society/sweden-gender-equality/. Retrieved July 17, 2018.

Swedish Secretariat for Gender Research. (2018). www.genus.se/kunskap-om-genus/fordjupning-skola/skolprestationer/. Retrieved September 3, 2018; in Swedish.

Tekla. (2018), www.teklafestival.se/in-english/. Retrieved August 23, 2018.

World Economic Forum. (2017). Global Gender Gap Report 2017. www3.weforum.org/docs/WEF_GGGR_2017.pdf. Retrieved August 10, 2018.

12

Portugal

Perspectives on Women in Computing

Arminda Guerra Lopes

INTRODUCTION

Historically, it is known that women had an important role in computing. History lessons on computer science narrate that women were some of the first software engineers until technology and practices changed the role of women as programmers.

Ada Lovelace is often called the first computer programmer by designing the first computer algorithm in 1843. Hedy Lamarr invented frequency-hopping technology, which was important for the invention of wireless signals. In 1952, Rear Admiral Grace Hopper created one of the world's first compilers. Adele Goldberg was one of the seven programmers that developed Smalltalk in the 1970s, among others (Gurer, 2002; Rolka, 2004). However, technology has been seen as a "thing of men." The majority of names associated with technology are those of men. In the beginning of the 1980s women started to increase their participation in programming. However, the number of women in computing changed at the end of this decade. There are no concrete answers for this situation but there are some events that possibly contributed to it. For example, personal computers began to be used as entertainment through games, which were mostly played by men.

Several countries have been affected by this and efforts have been made to study the contexts and reasons for the imbalance between men and women studying and working in the field. In the academic context I found numerous studies that presented results about salary discrepancy between women and men in computer science professions, disproportionate numbers of women in academic computer science and in the computer industry, and the declining enrollment of women in computer science programs, among others (Frenkel, 1990; Klawe et al., 1995; Frieze et al.,

2015; Kaiser, 2015). Nevertheless, there is evidence that in other studies, women appeared to be playing an increasingly significant role in computer science programs in colleges and universities, especially in Malaysia, India, and a handful of schools in the United States like Carnegie Mellon University and Harvey Mudd College. Despite this positive portrait, it is important to comprehend other possible ways to achieve better results.

There are three important aspects about computer science in Portugal to highlight: (1) The first commercial computer (NCR 315) was introduced in Portugal in the company CUF (Companhia União Fabril) in the early 1960s (Almeida, 2007). This company was an example of the application of typing, computer and data communication networks in Portugal, when universities were not yet interested in research and innovation. Men developed the computer's operation. (2) The first degree in computing was created in 1975 at the Universidade Nova de Lisboa (New University of Lisbon) (Sanches, 2015). (3) Considering computer science and the history of computers, there were people who thought that the history of computers was like the mini-skirt, a fashion that was going to pass. These three aspects show that computer science is very new in Portugal, which had repercussions for women choosing this subject.

Nowadays, side by side with universities there are professional associations that are concerned with the imbalance between men and women in computer science professions. Recently, the IEEE Computer Society Women in Engineering (WIE) started to recognize women's contributions to the computing profession, for example, in Portugal (IEEE WIE – Portugal, 2015). The same goes for the Association for Computing Machinery (ACM), which supports, celebrates, and advocates internationally for the full engagement of women in all aspects of the computing field (Microsoft, 2018).

In Portugal, the Women in Technology (WIT) group, which is part of the Microsoft Partner Network (IAMCP), was established in 2016. It is a "community of dynamic, creative women committed to the Microsoft ecosystem for the purpose of promoting mutual personal and professional goals in order to attract women to the area of Information Technology (IT)." The organization contributes "in this way to the diversity of gender, age and training of IT professionals in Portugal." The goal is to grow by integrating "high profile" professionals, including corporate CEOs, university professors, and lawyers, all linked to the IT area. Microsoft Portugal has created a challenge for more women to pursue careers in information technology. At Microsoft Portugal, 50% of executive directors are women, and they represent 31% of the totality of existing managers (Monteiro,

2017). Portugal is integrated in the Western Europe region, where there are twelve regions, seven of which are led by women (Panarra, 2018).

"Do It, Girls!" is a Portuguese program organized by Microsoft whose aims are to empower the next generation of women with the knowledge and resources to become more innovative in a world where technology is present in every aspect of life, demonstrating that this is an industry that offers numerous opportunities that go far beyond the more technical professions (Guerra, 2014; Fernandes, 2018). The initiative is committed to highlighting the achievements of innovative women who have been pursuing a career in this industry in an event that features roundtables with successful women with careers in the technological and digital world.

BACKGROUND AND GENDER ROLES

Women are the majority in regard to the population resident in Portugal, representing 53% of the total population. Data reveal that in 2009 there were 53.4% of women enrolled in the higher education degrees, and in that year 59.3% of the total graduates were women. In 1990 there was one female lawyer per every four lawyers; today that number has not changed much. However, there is near-equality in the medical profession. In 2009, the overall percentage of doctors shows that 49.5% are women (JN, 2011). Generally speaking, women in Portugal are more educated; they do more doctorates, but earn considerably less than men.

Women in Portugal have traditionally played supporting roles as wives and mothers with little independence and equality. The Portuguese saying, "O homem na praça, a mulher em casa," translates to "Man in the [outside] square and woman in the house." There is also a proverb that says, "Na casa quem manda é ela mas nela quem manda sou eu," which translates to "In the house she has the command, but it is I who command her" (Rodrigues, 1983). Women were especially impacted by the strict conservatism of the fascism regime and the colonial war (1933–1974). In the family, as well as in society, a woman was considered inferior to a man and dependent on the husband or father, who was the head of the family. This patriarchal vision was based on well-known fascist values, from the trilogy "God, Fatherland and Family." Certain professions were forbidden to women and all education was based on gender inequalities.

The colonial war was a field of affirmation for the masculine ideals of warriors defending the homeland, while war also affirmed the caring and supportive roles of women as wives, girlfriends, sisters, and especially of mothers, symbolically linked to the image of home (Vakil, 1999, p. 129) and historically linked to the idea of peace.

During this time some women, outside the social norms, were involved as smugglers, often a last resort for survival, making them tougher. But they dreamed of having children, especially girls, who would hold different positions in the future: becoming students and finding professional careers.

The revolution of 1974 brought the war and the fascist regime to an end. The Constitution of the Republic of 1976 was enshrined for the first time in Portugal, including the status of equality, which prohibited all discrimination. But there is still a long way to go before gender equality is the daily reality of our society.

STUDIES OF WOMEN IN COMPUTING IN PORTUGAL

This section offers two studies. The first investigated the perspectives of female computer science students at the high school level. The number of male students in each course was registered only to obtain the percentage of each gender. The second study was a quantitative study with data from the number of Portuguese female students that arrive at universities, as new students for the academic year of 2018–2019.

Study 1: Female Computer Science Students and Teachers at High School as Well as Women Working in the Field

The study was conducted with female students (aged 16–25) and teachers at high schools and universities. The questions for teachers focused on the following aspects: When and how did you first get interested in computers and computing? Why did you decide to major in computer science? What type of student is more predisposed to pursue a career in computer science?

In a second research stage, women working in the computer science field were questioned. The research questions to be answered were: "What makes a female student get into computer science studies and work in this field?" and "What is the positive aspect of having a career in computer science?"

I conducted three types of studies: (1) one was made with teachers and female students in the same high school, (2) another study was conducted in different academic institutions (high schools and universities), and (3) I questioned women working in the field. The data were obtained through questionnaires and interviews.

I designed a questionnaire, which was distributed through Google Forms. High schools were invited to disseminate the questionnaire among female students and teachers in the computer science/informatics field. The questionnaire comprised four sections: (1) background questions (e.g., Did you grow up with a computer in the house? Who used it most? Do you have your own computer? When did you get it? When and how did you first get interested in computers and computing? Why did you decide to major in computer science? Who was most influential in your decision to major in computer science?), (2) questions concerning the computer science female students' characteristics, (3) questions about female students' interests in computer science, and (4) questions about their thoughts on computer science.

The general context section aimed to discover what had aroused people's interest in computing. The second section aimed to characterize computer science female students, their position, first impressions about computer sciences, and stereotypes. The next section captured thoughts about the person's school journey. The last section aimed to draw conclusions about diversity in the area.

Participants were informed that survey responses would be strictly confidential and the data from the research would be reported only in aggregate. The participation was voluntary and they were free to stop at any point. The survey took approximately ten minutes to complete. The answers aimed to inform the researcher about student attitudes, experiences, and the computer science context. In order to complement data from the survey, I designed semi-structured interviews. These interviews were to obtain complementary information and the content was the same for teachers and students with appropriate changes. The main difference between those questions was in the content of the second set (women and their position about computer sciences). In the case of teachers, I wanted to know their relationships and professional experience. For students, I wanted to know the types of students who chose computer sciences in order to have a computer science career and the professional opportunities they can obtain.

Study 2: Female Computer Science Students at Universities and Polytechnics

The second study, with the objective of analyzing the number of women who are interested in completing a computer science degree or a degree in a similar area, was done based on the information collected through the Directorate General for Higher Education (DGES) website (www.dges .gov.pt). This site is the responsibility of the General Direction of Higher Education, being a Portuguese portal of the ministry of education and higher education. The data are accurate and available for free. The website was consulted for the purpose of knowing how many students are placed in the higher education degrees in the areas of computer science and similar. The total number of students placed in 2018–2019 was counted for each degree and the number of women was subtracted, since the placement lists are nominal.

This study involves all public higher education institutions in Portugal, both universities and polytechnics. While the data from the first study had a quantitative and qualitative analysis, the number of participants was small, and the context was secondary education, in the second study the data analysis followed a quantitative approach. In this case, students attended universities and polytechnics. I consider that the data are complementary, since they allow us to know, from high school until entering higher education, the number of women in the area of computer science.

To obtain more dynamic results, the data were analyzed considering students in computer science courses, students in related courses students in universities and in polytechnics, and students in institutions of different regions of the country.

RESULTS AND DISCUSSION

This section presents the results of the data obtained from the described case studies. Comments/critiques follow the results.

Study 1: Female Computer Science Students and Teachers at High School as Well as Women Working in the Field

The goal of study 1 was to examine the attitudes of young females and teachers in computer science (Lopes, 2019). The results are as follows. The main conclusion from this study, which does not explain the reasons, was that the number of females in computer sciences studies is increasing compared with males; however, more work should be done to improve their motivation. The majority of the female students grew up with a computer at home (96.6%), but only 42% of them used a computer. Those who used the computer the most, at home, were brothers followed by the father, and, finally, the mother. Having a personal computer in the home (or not having one) was not directly related to whether or not a computer was used during childhood.

Women showed interest in the area of computer science in some cases from when they were younger. The main reason to choose the computer science field was the employment opportunities, that is, the ability to find a job and the good salary after graduation. Other influencing factors were social media – 80% were influenced by social media to choose a course in computer science – and parents or brothers and sisters, who were also influencers in some cases. An interest in computers was the greatest factor pointed out by the participants for the decision of choosing the computer science area.

Concerning the skills that are needed to study computer science, a student of computer science has to work hard, be interested, have good perception, and be organized. Other personal skills listed were capability of problem solving, being analytical, and being focused. Some of the respondents still believe that there is prejudice in the area of computer science. For the question "How has it been, being a woman in the area?" professional women gave a range of answers: "Just like being a man"; "Horrible"; "Easy"; "Difficult, especially to be taken seriously and see the merit recognized, as well as having access to the same opportunities"; "Very challenging"; "I have been privileged but, in general, we have to try harder to prove that we can sit at the same table"; "I do not notice significant differences." These professional women think that some of them can suffer some kind of reprisal for entering a "masculine field." This can be an important factor in understanding the imbalance of men and female students/professionals in the field. To a certain extent this is also a reason related to pre-established stereotypes. Sometimes there is some condescension toward female students; however, both men and women believe that opportunities are similar and that effort and dedication contribute to overcoming this stigma. In relation to the stereotypes associated with computer sciences, in the students' general opinion society considers that those who study computer sciences are addicted to video games.

From the teachers' point of view, they have always had a fascination for computers and programming. And, in their opinion, the solution to increasing the number of women in computer science should be by demanding each school to advertise computer science degrees in different forms. This could also be done with more information about the professional market in the area. They consider that students could have an important role to play within the advertisement process.

The results are not very precise since the sample is small. However, this study helped us understand that more work must be done to obtain a larger amount of data to verify motivations and constraints within female students and teachers that are engaged in the field.

Study 2: Female Computer Science Students at Universities and Polytechnics

Table 12.1 presents the results of counting the number of students who started attending polytechnic education in the academic year of 2018–2019. For the purposes of this study, a decision was made to classify the courses (degrees) in those that are part of computer science and those that are related. It was considered that any course of informatics would be included in computer science, except those of telecommunications and informatics. The courses of computers, electronics, and telecommunications are designated as related to the computer science.

These numbers do not include students who have come through mobility programs. There were two application moments, the first phase and the second phase. The first phase is for those students who have accomplished the whole compulsory requirements until July/August. The second phase is for those who did not apply in the first phase, which occurs in September. Thus, according to the available data, in polytechnic education there are a total, in computer science degrees, of 1,188 students. From these, 825 men entered on the first phase and 261 entered on the second phase. The number of women is 78 in the first phase and 24 in the second phase. So, 91% were male students and 9% were women.

In relation to the number of students at Portuguese universities (Table 12.2), the total is 1,694 in computer science courses and 868 in other related courses. The number of women in computer science degrees is, in the first phase, 103 and 15 in the second phase, that is, 7% of women versus 93% of men. In comparative terms, the number of women in computer science in polytechnics is 102 in relation to 118 women at universities. This difference of choice is not very significant.

Without any judgment and based on Portuguese people's common sense, one could say that the stigma of studying at polytechnics instead of universities is no more relevant, since I found slight differences in the numbers. The same does not happen when considering similar degrees. In this case, 699 of men chose university against 152 who chose polytechnics; women at universities are 169 and just 12 at polytechnics. These numbers show that universities are preferred for degrees related to computer

Table 12.1 *Polytechnic institutes (academic year 2018–2019, placed students)*

	Degree	Total students		Men		Women		Total in computer science
		1st	2nd	1st	2nd	1st	2nd	
Computer science	Informatics engineering	590	169	544	155	46	14	**1,188**
	Information technologies	34	26	30	24	4	2	
	Information systems	47	15	40	14	7	1	
	Informatics systems	64	11	55	9	9	2	
	Informatics and computers	130	20	121	19	9	1	
	Informatics and multimedia	2	3	2	3	0	0	
	Informatics security and networks	20	5	18	5	2	0	
	Computer graphics and multimedia	7	13	6	12	1	1	
	Networks and computer systems	9	23	9	20	0	3	
		903	**285**	**825**	**261**	**78**	**24**	
								Total in others
Related degrees	Informatics and telecommunications	30	7	26	6	4	1	**164**
	Electronics, telecommunications, and computers	88	7	83	6	5	1	
	Electrotechnology and computers	10	22	10	21	0	1	
		128	**36**	**119**	**33**	**9**	**3**	

Table 12.2 *Universities (academic year 2018–2019, placed students)*

	Degree	Total students		Men		Women		Total in computer science
		1st	2nd	1st	2nd	1st	2nd	
Computer science	Informatics, networks, and multimedia	14	1	11	1	3	0	**1,694**
	Informatics engineering	959	124	878	116	81	8	
	Computational engineering	19	3	19	3	0	0	
	Computer engineering and telematics	94	14	93	13	1	1	
	Computer sciences	61	12	56	10	5	2	
	Informatics and computers	304	89	291	85	13	4	
		1,451	**243**	**1,348**	**228**	**103**	**15**	
Related degrees								**Total others**
	Electrotechnology and computers	419	129	304	118	115	11	**868**
	Telecommunications and informatics	148	24	131	22	17	2	
	Electronics and computers	104	40	84	36	20	4	
	Electronics and telecommunications	4	0	4	0	0	0	
		675	**193**	**119**	**33**	**9**	**3**	

sciences. The percentage in related degrees of students at universities is 51% versus 13% at polytechnics. When analyzing the numbers in computer science, the differences between polytechnics and universities is about 2% more at universities.

I was curious to know if each geographic region had any influence on the choice of the degree (course) (Table 12.3). The results of student enrollment in higher education institutions located in the major urban centers were withdrawn: from Porto in the north; from Coimbra, in the coastal center; and from Lisbon, in the south center. I wanted to know the distribution of students in the coastal regions and in the interior of the country. The regions of the interior have less population and those who are there are older. Despite excellent natural and economic resources, these regions are not appealing in terms of population permanence. The results indicated that, nowadays, the choice for an institution has nothing to do with its geographic situation. There are more students at the big centers, because there are more places in these institutions, and institutions are bigger. The distribution of students is similar in relation to both the coastal and the center regions. These results lead us to argue that the choices are made considering financial issues: it is cheaper to study in small urban centers regardless of their geographic location.

The results show that in relation to the polytechnics, the center region (including Lisbon) has greater demand than the other Portuguese geographic regions.

The results obtained from the universities (Table 12.4) are the following: if we do not consider the urban center of Lisbon, there are no significant results in terms of the student distribution per zone. The distribution of students per region is more or less similar, except for the south. The north region is in high demand. The region has no influence on the choice of the degree (course). One might think that the great urban centers or the coastal regions would be more attractive, but this is not true. The issue is, really, the desire and motivation to study computer science.

DISCUSSION

The history of women in Portugal shows that social and behavioral norms determined how they were positioned primarily in the home as housewife and support for husband and family. Socioeconomic situations about forty years ago also contributed to define women's behavior and thought. To work outside the home meant working as a domestic for wealthier people.

Table 12.3 *Placed students by geographic region (polytechnics) (academic year 2018–2019)*

	Geographic region	Degree	Total students		Men		Women	
			1st	2nd	1st	2nd	1st	2nd
Computer science	North	Informatics engineering	154	63	144	59	10	4
		Networks and computer systems	9	23	9	20	0	3
		Informatics security and networks	20	5	18	5	2	0
		Information systems	47	15	40	14	7	1
		Informatics systems	64	11	55	9	9	2
		Information technologies	17	13	15	12	2	1
		Computer graphics and multimedia	7	13	6	12	1	1
	Center	Informatics engineering	358	90	329	83	29	7
		Informatics and computers	130	20	121	19	9	1
		Information technologies	17	13	15	12	2	1
		Informatics and multimedia	2	3	2	3	0	0
	South	Informatics engineering	78	16	71	13	7	3
Related degrees	North	Electrotechnology and computer	1	0	1	0	0	0
		Informatics and telecommunications						
	Center	Electrotechnology and computers	6	7	6	7	0	0
		Informatics and telecommunications	30	7	26	6	4	1
		Electronics, telecommunications, and computers	88	7	83	6	5	1
	South	Electrotechnology and computers	3	15	3	14	0	1

Table 12.4 Placed students by geographic region (universities) (academic year 2018–2019)

Geographic region	Degree	Total students		Men		Women	
		1st	2nd	1st	2nd	1st	2nd
Computer science							
North	Informatics engineering	239	47	228	45	11	2
	Computational engineering	19	3	19	3	0	0
	Computer engineering and telematics	94	14	93	13	1	1
	Computer sciences	61	12	56	10	5	2
	Informatics and computers	94	27	89	27	5	0
Center	Informatics engineering	537	58	488	54	49	4
	Informatics and computers	210	62	202	58	8	4
South	Informatics engineering	115	10	101	8	14	2
Islands	Informatics, networks, and multimedia	14	1	11	1	3	0
	Informatics engineering	68	9	61	9	7	0
Related degrees							
North	Electrotechnology and Computers	144	44	111	42	33	2
	Telecommunications and informatics	36	6	32	6	4	0
Center	Electrotechnology and computers	275	85	193	76	82	9
	Telecommunications and informatics	112	18	99	16	13	2
Islands	Electronics and telecommunications	4	0	4	0	0	0

Nowadays, more women work outside the home but experience significant pressure by feeling that they are expected to be perfect mothers, devoted companions, competent professionals, and good friends; to be informed, bright, and with a sense of humor; to be beautiful and young, thin and well-dressed; and to be affable and caring. Women often are unable (or unwilling) to meet these expectations. Girls are still looked on as caregivers. And when they choose a science degree they are inclined to follow medicine, especially if they are good students.

Society today is very technological. Like men, women already use and depend on the technology in their day-to-day lives. Women are becoming more interested in the use and development of new tools that simplify their increasingly busy lives.

The mothers and fathers of today, as with twenty- or thirty-year-olds, have forgotten the traditional values and educate their children following other values, those of the internet. The internet is considered by them to be a modern source of information with updated advice to follow for their children's education. I believe that girls who will be adolescents in about ten years will choose computer science as a field of study and will be as interested, if not more so, than boys.

Salomi and Lee (2016) expected that by the end of 2016 "fewer than 25 percent of information technology (IT) jobs in developed countries would be held by women, i.e. women working in IT roles." To have this percentage, they suggested getting more girls and young women into streams that will lead to careers in IT. To improve gender parity in science, technology, engineering, and mathematics (STEM) at various levels in the education pipeline, it may take time for those improvements to translate into IT job parity.

Today, we found several studies with different numbers and discrepancies in the overall male–female ratio in IT. In the context of our study, it is argued that the problem is in the difficulties in changing society's mentality. We cannot expect to suddenly get women into studying for computer science degrees. We are on the way, but we must wait for the right time.

CONCLUSION

Gender relations are lived differently according to social class, ethnicity, and sexual orientation, along with broader social contexts such as generational, regional, national, and age.

Considering the described experiences of the Portuguese woman, she became adapted to being modest, linked to the home and to the education of the children, and, contrarily, less linked to public work. From the descriptions already presented in this chapter, it was already expected that the daughters of Portuguese women would be more interested in social sciences and professions with a dedication to the well-being of others (doctors, nurses, teachers) than in the areas of science. Computer science is not perceived as being aligned with these ideas. Their choices were based on the education they had in being good housewives, caring for children, learning to be obedient and humble, and behaving well. At the end of the fascist regime, other values emerged: education and professional occupations. The idea of gender equality is demarcated. There are cases where the daughters have followed exactly the path of the mothers, and, in other cases, they have become more rebellious, wanting to be independent professionally but always following the role of caretakers or cared-for "princesses."

At the same time, the computer science field is not thought of as a caring field. Computer science in Portugal is very new, since the first commercial computer was used by a chemical enterprise (CUF) in 1960, and the first degree in computing appeared in 1975 at Universidade Nova de Lisboa. So, with this in mind, it is not very surprising that women are at a disadvantage compared with men in the computer sciences. Moreover, it is important to point out the lack of inspiring role models; women do not have enough female role models. Men tend to speak of their experience, but women are less likely to do so.

The first study conducted at high schools gave few reasons for this imbalance between genders in computer science choices. The results were not very clear, but they suggest that a great deal of work should be done to motivate and engage women to pursue the computer science field. They suggested that government should take the lead by increasing the percentage of women in IT jobs in the public sector. Also, districts (regions) should provide extracurricular activities through either a computing or robotic club or a school-based business that requires application developers. Teachers must play a role in bringing about change. Schools could increase interest in computing among girls by inviting women who work in this field to discuss their experiences.

The second study presented above revealed that fewer female students are enrolled at the universities and polytechnics compared with male students. These numbers refer only to admissions in computer science degrees and in those with some affinity. The data were collected from public institutions only. The goal was to understand the depiction of the students, especially female students, who are presently interested in these subjects. The data show that in the year studied, 271 women will complete, for the first time, a computer science degree. The total number of women at polytechnics is 102 and at universities 169; this means that 9% chose to study in polytechnics and 10% at universities. The degrees related to computer sciences, which means those of electronics, telecommunications, and computers, in total, have 23% of men and 6% of women.

To complement the arguments obtained from the studies, no one escapes from their sociocultural background, and some gender norms are slower to change. However, from observing young girls playing with computers and mobile devices, today one can say that this new generation will be more motivated to study computer sciences. We are starting to listen and see women pursuing careers in the computer sciences field. Media are also releasing more information about computer sciences. The ecological problems that threaten us will be a source of motivation to learn and to manage several situations using information systems and technologies.

DISCUSSION QUESTIONS

1. What incentives were given, in childhood, to Portuguese women to pursue a career in computer science?
2. In what ways do Portuguese women make career choices based on traditional family values?
3. Who should be partners to spotlight computer science as a choice for women who want to pursue a higher education diploma or degree?
4. How can we end the stigma of women being less able than men to pursue a profession in computer science?
5. What role can female students already in computer science continue to play to encourage more women to enter in the field?

References

Almeida, J. M. F. (2007). *Historia da Informática em Portugal: o Subsistema de Informaçao da CUF/Quimical. Memórias das Tecnologias e dos Sistemas de Informação.* Editora Livros do Brasil.

Fernandes, J. (2018) Do It, Girls! Retrieved from https://wintech.pt/w-news/25078-do-it-girls-reune-mais-de-100-alunas-na-microsoft.

Frenkel, K. A. (1990). Women and Computing. *Communications of the ACM,* 11 (11), 34–46.

Frieze, C., and Quesenberry, J. (2015). *Kicking Butt in Computer Science: Women in Computing at Carnegie Mellon University*. Indianapolis, IN: Dog Ear Publishing.

Guerra, A.R. (2014). Tecnologia precisa de mais mulheres: Microsoft lança programa "Do IT, Girls." *dinheiro vivo*. Retrieved from www.dinheirovivo.pt/buzz/tecnolo gia-precisa-de-mais-mulheres-microsoft-lanca-programa-do-it-girls/.

Gurer, Denise. (2002). Women in Computing History. *SIGCSE Bulletin*, 34(2).

IAMCP Women in Technology. (2018). Retrieved from www.iamcp-wit.org/mission-vision-values/.

IEEE WIE – Portugal. (2015). http://sites.ieee.org/portugal-wie/index.php/ieee-wie-por tugal/.

JN. (2011). Retrato da Mulher Portuguesa Actual. Retrieved from www.jn.pt/sociedade/ interior/retrato-da-mulher-portuguesa-actual–1800079.html.

Kaizer, C. (2015). Do Women Who Succeed in Male-Dominated Domains Help Other Women? The Moderating Role of Gender Identification. *European Journal of Social Psychology*, 45, 599–608.

Klawe, M., and Leveson, N. (1995). Women in Computing: Where Are We Now? *Communications of the ACM*, 38(1), 29–35.

Lopes, A. (2019) "Women in Computing – Attitudes and Experiences." *International Journal of Technology and Human Interaction*.

Microsoft. (2018). "Women in Technology." Retrieved from https://partner.microsoft .com/en-US/community/wit#simple-tab-content-1.

Monteiro, M. (2017). "Woman in Technology Chega a Portugal." Retrieved from www .computerworld.com.pt/2017/03/08/woman-in-technology-chega-a-portugal/.

Panarra, P. (2018). Do It, Girls! Retrieved from https://tek.sapo.pt/opiniao/artigos/ opiniao-conselho-do-dia-do-it-girls.

Rodrigues, J. A. (1983). Continuidade e Mudanças nos Papéis das Mulheres Urbanas Portuguesas. *Análose Social*, 19, 77–79.

Rolka, G. M. (2004). *100 Mulheres que Mudaram a História do Mundo*. Editora Nova Fronteira.

Salomi, P., and Lee. P. (2016). Technology, Media and Telecommunications Predictions. Deloitte. Retrieved from www2.deloitte.com/content/dam/Deloitte/global/ Documents/Technology-Media-Telecommunications/gx-tmt-prediction-2016-full-report.pdf.

Sanches, Andreia. (2015). Primeiro curso de Informática tem 40 anos. Afinal os computadores nao eram como a mini-saia. Retrieved from www.publico.pt/ 2015/11/29/sociedade/noticia/primeiro-curso-de-informatica-tem-40-anos-afinal-os-computadores-nao-eram-como-a-minisaia-1715694.

Vakil, A. (1999). "At War with the Nation: Patriotism and the Gendered Discourse of Citizenship in WWI Portugal." *Ellipsis Journal of the American Portuguese Studies Association*, Special issue: Engendering the Nation, 1, 123–142.

13

Women in Computing

The Situation in Russia

Evgeniy K. Khenner

INTRODUCTION

Improving the gender balance among IT professionals by involving more women in IT spheres is a goal in many countries. In addition to achieving gender equality, it is of great economic importance, since there is a lack of IT professionals in many countries, including Russia. One possible solution to this problem is to increase the number of females in IT professions. This chapter will discuss the ICT education system in Russia, its history and major contributors to the field, careers in the field, and the relationship of these areas to gender issues. Below I give definitions of the main terms used in this chapter.

The term "computing" in Russian scientific and pedagogical literature is rarely used, while the term "informatics" is widely spread in the literature and is polysemantic in Russian; it is not an equivalent to the term "computing" in any of its meanings. In the following text, according to the Computing Curricula (2005), the term "computing" means "any goal-oriented activity requiring, benefiting from, or creating computers. Thus, computing includes designing and building hardware and software systems for a wide range of purposes; processing, structuring, and managing various kinds of information; doing scientific studies using computers; making computer systems behave intelligently; creating and using communications and entertainment media; finding and gathering information relevant to any particular purpose, and so on."

The IT (information and communications technology) specialist is "a professional who has the ability to develop, operate, and maintain ICT systems and for whom ICTs constitute the main part of the job" (Sgobbi, 2018). A set of European ICT professional profiles (European ICT Professional Profiles, 2012) is structured in six profile families: business

246

management, technical management, design, development, service and operation, support; within them, twenty-three concrete ICT professions are named. This is important to emphasize because sometimes, when people speak about IT professionals, in most cases, explicitly or implicitly, they mean program developers, which distorts the gender aspect of the problem of "women in IT," because the percentage of women among developers generally is less than in other IT professions, which are no less important.

COMPUTING IN RUSSIA: HISTORY AND MODERNITY

Development of computing technology in Russia (the Soviet Union) began immediately after World War II and was seen as an important strategic task. For about forty years, the Soviet Union was inferior only to the United States in this sphere; besides taking into account a high level of secrecy that reined in everything connected with computing during the first two decades of the computer era, the computer technology that was being created in the USSR at that stage was absolutely original. The situation changed in the mid-1970s of the twentieth century when the curtain of secrecy that used to cover the sphere of general purpose computers was slackened, and, along with producing domestic computer hardware, the USSR started a mass production of clones of the American IBM 360/370 and PDP-11 computers.

As for the theoretical and mathematical foundations of computing, such as mathematical logic and theory of algorithms, programming theory, computer mathematical modelling, and others, the level of research pursued in Russia (the Soviet Union) was not lower than abroad. The research work of such scientists as A. A. Lyapunov, L. V. Kantorovich, A. N. Kolmogorov, A. P. Ershov, and V. M. Glushkov is well known in their field all over the world. Many other researchers, albeit not so well known abroad due to partial or complete secrecy of their work, also performed theoretical and applied investigations at the forefront of computing. Note that the secrecy of this sphere in those years was everywhere and extended not only to applied but also to theoretical studies (e.g., some of the studies by American Claude Shannon on information theory were published in the United States ten to fifteen years after they were completed).

At this pioneering stage of computing development in Russia, women took a significant part in this process. In the 1960s to 1980s of the last century, *at least half of the university students majoring in specialties related to programming were women; and after graduation, almost all of them worked in their profession.* In computation centers of universities, research institute,s and industrial enterprises where mainframes were concentrated, *at least half of the staff including programmers was comprised of women.* Although key positions in this area belonged to men, history knows eminent female programmers and computer system designers.

For example, Kateryna Yushchenko was the first woman in the USSR to become a doctor of physical and mathematical sciences due to her innovative achievements in programming. She developed one of the world's first high-level programming languages with indirect addressing called the Address programming language. It was a breakthrough in the field of computer technology as this language provided the free location of a program in computer memory. Kateryna Yushchenko became a founder of the first Soviet scientific school of theoretical programming. She is the author of more than 200 studies and scientific papers, including twenty-three monographs and teaching aids.

One more example is Rosetta Zhilina, an outstanding mathematician and programmer. She developed and headed the development of many algorithms and program-solving problems in the field of physics, mechanics, heat conductivity, and ballistics of complex structures in the national defense industry.

Currently, the situation in computing in Russia is quite different. The country is no longer among leaders in this sphere. The overwhelming majority of computer hardware and software currently used in Russia is produced overseas. Recognition of the fact that this tendency contradicts the national interests resulted in 2016 in the adoption a long-term national program of import substitution of certain categories of software critical for information security.

Also currently, PC and server equipment and telecommunication systems used in government structures are to be gradually changed to hardware and software developed and produced in Russia. These and other circumstances have initiated a real boom in the demand for IT professionals. Their lack observed by all experts stimulated a desire to increase the number of female IT professionals.

According to a study performed in Russia by the recruiting agency GlobalCareer (2015), the structure of demand in the labor market for IT specializations is as follows (figures are percentage breakdowns of type of position of the overall IT labor market; e.g., developers account for 28% of the 100% of demand for labor market IT skills):

- Developers: 28%
- Automated systems: 14%

- IT sales managers: 13%
- Project managers: 11%
- System administrators: 7%
- Testers: 7%
- Analysts: 6%
- Mobile software developers: 5%
- Software architects: 4%
- Help desk technicians: 3%
- Oracle administrators: 2%

Developers are the most desired professionals in Russia; they account for more than a third of existing vacancies in the labor market. They are followed by experts on cloud technologies, Big Data, mobile developments, developments in the banking sector, etc. The number of vacancies in IT companies for developers constantly exceeds the number of those who want to take them up, which cannot be said about many other IT professions. The fact that the profession of developer is not in great favor among women partially explains the relatively small number of women in IT. Furthermore, it is significant that the salary of IT professionals is significantly higher than that of most other categories of employees. This is one more incentive to attract people to this industry.

EDUCATION IN THE FIELD OF COMPUTING AND GENDER ASPECTS

School Education

Russian schoolchildren start to study elements of informatics in primary school, where informatics either can be a separate subject or can be integrated into other subjects. It is about forming the foundations of logical and algorithmic thinking and learning initial elements of computer literacy.

In middle school, informatics is always a separate subject, compulsory for all students. The course of informatics introduces the basics of information science and information technologies.

In high school, school authorities decide whether "informatics" is to be taught or not taught at their school. Taking into account the popularity of the subject, most high schools include informatics in their programs. Most students who entered the university continued to study informatics in high school at a basic level; those students who study informatics at an advanced level, as a rule, plan to continue their education at university in the field of computing.

After high school is finished, students are supposed to take the Unified National Examinations. Depending on the results of the UNE, a secondary school graduate could be admitted to the university. Two exams are compulsory: mathematics and Russian. The rest are usually determined by his or her desire to choose a particular program at the university. Most of the university programs related to IT require the Unified National Exam in Informatics to be passed. During the last five years, 7–8% of secondary school graduates opted for the Unified National Exam in Informatics.

Statistics on the gender composition of students choosing an exam in informatics demonstrates the interest of women in IT professions. For instance, according to the Federal Institute of Pedagogical Measurements (2012), in 2012 women made up 27% of the total number of applicants taking the Unified National Examination in Informatics. The average score for informatics was 61 (out of 100 points), which is higher than for most other subjects. In general, women usually show slightly better results than men: women on average show 62 points and men 60 points. It allows us to conclude that at the level of studying informatics at school, women are no less successful than men, but this picture is seen against the background of the fact that the number of men who chose the Unified National Examination in Informatics is three times more than number of women. As already noted, the mere fact of choosing this or that National Examination tells a lot about the choice of subsequent professional education and professional careers. School education in informatics in Russia is described in detail by Khenner and Semakin (2014).

University Education

At present, professional training in Russia is mainly concentrated in higher education institutions, where about 80% of secondary school graduates enter. As a whole, in 2017, 1,026,086 students were admitted to higher education institutions of Russia, 538,095 of them females (52.4%). Considering that women within the age group of 15–24 make up a bit more than 50% of the country's population, it becomes clear that there is no gender discrimination in admission to universities. The fact that women are as successful as men in studying higher education programs is statistically proven: in 2017, women made up 56% among graduates.

Most of programs for training IT specialists in Russian universities include two stages of general university-level academic programs:

Table 13.1 *Training IT specialists, 2017*

Program	Enrollment for bachelor's degree programs, women (%)	Bachelor's degree program accomplished, women (%)	Enrollment for master's degree programs, women (%)	Master's degree program accomplished, women (%)
Math and computer sciences	36	41	38	47
Applied math and informatics	31	37	36	39
Applied informatics	30	38	42	49
Fundamental informatics and IT	25	24	25	30
Software and administration of IS	25	34	33	29
IS and IT	23	27	31	34
Informational security	22	25	27	24
Informatics and computer engineering	19	20	24	25
Software engineering	19	20	20	25
Total	**24**	**29**	**31**	**34**

bachelor's degree (four years) and master's degree (two years); and a part of these programs is based on a single-stage program of training a specialist (five years). Table 13.1 shows information on admission and graduation of students for the largest IT professional programs (according to data of Federal Ministry of Education and Science).

These figures allow us to draw the following conclusions.

1. The popularity of professional IT education among women is significantly lower than among men. This lays the foundation for a gender imbalance in the IT industry.
2. Of all the areas of IT education, the least popular among women are technical fields of study (informatics and computer engineering) and programming (software engineering).

3. Among women enrolled in a course preparing IT professionals (both bachelor's and master's programs), the dropout rate is significantly lower than among men (the dropout rate at bachelor's IT programs is quite high and can reach 30–40%).
4. The more options for choosing a future profession in a program, the more popular this program is among women. For example, the fields listed in the upper part of the table are less focused on specific professions than those ones in the lower part.

The popularity of professional IT education among women and men can be estimated from experience of some of the Russian universities – for instance, St. Petersburg National Research University of Information Technologies, Mechanics and Optics (ITMO University) – which many of the best high school graduates from all over the country are eager to enter, wanting to get a top-quality and prestigious IT education. The proportion of female students enrolled in IT programs at this university does not exceed 20%.

At the same time, as repeatedly noted in Russian and foreign literature, women are not inferior to men in studying the disciplines of professional training. I found this in my own analysis of the success in mastering the basic IT disciplines by women and men studying the programs of applied mathematics and informatics, fundamental informatics and information technologies, and information security at the Perm State University.

Here I am referring to the disciplines called algorithmization and programming, theory of information, programming languages, operating systems, computer networks and telecommunications, intellectual systems, and software engineering. These were not found to have statistically significant differences in the success of mastering any of these disciplines by women and men. This fact once again demonstrates the equal success of women and men in gaining new knowledge and skills in different IT disciplines, including programming (which is less popular among women when choosing a profession).

EMPLOYMENT OF WOMEN IN THE FIELD OF COMPUTING

IT Companies and Industry

According to an analysis carried out by the Higher School of Economics (2016), based on national statistics, by 2014 in the Russian Federation the percentages of women working in the IT industry and related organizations were as follows:

- Consulting on computer hardware: 18%
- Software development: 20%
- Data processing: 50%
- Development and use of databases and information resources, including internet resources: 35%
- Other activities related to the use of hardware and information technology: 23%

According to a survey conducted by the Institute for Internet Development (2016), a Russian non-profit organization for collecting and processing statistical and analytical information in the field of information technology, the respondents' opinions about the proportion of women in IT over the past three years were distributed as follows: has not changed (38%), increased (61%), and remained unchanged (1%). Thus, the majority of respondents note the positive dynamics of the process of women's involvement in IT.

According to this survey, the distribution of women working in Russia in different fields of IT is as follows:

- Project managers: 27%
- Sales managers: 21%
- Analysts: 10%
- Developers: 9%
- Designers: 9%
- Directors: 7%
- Consultants: 6%
- Testers: 5%
- Technical writers: 5%
- Engineers: 1%

Practically the same distribution of women's interests in the IT fields is noted by other Russian researchers.

Provided below are data on the employment of women in the IT fields in several large Russian companies, taken from the same source (Institute for Internet Development). In "Sberbank Technology" (which is a Russian IT company providing services in software development and implementation for Sberbank, the largest bank in Russian Federation and one of the largest in Europe), the number of women among IT personnel is at the level of 26–28%, and in absolute figures, within the period of 2015–2017 the number of women in the company has doubled.

At the Deutsche Bank Technology Center in Moscow, 20% of employees are women who work in different fields of IT: development, testing and quality control, business and functional analysis, and project management. Women manage big subdivisions; the general director of the center is a woman.

At Cognitive Technologies, a company dedicated to development and implementation of software, a leading developer of artificial intelligence for unmanned vehicles, the number of women in programming has recently increased. In complex projects led by the company, dedicated to high-level programming that involves complicated calculations and good mathematical background, the percentage of female employees increased to 35%.

At Technoserv Consulting, which is engaged in automation of medium and large businesses, currently the number of male and female employees is approximately 50/50, since the company deals not so much with classical programming as with introduction of large systems, where deep knowledge of business, processes, and approach to analysis is required. The personnel department of the company notes that the situation with female IT professionals in recent years has radically changed (fifteen years ago, one could hardly find a woman occupying an IT position in the company).

At InfoWatch, a group of companies developing information security software products, the ratio between males and females in IT positions looks something like this: developers 95:5, analysts 30:70, testers 60:40, technical writers 50:50, configuration management engineers 95:5, project managers 80:20, usability designers 50:50, linguists 70:30. These proportions remain the same over the past three to four years.

The information given above concerns big national companies (mostly based in Moscow and St. Petersburg) attracting specialists from all over the country. In other regions, the situation with IT personnel is more difficult. There is a shortage of specialists, especially highly qualified ones.

A group of companies, Information Computing Systems, is engaged in development and implementation of information systems, development of IT infrastructure, technical support, and services. Among its IT professionals there are currently 33% of women (ten years ago they were less than 20%). The company's management believes that the current ratio is optimal, and notes that there is a tendency to increase the percentage of women among IT specialists, and that professional qualities are the decisive factor when hiring an employee, but definitely not the gender of an applicant.

It is noted that women in the company are more interested in design and development, and less in technology management, maintenance service, and support.

Among IT specialists who occupy middle-management positions in the company, women make up 29%, while all top managers are men. The factor that constrains appointing women to leadership positions is that when a female leader takes a maternity leave, a substitute leader can change the team, change the working conditions of employees, and so on. In addition, it is noted that male leaders are easier to negotiate with other leaders.

In the CRM Expert company, a partner of Microsoft engaged in development of software for project management systems and implementation of those systems, currently 30% of IT specialists are women. The management of the company considers it desirable to increase this number to 40%. The reasons are as follows: (1) the desire to increase the role of women in generation and to search for new ideas in recent years and (2) the fact that in the presence of women, male colleagues become more hard-working and industrious and less coarse. According to the internal surveys of the company, among preferences of female IT professionals are development and technology management; women are much less inclined to work in the field of design and service and operation. Top management positions in this company are occupied only by 10% of female IT specialists. Directors of the company consider this quantity insufficient and are working on promoting more women to leadership positions, despite the fact that they have to overcome resistance of part of the team initiated by the stereotypes about female leaders.

Educational Institutions

In Russia, 32% of the population over the age of fifteen has a higher education (56% of women and 44% of men). Some 88% of schoolteachers are women, 12% are men. Among university teachers, 57% are women and 43% men. Their positions are distributed as follows: heads of departments: women 43%, men 57%; full professors: women 33%, men 57%; assistant professors: women 59%, men 41%; senior lecturers: women 70%, men 30%; assistants (teachers responsible only for laboratory work and practical classes): women 67%, men 33% (Federal State Statistic Service, 2016).

There are no statistics on the gender composition of schoolteachers of informatics. According to the author's estimation, the gender composition of teachers of informatics in Perm region is close to the general one listed above (i.e., females are significantly dominant). Among university teachers of computing occupying positions of full professors and assistant professors, the percentage of men is significantly higher.

Provided below are several specific examples taken from the websites of some of the leading Russian universities. Twenty-one faculty members work at the system programming department of the Faculty of Computational Mathematics and Cybernetics in the Moscow State University. Among them there are six full professors (all of them are men), and eleven assistant professors (only two are women). A bit more gratifying picture can be seen at the Department of Informatics of St. Petersburg State University (twenty-two faculty members in total, one woman out of five full professors, three women out of seven assistant professors). But there are no women among the heads of departments of computing in these universities. In the Higher School of Economics, a university established in the post-Soviet period when it had the opportunity to form its academic staff from scratch, there are eleven females out of forty-four faculty members (including one woman out of eleven full professors and one woman out of eleven assistant professors) in the Department of Software Engineering. A similar picture is observed in other departments that prepare specialists in computing. For example, in the Perm State University, there is not a single woman in the full professor position among fifty faculty members of computing (but 40% of the assistant professor positions are occupied by women).

EXAMPLES OF SUCCESSFUL PROFESSIONAL CAREERS FOR WOMEN

Many women in Russia have made an extremely successful career in the IT business, private and public. Below I give several examples – from federal structures and private business – which can be found as well as many other examples at http://wit.org.ru/ and http://tadviser.ru/a/268175.

Alisa Melnikova is the director of Financial Technology, Projects and Process Organization Department, at the Bank of Russia since 2017. Since 2000, she occupied leading positions in various transnational and Russian IT companies, including ISG, Egar Technology, and I-Teco. In these companies, she was responsible for the development of new competence centers and supervised the implementation of megaprojects in the field of technology support for business for the largest Russian and foreign banks.

Zulfiya Kakhrumanova is the head of the Information Technology Department of the Central Bank. In 2001 she started as a programmer in 1C, a large software company in Russia, then worked as a developer of databases and banking information systems.

Anastasia Chistyakova is the director of the Department of Information Technologies at Rosatom, the State Atomic Energy Corporation, since 2014. She started her career in IT in 2001 with SAP as an architect, project manager, and SAP support manager. Then she managed project IT offices of the multinational companies TNK-BP and SIBUR.

Natalia Kaspersky is president at InfoWatch, a company developing systems for protecting confidential information from internal threats, which now dominates the Russian IT market. For more than ten years she was the head of Kaspersky Lab.

Olga Uskova is president of Cognitive Technologies, a software and IT solutions developer. The company works both in Russia and in a number of other countries, specializing in software for unmanned vehicles. Uskova began her career in the 1980s as a developer of complex information systems. Repeatedly, according to various ratings, she was one of the top ten most successful businesswomen in Russia.

Ekaterina Voropayeva is president of GMCS (since 2010), one of the leaders in Russia in the implementation of business solutions and software development. She started her career in Rostelecom, Russia's biggest telecommunication company, as a project manager of ERP implementation. In 2004 she was appointed vice-president of GMCS.

Ekaterina Sannikova is general director of the technical center of Deutsche Bank LLC. She started her career with Deutsche Bank in 2007. Later she made a great contribution to the development, formation, and specialization of the center as a key IT structure of the investment business of Deutsche Bank. Previously, she occupied various positions at Credit Suisse (London), BSKYB (London), and Sun Microsystems (Moscow).

ASSESSING THE CAUSES OF GENDER IMBALANCE IN THE IT SECTOR AND PROSPECTS FOR IMPROVEMENT

Despite the above examples, gender imbalance obviously takes place in IT (it should be noted that most of Russian researchers and commentators analyzing the problem of "women in IT" refuse to see in this imbalance a deliberate violation of women's rights).

According to the Institute for Internet Development (2016), the assessment of the problems of women's work in IT includes the following categories: lack of career development, 24%; getting a wage lower than male employees in the same position, 24%; other factors, 15%. At the same time, 36% of respondents emphasized the absence of specific difficulties.

Below I give some opinions on the discussed issue from some female leaders in the IT industry, mentioned in the previous section.

Ekaterina Sannikova:

The imbalance exists and begins from the university. At the faculties of sciences, male students outnumber women, although the proportion of girls grows from year to year. Here I am dealing with historically established practices, as well as stereotypes and prejudices that have emerged in the profession for various reasons. These reasons have nothing to do with the capabilities, potential or level of professionalism of women. Our practice in attracting and developing employees confirm this.

The IT industry suits a women's job perfectly. Unlike many other areas, it allows a woman to combine her job and home: have flexible work arrangements, the ability to work from home. Working in this industry, women successfully cope with the tasks, and in some areas – such as quality control, requirements analysis, project management – are often superior to male colleagues. Unfortunately, there is a stereotype that this sphere is not for women, and it is pretty well imprinted on the brain of many girls who, having excellent analytical skills and interest in mathematics and logic, ignore the IT sphere when choosing a future profession.

Olga Rubtsova:

We are observing a situation when girls are actively entering the IT sphere and performing a large amount of work, often not directly related to software development. For example, they are excellent at solving problems concerning data analysis, analytics, consulting, customer service, sales. With the advent of women, the IT industry only wins. They are more diligent and more profound in working on tasks, a solution of which, in the end, becomes one of the main features of the project.

Now companies do not need just automation for automation. They need everything to be neat, beautiful, fast, convenient, and no man can match women in this.

The major difficulty is that not all women are perceived as professionals. As to sales, customer service, business consulting – there is no gender specificity. But if it is a deep technological task, very often women need much more time and energy to gain trust. On the contrary, men do not need to apply an effort; they are trusted by default.

Olga Uskova:

The gender approach is definitely not reasonable; only a professional approach is. We need a professional, and it does not matter whether this person is a boy or a girl or transgender.

CONCLUSION

Despite the above-mentioned reasons for gender imbalance in the IT sphere, why the situation remains is not quite clear. The reasons for this imbalance can be divided, in principle, into two categories: first, the explicit or implicit discrimination of women when applying for a job and getting enrolled in a college or university, and, second, the external influences that drive internal motivations such that women do not see themselves in IT.

In the sphere of both school and higher professional education, there are few differences in men and women's academic success in Russia; this is evidenced by numerous feedback of students and teachers, as well as by the author's extensive personal experience.

When hiring a woman, cases of latent gender discrimination are noted sometimes, especially in small firms, and are based primarily on employers' fear of being without a worker during maternity leave. However, this factor hardly explains the lack of interest of the majority of women in obtaining an IT profession, which, in particular, practically guarantees employment and relatively high wages. The author thinks it is more likely that social stereotypes and prejudices play a leading role. Overcoming this problem is very difficult, but definitely possible to solve.

The problem needs to be addressed early on, starting with school. It is necessary to seek changes in the National Curriculum so that all students – from elementary to high school – will have the opportunity to study informatics. In Russia, prerequisites for that have been already created: informatics is a recognized subject, with highly developed methodological support; surveys carried out among parents of primary school students, both boys and girls, indicate that a majority of them are in favor of studying informatics.

DISCUSSION QUESTIONS

1. Does your country's economy need to increase the inflow of women in the IT sphere?
2. How can your country's universities help to attract and motivate women to acquire an IT profession?
3. How do examples of successful careers of women in the IT industry contribute to improvement of gender equality in this sphere?
4. How does the neglect of female IT professionals affect the selection of future professions by women studying IT courses at universities?
5. How do public stereotypes and prejudices affect women's decisions not to choose professional careers in the IT sphere?

References

Computing Curricula. (2005). ACM, AIS, IEEE-CS (2005, September). Retrieved from www.acm.org/binaries/content/assets/education/curricula-recommenda tions/cc2005-march06final.pdf.

European Committee for Standardization. (2012, May). European ICT Professional Profiles. Retrieved from ftp://ftp.cen.eu/CEN/Sectors/List/ICT/CWAs/CWA% 2016458.pdf.

Federal Institute of Pedagogical Measurements. (2012). Final Analytical Report on the Results of the Unified National Examinations of 2012. Retrieved from http://fipi.ru/sites/default/files/document/1408709880/1_0.pdf (in Russian).

Federal State Statistics Service. (2016). Women and Men of Russia. Retrieved from www.gks.ru/free_doc/doc_2016/wo-man16.pdf (in Russian).

GlobalCareer. (2015, December). Review of Wages and Trends of the Russian Labor Market in the IT sector. Retrieved from http://docplayer.ru/36465709-V-sfere-informacionnyh-tehnologiy-tendenciy-na-rynke-truda-zarabotnye-platy-it-specialistov-rossiya-obzor.html (in Russian).

Higher School of Economics. (2016). Gender Aspect in the Digital Economy. Information Bulletin No. 3 (8). Retrieved from https://issek.hse.ru/data/2016/04/28/1128533054/%D0%9C%D0%BE%D0%BD%D0%B8%D1%82%D0%BE%D1%80%D0%B8%D0%BD%D0%B3_4.2_2016.pdf (in Russian).

Institute for Internet Development. (2016). Women in IT. Retrieved from www.tadviser.ru/index.php (in Russian).

Khenner, E., and Semakin, I. (2014). School Subject Informatics (Computer Science) in Russia: Educational Relevant Areas. *ACM Journal "Transactions on Computing Education" (TOCE)*. Special issue on Computing Education in K-12 Schools from a Cross-National Perspective, 14(2), 14:1–14:10.

Sgobbi, F. (2018). The Skills of European ICT Specialists. In Mehdi Khosrow-Pour (ed.), *Encyclopedia of Information Science and Technology*, 4th edition. Hershey, PA: IGI Global. Retrieved from www.igi-global.com/chapter/the-skills-of-european-ict-specialists/184183.

Part IV

Cultural Perspectives from Asia-Pacific

14

More Chinese Women Are Needed to Hold Up Half the Computing Sky

Ming Zhang and Yichun Yin

INTRODUCTION

Since Deng Xiaoping's economic reforms starting in 1978, the Chinese government has continuously improved the basic laws and regulations that guarantee women's economic rights and employment rights. Chinese women can participate equally in economic development, and enjoy the fruits of reform and development on an equal footing with men. In China (Aaltio and Huang, 2007), working women now account for 47.0% of the total labor force, higher than the world average of 40.8%. However, in the computing industry, the proportion of female practitioners in China is about 7% (Proginn and Juejin, 2017; Proginn, 2018), significantly lower than 17% in United States (Elizabeth, 2017). The problem of the small proportion of Chinese computing female practitioners should be remedied.

Women practitioners clearly play a crucial role in the development of China's computing industry. On the one hand, women infuse vitality into the computing industry, and influence and promote the sound development of computing. On the other hand, "Men and women work together, work is not tiring." There are many examples that show that work done in a diverse environment is more efficient and innovative, and this principle applies to the computing industry (Dike 2013). Men working with women will have a greater sense of accomplishment; women working with men will feel empowered and more secure. Collusions of different genders and different ideas will yield better results in the computing industry (Souhu News, 2017). Chinese traditional culture has held the belief that "Men's work centers around outside, women's work centers around the home" (男主外，女主内) and "a woman without talent is a virtue" (女子无才便是德). These beliefs continue to have a great influence on women's career choices. Currently, Chinese society demands even more from women: not only can they have a good career, but also they need to manage their families. Due to the pressure of social and cultural concepts in China, coupled with the demanding characteristics of careers in the computing industry, most women do not consider computing jobs when they choose to work. In China today, most women believe that computing is a field for men, and women do not have enough confidence in the development of their computing careers (Sun et al., 2018). At the same time, the high intensity and pressure of computing work also makes many female computing practitioners quit their jobs and put more energy into their families (Kaya, 2017).

Although the overall number of women practitioners in the computing industry is relatively small, there is also a surprising phenomenon in China: *the numbers of female entrepreneurs, who co-founded start-ups, are relatively high* (PRCSCIO, 2015), and the number of female managers in top positions in China is significantly higher than in other Western countries (Lacy, 2017). Chinese women have many unique advantages in the internet industry, which can help them discover and seize business opportunities in that domain. These senior female managers are generally highly educated and have high professional aspirations; their work has also been supported by the family, and, thus, they can successfully balance family and work conflicts. We will expand on this phenomenon later in the chapter.

In general, solving the problem of a small proportion of female comput-ing practitioners in China is still a long way off. Governments, schools, companies, and even families all need to make corresponding efforts.

CULTURAL INFLUENCES ON THE LOW RATIO OF CHINESE FEMALE PRACTITIONERS IN THE COMPUTING INDUSTRY

In 2018, Proginn.com, a popular online community, surveyed the current status of Chinese programmers. The participants included more than 150,000 Chinese programmers from twenty-eight provinces, municipalities, and special administrative regions. The survey reported that only 7.6% of programmers were female (Proginn and Juejin, 2017), which is surprisingly consistent with the number of 7.38% in the 2016 survey (Proginn, 2018). In the United States, the proportion of women in the computing industry is relatively higher but still less than 20%. Globally, at Twitter, there are 15% female technical practitioners; Microsoft and Google employ 19% and 20%, respectively (Microsoft, 2017; Kaya, 2017). According to professors from the top universities in China, the number of female students in computing majors is decreasing year by year (Souhu News, 2017).

The low proportion of female employees in the computing industry in China is an important issue that needs study and resolution. In this chapter, we study this problem in three aspects: (1) Chinese traditional ethics culture, (2) Chinese females' perception of the computing industry, and (3) pressure from the computing industry.

Chinese Traditional Ethics Culture

In the Chinese traditional patriarchal clan society, men are believed to be stronger than women in physical strength, and physical labor has been done mainly by men. Throughout China's history, war has been a frequent condition, with men serving as the main force throughout years of war while women did not participate in war. In order to maintain feudal rule, Confucian ethics, beginning in the seventh century BC, promoted a culture centered on male superiority and female inferiority. With the formation of the patrilineal inheritance system, married women follow men for their lives. After China came into the Spring and Autumn Period in the seventh through fifth centuries BC, woman's behavior was subject to various strict rules and restrictions by Chinese Confucianism.

The ideology of "men's work centers around outside, women's work centers around the home" is promoted in the "Book of Rites" and "Mencius," the Chinese Confucian classic books. In family life, women often play the role of the good wife. They are expected to help their husbands progress in their careers, education, and character, and to increase their husbands' position in society. At the same time, women are required to take up housework and take care of the children. In addition, there are extremely strict feudal rules that constrain women, such as the three obediences (to father before marriage, to husband after marriage, and to son after the death of husband) and the four virtues (morality, proper speech, modest manner, and diligent needlework). Over the past few thousand years, these unreasonable rituals have become ethical standards throughout China.

After the founding of the People's Republic of China in 1949, due to a series of national policies, the influence of traditional Confucian culture on women has changed (Wen and Cui, 2013). As mentioned earlier, Chairman Mao Zedong announced the policy that "women hold up half the sky" in 1955. In addition, the one-child policy further reduced the pressure on women to undertake family affairs. More and more women can enter the workforce. Today, Chinese women have been contributing nearly half of the labor force, a much higher proportion than in many Western countries (Aaltio and Huang, 2007). However, inequality still exists in actual work and family life: (1) Income inequality: the gap between men's and women's incomes is growing wider compared with the situation in 1990. In 2000, the annual income of middle-class women was 6.6% lower than men (Aaltio and Huang, 2007). (2) Housework inequality: working women spend about 2.9 hours a day on housework, which is 1.6 hours more than working men, according to the report from National Bureau of Statistics of China (NBSC, 2002). Traditional Chinese ethics culture still affects women's social behavior to a large extent and gender discrimination still exists to some extent. Moreover, modern society has higher requirements for ideal women and expects them to perform well both at home and at work. It can be said that Chinese modern women are under even more pressure than ever.

In the computing industry, it will be more difficult to become an "ideal woman" as expected by society, especially after child-bearing. Many female computing practitioners end up having to return to their families just when they are making advances in their careers, in order to take on the role of housewives. Now that China is opening up a second-child policy, women will devote even more energy to their family life, which will prevent them from choosing computer-related fields of work.

Female Chinese Students' Perceptions of the Computing Industry

To better understand why Chinese women are unwilling to choose computing, the Ada Workshop program, which was launched by Microsoft Research Asia to encourage and nurture female university students to pursue a core-tech position in their future career, investigated views of Chinese students on the capabilities required by the computing industry (Sun et al., 2018). This survey covered undergraduate, master's, and PhD students in computing fields of study, with a total of 373 students enrolled at the top thirty universities in China. The survey required respondents to compare the performance of different genders in various professional qualities: self-evaluation of scores and real capability, hands-on work, logical thinking, and willingness to take on challenges. The results of this survey are shown in Table 14.1. From the table, it can be seen that most male and female students believe that male students are better than female students in both hands-on work and willingness to take on challenges. Only 2.4% of the females believe that females are more willing to take on challenges, and no males think that females are more willing to take on challenges. Similarly, only 7.0% think that girls have an advantage in hands-on work. In logical thinking, the views of boys and girls are very different. Female students think they have the same logical thinking ability

Table 14.1 *Views of Chinese students on capabilities required by the computer industry*

Self-evaluation	Capability equals scores	Capability better than scores	Scores better than capability	Not sure
Female	25.6%	27.9%	27.9%	18.6%
Male	24.2%	50.9%	12.8%	12.1%
Hands-on work	Females equals males	Females are better	Males are better	Not sure
Female	26.7%	7.0%	65.1%	1.2%
Male	26.0%	7.6%	65.4%	1.0%
Logical thinking	Females equals males	Females are better	Males are better	Not sure
Female	48.8%	2.4%	48.8%	0.0%
Male	26.0%	0.0%	73.3%	0.7%
Willing to take challenges	Females equals males	Females are better	Males are better	Not sure
Female	38.4%	1.2%	60.4%	0.0
Male	24.9%	0.7%	72.7%	1.7%

Note: These capabilities required by the computer industry include: self-evaluation, hands-on work, logical thinking, and willing to take on challenges.
Source: Data from Sun et al., 2018.

as male students. However, most male students think they are better than females in logical thinking. In addition, 50.9% of male students think their own ability is higher than their score, and only 27.9% of females have an inflated belief about their abilities.

Based on the above results, we can infer the conclusion: both men and women believe that men are significantly better than women in hands-on work and in their willingness to take on challenges, both of which are important qualities for computing practitioners. These views directly reduce women's computer self-efficacy, an individual's perceptions of his or her ability to use computers in the accomplishment of a task (Compeau and Higgins, 1995). When women have low computer self-efficacy, they perceive that computing-related professions are more suitable to the opposite gender. Therefore, Chinese women may think that men will have a dominant position in the computing industry, and that it would be very difficult for them to gain a foothold in these areas of work.

Pressure from the Computing Industry

Today, computing technologies relying on the internet are experiencing rapid changes with each passing day, which puts higher requirements on computing practitioners than practitioners in other industries. It seems difficult for female computing practitioners to deal successfully with these trends. The Committee for Women in Computing, China Computer Federation, conducted two surveys on female computing practitioners in 2015 and 2016, and found that the pressure on these female practitioners comes from the rapid pace of technological change, the heavy workload, and the high level of difficulty of computing-related work (Kaya, 2017). Because of the Chinese long-held traditional ethical values, such as the concept of "Men's work centers around outside, women's work centers around the home," women's perceived and real lack of initiative in learning new technologies and new opportunities, as well as their lack of enthusiasm for realization of their potential, put them under pressure in their work. These pressures make it easier for women than men to quit their jobs and leave the computing industry. These pressures are forcing women to quit their jobs and leave the computing industry.

MEASURES TAKEN TO IMPROVE CHINESE FEMALE PRACTITIONERS IN COMPUTING

In order to protect women's equal employment rights, China has formulated and improved laws and regulations to promote fair employment and to eliminate gender discrimination in employment (PRCSCIO, 2015). The Employment Promotion Law of the People's Republic of China, which was released in 2007, has a special section on "Fair Employment," which emphasizes the equal employment rights of men and women. The Law of the People's Republic of China on the Labor Contract Law, which was released in 2007, clearly stipulates the establishment of special collective contracts for the protection of the rights and interests of women practitioners. China stipulated, revised, and implemented the Special Regulations on the Protection of Female Employees, which was released in 2012, to support the growth of female scientific and technological talent and to promote the equal employment of female university students, by creating favorable conditions for women's employment and career development. In response to the difficulties faced by different groups of women in employment and entrepreneurship, China introduced supportive policies and measures. Women college students' employment and entrepreneurship support activities were implemented to provide female college students with employment training, entrepreneurship guidance, and apprenticeships.

Under the protection of these measures, the employment and entrepreneurial environment of Chinese women has greatly improved. In 2013, the

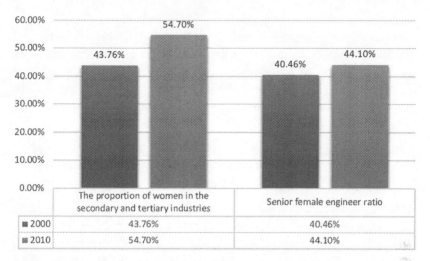

Figure 14.1 Comparison of data between 2000 and 2010: the proportion of women in the secondary and tertiary industries and senior female engineer ratio
(data from CWRN, 2010).

number of women employed nationwide was 346.4 million, accounting for 45% of the total employment. The latest survey in 2010 on the professional status of Chinese women (CWRN, 2010) showed that women's participation in the secondary and tertiary industries was 14.5% and 40.2%, respectively, an increase of 25% from ten years earlier. The number of female senior professional technicians reached 6.61 million, accounting for 44.1% of the total senior professional technicians, which was nine percentage points higher than in 2000 (Figure 14.1). The group of women entrepreneurs in China is growing, and women entrepreneurs account for about one-quarter of the total number of entrepreneurs. It can be said that in China today, compared with the past, Chinese women have a better employment and entrepreneurial environment in various industries, especially in the computing industry (new industries) that the country strongly supports.

The China Computer Association (CCF) established the Committee for Working Women in 2014 to focus on the education, scientific research, academic and professional status, and living conditions of female computing practitioners. It advocates that Chinese society pay attention to and care for female computing practitioners and provide protection and support in terms of female employment, salary, and career development. At the same time, CCF has been committed to discovering and recommending future female stars, and to providing employment guidance for female college students. So far, the CCF Women's Working Committee has convened three influential Female Elite Forums (October 20, 2016, and May 6 and October 26, 2017), similar to the Grace Hopper Conference in the United States. At these conferences, successful women in computing share their own experiences and make suggestions to address various problems encountered by Chinese women computing practitioners.

CULTURAL INFLUENCES ON THE RATIO OF CHINESE FEMALES IN TOP POSITIONS AND AS COMPUTING ENTREPRENEURS

According to the 2015 white paper "China's Gender Equality and Women's Development," 55% of entrepreneurs in the internet industry are women (PRCSCIO, 2015), who have become the main force of entrepreneurship in the internet field. A study by the Silicon Valley Bank also reports anecdotal evidence that about half of the American technology companies surveyed have at least one woman in an executive position (C-level jobs, such as CEO, COO, CFO, or CTO), while in China it is closer to 80% (Lacy, 2017). It can be said that among internet companies, the proportion of Chinese female entrepreneurs or females in top positions is very high. In the next section, we discuss some of the reasons for this phenomenon, that is, that women in China have many unique advantages that are suitable for the development of the internet industry. At the same time, these women entrepreneurs or women in top positions are better able to balance home and work than other Chinese female practitioners in computing.

Chinese Women's Advantages in Computing Entrepreneurship

China's internet entrepreneurship has exploded in recent years. According to a study by the Zhejiang Provincial Administration for Industry and Commerce, women have some unique advantages that have brought them success as entrepreneurs (Zhejia News, 2017). (1) Subversion and dissatisfaction are critical entry points for internet entrepreneurship. Women in China are the main buyers and users of internet goods and services (CBNData, 2016), so they are likely to first discover that a given product is "unsatisfactory" and then propose improvements, leading to successful entrepreneurship. (2) The handling of social relationships plays a key role in the success of internet entrepreneurial projects. Some examples include social marketing, social communication, and team relationship processing. Chinese women have been shown to excel in these arenas. (3) Chinese women appear to have a strong ability to integrate resources, providing another unique advantage for women as entrepreneurs. Some entrepreneurial service platforms launched by the Chinese government, industry associations, social organizations, etc. create conditions for the connection and integration of such entrepreneurial resources. It is through these platforms that many women entrepreneurs find the resources needed for entrepreneurship.

Work–Life Balance of Chinese Female Entrepreneurs and Leaders in Computing

Because computing is a global technology-oriented industry, compared with other industries, Chinese women entrepreneurs and leaders have more in common culturally with women in other countries. These women are young, well educated, well paid, and have a strong sense of professionalism and independence (Aaltio and Huang, 2007). They have high career expectations for themselves, and want to let others know that they can be "as good as men." These women are also very clear about their roles as wives and mothers. Fortunately, because their families and spouses are also more highly educated, they also have good support from their families, which makes it possible for them to focus on career development (Aaltio and Huang, 2007). They usually have parents or maids (home helpers) to help them with housework and/or childcare, or tutors to help their children with homework. They do not believe that work and family life interfere; in fact, they believe that their work can help and shape their personal and family life, and vice versa.

SUGGESTIONS TO INCREASE THE RATIO OF CHINESE FEMALE PRACTITIONERS IN COMPUTING

From the above discussion, we see that although the working environment of the entire computing industry in China has been greatly improved, women's misunderstanding of the computing industry may have caused many women to reject computing-related jobs. Long-held traditional Chinese ethical values, such as the concept of "Men's work centers around outside, women's work centers around the home," is still relatively common. In addition to a demanding workload, most women in computing bear the greater responsibility compared with their husbands regarding housework and care of the children. In China as elsewhere in Asia, children are under enormous pressure to perform academically, and the mother is generally the one the children turn to for help with their studies. Work and life are difficult to balance, and many computing women practitioners give up their jobs. There is still a long way to go to solve the problem of fewer female practitioners in the computing industry in China. Efforts must be made by governments, schools, companies, and families.

Suggestions to Government

The government plays an important role in solving the problem of fewer female computing practitioners in China. Some areas in which the government can and should take action include the following: (1) formulate more basic laws on women's rights to protect the basic interests of computing women practitioners in their work and life, (2) use the power of propaganda to guide the public's values and ease the pressure on female practitioners from the outside world; (3) play a guiding role and motivate the various functional departments of society to pay attention to this problem and solve it together; and (4) establish some basic service agencies to effectively ease the pressure of female computing practitioners from housework and children.

A survey conducted by the Chinese National Bureau of Statistics (NBSC, 2002) shows that the Chinese public has significantly improved their awareness and recognition of the Women's Rights and Interests Protection Law and the basic national policy of equality between men and women. At the same time, the government can use its own power to promote awareness and principles of gender equality among educators and media practitioners, strengthening the guidance and supervision of mass media, especially television and the internet, to counteract and eliminate discrimination and prejudice against women in the computing industry. The government should vigorously develop public childcare services to alleviate the problem of balancing work and family for female practitioners in the Chinese computing industry.

Suggestions to Schools

Everyone in China experiences a long and intense period of education. In this process, the information the school communicates to students will deeply affect their future choices, including the students' career choices. Chinese schools can take a significant role in promoting the computing industry for female students, highlighting the unique advantages of females in the computing industry, and reducing their misconceptions about the computing industry. Currently, programming courses are optional, not compulsory, in junior and senior high schools. Further, schools should offer a rich array of computing courses (not only programming classes, but also classes such as front-end, user interface design courses) that can attract more diverse student interests in computer science. In universities, the schools can invite successful women in the computing field to share their own experiences, address students' doubts about the computing industry, and establish a more realistic understanding of the computing industry. At the same time, teachers can create a more diverse environment for students in their team work projects so that females can better participate in and establish their confidence in the computing industry.

Suggestions to Companies

Computing industry companies should also recognize the importance of gender diversity in companies, in addition to abiding by the country's basic rights and interests laws that protect women practitioners. The company can provide a comfortable working environment for women while improving the proportion of women in the company. (1) Companies need to eliminate gender discrimination, and in the premise of equal treatment, formulate favorable incentive policies for female practitioners (e.g., equal pay); (2) companies can set up special teams to help women practitioners solve work and life problems and give them more care; and (3) companies can partner with universities to promote company culture and provide more opportunities for internships to women, increasing the number of female practitioners when recruiting.

Suggestions to Family

Affected by traditional culture, Chinese people have strong family values and family harmony is important to everyone. Due to the nature of the computing industry itself, overtime hours and work pressures are relatively high, so women practitioners will have relatively less time for family life. Therefore, families with women in the computing industry face a more serious problem of work–life balance than other industries. For family harmony, other members of the family should revise China's traditional family attitudes, adopt a tolerant and understanding attitude toward female practitioners, and take more homework and childcare tasks in family life. When both parents are busy, they should have access to resources that can help to assist in family affairs. Female practitioners should be supported so they can spend as much time as possible to be with their families, so that work and family are complementary.

CONCLUSION

The current number of women in the computing industry as a whole is inadequately low due to deeply rooted attitudes from China's traditional Confucian-based ethics, the intense pressures of balancing work and home, and the prevailing male-dominated environment in the computing industry.

There are many positive lessons to be learned from the surprisingly high number of women entrepreneurs, which offers promise that the goal of a major shift in diversity in this industry can be achieved. Many of these accomplishments should be focused on culture. However, there are many situations that need to be addressed to improve the ratio of female practitioners. Also, these cultural influences can be improved to have a positive role in recruiting and retaining women in the computing industry. While significant strides have been made over the past half-century, much more needs to be accomplished through a partnership among the Chinese government, educational institutions, and the computing industry.

China has made significant strides through legal protection of women's economic rights overall and through promotion of diversity, specifically in the computing industry. China is moving in the right direction to achieve the goal that "Women hold up half the (computing) sky!"

DISCUSSION QUESTIONS

1. What are the reasons for the low proportion of Chinese female practitioners in the computing? Are there other reasons besides those named in this chapter?
2. Discuss the benefits of gender diversity to the computer industry.
3. Why is the proportion of female entrepreneurs or females in top positions relatively high in China than in other countries?
4. Do you have any other suggestions for increasing the proportion of Chinese female practitioners in computing?
5. Do you think the proportion of female computer practitioners in China will increase in the future? Provide your reasons.
6. Do you have any encouraging words to Chinese female computing practitioners?
7. If you are a decision maker, how do you determine the gender ratios of participants based on the project requirements?

References

Aaltio, I., and Huang, J. (2007). Women Managers' Careers in Information Technology in China: High Flyers with Emotional Costs? *Journal of Organizational Change Management*, 20(2), 227–244.

CBNData. (2016). Report on Chinese Women's Consumption Market. www.yicai.com/news/5080567.html (accessed August 31, 2018).

Chinese Women's Research Network. (2010). The Main Data Report of the Third Survey of the Status of Chinese Women. www.wsic.ac.cn/staticdata/84760.htm (accessed June 26, 2018).

Compeau, D. R., and Higgins, C. A. (1995). Computer Self-Efficacy: Development of a Measure and Initial Test. *MIS Quarterly*, 189–211.

Dike, P. (2013). The Impact of Workplace Diversity on Organisations. *ARCADA*, 1(1), 1–52.

Elizabeth, J. (2017). The 17% Problem: Why Does the Percentage of Women in Computer Science Stop There? *JaxEnter*. https://jaxenter.com/women-in-computer-science-majors-133646.html (accessed June 29, 2018).

Kaya, Y. (2017). Google Struggles to Increase Workforce Diversity. *CNN Tech*. http://money.cnn.com/2017/06/29/technology/google-diversity-report/index.html (accessed June 27, 2018).

Lacy, S. (2017). Women in Tech Are Rising Higher in China than in the US. *The Atlantic*. www.theatlantic.com/technology/archive/2017/11/women-china-tech/545588/ (accessed June 26, 2018).

Microsoft (2017). Microsoft Global Diversity and Inclusion: Inside Microsoft. *Microsoft*. www.microsoft.com/en-us/diversity/inside-microsoft/default.aspx#epgDivFocus Area (accessed June 27, 2018).

National Bureau of Statistics of China. (2002). The Major Data Report of Second Spot Check of Chinese Women's Social Status. www.stats.gov.cn/tjgb/qttjgb/qgqttjgb/t20020331_15816.htm.

People's Republic of China State Council Information Office. (2015). China White Paper on Gender Equality and Women Development.

Proginn and Juejin. (2017). A Survey Report on Computer Science Engineers in China (2017). www.sohu.com/a/165615021_475887 (accessed June 27, 2018).

Proginn. (2018). 2018 Chinese Programmer's Salary and Life Survey Report. https://blog.csdn.net/helloxiaozhe/article/details/80510504 (accessed June 27, 2018).

Souhu News. (2017). Why Female IT Practitioners Account for a Low Proportion. www.sohu.com/a/201304649_267106 (accessed June 27, 2018).

Sun, L., Ma, X., Zhang, M., and Pan, T. (2018). Ada Workshop: Study and Practice on Improving Gender Diversity in Computer Science Industry.

Wen, H., and Cui, F. (2013). An Analysis of Women's Political Emancipation in the Early Period of the Founding of New China: A Perspective from the People's Daily, 1949–1956. *Monthly Research Theory of Marxism*, 38–41.

Zhejiang News. (2017). Is Internet Business More Suitable for Women? https://zj.zjol.com.cn/news/577640.html (accessed on June 26, 2018).

15

How the Perception of Young Malaysians toward Science and Mathematics Influences Their Decision to Study Computer Science

Mazliza Othman and Rodziah Latih

INTRODUCTION

It has been twelve years since our article "Women in Computer Science: No Shortage Here!" (Othman and Latih, 2006) was published. It is disheartening that after more than a decade, gender disparity in computer science (CS) is still an issue. *Among important findings of our previous study is that young Malaysian females and males have a markedly different attitude toward science and mathematics compared with their Western counterparts.* CS and information technology (IT) is not viewed as a masculine field by young Malaysians, which is a key reason why this nation does not encounter the problem of too few females being interested in pursuing a degree in CS/IT.

The following is an anecdote from an American woman who graduated from Yale in 1978 (Pollack, 2013): "I attended a rural public school whose few accelerated courses in physics and calculus I wasn't allowed to take because, as my principal put it, 'girls never go on in science and math.'" It is sad that Cheryan et al. (2015) found that girls are still steered away from CS and engineering by parents, teachers, and others who think that it is more suitable for boys.

While some universities (e.g., Norway University of Science and Technology and Carnegie Mellon University) have been successful in attracting more female students into their CS programs, others continue to struggle (Bartilla and Köppe, 2015). In the Netherlands, the Girls Day initiative to attract more females to study CS achieved little success – the numbers of female CS students remain very low.

WOMEN IN COMPUTING IN THE WEST

In the United States, in the science, technology, engineering, and math (STEM) fields, women obtain the majority of undergraduate degrees (59%) in biology and nearly half in chemistry and math, but they earn less than 20% of undergraduate degrees in computer science and engineering (Cheryan et al., 2015). Cheryan et al. list the following as reasons:

1. Girls may be steered away from CS and engineering by parents, teachers, and others who think that these careers are more suitable for boys.
2. Underrepresentation might perpetuate future underrepresentation. If girls do not see computer scientists and engineers as people with whom they feel similar, they may be more reluctant to enter these fields.
3. Girls underestimate how well they will do in these fields, resulting in a lower interest in entering them.
4. Girls may anticipate encountering greater work–family conflicts in these fields.
5. There is discrimination in these fields that prevents qualified women from receiving the same opportunities as their male counterparts.
6. Women who enter traditionally masculine domains can be socially and professionally penalized for exhibiting competence and leadership qualities.

These are barriers that contribute to why some women choose not to enter and persist in fields like CS and engineering in some cultures and countries. These are the same barriers that have been persisting in other male-dominated fields that women have entered. A key question remains: What has allowed other fields to welcome more women while computer science and engineering continue to lag behind?

Cheryan et al. (2015) report that among high-school students, girls are significantly less likely to take a computer programming class than boys, less likely to take the CS Advanced Placement test than boys, and express less interest in pursuing careers in CS and engineering than boys. By the time they enter college, men are already more than four times as likely to have an intention to major in CS and engineering than women. Even if every woman who intended to major in CS and engineering on entering college was retained in these fields, men would still be significantly more likely to earn a degree in these fields than women.

Kendall (2016) pointed out that in this age, the decreasing percentage of female intake is depressing, especially because being a "computer scientist" rather than just "computer literate" is becoming increasingly important. As deep learning and Big Data become common, it is useful for all genders to have an appreciation and engagement with these technologies – not just the males.

Taylor (2015) suggests that this issue be addressed as early as possible in the education cycle. We need to get young women excited about math, science, and technology, including computer science, long before they enter college. For example, the stereotypes that still make women feel unwelcome in the computer science industry need to be eliminated. One of the biggest stereotypes is that only men can be computer scientists, which makes it challenging for women to break through, and leads to the belief that women simply are not as good as men in computer science (Larson, 2014).

Unfortunately, Jung (2017) found that exposure to computer courses at the school level did not positively improve women's decision to major in technology. One of the influences that has been cited as contributing to the educational gender gap in technology is the lack of female role models (Jung, 2017). It is hard to identify women in technology – television and the media often feature men in technology, not women. This lends credibility to the assumption that women rarely excel in technology, resulting in few women choosing to major in this field.

Media can also have a strong influence on a girl's impression of computer science and technology. In the 1980s, forensics was a field dominated by men, but now it is one of the few sciences that are dominated by women (Potter, 2015). This increase could be attributed to primetime shows, such as the crime drama series *CSI*,[1] which are populated with female crime scene investigator role models, such as Sara Sidle, Catherine Willows, and other fictional characters, that have become very popular.

The fact that there are not many women teaching CS at the secondary school level is another reason. Girls who have women teaching them are more likely to be interested in pursuing CS (Goldman, 2016). Boys, on the other hand, seem equally engaged in computer science regardless of the teacher's gender.

A study conducted by Google in 2014 found women who were CS graduates were more likely to have their mother or father encouraging them to study CS compared with graduates from other degrees (Google, 2014). Another study by NCWIT showed that women most frequently chose their fathers (37%) or mothers (29%) as the most influential person in their decision to pursue a computing career (Ashcraft et al., 2012).

Owolabi et al. (2014) found math to be a good predictor of success in CS – someone who is good in math is more likely to be good in programming because both involve the ability to understand abstract concepts in solving problems. However, both adults and children in the United States believe that math is a stereotypically male domain (Cvencek et al., 2011). If girls are influenced to believe that they cannot be as good as boys in math, this would certainly influence their decision in what field of study to pursue later at university.

There have been heated debates about whether mathematical and scientific competency is biologically or socially/culturally determined (Damarin and Erchick, 2010). For instance, the former president of Harvard University, Lawrence Summer, sparked controversy when he remarked that women's scarcity in Harvard science departments was due to biological differences between women and men.

In a debate between Pinker and Spleker (2005), Spleker argued that there is no difference in the overall aptitude for science and mathematics between men and women. If we add up all the things that men are good at and all the things that women are good at, there is no overall advantage for men that would put them at the top of the fields of math and science. There are variations in the approach that males and females prefer in solving mathematical problems, but this does not result in one outdoing another in their problem-solving ability. While there are differences between the genders, the differences do not add up to an overall advantage of one over the other.

Spleker's argument is supported by a study conducted by Hyde et al. (2008) in the United States. In previous decades, girls took fewer advanced math and science courses in high school compared with boys, which led to superior male performance in standardized tests in high school. By 2000, girls were taking calculus at the same rate of boys. Now 48% of graduates in mathematics are women. Hyde et al.'s analysis of showed that for grades 2–11, there was no gender difference in math skills. Mathematical skill cannot be said to be the only factor that leads to gender disparity in STEM fields.

WOMEN IN CS IN MALAYSIA: OUR EARLY STUDY

The total Information and Communication Technology (ICT) market value in Malaysia for 2015 is RM155.2 billion (approximately US$38 billion). The share of the overall ICT industry in the economy expanded from 16.5% in 2010 to 17.6% in 2015, and is on track to reach 20% by

2020.[2] Given the size and rapid growth of this industry, investment in human capital is important to ensure that progress is not hampered.

The results of our previous study (Othman and Latih, 2006) showed that young Malaysians do not subscribe to many of the stereotypes of their Western counterparts. There was little difference in mathematic competency of male and female students. For example, 37% of the females strongly agreed that CS/IT is suitable for women, compared with 5% of the males. Further, 44% of females strongly agreed that they will work in the CS/IT industry after graduation, compared with only 29% males. This indicates that female students do not experience demoralization while pursuing their study and, as a result, are keen to pursue a career in a related field.

Table 15.1 shows the undergraduate intake for CS/IT programs at the Faculty of Computer Science and Information Technology, University of Malaya (UM), and the Faculty of Information Science and Technology, University Kebangsaan Malaysia (UKM) from 2010 to 2018. At UM, the difference between the percentage of male and female intake is mostly negligible. At UKM, there were years where female students outnumbered the males significantly.

WOMEN IN CS IN MALAYSIA: OUR LATEST STUDY

In March 2018, a hard-copy questionnaire was distributed to eighty second- and third-year undergraduates (61% female and 39% male) at the University of Malaya (UM) and the University Kebangsaan Malaysia (UKM). The respondents were from the computer science program (73%), the information technology program (25%), and the software engineering program (2%). The questionnaire is similar to the one we used in our 2006 study with a few additions to take into account technology progress since then (e.g., operating systems and devices respondents have experience using). T-tests were carried out at the significance level of 0.05. Where the results differ from our previous study, we discuss on which aspects they differ.

Family Background

When asked why they chose their current degree program, 92% female and 84% male said they chose it out of interest (Table 15.2). The respondents have educated parents and at least finished secondary school. A few respondents have parents with master's degrees. About half of respondents have a family member working in a CS-related field (Table 15.3). A slight

Table 15.1 *Student intake of undergraduate CS/IT programs at UM and UKM, 2010–2018*

Academic year	UM				UKM			
	Female		Male		Female		Male	
	Number	Percentage	Number	Percentage	Number	Percentage	Number	Percentage
2017–2018	207	50	203	50	141	54	122	46
2016–2017	70	46	83	54	125	56	98	44
2015/2016	37	40	56	60	138	63	81	37
2014–2015	61	51	59	49	167	69	76	31
2013–2014	27	51	26	49	137	74	47	26
2012–2013	43	51	41	49	117	61	74	39
2011–2012	37	44	48	56	122	58	88	42
2010–2011	45	49	47	51	125	64	71	36

Table 15.2 *Reason for choosing this program*

Gender	Interest (%)	Family (%)	Selected (%)
Female	92	2	8
Male	84	3	13

Table 15.3 *Has family member working in computer science–related field*

Gender	Yes (%)	No (%)
Female	55	45
Male	45	55

Table 15.4 *SPM mathematics grade*

Gender	Grade A (%)	Grade B (%)	Grade F (%)	No answer (%)
Female	86	6	0	8
Male	42	16	3	39

Table 15.5 *STPM mathematics grade*

Gender	Grade A (%)	Grade B (%)	Grade C (%)	Grade D (%)	No answer (%)
Female	45	27	2	2	24
Male	32	7	0	0	61

majority, or 55%, of female respondents have a family member whose work is related to CS. While this might influence their decision to study CS, it probably is not the only factor influencing their decision. For respondents who have learned programming languages prior to starting their degree programs, this contributes to their interest in pursuing a degree in CS (more about this when discussing the results shown in Tables 15.9 and 15.12).

Mathematics

We asked respondents about their mathematic grades for SPM[3] (equivalent to O-level[4]) and STPM (equivalent to A-level). Our findings show there is a significant difference in mathematical competency between male and female students (Tables 15.4 and 15.5). Twice as many female students earned an

Table 15.6 *Grade in programming subject (%)*[a]

	A		B		C		D		E	
Subject	F	M	F	M	F	M	F	M	F	M
Java	18	13	16	9	6	1	1	0	0	2
C/C++	12	6	12	7	6	2	2	0	0	0
VB.net	2	3	1	0	1	0	1	0	0	0
PHP/HTML	21	7	10	5	3	0	1	0	0	1

[a] F, female; M, male.

Table 15.7 *Has taken computer courses prior to enrolling in program*

Gender	No (%)	Yes (%)
Female	35	65
Male	52	48

A grade for mathematics in SPM and more females received an A grade in STPM. In fact, when asked whether they agree with the statement "I like mathematics" (Table 15.13, below), 88% of the females "strongly agreed/agreed" compared with 74% of the males.

If we were to go by Owolabi et al.'s (2014) finding that someone who is good in math is more likely to be good in programming, then the female respondents would have no trouble succeeding in CS study.

Computer and Programming Skills

We asked respondents their grades for programming courses taken and found no significant difference in programming achievements (Table 15.6).

We asked respondents to specify how they attained their computer skills prior to beginning their degree program. We found that 65% of the female respondents took programming courses before they enrolled in the current program as compared with only 48% of male respondents (Table 15.7). They took courses like programming, computer software packages, and networks.

When our respondents were in secondary school (before 2015), computer subjects were not taught as part of the standard school curriculum. Some schools taught programming as an extra-curricular activity offered by the Computer Club. Either they learned programming (and other computer subjects) through classes conducted by the Computer Club or they took private lessons offered by vocational training centers.

Table 15.8 *Time spent on activities*

	Female	Male
a. Playing computer games[a]	2.7	3.0
b. Surfing the internet	3.8	3.8
c. Writing programs (other than coursework)	2.4	2.5
d. Doing assignment using a computer	3.4	3.6
e. Hacking computer systems[a]	1.2	1.4

[a] z-test indicates a significant difference.

Table 15.9 *Computers used prior to beginning degree program*

	Female	Male
a. Personal computer/laptop	3.3	3.2
b. Macintosh	1.7	1.7
c. Mini computer (UNIX, VAX, etc.)	1.8	1.7
d. Smart phone/tablet[a]	3.7	3.4

[a] z-test indicates a significant difference.

Respondents were asked how much time they spend doing the activities listed in Table 15.8 (never, less than 1 hour/week, 1–2 hours/week, more than 2 hours/week). The only significant difference was the amount of time playing computer games and hacking computer systems.

When asked them to rate their skills (1, novice; 2, competent; 3, proficient; 4, expert) in using computers prior to starting their degree programs (Table 15.9), overall the female respondents rated themselves higher than the males. This correlates with the result shown in Table 15.13 (below), where more females agree with the statement that "Computer skills are important."

We asked respondents to rate their competency with operating systems (Windows, Unix/Linux, iOS, and Android), programming languages (Java, C, or C++) and several computer applications like word processors, spreadsheets, and databases (Table 15.10). Note that there is a significant difference for all but two, with female respondents feeling more confident of their competency. This is different from our previous finding, where male respondents were more confident of their skills. After comparing the responses from our previous and current studies, we are unable to pinpoint what led to female respondents to be more confident.

Respondents learned programming languages like Java, C/C++, VB.net, PHP, Python, and HTML in their current program. We asked respondents to rate their familiarity with programming constructs like control structure, looping, array, procedure, and pointer. The results show that the male

Table 15.10 *Skill in operating systems, computer languages and applications before commencing current program*

	Female	Male
a. Windows[a]	3.4	3.1
b. Unix/Linux[a]	2.1	1.9
c. iOS	2.4	2.5
d. Android[a]	3.2	2.9
e. Java[a]	2.6	2.3
f. C or C++	2.6	2.5
g. Word processor[a]	3.5	3.2
h. Spreadsheet[a]	3.3	2.9
i. Databases[a]	2.9	2.3

[a] z-test indicates a significant difference.

Table 15.11 *Familiarity with programming construct*

	Female	Male
a. Control structure (if-else)	2.8	2.9
b. Loop (while, for)[a]	2.7	3.0
c. Array[a]	2.6	2.8
d. Procedure/function[a]	2.5	2.7
e. Pointer	2.4	2.3

[a] z-test indicates a significant difference.

students claim to understand programming constructs better than females (Table 15.11). Even though there is a small difference between female and male opinions, female respondents proclaim that they can program well compared with male respondents (Table 15.13). Compared with our previous study, even though male respondents still rate themselves higher, current female respondents rate their understanding higher than female respondents in the previous study.

Skill Acquisition

We asked respondents how they acquired their computer skills (Table 15.12) prior to beginning their degree programs. The results are very different from our previous study, where the only significant difference was acquired skills via self-teaching, with more male respondents self-teaching themselves. In this study, there is no difference in self-taught skill acquisition. Other significant differences are acquired skill at school, private lesson, friends, family, and work.

Table 15.12 *Acquisition of computer skills*

	Female	Male
a. Secondary school[a]	3.2	2.7
b. Self-taught	3.5	3.5
c. Private lesson[a]	3.1	2.5
d. Books and magazines	2.7	2.5
e. Internet	3.7	3.6
f. Friends[a]	3.3	3.0
g. Family[a]	3.1	2.7
h. Work[a]	3.3	2.7
i. Hacking	1.8	1.9

[a] z-test indicates a significant difference.

Our previous finding that more males self-taught themselves did not surprise us because it corroborated other findings that boys liked to explore and, therefore, are more likely to self-teach themselves. The proliferation of online resources makes it easy for anyone interested in learning programming to do so and teach themselves. The widespread use of mobile devices also contributes to exposing young people to mobile apps, hence increasing their curiosity about how apps are developed. We speculate that this may lead to more females self-teaching themselves.

Unlike the finding of Cheryan et al. (2015) that among high-school students, girls are significantly less likely to take a computer programming class than boys, more female respondents acquired their computer skills while in secondary school and through private lessons. This indicates that they did not see computer skills as something that only boys do or only boys can become good at. Therefore, it is hardly surprising when 92% of females chose to study CS (Table 15.1) out of interest – they do not have the same inhibitions as their Western counterparts.

Perceptions toward CS

We asked respondents to rate their agreement (1, no opinion; 2, disagree; 3, mildly disagree; 4, agree; 5, strongly agree) with a set of statements (Table 15.13). Both male and female respondents agreed that they enjoy a challenging environment and that computers are fun. Females agree more strongly that CS is suitable for women, and this is reflected in their agreement that they will work in the computer industry after graduation. In fact, more females than males stated that they will work in the industry.

Table 15.13 *Degree of agreement with statements*

	Female	Male
a. I enjoy a challenging environment	3.8	3.8
b. Computers are fun	4.3	4.2
c. CS/IT is suitable for women[a]	4.2	3.7
d. I was prepared for the program	4.1	4.0
e. Other people seem more prepared[a]	4.3	3.9
f. I like mathematics[a]	4.2	3.9
g. I can program well[a]	3.6	3.4
h. I will work in computer/IT industry after graduating[a]	4.1	3.8
i. Computer skills are important	4.6	4.5
j. Men are more skillful than women in using computers[a]	3.9	3.4

[a] z-test indicates a significant difference.

It is interesting to note that female respondents agree more strongly that "Men are more skillful than women in using computers."

We have been asked several times how many CS/IT female graduates actually continue with a career in a related field. We too have pondered this matter. Unfortunately, we have been unable to provide a definitive answer because tracking down alumni has proved to be a non-trivial task. We also have not been able to find any official data (either no study has been conducted by the government or the data are not made available to the public).

There is no significant difference when asked whether they feel prepared for the program. Both respondents agree with the statement. Unfortunately, the female students feel more strongly that "other people seem more prepared" compared with the male students.

Compared with the results of our previous study, where there was no difference in the agreement to "I can program well," more females in this study believe that they can program well. Also, it is interesting to note that while previously there was no difference in the agreement with "Men are more skillful than women in using computers," there is now a significant difference, with females agreeing more strongly with this statement.

CONCLUSION

Once again, our survey shows that young Malaysian men and women do not hold a different perception in terms of their ability to succeed in CS. Math and science are not seen as masculine fields dominated by men. In fact, our study shows that female respondents do better in mathematics.

Referring to the anecdote we shared in the Introduction section, we know from personal experience that the education culture in Malaysia does not discriminate when helping students excel in the subjects they choose to study. Boys and girls are given equal opportunity and encouragement to succeed. Consequently, they do not grow up with a preconceived belief that one gender is better suited for certain fields and, therefore, more likely to succeed in those fields.

The lack of women in computer science, and STEM in general, is not due to an innate inability of women to excel in this field but, rather, due to cultural and societal "programming." Figure out a way to deprogram this belief, and the problem will be solved. We hope that a decade from now, we will no longer be discussing how to attract young women to pursue a study, and later a career, in STEM.

DISCUSSION QUESTIONS

1. Identify the root cause of the belief that males are better at mathematics and science. What can be done to rectify this belief?
2. Compare the performance of male and female students majoring in computer science. Is there a significant difference?
3. A number of studies show that the culture of a country influences females' perception of computer science. Discuss how the culture in your country encourages or deters women from studying computer science.
4. The proliferation of mobile devices and the popularity of social media websites have created a generation of computer-literate users. How, in your opinion, can this be used to cultivate the interest of young females to major in computer science in the university?
5. If you know a woman who works in the computer industry, interview her about any difficulties she might have experienced during her study and career.

References

Ashcraft, C., Eger, E., and Friend, M. (2012). *Girls in IT: The Facts*. Boulder, CO: National Center for Women and Information Technology.

Bartilla, A., and Köppe, C. (2015). Awareness Seeds for More Gender Diversity in Computer Science Education. In Proceedings of the 20th European Conference on Pattern Languages of Programs, July 8–12, 2015, Kaufbeuren, Germany.

Cheryan, S., Master, A., and Meltzoff, A. N. (2015). Cultural Stereotypes as Gatekeepers: Increasing Girls' Interest in Computer Science and Engineering by

Diversifying Stereotypes. *Frontiers in Psychology*, 11, article number 49. https://doi.org/10.3389/fpsyg.2015.00049.

Cvencek, D., Meltzoff, A. N., and Greenwald, A. G. (2011), Math-Gender Stereotypes in Elementary School Children. *Child Development*, 82(3), 766–779.

Damarin S., and Erchick, D. B. (2010), Toward Clarifying the Meanings of "Gender" in Mathematics Education Research. *Journal for Research in Mathematics Education*, 41(4), 310–323.

Forrest, C. (2014), Media Portrayals of Women in Tech: Google Joins Non-profits to Drive Change. *TechRepublic*. www.techrepublic.com/article/media-portrayals-of-women-in-tech-google-joins-non-profits-to-drive-change/, accessed July 6, 2018.

Goldman, J. (2016). Why It's Getting Harder, Not Easier, to Find Women with Computer Science Degrees. www.inc.com/jeremy-goldman/why-its-getting-harder-not-easier-to-find-women-with-computer-science-degrees.html, accessed July 3, 2018.

Google. (2014). Women Who Choose Computer Science – What Really Matters. https://static.googleusercontent.com/media/edu.google.com/en//pdfs/women-who-choose-what-really.pdf, accessed July 7, 2018.

Hyde, J. S., Lindberg, S. M., Linn, M. C., Ellis, A. B., and Williams, C. C. (2008). Gender Similarities Characterize Math Performance. *Science*, New Series, 321(5888), 494–495.

Jung, L., Clark, U., Patterson, L., and Pence, T. (2017). Closing the Gender Gap in the Technology Major. *Information Systems Education Journal (ISEDJ)*, 15(1), 26–41.

Kendall, G. (2016). Why Girls Are Put Off Studying Computer Science. *The Conversation*. https://theconversation.com/why-girls-are-put-off-studying-computer-science-70691, accessed July 3, 2018.

Larson, S. (2014). Why So Few Women Are Studying Computer Science. *ReadWrite*. https://readwrite.com/2014/09/02/women-in-computer-science-why-so-few/, accessed July 3, 2018.

Othman, M., and Latih, R. (2006). Women in Computer Science: No Shortage Here. *Communications of the ACM*, 49(3), 111–114.

Owolabi, J., Olanipekun, P., and Iwerima, J. (2014). Mathematics Ability and Anxiety, Computer and Programming Anxieties, Age and Gender as Determinants of Achievement in Basic Programming, *GSTF Journal on Computing (JoC)*, 3(4), 109–114. Doi: 10.5176/2251-3043_3.4.296

Pinker S., and Spleker, E. S. (2005). The Science and Gender of Science: Pinker vs. Spleker – A Debate. *Edge: The Third Culture*, May 16. www.edge.org/3rd_culture/debate05/debate05_index.html#s2, accessed July 5, 2017.

Pollack, E. (2013). Why Are There Still So Few Women in Science? *New York Times*, October 3.

Potter, D. (2015, September 15). More Women Examine a Career in Forensic Science. ABC News. ABC News Network.

Taylor, R. (2015). How Early Education Can Close the Gender Gap in STEM, *Fortune*. http://fortune.com/2015/10/28/early-education-gender-gap-stem/, accessed 4 July 2018.

16

Women as Software Engineers in Indian Tamil Cinema

Joyojeet Pal

INTRODUCTION

Prior to the 2010 World Classical Tamil Conference[1] in Coimbatore, a music video called "Semmozhiyaan Tamil Mozhiyaan" made its way to television networks across Tamil Nadu. The video was shot by Gautham Menon and had music composed by A. R. Rehman – both leading figures in the Tamil film industry at the time, with lyrics penned by the then chief minister and Dravida Munnetra Kazhagam (DMK) headman Muthuvl Karunanidhi. The song was intended as an anthem for the conference, but soon started being referred to as the state anthem.

The visuals of the music video had an anthem feel, in that they showcased the state and its people, featuring several iconic images from ancient tablets of classical Tamil text to modern urban infrastructure, lush landscape images, and a range of well-known performers making cameo appearances through the song. Images of a harmonious society included a wedding, religious ceremonies, classical performances, and children being taught in school. Outside of the performances themselves, there are only three images of vocations: a farmer, a teacher, and a computer programmer. The selection of the images is deliberate, and captures the political message of DMK through the anthem – earth, knowledge, and modernity.

The computer programmer is shown as a young middle-class woman, awed by the environment in which the company is housed, but instantly content with her surroundings as she settles into her cubicle. As she enters the building, others entering around her are women in salwaar kameezes like her, and around her cubicle we also see women at work. There is then a close-up of her computer screen, and we see her do a search using a Google Tamil interface, which leads her to a Wikipedia page about computing in

Tamil. Further down in the film, we see people use cellphones to send messages, typing in Tamil.

The use of Tamil script on the screen of the computer and phone signify the compatibility of the language and tradition with high technology. The office of the technology firm suggests modernity – a glass tower with computers and spacious modern furnishings – but the woman in the office is pointedly middle-class, as are the others we see in the images. There are no men in suits walking about and the focus is on the accessibility of the space to the average Tamilian. She is a young girl, presumably unmarried – given that the other women in the rest of the video wear sarees, and are probably married – and has a career. Despite the artifacts of modernity all around her, tradition and moral order are not threatened by an important site of relevance – her physical appearance. But the emphasized bottom line is that a young woman's career is not incompatible with the ideal of Tamilness. It also helps that the message is endorsed by the mouthpiece of Tamil establishment of the time.

COMPUTING, CINEMA, AND ASPIRATION IN INDIA

Much recent work has examined the role of technology in career aspirations in India. The young woman in the Semmozhiyaan video was one among a large number of mainstream media depictions of women in technology jobs in India. This is part of a larger discourse on technology and development that has captured India since the late 1990s. From special economic zones promoting technology companies to lead characters in movies as software engineers, or politicians promoting themselves as technocrats in the media, the idea of technology as central to an aspirational discourse of development has been ubiquitous in the public sphere. Working in the technology sector, both in India or preferably abroad, has been a central marker of middle-class upward mobility. Indeed, there are few greater markers of the role of technology in Indian development than the prime minister, Narendra Modi, who has crafted an identity for himself as a tech-savvy politician with an eye on a technology-driven vision of Indian development during his tenure.

The Semmozhiyaan video is arguably part of a larger belief that the role of technology has been positive overall for issues of gender equity in India. While this is extremely difficult to measure, there are some preliminary measures that may be helpful in approaching gender questions as they relate to the technology industry. Engineering education, for instance, has much greater gender equity in India on par with males at several levels of post-secondary education compared with the United States (Zweben and Bizot, 2018). This is additionally important because females' access is otherwise significantly less than that of males in the Indian higher education system. Needless to say, not all is entirely positive – for instance, marriage dowries (which are still an important part of the Indian social structure) for software engineers are high among professionals (Biao, 2005), especially if they are global professionals (Yakaboski, 2013).

CINEMA AND MIDDLE-CLASS ASPIRATION IN INDIA

Cinema has long served as a mirror for Indian society's aspirations, prejudices, and fears alike. The largest feature film industry in the world, the Indian film industry produces content in various languages. In the south Indian state of Tamil Nadu, where this research was conducted, cinema is central to both the political and social lives of people. For more than five decades, the elected heads of government in the state have only been people from the film industry. Film stars from the state routinely transition to mainstream politics, and suffer what has been referred to an "image trap," which is being stuck in playing roles that comply with righteous visions of what is socially desirable (Pandian, 1992).

The existence of this image trap has meant that filmmakers must carefully tread a line between what is interesting narrative and what is aligned with social aspirations of the time, particularly among middle-class Tamil people. This has long meant that despite the presence of women in the workforce, the portrayal of females in the workforce remained a complex issue, such that most film scripts have taken conservative, recidivist positions. With a solid history of protest and manufactured outrage, filmmakers needed to be careful about how they portrayed morality, and actors themselves needed to be careful about choices that led them to typecasting.

In this environment, the turn to depicting women who work in technology in a positive light is a particularly important change in Tamil cinema. In the past, a woman in the workforce was invariably accompanied by the failure of patriarchy – a dead husband, a disabled father, or an irresponsible husband whose actions pushed a virtuous woman into the workforce. Technology changed this. To understand this evolution, we will examine the history of women in the workforce on screen in Tamil cinema and combine depictions into categories with the goal of describing the ways in which this change is significant.

AT HOME AND IN THE WORLD

In 1973, K. Balachander directed *Arangetram*. In the film, the eldest daughter of a rural orthodox Brahmin family moves to the city to get a job. She earns a living as a prostitute, works her family out of poverty, and is eventually rejected by her family. In 2000, Rajiv Menon directed and co-wrote *Kandukondain Kandukondain*. A rural Brahmin family is likewise impoverished, and the eldest daughter must negotiate life in a city to earn a living. She gets a job as a software engineer, and works her family out of poverty. In an interview, Menon noted that he was very deliberate about casting the lead female as a computer engineer, because he saw it as a meritocracy, and as a departure from the dominant "angelic face of rural ethic" that had dominated Indian cinema in the past.

Females have traditionally been part of the workforce throughout South India, irrespective of the cinematic tropes that undermine the legitimacy of a working woman. Gender and film studies scholars have long argued that the notion of a good woman was modeled on the mythical goddess. While she possessed the virtues of love, domesticity, and morals, she was often defined in part by what she did not possess – the corrupting Western influence, of which a Western education was an inherent part (Lakshmi, 2008). A Western education gives women both Western ideas and, when they arrive at the workplace, access to westernized spaces. Thus, both *Kandukondain Kandukondain* and the song "Semmozhiyan" offer an important path away from the traditional lines of what good women were meant to be; the reason "Semmozhiyan" was particularly important was that it was penned by the very politician-writer who wrote the same screenplays that would come to define the good Tamil woman. To contextualize this, we begin by thematically summarizing the woman at work in Tamil cinema throughout the years.

THE GODDESSES

Two key mythological characters, the Tamil folklore character Kannagi and the Hindu goddess Durga/Kali, provide the normative basis for an important female characteristic – anger. In their respective tales, both Kannagi and Durga/Kali have moments of culmination in their characters, where the male companion is diminished or missing, and the woman's act of righteous aggression brings woe to their antagonists. Durga and Kali are the angry/destructive avatars of Parvathi, Shiva's consort in Hindu mythology.

This avatar of righteous anger and capability of destructive power was worked into screen characters where the protagonist's righteous anger toward social ills is central to her characterization. These films include crusading journalists (*Niraparaadhi*, 1984; *Moondru Mugam*, 1982; and *Indran Chandran*, 1989), righteous rebels (*Kannathil Muthamittal*, 2002), magistrates or other powerful civil servants (*Vanavil*, 2000, and *Kadhalan*, 1994), and the most frequent character, policewomen (*Citizen*, 2001; *Pen Singam*, 2010; and *Bhavani IPS*, 2011). This avatar was sometimes complicated by both its roots in Western education and its opening of male spaces to female protagonists.

The second goddess prototype derives from the avatars of Parvathi, such as Meenakshi or Sati, that focus on maternal or familial qualities. These include professions that are legitimized by their focus on caregiving – such as nurses (*Paalum Pazhamum*, 1961, and *Deiva Thai*, 1964) and doctors (*Pudhiya Mugam*, 1993 and *Vetri Vizha*, 1989). These professions highlight love, demure behavior, a standardized function in society, and the trappings of modesty including conservative dress, tied-back hair, etc. The vast majority of screen roles featuring nurses or doctors tend to present the work as appropriate, or at least not as explicitly problematic.

The third and perhaps most complex symbolic heroine is the goddess Saraswathi, who represents knowledge and the arts. These jobs include teachers, who represent knowledge but also motherhood, in that the teachers become surrogates for parental influence (*Teacher Amma*, 1968, and *Naane Raja Naane Mandhiri*, 1985). But while the teacher in school presents an extension of a woman's natural role around young children, teachers around grown-ups (such as college students) are often presented as framed within the sexual risks of being around young males (*Nammavar*, 1994). The Saraswathi personification extends to the artist – thus including the Carnatic singer/performer or the Bharatnatyam dancer.

THE ANTI-GODDESSES

The Saraswathi personification is further emphasized by what does not qualify as legitimate art. The "Western" performer, who deviates from tradition, is almost always portrayed in negative light. The woman in a "westernized profession" can also be depicted as a site of sanctioned violence. When a woman is murdered in a Tamil film such as in *Kalaignan* (1993), *Pulan Visaranai* (1990), *Oomai Vizhigal* (1986), or *Tik Tik Tik* (1981), the victim is frequently employed as a model or a dancer. The working woman in *Tik Tik Tik*, for instance, is shown as dressing suggestively, fantasizing about men while lying on a swing. In Silambarasan's *Manmadhan* (2004), even though the protagonist is a psychopath who murders "westernized women," the tagline of the film is "Only God can judge him" – implying that it is arguable whether or not the women got what they deserved.

Class offers an exception to most rules of acceptable female profession on screen. Since the earliest days of cinema, females have been cast as domestic or farm laborers. While some of these attempted to highlight class inequality (e.g., *Velaikkaari*, 1949), the vast majority of films that have historically cast women in these roles have simply accepted working-class poverty as a justification for women in the workforce.

AT HOME IN THE WORKPLACE

The discussion of women on the screen as a starting point for thinking about gender and technology is best understood through how the office workplace has traditionally been depicted. The office secretary has been a stereotypically gendered occupation, often the starting point of female depictions in the white-collar office. The female office secretary poses no serious threat to the professional supremacy of a man in the workplace, since, typically, she reports to a man. Secretarial jobs have traditionally been sexualized – in *Uthama Purushan* (1989), *Bharatha Vilas* (1973), and *Thodarum* (1999), an attractive office secretary is the starting point for a man's temptation. To emphasize the foreignness of such workplaces, secretaries often had Christian names, to suggest a further separation from authentic Tamilness (e.g., *Ulagam Sutrum Valiban*, 1973).

The vast majority of private sector workplaces were similarly problematic. In films that featured women who replaced men in positions of professional power, such as female managers or owners of businesses, the gender dynamics were invariably problematic for the woman. The focus was not only on the sexual complexity of a woman in the male domain of offices, but also on her neglect of her duties as a wife, daughter, daughter-in-law, or mother if her attention is focused on a professional career. Women in business may be depicted as competent, in which case the characterization is often of arrogance such as the common trope of an heiress (thus not self-made) businesswoman in *Sandai* (2008) or *Arumugam* (2009), who is eventually tamed by being pushed into greater femininity by the hero or, more commonly, of an incompetent, accidental professional who is exposed to exploitation by a crafty male relative (*Vettaikaran*, 1964).

In *Sigappu Rojakkal*, a group of women are waiting to be interviewed, and an administrator comes into the room asking the girls for pre-interview details in a lewd manner. None of the girls is offended at his behaviour, thus implying that such treatment of women in an office space ought not to be seen as surprising. Further, one of the girls is not bothered by the advances, is confident and outspoken, and in the interview comes across as modern and goal-driven. This girl gets the job, but is murdered later on, alongside other women who fit her modern profile.

The consistent theme over the years has been that a professional, private sector office space is outside the realm of the ideal use of a woman's time. While the goddess prototypical jobs are clearly legitimate, those driven by poverty such as labor jobs are to be tolerated, since they are driven by need, while the anti-goddess jobs clearly represent social decay. The office job is a much more problematic space because it represents a fundamental failure of masculinity.

THE GODDESS GOES TO WORK

The turning point of Rajiv Menon's *Kandukondain Kandukondain* was the scene in which the female protagonist goes from being an office secretary to a software engineer. The woman, Sowmya, leaves her village for a city to work as a receptionist at a software company. When her boss discovers that she has been moonlighting, learning programming on the job, he promotes her to a technical position. In the scene when she is promoted, Sowmya can barely hide her excitement, and drops her typically demure and traditional demeanor to reach out and shake hands with her boss. The scene is shot to present the handshake with a man as a transition away from the traditional folded hands. Sowmya, however, remains the demure, talented Brahmin girl, who gives up only as much of her orthodoxy as is needed to support the family with no male heirs.

Sowmya's workplace is not the stereotypical sexualized space of past office space movies. *Kandukondain Kandukondain* was a precursor to the DMK anthem a decade later, and Sowmya was the new age avatar of the goddess Saraswathi. A number of films featured females in tech sector jobs in the decade to follow (*Unnale Unnale*, 2007; *Yaradi Nee Mohini*, 2008; and *Vinnaithandi Varuvaya*, 2010), in which the woman's work was generally a positive force in her life, and where she straddles tradition and modernity effortlessly. Around this time, research on women and careers in Tamil Nadu showed evidence that women and parents alike felt that working in the tech industry was different from working in any other workplace (Pal, 2010). It helped that the tech sector in India came with some measure of gender-conscious benefits – more women in the workplace, access to safe transportation (since many tech firms offered pick-up and drop-off services for employees), and a work environment that, at least in the popular imagination, involved dealing with machines rather than with people.

Perhaps one of the most significant and successful films in this genre was *Yaradi Nee Mohini* (2008), in which a jobless alcoholic male protagonist turns his life around after falling in love with a female software engineer. The film is loaded with the artifacts of modernity as understood in relation to the tech sector in India – computers, employees wearing lanyards, and foreign trips for young engineers. But most importantly, the film was about an educated, competent woman, who helps turn around a fool.

The idea of a no-good male being "fixed" by a good woman is a fairly common idea in Tamil cinema, but contrary to the past when the care aspects of a woman's personality were the drivers of what made a man want to be better, in *Yaradi Nee Mohini*, she epitomizes Saraswathi in that she teaches the man to be an engineer, and yet remains modern and also traditional through it. Unlike the screen secretaries of the past whose Western dressing was an expression of their distance from traditional womanhood, the Mohini's Western dressing alternates with her traditional characteristics and signifies her ability to evolve. The software engineer has evolved to be the newest addition to the Saraswathi character.

CONCLUSION

Much of the change in the portrayal of working women in Tamil Nadu is related to the kinds of opportunities available to middle-class Tamilians. The woman engineer in the urban tech workplace is not an anomalous sight in the real world, though arguably the woman in the urban office was no more an anomalous sight through much of the 1970s and 1980s when the office space was being demonized on screen. The difference is that the barriers to women's successes in the workplace have been laid open in ways that were less obvious in the past.

What has also changed in India is the nature of male aspiration. The technology office in the "Semmozhiyaan" anthem is part of the larger vision of the future of the Indian workplace and social aspiration. And while the image of women in the economy may be finding new sanction in these images, a paradox of misanthropy lies underneath. At the same time as the prime minister, Narendra Modi, runs a Digital India online campaign to turn the country to a technology hub, promotes the role of women in these transformations, and runs a prevention campaign called #BetiBachao (save our daughters), he also oversees a culture that includes female infanticide.

DISCUSSION QUESTIONS

1. How does film influence our social perceptions of gender and careers?
2. What is the typical perception of the computing field as portrayed in Indian Tamil film?
3. How are female computing professionals depicted in Indian Tamil film?
4. In what ways is a computing career attrative to women in India?
5. What challenges do women in India face in pursuing a computing career?

References

Biao, X. (2005). Gender, Dowry and the Migration System of Indian Information Technology Professionals. *Indian Journal of Gender Studies*, 12(2–3), 357–380.

Lakshmi, C. (2008). A Good Woman, a Very Good Woman: Tamil Cinema's Women. In S. Velayutham (ed.), *Tamil Cinema*. New York: Routledge, 16–28.

Pal, J. (2010). Of Mouse and Men: Computers and Geeks as Cinematic Icons in Age of ICTD. In *Proceedings of the 2010 iConference*, 179–187.

Pandian, M. S. S. (1992). *The Image Trap: MG Ramachandran in Film and Politics*. New Delhi: Sage Publications India.

Yakaboski, T., Stout, R., and Sheridan, K. (2013). U.S. Engineering Degrees for Improving South Indian Graduate Students' Marriage and Dowry Options. *Journal of Studies in International Education*, 18(1), 45–63.

Zweben, S. and Bizot, B. (2018). Another Year of Record Undergrad Enrollment: Doctoral Degree Production Steady While Master's Production Rises Again. *Computing Research Association (CRA) Bulletin*, May 21, Washington, DC. Retreived from https://cra.org/2017-cra-taulbee-survey-another-year-of-record-undergrad-enrollment-doctoral-degree-production-steady-while-masters-production-rises-again/.

17

Women in Computing Education

A Western or a Global Problem? Lessons from India

Roli Varma

INTRODUCTION

Graduation trends in the last twenty-five years show that majors in computing-related fields have had low popularity among female students in the United States and Europe. For instance, in 2015, US women earned a mere 18% (9,209) of bachelor's degrees in computer science (CS), which is less than the number earned in 1985 (14,431) (National Science Board, 2018). Similarly, in Europe women represented 16.7% of total graduates in information communication technology (ICT) in 2016 (European Commission, 2018). Low participation of women in computing education has been a pressing problem in Western countries. Gender diversity in computing is imperative as it will increase the skilled labor force pool, enrich innovation, and foster social justice. Most importantly, there is a high demand for people with computing skills. The number of ICT specialists in the European Union grew by 36.1% from 2007 to 2017, more than ten times as high as the increase (3.2%) for total employment (Eurostat, 2018). Employment in computing-related occupations in the United States is projected to grow 13% from 2016 to 2026, which is faster than the average for all occupations. This is expected to add about 557,100 new jobs (US Department of Labor, 2017). Often such growing needs are met by foreign skilled workers, mostly from Asian countries. It is, there-fore, no surprise that a number of governmental and corporate initiatives exist in the United States and in Europe to empower students with the computing skills to thrive in a global economy.

Women's underrepresentation in computer science and computer engineering (CS/CE) education has been scrutinized from many angles during the last two decades (Ahuja, 2002; Cohoon and Aspray, 2006; Singh et al., 2007; Beyer, 2015; Aspray, 2016). Scholars have identified a range of factors that may be divided into three themes. First, objective conditions, including the small proportion of women among CS/CE faculty and student populations, differential treatment by male peers, and economic impediments that limit access to ICT and/or competent preparatory education (Varma, 2002a; Katz et al., 2003; Kahle and Schmidt, 2004; Lang, 2010; Good, Rattan, and Dweck, 2012; Beyer, 2016). Second, women's subjective evaluations of their self-efficacy leads to alienation and a pervasive sense of not belonging (Margolis and Fisher, 2002; Hyde et al, 2008; Varma, 2010; Quesenberry and Trauth, 2012; Beyer, 2014). Third, gendered socialization and masculine culture that affect women's affinity for CS/CE study (Larsen and Stubbs, 2005; Varma, 2007; Papastergiou, 2008; Cheryan, 2011).

In contrast, women in many developing countries have increased their presence in CS/CE (Shashaani and Khalili, 2001; Adam et al., 2003; Lee, 2003; Fan and Li, 2004; Lagesen, 2008). A study conducted by the author in India shows that CS/CE is a popular major among women. Recent enrollment data show that women constitute approximately 40% of students in CS/CE at the undergraduate level, 65% at the master's level and 50% at the doctorate level. During the 2016 fiscal year, approximately 813,000 male and 792,000 female students graduated from CS/CE disciplines (Statista, 2018). This is despite the fact that Indian women socially have fewer rights and opportunities in comparison to the United States and Europe. Despite economic and social advantages in the United States and Europe, women in India seem to have levels of success in computing education that appear to somewhat surpass those of American and European women.

This chapter presents a case study of women in CS/CE education at the undergraduate level in Indian institutions of higher education. Enrollment data show that the CS/CE field appears to be a "woman-friendly" field in India. The question of importance is: How is it that women in India have managed to outperform their peers in Western countries in studying CS/CE? This chapter argues that gender remains an important factor, even though CS/CE does not appear to be a male-dominated field in India. It shows a contradiction since female students seem to be empowered with a degree in CS/CE, yet they remain sidelined within Indian social structure. At the same time, it questions the Western portrayal of CS/CE as a masculine field mostly due to the low number of women. An analysis of the Indian context for CS/CE and the cultural/social meaning of gender in India provides a better understanding of the reconstruction of gender and CS/CE.

INDIAN WOMEN AND COMPUTING EDUCATION

In 1947, India declared independence from the British, emerging as economically and technically underdeveloped in relation to the West. Since then, India has sought to catch up to scientific and technological advances made in the West with its industrialization policies. However, until 1990 India had controlled its industrialization with licenses and regulations. In 1991, India implemented economic liberalization reforms to provide favorable business environments to national and multinational corporations. The Indian government has made the ICT industry a viable option to strengthen its national economy and emerge as a "soft power," a term coined by Joseph Nye of Harvard University. The Indian ICT sector has grown tremendously. According to one estimate, in 1986–1987, there were only 6,800 IT workers in India (Basant and Rani, 2004); currently, the ICT industry is creating more than 3.7 million jobs per year (Statista, 2018). The ICT industry is expected to provide quality employment to a large number of qualified people in the coming years. Indian people, especially women, are well aware of a bright future with CS/CE education.

Gender Socialization

Socially, women have had fewer opportunities in every country. The stereotype that a "woman's place is in the home" has assigned their social role. Consequently, formal education for girls was secondary to that for boys. In the last 100 years, Western countries have moved toward an egalitarian form of social organization. This is not to deny that subtle gender biases in socialization, lack of encouragement for girls to purse science and engineering fields, and gender stereotypes exist. In India, patriarchy – a system of male dominance legitimized within the family and the society through superior rights, privileges, authority, and power – is prevalent (Sarshar, 2010). Basically, Indian tradition holds that a woman's place is under her father while she is unmarried, under her husband after her marriage, and under her sons if she is a widow. Most importantly, all property is vested in, exercised through, and transferred through patrilineal descent. A male is considered an asset, who will compound the family wealth, whereas a female is considered a liability, who will consume the wealth in the form of dowry on her marriage (Varma, 2002b). Because chastity is necessary for a woman to be marriageable, families control all aspects of their daughters' lives. In such a social system, girls grow up with multiple restrictions. Though both boys and girls attend school, the experience of the two radically differ. Girls attend school with the knowledge that ultimately their proper place is going to be in the home to fulfill domestic duties, while boys attend school so they can become providers for their families. It is, therefore, no surprise that female students view education as a means of obtaining greater strength to stand up to the Indian social system, which is not friendly to them.

Early Exposure

It is believed that if female students have early access to and better use of computers at home and in schools, they are likely to pursue a CS/CE major at the university level. Since India has a huge agrarian sector, a digital divide is seen mostly between rural and urban India, rather than along gender lines. Even among a large section of the urban population that knows English, female students face a digital divide at home and in schools (Varma, 2010). This is mostly because family members have yet to see the importance of purchasing or renting a computer at home, which is rather expensive even for the middle class. Schools do have computers, which are typically situated in the laboratory. In fact, a computer course is introduced during sixth grade in schools, which follow the National Council of Education and Training (NCERT) curriculum. However, schools lack a strong telecommunications infrastructure with adequate reliable bandwidth for internet connection. Furthermore, electricity remains unreliable with fluctuations in voltage and frequency. Though such economic barriers apply to all students, there are social and cultural barriers that relate only to female students. It is common for teachers to direct or encourage male students to use computers and female students to watch male students' activities. Parents and relatives tend to keep an eye over female students' use of the internet to make sure they are not on a "wrong path."

Confidence in Mathematics

A certain level of "mathematical sophistication" is seen as necessary for a CS/CE major (ACM and IEEE Computer Society, 2005). Historically, lack of proficiency in mathematics has been seen as an obstacle to deal with in the underrepresentation of women in science and engineering in the United States and Europe. Even though mathematics scores show no gap between boys and girls (Hyde et al., 2008), it has been found that women tend to lack confidence in their mathematical skills when compared with men (Margolis and Fisher, 2002). Due to the introduction of computing as a subject in schools, female students in India have an early exposure to the field. Most importantly, they are confident about their mathematical training and thus believe in their ability to do well in CS/CE at the university level (Varma, 2011). Typically, female students are rarely concerned about their ability to do challenging computing and mathematical work either in an absolute sense or relative to male students. Academically, female students compare rather well with their male peers. There is a general belief that gender is not the main factor in determining who does well in CS/CE courses. This is not to deny that more opportunities are available to men than women, causing some men to perform better than women. It is, therefore, no surprise that once female students join CS/CE, they seldom change their major to something else.

Preference for CS/CE

Typically, enrollment in institutions of higher education in India is on the basis of the scores students receive in state and/or national entrance exams. Technical fields are typically seen as suited for men, while women are expected to study feminine fields such as medicine, commerce, arts, or social studies. Now CS/CE has emerged as the highest pursued major for those who do not wish to a pursue medical or social sciences track. CS/CE is preferred by and for women mostly for three reasons: economic benefits, suitable work environment, and social advantages (Varma, 2015a; 2015b). Economic benefits for a woman with a CS/CE degree appear to be much higher than for those with a degree in other fields. Not only will women have high-paying job opportunities with a CS/CE degree, they could get employment in multiple sectors, fields, and locations, including in large national and multinational companies. Due to the remarkable growth in the ICT sector, they could take a job soon after graduation. Undoubtedly, high-paying jobs offer women a better standard of living for themselves and their families. Such economic benefits tend to alleviate concerns their families have about marriage and dowry. In addition to the potential for job opportunities with a CS/CE degree, women will be working mostly in offices and laboratories rather than male-dominated shop floors or construction sites. CS/CE jobs are seen as white-collar positions at desks in secure indoor offices, with air conditioning. It should be noted that female toilets are not easily available on outdoor jobs. Furthermore, computing jobs tend to have flexible regular daily hours, rather than arbitrary hours and locations associated with medicine, which has been historically considered a suitable profession for women. Finally, there has been tremendous appreciation for women with a CS/CE degree inside and outside institutions of higher education. Women eventually enjoy a higher social status due to their ability to perform technical tasks, which results in women accessing greater autonomy and self-confidence. For all these reasons, female students have strong support from parents, family members, friends, and community for their CS/CE study. In fact, families put pressure on young women to enter into computing.

Images of Those in the Computing Profession

In the Western countries, the prominent image of people in computing is of geeks (Margolis and Fisher, 2002; Wajcman, 2004; Varma, 2007). Traditionally, geeks are seen as eccentric people who are obsessed with computers, fall in love with computers with their first exposure, are overly smart in breaking codes, knowledgeable in the inner workings of computers, and socially awkward. Geeks have become more acceptable over a period of time, yet the association with them remains derogatory and thus not desired by women in the West. Contrary to the West, the image of people in computing is positive in India. They are considered dedicated, hard-working, intelligent, meticulous people (Varma, 2015a). These people score very high in mathematics and sciences, while being very detail-oriented, which are both needed in CS/CE. They are an inspiration for others, so it is considered pleasant to be around them. Most importantly, they are socially and culturally active, like anyone else. Basically, they are role models for young male and female students. Male students' attraction to CS/CE has little to do with the geek culture; instead male students are pulled toward CS/CE because it offers many high-paying job opportunities inside and outside India. In India, parents raise their sons to pursue fields that have high income potential since they must financially support their families.

Gender Issues

Does the above mean that female students do not experience any obstacles in pursuing a CS/CE degree? In the Indian patriarchal social system, a man is the head of the family, who controls a woman's education, mobility, labor participation, reproduction, and sexuality (Sarshar, 2010). Patriarchy results in a strong preference for sons over daughters. As a result, female students experience problematic social perceptions, the dearth of financial support, and family restrictions due to their gender (Varma, 2016). They receive less support than their male siblings in the form of financial assistance and encouragement for higher education. A family considers the sons' role as staying home to provide for the family, whereas girls are expected to leave home after marriage to raise a family. Teachers have greater expectations for the education of male than female students; thus, women have to work harder and perform better to achieve the same acclaim. Because of their gender, female students face curfews at their hostels and at home (typically, 8 p.m.). Furthermore, male and female students cannot enter each other's hostels or homes before curfew time. Consequently, the system has created a gendered restriction that curtails a female students' ability to stay in laboratories longer to complete group projects and network with male peers. It also gives male students an edge with regard to hard assignments and group work. During job placements on campus, it is common for employers to ask whether female students have their parents' permission to work, as well as about their marriage plans. Because women are not expected to travel alone, female students cannot travel for a possible internship, additional training, and job interviews. In other words, female students are forced to make compromises with regard to family in educational institutions and in seeking employment.

After CS/CE Degree

The above shows that female students have an affinity toward CS/CE education, as it leads to better occupations. They select a CS/CE major after going through competitive admission to institutions of higher education, then they seek to finish required courses and training. The attainment of a CS/CE career is the final outcome. However, their CS/CE career preference is affected substantially by the constraints imposed by parents and society (Varma, 2010). In India, girls are under tremendous pressure to get married as soon as they finish their undergraduate degree. However, by taking a job, they end up having some financial independence thus are able to avoid pressure from parents to get married. Thus, when company representatives come to campus to recruit students as soon as they graduate, women with CS/CE degrees will then typically take a job in the ICT sector. Even if women have marriage in mind, they believe their earnings will reduce the financial burden of their families for their marriage; in India, a person commonly spends one-fifth of the total wealth accumulated on the wedding. In addition, increasingly, women with employment potential are viewed as desirable marriage partners.

Some female students opt for graduate education. Interestingly, there is a preference to do a master's in business administration (MBA), as it would result in a higher pay scale than with a CS/CE degree (Varma and Kapur, 2010). These female students prefer to take managerial or financial positions within the ICT sector rather than being computer scientists or computer engineers. Nevertheless, Indian women in graduate schools are often seen as passing time until they find a suitable marriage partner.

CONCLUSION

Much scholarly research in the West has shown how women have been excluded from the computing and other technology fields, as well as how such exclusion has given these fields masculine characteristics. It has been argued that stereotypes of masculine/geek images in computing result in fewer females enrolling in CS/CE. Those who do join the program begin to question their position in the field and typically leave before completing the degree. Even though in the West women are underrepresented in computing, this is not the case in India. Enrollment trends by gender show a decline in the number of women in the CS/CE fields in the United States and Europe, and an increase in India. Many women in the Western countries avoid computing and prefer other vocations; in contrast, computing is a magnet for women and their families in India.

Indian women see CS/CE degrees as an opportunity for a bright future. They are attracted to CS/CE mostly due to the strong possibilities for future employment and the potential of high-paying jobs. Living in the patriarchal milieu, Indian women desire financial independence from families to avoid any future social restrictions. With a high-paying job in the ICT sector, they can look forward to standing on their own feet instead of being homemakers; even after marriage, they can anticipate a high social status by supplementing the household income. Furthermore, they view ICT-related jobs as rather safe for themselves. For Indian women, being indoors in an office in front of a computer and interacting with a small number of professionals means they are protected from outsiders. Physical safety is a very important consideration for parents who let their daughters work outside the home. Parents seek for their daughters to be protected from sexual assaults, which is seen as a threat at construction sites and in factories. This is in contrast to the case for Western women, for whom working indoors in an office is considered normal, and, thus, there is little excitement for it. Sitting in front of a computer and being confined to a desk does not go well with their desire to interact with people. The fields of biology, psychology, and social sciences are seen as people-oriented fields and, thus, are preferred by women in the United States and Europe.

The reasons CS/CE is viewed as well suited for women is not in contradiction with the Indian social context. Parents favor CS/CE in lieu of engineering because it agrees with their perception of the type of work girls should be allowed to do. Parents typically do not approve of other engineering fields since girls would be outside and involved in physical activities, which they consider unsafe for women. Without parental permission, girls could not have enrolled to study CS/CE. In fact, their preference for CS/CE is closely linked with the family preference for CS/CE. Although this suggests a gendered construction of CS/CE, albeit different from the United States and Europe, it should be noted that women themselves view the field as giving them independence from the social obligations imposed on women in India. The possibility of women going against their families' wishes for them to get married is impossible without the economic security attained through a well-paying job, which is what a CS/CE degree can provide. It should also be noted that there is little special provision for women in higher education by the Indian government.

To sum up, masculinity and gender issues are prevalent in Western and non-Western countries, but in different forms. The gender imbalance in Western countries seems to be specific to their social context; it is not a universal phenomenon as it has been presented in scholarly literature. The Indian experience shows that gender is divisive in CS/CE, not because of the nature of the field but mostly because of the Indian patriarchial system. Even with the gendered treatment of women by family members and society as a whole, women do not doubt the appropriateness of CS/CE major for them.

DISCUSSION QUESTIONS

1. How do high school classes prepare Indian girls to do well to study CS/CE at the university level?
2. Why do female students in India not consider changing their major from CS/CE to something else?
3. What is the typical perception of the computing field in India and in Western countries?
4. How are people in the computing field perceived in India in comparison to the perception in Western countries? What are their characteristics?
5. Are careers with a computing degree attractive to women in India and the United States?

6. What are similarities/differences between women in India and the United States with respect to attitudes/beliefs toward careers with a computing degree?
7. Why do you think there are so few women that study CS in the West?
8. What attracts men to study CS/CE in Western countries?
9. Do women encounter obstacles that men do not in the CS/CE programs? Give some examples.
10. Why would some Indian female students not want to pursue CS/CE after attaining their undergraduate degree?

References

ACM and IEEE Computer Society. (2005). *Computing Curricula 2005 – The Overview Reports.* New York: Authors.

Adam, J. C., Bauer, V., and Baichoo, S. (2003). An Expanding Pipeline: Gender in Mauritius, *SIGCSE Bulletin*, 35(1), 59–63.

Ahuja, M. K. (2002). Women in the Information Technology Profession: A Literature Review Synthesis and Research Agenda. *European Journal of Information Systems*, 11, 20–34.

Aspray, W. (2016). *Women and Underrepresented Minorities in Computing: A Historical and Social Study.* Switzerland: Springer.

Basant, R., and Rani, U. (2004). Labour Market Deepening in India's IT: An Exploratory Analysis. *Economic and Political Weekly*, 39(50), 5317–5326.

Beyer, S. (2014). Why Are Women Underrepresented in Computer Science? Gender Differences in Stereotypes, Self-efficacy, Values, and Interests and Predictors of Future CS Course Taking and Grades. *Computer Science Education*, 24, 153–192.

Beyer, S. (2015). Women and Science, Technology, Engineering, and Math (STEM). In S. Dunn (ed.), *Oxford Bibliographies in Psychology.* New York: Oxford University Press.

Beyer, S. (2016). Women in CS: Deterrents. In P. A. Laplante (ed.), *Encyclopedia of Computer Science and Technology.* CRC Group.

Cheryan, S. (2011). Understanding the Paradox in Math-Related Fields: Why Do Some Gender Gaps Remain While Others Do Not? *Sex Roles*, 66, 184–190.

Cohoon, J. M., and Aspray, W. (eds.). (2006). *Women and Information Technology: Research on Underrepresentation.* Cambridge, MA: MIT Press.

European Commission. (2018). *Girls and Women Underrepresented in ICT.* https://ec .europa.eu/eurostat/web/products-eurostat-news/-/EDN-20180425-1?inheritRe direct=true.

Eurostat. (2018). *ICT Specialists in Employment.* https://ec.europa.eu/eurostat/statistic sexplained/index.php/ICT_specialists_in_employment.

Fan, T. S., and Li, Y. C. (2004). Gender Issues and Computers: College Computer Science Education in Taiwan. *Computers & Education*, 44, 285–300.

Good, C., Rattan, A., and Dweck, C. S. (2012). Why Do Women Opt Out? Sense of Belonging and Women's Representation in Mathematics. *Journal of Personality and Social Psychology*, 102, 700–717.

Hyde, J. S., Lindberg, S. M., Linn, M. C., Ellis, A. B., and Williams, C. C. (2008). Gender Similarities Characterize Math Performance. *Science*, 321(5888), 494–495.

Kahle, J., and Schmidt G. (2004). Reasons Women Pursue a Computer Science Career: Perspectives of Women from a Mid-sized Institution. *Journal of Computing Sciences in Colleges*, 19, 78–89.

Katz, S., Aronis, J., Allbritton, D., Wilson, C., and Soffa, M. L. (2003). Gender and Race in Predicting Achievement in Computer Science. *IEEE Technology and Society Magazine*, 22(3), 20–27.

Lagesen, V. A. (2008). A Cyberfeminist Utopia? Perceptions of Gender and Computer Science among Malaysian Women Computer Science Students and Faculty. *Science, Technology & Human Values*, 33, 5–27.

Lang, C. (2010). Happenstance and Compromise: A Gendered Analysis of Students' Computing Degree Course Selection. *Computer Science Education*, 20, 317–345.

Larsen, E. A., and Stubbs, M. I. (2005). Increasing Diversity in Computer Science: Acknowledging Yet Moving beyond Gender. *Journal of Women and Minorities in Science and Engineering*, 11, 139–169.

Lee, A. C. K. (2003). Undergraduate Students' Gender Differences in IT Skills and Attitudes. *Journal of Computer Assisted Learning*, 19, 488–500.

Margolis, J., and Fisher, A. (2002). *Unlocking the Clubhouse: Women in Computing*. Cambridge, MA: MIT Press.

National Science Board. (2018). *Science and Engineering Indicators*. Arlington: National Science Foundation.

Papastergiou, M. (2008). Are Computer Science and Information Technology Still Masculine Fields? *Computers & Education*, 51, 594–608.

Quesenberry, J. L., and Trauth, E. M. (2012). The (Dis)placement of Women in the IT Workforce: An Investigation of Individual Career Values and Organizational Interventions. *Information Systems Journal*, 22, 457–473.

Sarshar, M. (2010). *Patriarchy: The Indian Experience*. New Delhi: BePress.

Shashaani, L., and Khalili, A. (2001). Gender and Computers: Similarities and Differences in Iranian College Students' Attitudes toward Computers. *Computers & Education*, 37, 363–375.

Singh, K., Allen, K. R., Scheckler, R., and Darlington, L. (2007). Women in Computer-Related Majors: A Critical Synthesis of Research and Theory from 1994 to 2005. *Review of Educational Research*, 77, 500–533.

Statista. (2018). Number of Students Who Graduated in Computer Science Engineering Stream across India in FY 2016, by Gender (in 1,000s). www.statista.com/statistics/765577/india-number-of-students-graduated-in-computer-science-engineering-stream-by-gender/.

US Department of Labor. (2017). *Employment Projections: 2016–26 Summary*. www.bls.gov/news.release/ecopro.nr0.htm.

Varma, R. (2002a). Women in Information Technology: A Case Study of Undergraduate Students in a Minority-Serving Institution. *Bulletin of Science, Technology & Society*, 22, 274–282.

Varma, R. (2002b). Technological Fix: Sex Determination in India. *Bulletin of Science, Technology & Society*, 22, 21–30.

Varma, R. (2007). Women in Computing: The Role of Geek Culture. *Science as Culture*, 16, 359–376.

Varma, R. (2009). Exposure, Training and Environment: Women's Participation in Computing Education in the United States and India. *Journal of Women and Minority in Science and Engineering*, 15, 205–222.

Varma, R. (2010). Computing Self-Efficacy among Women in India. *Journal of Women and Minorities in Science and Engineering*, 16, 257–274.

Varma, R. (2011). Indian Women and Mathematics for Computer Science. *IEEE Technology and Society Magazine*, 30, 39–46.

Varma, R. (2015a). Decoding Femininity in Computer Science in India. *Communications of ACM*, 58, 56–62.

Varma, R. (2015b). Making a Meaningful Choice: Women's Selection of Computer Science in India. In Willie Pearson, Lisa M. Frehill, and Connie L. McNeely (eds.), *Advancing Women in Science: International Perspectives*. New York: Springer.

Varma, R. (2016). Paradox of Empowerment and Marginalization: Indian Women in Computer Science. In Helen Peterson (ed.), *Gender in Transnational Knowledge Companies*. New York: Springer.

Varma, R., and Kapur, D. (2010). Access, Satisfaction, and Future: Undergraduate Studies at the Indian Institutes of Technology. *Higher Education*, 59(6), 703–717.

Varma, R., and Kapur, D. (2013). Comparative Analysis of Brain Drain, Brain Circulation and Brain Retain: A Case Study of Indian Institutes of Technology. *Journal of Comparative Policy Analysis*, 15(4), 315–330.

Wajcman, J. (2004). *Technofeminism*. Cambridge: Polity Press.

18

Challenging Attitudes and Disrupting Stereotypes of Gender and Computing in Australia

Are We Doing It Right?

Catherine Lang

INTRODUCTION

This chapter will provide a current perspective of the gendered nature of computing in Australia. The underrepresentation of women is the most visible issue in this discipline, and may well be a product of the unique culture of the country that is at odds with the multicultural nature of the population. Many initiatives and interventions have been and still are in operation to encourage girls to consider a computing career. However, the proportional numbers of males and females in the discipline in universities and the workforce remains a concern in 2018.

Australia's workforce is highly gender segregated. The Australian Government Workforce Gender Equity Agency (WGEA, 2018) reported on International Women's Day that: "Women and men in Australia's workforce are concentrated in different industries, with most industries being dominated by male employees. . ... Women are most concentrated in Health Care and Social Assistance (80.2% female) and Education and Training (63.4% female)."

The Australian Computing Society provides an annual report on "Australia's Digital Pulse." In 2018 this report noted that "28% of Information and Communication Technology workers are women and only 12% are aged over 55, compared with 45% and 15% respectively in all professional industries" (ACS, 2018, p. 3). This appears to be a reasonably healthy percentage, given that Valian (1999) ascribed 25% as a critical mass for gender or minorities. Below this proportion women or minorities are seen as outside the norm because of their gender or difference; above this percentage they are more likely to be perceived to belong to the general cohort. A closer look at these statistics shows that they include workers in many of the less technical aspects of computing, such as sales.

Only 19.4% of students enrolled in computing courses in universities in Australia are female, with one-third of these being domestic students and two-thirds being international (ACS, 2018). Statistics show that the percentage of female students (19.4%) in all courses has remained the same since 2012, but the percentage of these who are domestic students has declined by 1.1% in the same time frame (ACS, 2018).

I present these statistics at the start of this chapter for several reasons. As a researcher in gender and computing for the last twenty years, I have concluded that while intervention programs (including mine) to challenge stereotypes are needed, the outcomes are often localised and the breadth of impact is not being seen in proportional percentage changes of women at university or in computing careers. While the raw numbers of female students enrolled are increasing (9,723 in 2012 to 12,918 in 2016) the numbers of males are also increasing at a similar rate, so proportionally computing is still a male discipline. It is apparent that the underrepresentation of women in computing is a multifaceted social situation.

In this chapter I will present a current scan of the computing landscape in Australia drawing on several past and some current initiatives to challenge attitudes and disrupt societal stereotypes. In doing so I raise the question "Are we doing it right?" because more than twenty years of interventions has made little impact on the perception that computing is male. I will present my suggested solution to attacking the issue at a ground level at the conclusion of the chapter.

NOMENCLATURE CONFUSION

In the last twenty-five years there have been several shifts in nomenclature of computing courses and disciplines. I argue that this creates a confusion in parents and students, with many students leaving because they are not sure what the discipline contains. For clarity and flow in this chapter, I use "computing" as the collective term for computer science, information and communication technologies, digital technology, and information systems as much as possible. However, in this section I present an example of how trending acronyms confuse the issue of the lack of women in the discipline.

In Australia, as is the case in the United States, the government and the media have adopted the acronym STEM (for science, technology, engineering, and maths) particularly when commenting on future employment skills. Conflating computing into this acronym, if one assumes the "T" is referring to digital technology, is problematic, demonstrated by the following quote: "Every time I hear STEM (Science Technology, Engineering, and Math), I wish we could focus the conversation on computer science" (Partovi, n.d.).

Partovi is the founder of Code.org and is considered an important influencer in computing in the United States. His reasoning is based on future employment predictions, the current gender imbalance in computing, and the confusion around nomenclature: "Computer Science is the only industry where there are more annual job openings than students . . . the gender gap is in computer science, not STEM . . . no one really knows what STEM is" (Partovi, n.d.).

Interestingly, Australia's Chief Scientist in his 2016 report on the future of the Australia's STEM workforce includes agricultural and environmental sciences within this acronym. Conflating these disciplines within STEM not only confounds nomenclature but also does little to shed light on the gendered employment issues in computing and engineering. Taken together, these five disciplines show that the proportion of women with bachelor's degrees and above in the workforce is only 10%. However, when the disciplines are taken separately it is clear to see that the deficit resides in engineering (2%) and computing (15%). The proportion of women in science and maths is very healthy at 41% and 38%, respectively.

I have introduced the current state of computing in Australia by presenting these statistics and the confusion around nomenclature at the start of this chapter with the purpose of framing the complex sociocultural situation that contributes to the underrepresentation of women in computing courses and careers. In the next section I present a commentary on the cultural stereotypes associated with the discipline in Australia and in most Westernized nations.

CULTURAL STEREOTYPES

Women's participation in the workforce has been increasing since the 1950s, so it is puzzling why computing remains a masculine domain despite the growing egalitarian society that Australia purports to be. An explanation may lie in the degree of choice given to young women, often at key areas in their education journey, as a factor to them fulfilling traditional cultural stereotypes: "For women in affluent societies, freedom of choice . . . implies both the right to be free from overt discrimination (should they elect to pursue a traditionally male-dominated field of study)

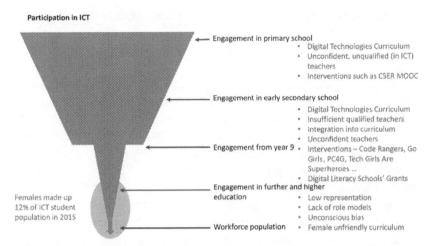

Figure 18.1 The ever-shrinking pipeline of participation in ICT by girls and women.
Reproduced with permission from J. Coldwell-Neilson, Equity and Diversity in ICT, presentation at the ACDICT Academy Learning and Teaching Forum (ALTA) at UNSW, April 5–6, 2018.

and the right to choose poorly paid female-labelled career paths, if they so desire" (Charles and Bradley, 2006, p. 196).

Charles and Bradley (2006) found that countries that prevented students from choosing preferences during their secondary education had a greater gender balance in computer-related courses at university. This research suggests that where students select courses early in their school years, young girls self-select what they perceived to be "gender-appropriate" options.

The STEM statistics in Australia presented in the Introduction section indicate that while there have been major inroads to female participation in education and the workforce, there are still strong, culturally embedded stereotypes associated with gender and computing. Figure 18.1 demonstrates this decline in participation at key points in education.

Coldwell-Neilson visually displays the shrinking pipeline of female participation and exposure to computing through their schooling to the workforce in Figure 18.1. The horizontal arrows in the diagram relate to the key points in the Australian education system where changes in schooling contribute to declining female student enrollment numbers in computing. The bulleted points on the right-hand side indicate the enablers and the barriers that influence the female student experiences in this discipline. The material in Figure 18.1 is explained in more detail in the next few paragraphs.

The federal body that determines school curriculum, the Australian Curriculum, Reporting and Assessment Authority (ACARA), released a new curriculum for 2016 that required all teachers, regardless of discipline specialization, from foundation year to year 10, to use digital technologies in their teaching (ACARA, 2015). The reasoning provided for this is: "It ensures that all students benefit from learning about, and working with, traditional, contemporary and emerging technologies that shape the world in which we live. In creating solutions, as well as responding to the designed world, students will contribute to sustainable patterns of living for themselves and others" (ACARA, 2015).

In primary schools (foundation to year 6), while the curriculum is mandated to include digital technology across all subjects, the levels and the type of exposure to computing are strongly dependent on the digital technology skills of primary school teachers. In Australia the majority of primary school teachers are trained as curriculum generalists. In my own university there are twenty-four core subjects in the primary teaching degree, and only one first-year subject is related to teaching with digital technology. Consequently, many primary teachers lack the confidence and competence to teach creatively with digital technologies. There are some interventions available to those teachers who have the inclination and time to upskill in these areas, and the Computer Science Education Research group online course CSER MOOC is one such example. This would be classified as a professional development activity and in most cases would be completed on the teacher's own time.

To teach in a secondary school (years 7–12) teachers are required to have up to two discipline specializations. Many universities are not offering digital technology (computing) as a teaching discipline in their teacher education courses. This is the case in my own university, because of the economic pressures of delivering courses to a small cohort of students. The flow-on effect is that secondary schools also have issues of insufficiently qualified teachers. Once in the classroom, the ACARA curricula are also prescribed up to year 10. The mandated integrated approach to digital technologies means that computing is diluted throughout the curriculum, depending again on the subject content and the confidence of the teachers. Many students are exposed to digital technologies in science and maths and in some schools have elective subjects focusing on coding, creating, and makerspaces, for example.

The next point of decline (see Figure 18.1) is engagement from year 9 where the silos of discrete subjects in the senior school curricula (years 11 and 12) start to emerge. Student subject choices are narrowed to fit future career paths. At this point students have the "luxury of choice" referred to by Charles and Bradley (2006) and often self-select away from the more technical subjects. These students are in the 14–16 age bracket and may be strongly influenced by social groups and peer pressure in making these subject choices. Hodkinsen and Sparkes (1997) in their career choice research reported that not all career choices are considered by young people because they may not be appropriate within particular social groups. This is particularly relevant to this stage of decline in female student interest in computing in Australia because of the social construction of computing as a male space (Wajcman, 2000).

In this senior secondary curriculum English and maths are compulsory for all students, leaving the options of a selection from the sciences, humanities, arts, health, and other disciplines. The common course load is five subjects that vary depending on the school size and subjects on offer. Teenagers do not tend to select computing, now called digital technology in the senior Australian Curriculum, and it is clear from subject completion data that it is not particularly attractive to girls. For example, in 2014 only 216 girls in the state of Victoria successfully completed the final information technology exam (VTAC, 2018), out of more than 50,000 students who sat final year exams in all subjects that year.

There are government intervention programs to encourage schools to upskill their workforce (Digital Literacy Schools' Grants are named in Figure 18.1). There are also many outreach and co-curricular programs and activities for students to engage with (Code Rangers, Go Girls, PC4G, Tech Girls Are Superheroes). The extracurricular nature of these programs may in themselves contribute to computing being perceived as something other than mainstream to female students. To add another question to the one posed in the title of this chapter, "Are we doing it right?": Is the extra curricular focus the best way to promote this discipline and career path to girls?

GIRLS-ONLY COMPUTER PROGRAM IN THE CURRICULUM

After many years of conducting research into why girls are reluctant to choose computing courses and careers, the Digital Divas Club curriculum-based program was developed by the author and three like-minded colleagues, Professor Julie Fisher and Professor Helen Forgasz from Monash University and Associate Professor Annemieke Craig from Deakin University. This research project was funded by an Australian Research Council grant and the program was developed, delivered in ten schools, and critically evaluated over a four-year time period, 2009–2012.

A total of 265 female students participated in the data collection cycles of the research project. The findings as well as an examination of the process of conducting longitudinal programs in schools were published in book form and online (Fisher et al., 2016).

The critical evaluation and reflection of the program provided insight into "what worked" in the project. A summary is provided below regarding how and why a curriculum-based program is perceived as more effective than co-curricular and outreach programs.

- Teachers learned beside their students through the provision of prewritten modules of work that they could use with little background preparation. This included project suggestions, assessment suggestions, and, as the Digital Divas program matured, samples of student work and marking rubrics. This catered to the busy life of teachers and also addressed some of the issues around lack of confidence with computing.
- In-class support was provided by university students studying computing, for at least one lesson a week. In the Digital Divas Club project we employed current female university students studying a computing degree to do this; we called them "Expert Divas." They were provided with training in the curriculum modules being presented, so they could help the teacher with programming concepts, for example. A second advantage of this university–school connection was that they acted as informal role models to the middle school students.
- All-girl computing classes were designed to moderate the years of societal perceptions that only boys do computing. These classes employ pedagogies that are suited to female learning styles, such as group work. Music was played in class, and a colourful environment with graphics and design was created. In the evaluation of the Digital Divas program the removal of the dichotomy of gender was regarded as positive by both teachers and students.
- The curriculum was focused on broader interests, for example, students were introduced to computing through graphics, story-telling, menu creation, and design concepts. Project-based modules for topics were used. We deliberately did *not* teach programming for programming's sake but introduced it through a design project (Fisher et al., 2016).

We learned a lot through this project, and, informed by our prior research, we were confident that we could change female student perceptions about computing. We were also surprised by some of the unintended findings, which helped us understand that even with a curriculum-based program, external factors influenced student course choices. The most significant findings were the following.

- Not all teachers allocated by their principals to teach in the Digital Divas program had a computing background. We were unaware that there was so much "teaching out of field," so this was an eye-opener. The program was primarily delivered to year 8 and year 9 students, so many teachers with an interest in computing were able to pick up our materials.
- A positive outcome related to the previous finding was that because our program had in-built scaffolding for teachers and students, it contributed to building teacher computing self-efficacy. Some teachers added to our materials, personalized them, and then shared with us.
- We found that the common response from girls in schools with high socioeconomic rankings was that they would not consider a computing degree, even though they loved the program and were often the most tech-savvy. These students were more focused on high-prestige careers such as in law and medicine (pp. 147–148).

The lasting impression of this project was the importance of teachers in the success of any intervention program to encourage girls to study computing. Earlier research had already indicated that teachers are often second only to parents or close family members in influencing student course and career choice (Lang, 2010). The outcomes from the Digital Divas Club project led to a greater understanding of the importance of including not only teachers, but preservice teachers in intervention and outreach programs.

THE FUTURE TEACHERS AS INFLUENCERS

The influence of teachers in female students' course and career choices cannot be underestimated. A qualitative study carried out with secondary students in Australian schools supports this claim (Lang, 2012). The findings from this research indicated that computing rarely entered the possible career choices of females. It also identified a pattern of factors that had a strong inhibitive effect on females choosing this career path. These were identified as computing being "not cool," "not cool to be a geek," "not cool to be considered IT capable" (Lang, 2012, p. 293). When female students who were already enrolled in computing degrees were interviewed to determine what influenced their career choice, the majority said they were influenced by "happenstance" (Lang, 2010, p. 332). In most cases the computing degree was not their first choice and was considered only when a family member, schoolteacher, or significant other suggested it to them.

The outcomes from this research confirmed the importance of integrating technology into the curriculum, delivered by competent, confident, and creative teachers. The focus of further research shifted from influencing students to influencing and upskilling practicing teachers (Lang et al., 2017). The result was a pedagogy for outreach activities in information and communication technologies (computing) as a collaborative student-led program where university-based teacher educators and preservice teachers explored and created alongside current schoolteachers and computing professionals to deliver engaging and exciting curricula in secondary schools. This model of outreach promotes a community of learners that collaborate to disrupt the current social stereotype that computing is male (Lang et al., 2017).

Rather than co-curricular outreach activities, embedding opportunities for student-led practice and peer-to-peer learning within the curriculum in schools ameliorates the problem of less confident computing teachers. Linking schools with university teacher education faculties provides further opportunity for authentic real-life experiences for preservice teachers. Furthermore, intentional role-modeling using female university students where possible also helps to disrupt cultural and social stereotypes. Unfortunately, these programs are time-consuming to establish and are influenced by geographical location as well as relationships between teachers and teacher educators. The model, however, can produce ongoing outcomes given the reach and importance of teachers in their role as influencers of student course and career choices. I suggest this is a more efficient and powerful way of influencing female or any student interest in computing.

BROADENING INDIGENOUS STUDENT PARTICIPATION IN COMPUTING

In Australia, indigenous youth (male and female) are underrepresented in computing; in fact, they are much less likely to be in education generally than non-indigenous youth (Venn, 2016, p. 2). An analysis of 2016 Census data shows that there has been some improvement in the participation of indigenous students in education at every level. Biddle and Markham (2018) reported the following:

- The percentage of three- to five-year-olds who are not already at primary school that were attending preschool is up from 43.5% in 2011 to 48.5% in 2016.

- At the secondary school level, 59.7% of indigenous people aged 15–18 were attending school. This is up from 51.2% in 2011.
- The percentage of indigenous people aged 15 or more who have completed year 12, the final year of secondary school, rose to 34.6% in 2016 from 28% in 2011.
- The proportion of indigenous 15- to 24-year-olds undertaking tertiary education has grown from 14.1% in 2011 to 16.2% in 2016.

Furthermore, industry statistics gleaned from the 2016 Census show that the majority of indigenous males in the 15–29 age group are employed in the construction industry (20.5) and only 1.1% in information, media, and telecommunications. The majority of females in the same age range are employed in health care and social assistance (19.8%) with 1% employed in information, media, and telecommunications (Venn, 2016).

A more detailed analysis of indigenous student participation in computing shows that the raw numbers were shown to be on the rise from the period of 2005–2013 (Anderson, 2014). While still very small numbers, they grew from just over 120 to 200 students in this eight-year time period. As a comparison, the enrollments of non-indigenous students fell from just under 65,000 to 54,000 over the same period (Anderson, 2014). These numbers include both male and female students.

While the growth in raw numbers of indigenous students undertaking computing courses at universities is on the rise, they remain very low. There is no empirical evidence related to the experiences of these indigenous youth in computing courses. Most Australian universities have an Indigenous Office that provides social and academic support to students. An interview with an indigenous academic resulted in the following comment, indicating the level and depth of barriers that indigenous youth feel in university:

Within the Aboriginal Community there are in fact amazing role models and in fact the Aboriginal Community often offers incredible support for each other and our kids.. . . The difficulty comes from the feeling of safe or not safe. Many of us find it hard working, studying, and living within the Western Worldview or lens. As we see the world through the Indigenous Relational Worldview. Because we aren't part of the dominant culture it is often hard to be in this world.

(K. Coff, personal communication)

This is very important regardless of discipline because research indicates that minority groups will leave a discipline at a faster rate, and take longer to return to their studies, than the dominant group (Faulkner, 2018).

CONCLUSION: ARE WE DOING IT RIGHT?

In this chapter an overview of the current Australian situation around gender and computing has been presented through enrollment and work-force participation statistics. It is clear that proportionally there has been little change in society's perception that computing is predominantly male. A discussion has been provided related to the nomenclature issues associated with computing, which continue into the current STEM debate. This nomenclature confusion does little to demystify the career path and does nothing to address the persistent cultural stereotypes of gender in Australia.

The education system allows for a dilution of computing as a stand-alone subject, and while there are many co-curricular programs to encourage female students to study computing, the argument is made for curriculum-based interventions, particularly those that involve schoolteachers, preservice teachers, and teacher educators working together. Currently, Australian female students have many career choices presented to them, a luxury not always available in other cultures. While they are embracing computing as users, they are showing little interest in becoming creators, resulting in a lost pool of creativity and talent. It is also clear that the lack of qualified and trained computing teachers contributes to this problem.

We have a long and rocky road ahead before we can achieve a critical mass of women in all facets of computing; however, creative and confident computing teachers in all schools will provide the first step. Teachers are already strong influencers in student course and career choices, and can engender student interest and curiosity in the discipline both in schools and in universities.

The chapter question "Are we doing it right?" begs a response. It is apparent that we are growing the number of female students undertaking computing courses and careers, but making no change to the proportional representations. Societal beliefs that computing is a male industry remain very strong in Australia. It is also apparent that the number of indigenous youth selecting computing courses at university is also growing; however, their numbers are very low. There are also ingrained societal beliefs that need addressing related to our First Peoples. "The other thing that Indigenous students find difficult is the huge assumptions the 'other Australians' still hold about us. It feels at times there needs to be a lot of change in belief systems to still occur" (K. Coff, personal communication). Despite many interventions and goodwill, the answer to the question "Are we doing it right?" is in fact, "No, we are not doing it right."

We are leaking talent along the education pipeline. We are addressing the root of the problem by building computing competence *and creativity* in our in-service and preservice teachers. The challenge remains for universities and schools to break down silos between computing disciplines and education disciplines, and work with our professional organizations to upskill and grow the pool of talent in computing to satisfy future job demands.

DISCUSSION QUESTIONS

1. What is the difference between equality and equity? How might this differentiation influence policies related to gender and computing in government and universities?
2. What is the employment and education data for gender and computing, and indigenous youth and computing, in your own country?
3. Are there detractors to women studying in non-traditional fields that are attractors for men? Draw on your own experiences as well as research in this area.
4. Investigate your own education system. Are there "transition" areas where female students can exit the computing pipeline similar to those illustrated in Figure 18.1 of this chapter?
5. In the message "All students should learn to code," substitute "code" with "write," "think," and "create." Does making something compulsory make it of a higher value in society? Discuss.

References

Anderson, I. (2014). Broadening Indigenous Participation across the Disciplines. Address to the Australian Council of Deans of ICT Annual Council Meeting, July 2014. www.acdict.edu.au/documents/ONPresentationtoACDICT7Final.pdf, accessed August 2018.

Australian Computer Society (ACS). (2018). Australia's Digital Pulse: Driving Australia's International ICT Competitiveness and Digital Growth. www.acs.org.au/content/dam/acs/acs-publications/aadp2018.pdf, accessed August 28, 2018.

Australian Curriculum, Assessment and Reporting Authority (ACARA). (2015). Australian Curriculum. www.acara.edu.au/curriculum, accessed April 2017.

Australian Government. (2018). Workplace Gender Equality Agency. www.wgea.gov.au/wgea-newsroom/iwd-2018-key-facts-about-women-and-work, accessed July 25, 2018.

Australian Government, Office of the Chief Scientist. (2016). Australia's STEM Workforce: Science Technology Engineering and Mathematics. www.chiefscientist.gov.au/2016/03/report-australias-stem-workforce/, accessed August 2018.

Biddle, N., and Markham, F. (2018) Census 2016: What's Changed for Indigenous Australians? *The Conversation*. https://theconversation.com/census-2016-whats-changed-for-indigenous-australians-79836, accessed August 2018.

Charles, M., and Bradley, K. (2006). A Matter of Degrees: Female Underrepresentation in Computer Science Programs Cross-Nationally. In *Women and Information Technology*, J. M. Cohoon and W. Aspray (eds.). Cambridge, MA: MIT Press, 183–203.

Coldwell-Neilson, J. (2018, April). Equity and Diversity in ICT. Presentation at Australian Council of Deans in ICT (ACDICT) Academy Learning and Teaching Forum (ALTA). University of New South Wales. www.acdict.edu.au/documents/ACM2017/ColdwellN-Equity+DiversityinICT.pdf, accessed July 2018.

Faulkner, K. (2018, April). Equity and Diversity in ICT. Presentation at Australian Council of Deans in ICT (ACDICT) Academy Learning and Teaching Forum (ALTA). University of New South Wales. www.acdict.edu.au/documents/ALTA2018/Falkner-Enrolment%20Data%20Update.pdf, accessed April 16, 2019.

Fisher, J., Lang, C., Craig, A., and Forgasz, H. (2016). *Digital Divas: Putting the Wow into Computing for Girls*. Melbourne: Monash University Publishing.

Hodkinson, P., and Sparkes, A. C. (1997). Careership: A Sociological Theory of Career Decision Making. *British Journal of Sociology of Education* 18(1): 29–44.

Lang, C. (2010). Happenstance and Compromise: A Gendered Analysis of Students' Computing Degree Course Selection. *Computer Science Education* 20(4): 317–345.

Lang, C. (2012). Sequential Attrition of Secondary School Student Interest in IT Courses and Careers. *Information Technology and People* 25(3): 281–299.

Lang, C., Craig, A., and Casey, G. (2017). A Pedagogy of Outreach Activities in ICT: Promoting Peer to Peer Learning, Creativity and Experimentation. *British Journal of Educational Technology* 48(6): 1491–1501.

Partovi, H. (n.d). What % of STEM Should Be Computer Science. www.irvine chambereconomicdevelopment.com/media/userfiles/subsite_132/files/rl/evc/library/computer_science_vs_stem1.pdf, accessed August 29, 2018.

Valian, V. (1999). *Why So Slow?: The Advancement of Women*. Cambridge, MA: MIT Press.

Venn, D. (2016). Indigenous Youth Employment and the School to Work Transition, CAEPR 2016 Census Paper No. 6. Australian National University. http://caepr.cass.anu.edu.au/sites/default/files/docs/2018/6/CAEPR_Census_Paper_6_2018_0.pdf, accessed 28 August 2018.

Victorian Tertiary Admission Centre. (2018). VTAC Annual Report and Statistics. Section D Completion by Subject. www.vtac.edu.au/statistics/stats13-14.html, accessed August 2018.

Wajcman, J. (2000). Reflections on Gender and Technology Studies: In What State Is the Art? *Social Studies of Science* 30(3): 447–464.

Workplace Gender Equality Agency (WGEA). (2018). Australia's Gender Equality Scorecard. www.wgea.gov.au/sites/default/files/documents/2016-17-gender-equality-scorecard.pdf, accessed April 16, 2019.

Conclusion

As we close this collection of many perspectives from multiple cultures and countries we hope to have shown that women's participation in computing is largely determined by cultural factors. We hope this book has provided a convincing argument that alternative ways of thinking about, and acting on, gender and computing issues could benefit both the field and the people in it. We have argued for the examination of *variables outside a gender dichotomy* as possible sources of differences in women's participation in computing. In particular, we have suggested and illustrated that *a cultural approach*, an approach that pays close attention to culture and environment, focuses on the many factors that can allow for, or hinder, women's participation.

At the same time, we should not look at women as a single category but in light of their own views, backgrounds, and lived cultural experiences. Trauth reminds us that even when women are exposed to the same environment they may experience it differently because of personal influences and characteristics (Trauth, Chapter 3). The chapter on women with disabilities is a good example of this, where we see that disability often impacts women's careers more prominently than their gender (Blaser et al., Chapter 9).

Different countries and cultures illustrate a wide range of *catalysts* and *disincentives* to women's participation most commonly shaped by cultural norms and expectations. Worldwide we see how gender norms and lingering patriarchal controls influence women's behavior and expectations. But we also learn from history that gender norms can change. For example, women were once considered better suited for programming than men. We also know women played a critical role as code breakers during World War II (Frieze and Quesenberry, Chapter 10). Khenner explains that the low level of women's participation in computer science in Russia (currently at 20%) was not always the case: "In the 1960s to 1980s ... at least half of the university students majoring in specialties related to programming were women; and after graduation, almost all of them worked in their profession" (Khenner, Chapter 13). We also know that gender norms are not universal. A study of the small island nation of Mauritius found that women were participating and graduating in computer science in numbers representative of the general population. The researchers concluded that "while the problem is wide-spread, the under representation of women in computer science is not a universal problem. It is a problem confined to specific countries and cultures" (Adams et al., 2003, p. 59).

In Western cultures, especially, it seems particularly urgent that we challenge stereotypes and recognize the tendency of families, peers, educators, and the media to perpetuate the *pink brain, blue brain* mentality. This is often the result of an entrenched belief that men and women are significantly different in just about everything they do. Added to this we risk having members of the male-dominated Silicon Valley culture tighten their hold on computing globally as cultural attitudes, beliefs and meanings about themselves and others, migrate with them (Applin, Chapter 8). When we see few women entering the field of computer science in Western countries, it's an easy jump to assume that computing is not for women. But findings from some non-Western cultures and our studies at Carnegie Mellon University advise caution in generalizing about women in computing. At Carnegie Mellon we saw increased interest and engagement as women became central to changing the culture and as "leveling the playing field" programs were established. Cordelia Fine (2010) argues that so much of what we have come to believe about the brain is neurosexism creating differences where none may exist. In reality "our brains, as we are now coming to understand, are changed by our behavior, our thinking, our social world" (pp. 176–177). In the United States the gender divide starts early: "what is perhaps most striking in today's world is that parents continue to stereotype their infants, beginning even before they are born" (Eliot, 2009, p. 102). Clearly, we need to see human intellectual potential not as hardwired but as a spectrum of possibilities, limited or accelerated, by social and cultural conditions and behaviors (Jordan-Young, 2011).

This book seeks not only to challenge "gender difference thinking" as a way to understand women's low participation in computing but also to act as a wake-up call – as computing becomes more ubiquitous we need to know what is happening to women in computing. We need to know which factors are helping to advance women or holding them back when careers in computing fields are becoming more and more plentiful, and rewarding.

So why are women so poorly represented in computing when in many countries women are exceeding their male peers in gaining bachelor's degrees in other subjects? We have said *there is no simple answer*. While that is clearly true, *and not unexpected*, we can increase our understanding of the situation, and indeed we see many factors emerge and some major themes surface in several of our chapters.

WOMEN IN COMPUTING: OBSTACLES AND CATALYSTS

The Double Workday

To most of us it comes as no surprise to hear that the double workday of family and professional responsibilities is noted most frequently as a major obstacle to women's professional lives (Huyer, Chapter 2). In many, if not most, cultures women are seen to have far more family responsibilities than men, and spend much more time on housework duties, childcare, and care for the elderly than men.

In some Eastern cultures "tradition holds that a woman's place is under her father while she is unmarried, under her husband after her marriage, and under her sons if she is a widow" (Varma, Chapter 17). This places a very high bar for working women with families, who are expected to perform well in the home and in their careers. In China, for example, modern working women, including single women, are expected to conform to the traditional "ideal" woman. Brazilian women, especially single black women, "are told to be dutiful and obedient," a characteristic of the positive marianismo ideology and behavioral norms (quoted from Diekman et al., 2005, in Buttles and Vladez, Chapter 4). Such high pressure has been blamed for many leaving the computing workforce (Zhang and Yin, Chapter 14). For some women, staying in computing under unrealistic family expectations or working under adverse conditions can demand tremendous "grit and resilience" (Adya, Chapter 7). Nevertheless, many women do persist and become great role models for "countering negative cultural effects" (Adya, Chapter 7).

Family

But "family" in itself is not always an obstacle. Indeed, family encouragement is particularly important and we found this catalyst to be evident in many cultures. For instance, high levels of encouragement from family were found to be a major factor contributing to the high levels of Arab Israeli high school women studying computer science, compared with their Jewish Israeli counterparts (Hazzan et al., Chapter 5). Chinese women represent 55% of entrepreneurs in the Chinese internet industry, and for many their success rests on having the support of their partners and families (Zhang and Yin, Chapter 14). Further, in India the support of family emerges as a major factor in increasing the participation of women in computing. Computing is seen as "a magnet for women and their families," and female students have strong support to study computing fields (Varma, Chapter 17). For many Indian women, entering the computing workforce can lead to independence and freedom for those who feel the constraints of family duties and traditional patriarchal control over their lives.

Intellectual Potential

India is a good example of a culture that does not conflate *intellectual* and *social* norms and expectations. By this we mean women may be constrained by strict gendered social expectations, as well as limitations on what Westerners may see as their freedom, but they are not regarded as having different intellectual abilities or innate academic inclinations. We see this in Saudi Arabia too where women's rights are strictly controlled by religious laws. Indeed, Saudi Arabia ranked 141 out of 144 countries for gender parity according to the World Economic Forum Report (2016). The country hit the news in 2018 when women were given the right to drive. At the same time women outnumber men in computer science education. One study found that "[i]n 2014, 59% of students enrolled in CS-studies in government universities in Saudi Arabia were women" (Alghamdi, 2016, p. 1). The researchers suggest that this has a lot to do with women staying close to home while men can study abroad. But we also see that there are government efforts to encourage women in computing that appear to be paying off. In Saudi Arabia, as in India, it is not assumed that computing is a boys' field or that it is beyond women's intellectual capabilities.

Stereotypes

Another recurring theme is how computing and the people in the field are represented and perceived. The unattractive stereotype of the anti-social, geeky male with poor hygiene, coding in isolation, is a popular representation of computer scientists in the West. Variations of negative stereotypes are embedded in Latin American culture and clash with marianismo stereotypes: "[t]he feminine, sexy, and people-oriented computing stereotypes are in direct conflict with the negative marianismo stereotypical behavioral norms, especially those portrayed in mass media, including geekiness, poor hygiene, and sloppy dress" (Buttles and Valdez, Chapter 4).

Stereotypes also form the basis of how women, *and their computing skills*, are perceived in the male-dominated field of computing. Women report being pigeonholed into softer technical roles and not trusted to solve complex questions (Adya, Chapter 7). This can lead to women questioning their self-efficacy and a general sense of non-belonging or imposter feelings.

The field itself is also subject to stereotypical, misleading representations with computer science most commonly being defined narrowly as coding. The idea that programming pretty much defines the field is particularly misleading. At Carnegie Mellon we found that almost *all students* reported programming as *one part* of their computer science interests, and they viewed programming as a *tool* for developing *applications* – frequently their primary motivation for being in the field. With increased exposure and deepening understanding, students come to see computer science as a challenging and complex field requiring multiple skill sets and diverse interests. This is a significant difference from the general public's view where stereotypes persist and where computer science is narrowly viewed as "computer programming by male nerds." Such stereotypes, perpetuated in popular media, can be a major deterrent to young people especially if they have little to no access to computing classes in their schools.

Gendered expectations and behavioral norms are influenced by such stereotypes and play a strong role in the attitudes of parents and guardians. If computing is perceived negatively and represented as a boys' field, girls can all too easily be discouraged and miss out. Girls and women need to see themselves as *belonging* in the field. As Gloria Steinem, a global feminist icon, once said, "If you can't see it, you can't be it – so unless you see your life and your group and your experience reflected, you think you don't belong, you're powerless, you can't act – consciousness comes before practical change usually. And the media is our consciousness" (quoted in Schnall, 2014).

In cultures where the perceptions of computer science are positive, girls and women are more likely to participate. Malaysia is a good example. Children "do not grow up with a preconceived belief that one gender is better suited for certain fields," and "young Malaysians do not subscribe to many of the stereotypes of their Western counterparts" (Othman and Latih, Chapter 15). In India, computing is not considered to be a masculine field, and the people in the field are seen very positively. "They are considered dedicated, hardworking, intelligent, meticulous people" (Varma, Chapter 17). In studies of South Indian movies, the representation of women as software engineers, and even the simple association of women as computer users, has been shown to contribute to aspirations and high regard for computing even among populations who have little to no experience or understanding of the field (Pal, 2010; Pal, Chapter 16).

It is worth noting that the Unstereotype Alliance,[1] in concert with the United Nations women's organization UN Women,[2] is monitoring stereotypes around the world and is working to eradicate harmful gender-based stereotypes particularly in advertising and the media. Audrey Azoulay, Director-General of UNESCO, and Phumzile Mlambo-Ngcuka, Executive Director of UN Women, point out that "[i]t is difficult for girls to believe in themselves as scientists, explorers, innovators, engineers and inventors when the images they see on social media, in textbooks and in advertising reflect narrow and limiting gender roles" (Azoulay and Mlambo-Ngcuka, 2018, para. 5).

Other challenges to stereotypes often emerge from individual experiences. Personal accounts of women in the field of computing from countries with low female participation show that they too, not surprisingly, had stereotypical expectations of the people in the computing field. One computer scientist expected them to be "dry, anti-social and generally severely lacking in life skills" but found she was quite wrong – she met many interesting people. Similarly, her expectations for programming were debunked when she found it unexpectedly creative: "Learning the tools to construct something out of nothing more than my own thoughts and ideas was exhilarating" (Lindquist and Melinder, Chapter 11).

Implicit Bias

While there is little solid evidence for gender differences in the brains of very young children, the *pink brain, blue brain* difference mentality has become embedded in American culture. It feeds our stereotypes and it starts early: one study found that "6 year-old girls are less likely than boys to believe that members of their gender are *really, really smart*" (Bian, 2017, p. 1). In so many chapters, and so many cultures, we see how stereotypes impact women's participation in computing. But how do stereotypes inform our thinking so dramatically and yet so subtly?

Stereotypes trigger our biases, both explicit and implicit. Implicit biases are particularly insidious because they represent the more subtle, "hidden" forms of discrimination. They are fast, automatic, and unintentional, and often do not align with our values. While implicit biases are critical to our survival they can also lead to misguided judgments that can have negative consequences in our decision-making without us being aware (Devine et al., 2013). For women implicit gender bias can threaten self-esteem, confidence, and sense of belonging. In male-dominated fields like computing these factors can contribute to high attrition levels and discouragement. Also, because of their automatic characteristics, implicit biases can be perpetrated unknowingly on a daily basis by those most committed to the welfare of children. This is beautifully articulated by Adam Mastroianni and Dakota McCoy, discussing women in STEM in the *Scientific American* blog: "Early in school, teachers' unconscious biases subtly push girls away from STEM. By their preteen years, girls outperform boys in science class and report equal interest in the subject, but parents think that science is harder and less interesting for their daughters than their sons, and these misconceptions predict their children's career choices" (para. 4).

We suggest implicit gender bias represents a major obstacle to gender balance in the field of computing. Thankfully, the research of Patricia Devine and colleagues provides optimism (Devine et al., 2013). While we cannot "fix" or eliminate bias, we can mitigate implicit bias by raising awareness in ourselves and others, by intentionally building relationships with groups unfamiliar to us, by seeing bias as a mental habit, and by using interventions to retrain the brain and break the habit. Several of the major tech companies and computing industries (e.g., Google, Facebook) are now taking steps to ensure their employees are made aware of how implicit bias works along with strategies to help mitigate the negative effects of bias in the workforce.

Choice

In the individualistic culture of the United States we tend to assume we make our own choices and decisions. Many among us, including some academics, believe women and minorities *simply do not choose to study computing*: it's simply not what they want to do, they choose subjects they love. But let us stop and consider the issue of "choice" (e.g., Reges, 2018). In countries like the United States, where computing is generally considered a boys' field, choosing to do computing can also mean going against gender norms. For the most part, men and women are "freely choosing" to enter studies and occupations that sit well with cultural definitions of what is appropriate for men and for women, a situation that can have negative repercussions for many women who are more likely to occupy poorly paid, low prestige work. Charles and Bradley put this most succinctly: "For women in affluent societies, freedom of choice ... implies both the right to be free from overt discrimination (should they elect to pursue a traditionally male-dominated field of study) and the right to choose poorly paid female-labelled career paths, if they so desire" (Charles and Bradley, 2006, pp. 195–196).

We also have to consider "choice" in the framework of who has access to computing education. Many children and young people around the world do not have access to education at all. Studies by Sanchez and Singh found "important inequalities in access to higher-education arising from parental background, household wealth, location, and gender" (Sanchez and Singh, 2016). Many schools in the United States do not have computer science on their curriculum, yet we know that student exposure to the field is critical. "American girls who aim to 'study what they love' might be just as passionate about computer science and engineering as they are about teaching and nursing if they had more chances to find out whether they love these STEM fields" (Thébaud and Charles, 2018, p. 12). Lang reminds us that teachers, who have such a strong influence over their students, can play an important role in encouraging student interest and curiosity in computing as a choice of study and career (Lang, Chapter 18). That said, teachers could be helped in this effort if educational policies "weaken emphasis on individual curricular choice" (Chow and Charles, Chapter 1).

In many cultures choice is most commonly influenced by economic factors, such as the need to find employment to help support families and/ or for economic independence (e.g., Abu-Lail et al., 2012). We see examples of how this plays in Indian film where changing portrayals of what is considered valid vocation for women underlines the tension between patriarchal constructions of a woman's place in society and the economic realities of workforce participation in STEM occupations (Pal, Chapter 16). In some countries men can choose to study overseas, a "choice" denied to many women. Choice is not situated in a level playing field and a multitude of factors determine what we all too easily call "choices" – biological, educational, psychological, socioeconomic, media, political, etc. Even physical cues in the environment "can act like gatekeepers by preventing people who do not feel they fit into those environments from ever considering membership in the associated groups" (Cheryan et al., 2009, p. 1045).

Other Factors

Other factors impacting girls and women's participation in computing emerge in several chapters. Travel restrictions, be they financial or social, have been shown to limit the academic and professional progress of women, especially where women's safety is a priority (Varma, Chapter 17). For women with disabilities we need greater understanding about accessibility and we need to ensure they are included in diversity efforts (Blaser et al., Chapter 9). In some countries computing is seen as attractive by providing a clean, safe environment for women. Female role models are thought to play an important role in Western cultures, while in Malaysia with its high rates of women studying computer science we see surprisingly few female professorial role models (Othman and Latih, Chapter 15).

Flexible work hours have been found to contribute to women's retention in computing careers (e.g., Ferrante, 2018; Guy, 2018; Quesenberry and Trauth, 2008). Thoughtful policy interventions that include women's recommendations, along with enforcement, can also make a difference. Indeed, as Zhang and Yin remind us, meaningful partnerships among government, educational institutions, and the computing industry could well contribute to improving gender balance in the field (Zhang and Yin, Chapter 14).

Socioeconomic factors play a major role in most areas of life and computing is not exempt. More affluent women are not only more likely to have access to study computing, they are also more likely to afford paid help for childcare. Added to this, "the gender expectations placed on a poor woman by society or culture may be quite different for a middle-class woman" (Buttles and Vladez, Chapter 4). The inequity in representation and participation in computing often disadvantages those most disadvantaged already by inequities in society.

FUTURE EFFORTS AND THE WORK AHEAD

One thing we know – *Darwin (and others) got it wrong regarding women's intellectual ability*. Women's intellectual potential is equal to that of men and when conditions allow, men and women can perform equally well. All men and women have the *potential* to be multi-dimensional – capable of spanning genders through a spectrum of perspectives – but much work is still needed to remove obstacles and embrace catalysts, to help ensure women feel welcome to participate in computing. Women need to see computing as a "natural" possibility for their studies and careers, and for *everyone* to see women as belonging in the field.

In the meantime, various organizations offer free online resources providing data and opportunities we can use to help with our efforts. The Anita Borg[3] Institute's Grace Hopper Celebration of Women in Computing Center is now famous worldwide and supports local area celebrations. Other well-known organizations noted for their international efforts, *but by no means all*, include the Association for Machinery's Women in Computing Committee (ACM-W)[4] and Women in Computing Research (CRA-W)[5]. Other organizations work broadly on diversity and inclusion. For example, the National Center for Women and Information Technology (NCWIT)[6] works with academia and industry in the United States to promote gender equity in information technology and computing at both the local and policy levels. Also, in the United States, the National Center for Minorities and People with Disabilities in Information Technology (CMD-IT)[7] and the AccessComputing Alliance[8] work to increase the participation of people with disabilities in computing fields. There are also many other programs throughout the world not specifically related to computing that are working to ensure that opportunities and resources in math and science are made available to girls and women.

We hope this global collection furthers our understanding of the various factors that help determine women's participation in computing. Othman and Latih (Chapter 15) sum up our initial thesis optimistically in words most befitting the subject matter "The low representation of women in computer science. . . . is not due to an innate inability of women to excel in this field, but rather, due to cultural and societal 'programming'. Figure out a way to de-program this belief, and the problem will be solved". Also, most importantly in the work ahead, Adya (Chapter 7) reminds us that finding solutions to increase the participation of women in computing is "not merely a charge to women but also to men". Men need to be on board as allies with potential solutions or remain as part of the problem.

Women, *and all who are underrepresented* in computing, do not need academic handholding to succeed but they do need a level playing field, a respected voice, and much needed cultural change. After all, increasing the representation of women in computing is not an end in itself. For people to thrive in the field we need to pay close attention to culture and environment. We believe this collection of perspectives on women in computing has clearly demonstrated that it is at the level of culture and environment – local, institutional, and global – that change can be fostered and accelerated.

References

Abu-Lail, N., Phang, F., Ater Kranov, A., Mohd-Yusof, K., Olsen, R. G., Williams, R., and Zainal Abidin, A. (2012). Persistent Gender Inequity in U.S. Undergraduate Engineering: Looking to Jordan and Malaysia for Factors to Their Success in Achieving Gender Parity. In *Proceedings of the American Society of Engineering Education Annual Conference*, 1–34.

Adams, J., Vimala, B., and Baichoo, S. (2003). An Expanding Pipeline: Gender in Mauritius. In *Proceedings of the 34th ACM SIGCSE Technical Symposium on Computer Science Education*, 59–63.

Alghamdi, F. (2016). Women in Computing in Saudi Arabia. In *Proceedings of the 3rd ACM-W Europe Celebration of Women in Computing*. Retrieved from https://uu.diva-portal.org/smash/get/diva2:971716/FULLTEXT01.pdf.

Azoulay, A., and Mlambo-Ngcuka, P. (2018). Joint-Message from Audrey Azoulay, Director-General of UNESCO, and Ms Phumzile Mlambo-Ngcuka, Executive Director of UN Women, on the Occasion of the International Day for Women and Girls in Science. United Nations Educational, Scientific and Cultural Organization (UNESCO), February 11. Retrieved from https://en.unesco.org/commemorations/womenandgirlinscienceday.

Bian, L., Leslie, S., and Cimpian A. (2017). Gender Stereotypes about Intellectual Ability Emerge Early and Influence Children's Interests. *Science*, 355, 389–391.

Charles, M., and Bradley, K. (2006). A Matter of Degrees: Female Underrepresentation in Computer Science Programs Cross-Nationally. In J. M. Cohoon and W. Aspray (eds.), *Women and Information Technology*. Cambridge, MA: MIT Press, 183–203.

Cheryan, S., Plaut, V. C., Davies, P. G., and Steele, C. M. (2009). Ambient Belonging: How Stereotypical Cues Impact Gender Participation in Computer Science. *Journal of Personality and Social Psychology*, 97(6), 1045–1060.

Devine, P. G., Forscher, P. S., Austin, A. J., and Cox, W. T. (2013). Long-Term Reduction in Implicit Race Bias: A Prejudice Habit-Breaking Intervention. *Journal of Experimental Social Psychology*, 48(6), 1267–1278.

Diekman, A. B, Eagly, A. H., Mlandinic, A., and Ferreira, M. C. (2005). Dynamic Stereotypes about Women and Men in Latin America and the United States. *Journal of Cross-Cultural Psychology*, 36(2), 209–226.

Eliot, L. (2009). *Pink Brain, Blue Brain: How Small Differences Grow into Troublesome Gaps – And What We Can Do about It*. New York: Houghton Mifflin Harcourt.

Ferrante, M. B. (2018). Three Ways to Ask for a Flexible Work Schedule. *Forbes*, October 20. Retrieved from www.forbes.com/sites/marybethferrante/2018/10/20/3-ways-to-ask-for-a-flexible-work-schedule/1#656c5e391246.

Fine, C. (2010). *Delusions of Gender: How Our Minds, Society, and Neurosexism Create Differences*. New York: W. W. Norton.

Guy, S. (2018). Flexible Work Arrangements: A Growing Trend for Engineers. *SWE Magazine*, May 7. Retrieved from https://alltogether.swe.org/2018/05/flexible-work-arrangements-a-growing-trend-for-engineers/.

Jordon-Young, R. M. (2011). *Brain Storm: The Flaws in the Science of Sex Differences*. Cambridge, MA: Harvard University Press.

Mastroianni, A., and McCoy, D. (2018). Countries with Less Gender Equity Have More Women in STEM – Huh? *Scientific American, Voices*, May 17. Retrieved from https://blogs.scientificamerican.com/voices/countries-with-less-gender-equity-have-more-women-in-stem-huh/.

Pal, J. (2010). Of Mouse and Men: Computers and Geeks as Cinematic Icons in the Age of ICTD. In *Proceedings of the 2010 iConference*, 179–187.

Quesenberry, J. L., and Trauth, E. M. (2008). Revisiting Career Path Assumptions: The Case of Women in the IT Workforce? *International Conference on Information Systems (ICIS)*, Paris, Paper 150.

Reges, S. (2018). Why Women Don't Code. *Quillette*, June 19. Retreived from https://quillette.com/2018/06/19/why-women-dont-code/.

Sanchez, A., and Singh, A. (2016). Accessing Higher Education in Developing Countries: Panel Data Analysis from India, Peru, and Vietnam. Young Lives, Working Paper 150, May. Retrieved from https://europa.eu/capacity4dev/file/31987/download?token=ztUbIV7A.

Schnall, M. (2014). Celebrating Gloria Steinem's 80th Birthday. *Huffpost*, May 24. Retrieved from www.huffingtonpost.com/marianne-schnall/gloria-steinems-80th-birthday_b_5009045.html.

Thébaud, S., and Charles, M. (2018). Segregation, Stereotypes, and STEM. *Social Sciences*, 7(7), 111.

World Economic Forum (2016). The Global Gender Gap Report 2017. Retrieved from www.weforum.org/reports/the-global-gender-gap-report-2017.

Notes

INTRODUCTION

1 Both Aristotle and Plato discussed women's inferior intelligence, which was also perpetuated by early Christianity.
2 https://en.wikipedia.org/wiki/Men_Are_from_Mars,_Women_Are_from_Venus.
3 Neuroscientist Lise Eliot (2009) coined the phrase with her book title *Pink Brain, Blue Brain.*
4 We use the term "computing" as an umbrella term to be inclusive of various fields and terminology, e.g., computer science; informatics, information, and communication technologies; information systems; information technology; and related fields.
5 Iceland was ranked 1st and the United States was 45th; retrieved from http://reports.weforum.org/global-gender-gap-report-2016/rankings/.
6 https://ghc.anitab.org/.
7 This refers to our book *Kicking Butt in Computer Science: Women in Computing at Carnegie Mellon University*; http://women-in-computing.com.
8 Here we include Russia as part of Europe as our Russian contributor is from Perm in the European region of Russia.

1 AN INEGALITARIAN PARADOX

1 In India, about 42% of undergraduates enrolled in information technology and computer science were women during the 2017–2018 academic year, with even higher proportions pursuing advanced degrees in the field (Ministry of Human Resource Development 2018: 109).
2 Underlying these theories is the argument that discrimination becomes more costly in advanced industrial economies and/or that democratic, egalitarian values, including gender-egalitarianism, become more widespread with rising material security (Treiman 1970; Jackson 1998; Inglehart and Norris 2003).
3 Exceptions are El Salvador (2016), Ethiopia (2013), Liberia (2010), Mauritius (2016), Panama (2014), and Thailand (2016).
4 Cross-national comparisons of workers at the unit- and minor-group levels are still not possible with these data. Our figures therefore exclude a few ICT occupations

that are classified under other sub-major groups (e.g. telecommunications engineers, housed under sub-major group 21, "Science and Engineering Professionals").

5 We replaced missing values with zeros for individual sub-major categories not related to ICT.

6 ILO statistics show women comprising 56% of the formal labor force and 87% of professional ICT workers in Peru. We were unable to verify these very high values through other sources.

7 For example, a professional ICT sector comprised of 20% women might be described as less gender segregated in a country where women made up 20% of the professional labor force than in a country where women made up 40% of the professional labor force. Charles and Grusky discuss the advantages of using odds ratios for cross-national comparisons (2004; see also Charles and Bradley 2006).

8 For each country, women's share of ICT professionals is calculated as (W_{P_ICT} / (M_{P_ICT} + W_{P_ICT})) * 100, where W_{ICT_P} and M_{ICT_P} denote the number of women ICT professionals and the number of men ICT professionals, respectively. Odds ratios for ICT professionals are calculated as (W_{P_ICT} / M_{P_ICT}) / (W_{P_NonICT} / M_{P_NonICT}), where W_{P_NonICT} and M_{P_NonICT} denote the number of women professionals and men professionals who are *not* in ICT, and the other terms are defined as above. Gender segregation in the associate professional ICT workforce is measured using analogous measures (e.g., W_{AP_ICT} and M_{AP_ICT} for women and men in associate professional ICT occupations).

9 Values are for 2017 and were taken from the Polity Project (2018).

10 Data on women's share of the labor force are taken from ILO (2018) and cover the same survey year as the occupational breakdowns. Data on university degrees and ICT degrees are from UNESCO (2018, for the last available year, which ranges from 2014 to 2017). Data on women's share of parliament are from the UNDP (2018 for the year 2015).

11 The values in Table 1.3 are computed by averaging country scores within regions. They are therefore not affected by differences in the sizes of national labor forces (i.e., large and small countries are weighted equally).

12 It is noteworthy that the negative correlations are especially strong when ICT representation is measured using odds ratios (see Table 1.6, row 7). With increasing female educational attainment, more women work in the professions and associate professions, but their representation in ICT decreases, *relative to that in other professional and associate professional occupations*. This points again to the multi-dimensional nature of women's status (Charles, 2011b).

2 A GLOBAL PERSPECTIVE ON WOMEN IN INFORMATION TECHNOLOGY

1 UNESCO Institute for Statistics, June 2018.

2 www.oecd.org/education/eag2017indicators.htm.

3 Prepared for the 62nd Session of the Commission on the Status of Women in March 2018.

4 R is a programming language and free software environment for statistical computing and graphics. The R language is widely used among statisticians and data miners for developing statistical software and data analysis.

5 This section summarizes Abreu, 2012; Kim and Moon, 2011; Nair, 2011, and Zubieta and Herzig, 2015.

6 Defined as a work undertaken in different times and/or places on a regular basis. It can refer to the *scheduling* of hours worked (e.g., flex-time and compressed work weeks), and arrangements regarding shift and break schedules; the *amount* of hours worked, such as part-time work and job sharing; and the *place* of work, such as working at home or at a satellite location (Georgetown University Law Center, 2006).

5 A GENDER PERSPECTIVE ON COMPUTER SCIENCE EDUCATION IN ISRAEL

1 Our nation-level data analysis is based on a variety of resources from 2016 and 2017.

2 Source: *TheMarker*, May 23, 2018: www.themarker.com/technation/.premium-MAGAZINE-1.6112352.

3 *TheMarker* is a daily Hebrew-language business newspaper. *TheMarker*'s prolonged campaigns, usually consisting of dozens of long-form essays, articles, and analyses packed with data, were able to put issues on the agenda; prime them to attract the attention of the public, regulators and politicians; and present them in a way that would garner support. See https://en.wikipedia.org/wiki/TheMarker.

4 Source: the Council of Higher Education, at www.themarker.com/technation/1.4367003.

5 See http://meyda.education.gov.il/files/shivion/Hi-Tech.pdf.

6 See, e.g., www.nextgenskills.com/israel-leads-the-way-on-computer-science-in-schools/.

7 See www.cbs.gov.il/reader/?MIval=cw_usr_view_Folder&ID=141.

8 See www.themarker.com/technation/.premium-MAGAZINE-1.6112352.

9 See, for example, the 2014 rating of CS department: www.shanghairanking.com/Shanghairanking-Subject-Rankings/computer-science-engineering.html; www.shanghairanking.com/SubjectCS2014.html#; 2018: www.shanghairanking.com/Shanghairanking-Subject-Rankings/computer-science-engineering.html.

10 Source: www.themarker.com/career/1.6342025 . In the following description of the Technion, we do not address the sector perspective since the Technion does not collect these data.

11 Source: www.timeshighereducation.com/features/which-countries-and-universities-produce-most-employable-graduates#survey-answer.

12 Source: www.technion.ac.il/en/technion-alumni-impact/.

13 She Codes, founded in 2013 by Ruth Polachek, is a community of women established with the goal of reaching 50% women software developers in the Israeli high-tech scene in the next decade. https://she-codes.org/about/.

14 It is reasonable to assume that this percentage is, in fact, higher. The reason is that about 30% of the undergraduate CS students study in a special program – Atuda – which means that they begin their undergraduate studies before they start the compulsory army service. Furthermore, most probably, they will work in a CS-related profession in the IDF service after graduation.

15 See the 2018 event: www.technion.ac.il/2018/03/tech-women-2018/.

16 See https://women.technion.ac.il/.

17 Google established the Anita Borg Memorial Scholarship in 2003 to encourage undergraduate and graduate women completing degrees in computer science and

related fields to excel in computing and technology and become active role models and leaders in the field. See www.womentechmakers.com/scholars.

18 Technion CS students who received Google's scholarship appear at www.cs .technion.ac.il/news/2018/1004/.

19 The Knesset homepage: http://knesset.gov.il/main/eng/home.asp.

20 The Knesset Research and Information Center homepage: http://knesset.gov.il/ mmm/eng/MMM_About_eng.htm.

21 Source: www.knesset.gov.il/mmm/data/pdf/m04224.pdf, p. 10.

22 Leadership workshop for female doctoral students: https://women.technion.ac.il/ events/%D7%A1%D7%93%D7%A0%D7%AA-%D7%93%D7%95%D7%A7%D7% 98%D7%95%D7%A8%D7%A0%D7%98%D7%99%D7%95%D7%AA-%D7%9C% D7%9E%D7%A0%D7%94%D7%99%D7%92%D7%95%D7%AA/.

23 Source: www.knesset.gov.il/mmm/data/pdf/m04224.pdf, p. 15.

24 Source: www.ite.poly.edu/htmls/role_israel0110.htm.

25 Source: www.smartcodecorp.com/about_us/israel_profile.asp.

26 Source: The National Economic Council report *Students to the High-Tech Professions – A National Target and Practical Recommendations.* http://meyda .education.gov.il/files/shivion/Hi-Tech.pdf.

6 FACTORS INFLUENCING WOMEN'S ABILITY TO ENTER THE INFORMATION TECHNOLOGY WORKFORCE

1 The gender gap in mobile ownership is lower in Kenya than other countries in the region, at 7%.

2 www.nationsencyclopedia.com/WorldStats/Gender-female-professional-workers.html.

7 AGAINST ALL ODDS

1 Names of participants of this study have been changed to preserve confidentiality.

2 www.pwc.co.uk/who-we-are/women-in-technology/time-to-close-the-gender-gap .html.

3 www.worldbank.org/en/topic/education/publication/missed-opportunities-the-high- cost-of-not-educating-girls.

4 The village school went up to grade eight due to constrained resources. Most children who wanted to completed their high school at another institution. Initially, Bela struggled in her high school socially because of her unrefined English-speaking skills as well as limited family resources to support her education. However, she went on to complete high school successfully and obtain admission to a three-year college.

8 CULTURES AND CONTEXT IN TECH

1 A sweatshirt with a zipper up the front and a hood, brought to prominence via characterization of "the hacker" archetype and worn frequently by Mark Zucker- berg, founder of Facebook.

9 PERSPECTIVES OF WOMEN WITH DISABILITIES IN COMPUTING

1 This work is supported by National Science Foundation Grant CNS-1539179. Any opinions, findings, and conclusions or recommendations expressed in this article are those of the authors and do not necessarily reflect the views of the National Science Foundation.
2 Comparatively, 12.8% of the population has a disability (Erickson, Lee, and von Schrader, 2017) and 3.7% of the workforce age sixten and over has a disability (Bureau of Labor Statistics, 2018).

10 AN INTERVIEW WITH DR. SUE BLACK, OBE, COMPUTER SCIENTIST AND COMPUTING EVANGELIST

1 Sue Black, *Saving Bletchley Park* (Random House UK, 2016).
2 See https://bletchleypark.org.uk/.
3 www.hesa.ac.uk/search/site/computer%20science; www.hesa.ac.uk/news/11-01-2018/sfr247-higher-education-student-statistics/subjects.

15 HOW THE PERCEPTION OF YOUNG MALAYSIANS TOWARD SCIENCE AND MATHEMATICS INFLUENCES THEIR DECISION TO STUDY COMPUTER SCIENCE

1 *CSI* is an American forensics crime drama television series. More information at https://en.wikipedia.org/wiki/CSI:_Crime_Scene_Investigation.
2 ICT Sector Report, www.bmcc.org.my/vault/publications/ict-sector-report-2017-2018, accessed 31 July, 2018.
3 In Malaysia, education is divided into four stages: early childhood education (4- to 6-year-olds), primary school (7- to 12-year-olds), secondary school (13- to 17-year-olds), and tertiary education (college or university). Secondary school stage is divided into two levels: lower and upper secondary school. Only primary school is compulsory. After each stage, there is a national examination: Primary School Assessment Test (UPSR), Form Three Assessment (PT3), and Malaysian Education Certificate (SPM). For those who want to go for tertiary education, they can choose to go to Form Six, matriculation, or diploma at any institution, such as polytechnics. After Form Six, they have to sit for another national examination called the Malaysian Higher Education Certificate (STPM). The admission requirement for Malaysian universities is either STPM, matriculation, or diploma.
4 O-Level (Ordinary Level) is one of the two-part General Certificate of Education (GCE). The other part of GCE is A-Level (Advanced Level), which students enter after completing O-Level. O-Level is the final certification for secondary school, to be taken at fifth form or year 11 at approximately age 17 (or age group 14–16). A-Level (Advanced Level) is the second part of GCE taken by students of Year 12 and 13 (or sixth form) from the age group 16–18.

16 WOMEN AS SOFTWARE ENGINEERS IN INDIAN TAMIL CINEMA

1 The World Classical Tamil Conference 2010 was an international gathering of scholars, poets, political leaders, and celebrities with an interest in Tamil people, the Tamil language, and Tamil literature.

CONCLUSION

1 www.unstereotypealliance.org.
2 www.unwomen.org.
3 http://anitaborg.org/.
4 http://women.acm.org/?searchterm=ACM-W.
5 http://cra-w.org/.
6 NCWIT: http://www.ncwit.org/.
7 http://www.cmd-it.org/about.html.
8 http://www.washington.edu/accesscomputing/get-involved/students/join-access computing-team.

Index

Printed in the United States
By Bookmasters